T0325263

Advance Praise for *The Israeli Century*

"*The Israeli Century* is one of the most important books of our generation, emphasizing how Israel is becoming the center of the Jewish People's existence and is laying the solid foundations for its future."

—Isaac Herzog, President of the State of Israel

"*The Israeli Century* is an excellent book that transforms a sweeping and wide ranging story of Jewish history into a coherent narrative. Shain shows how Israel came to surpass and dominate all diaspora alternatives, and how Zionism's 'negation of exile' still remains highly relevant today."

—A. B. Yehoshua, *Haaretz*

"With a broad and profound historical perspective, in his new and compelling book, Professor Shain explores Jewish history from its inception and invites the reader to understand the present era as a brand new development: the 'Israelization of Judaism,' which largely also defines what it means to be a Jew beyond Israel's borders."

—Dr. Avi Shilon, *Haaretz*

"Yossi Shain...engages the underlying foundations of the contemporary relationship between Israeli and American Jews through a truly provocative 'paradigm-changing' thesis...[He]challenges the notion that Israel and the Diaspora are 'two worlds of Judaism.' Rather, he presents a picture of a Jewish globe with Israel at its center. What characterizes the 'Israeli century' is...not that the State of Israel is incrementally achieving consensus among all Jews. The main change is that regardless of whether one lives in Israel or not, or identifies with the Zionist project or not, Israel has become the central issue around which both Jews and non-Jews worldwide engage Judaism."

–Adam Ferziger, *Contemporary Jewry*

THE ISRAELI CENTURY

HOW THE ZIONIST REVOLUTION CHANGED HISTORY AND REINVENTED JUDAISM

by Yossi Shain

Translated from Hebrew by
Eylon Levy with Ronnie Hope

WICKED SON

A WICKED SON BOOK
An Imprint of Post Hill Press
ISBN: 978-1-64293-845-6
ISBN (eBook): 978-1-64293-846-3

The Israeli Century:
How the Zionist Revolution Changed History and Reinvented Judaism
© 2021 by Yossi Shain
All Rights Reserved

Cover Design by Tiffani Shea

Post Hill Press
New York • Nashville
posthillpress.com

Published in the United States of America
1 2 3 4 5 6 7 8 9 10

This book is dedicated to Vered Fishbein, my love.

Also by Yossi Shain

The Frontier of Loyalty: Political Exiles in the Age of the Nation-State

Governments-in-Exile in Contemporary World Politics

Between States: Interim Governments and Democratic Transitions (with Juan J. Linz)

Marketing the American Creed Abroad: Diasporas in the U.S. and Their Homelands

Kinship and Diasporas in International Affairs

The Language of Corruption and Israel's Moral Culture (in Hebrew)

Table of Contents

Introduction: The Israeli Century and the Israelization of Judaism

The Israeli Century has been the most dramatic period in all of Jewish history. Over the course of a single lifetime, the Jewish people have moved from two millennia of statelessness to a life defined by the sovereignty of the State of Israel. During this short period, the entire Jewish people has undergone a metamorphosis. Israel has gradually become the most important force in all areas of Jewish life. In the last two decades especially, Israel has consolidated its hold as the most dominant entity in the Jewish experience, defining and determining Jewish identity, memory, and the place of Jews and Judaism among the nations. The Jewish center of gravity—cultural, religious, political, demographic, and even economic—has decamped from New York, and is now to be found in Jerusalem and Tel Aviv for the foreseeable future.

In May 2006, the celebrated Israeli author A. B. Yehoshua sparked a ferocious controversy when he told delegates to the American Jewish Committee's week-long centennial celebration that, "If, in one hundred years, Israel will exist, and I will come to the Diaspora and there will not be any Jews, I would say it's normal. I will not cry for it. Because it's very natural that every one of you will be American.... Being Israeli is my skin, it's not my jacket. You are changing jackets." Diaspora Judaism, Yehoshua added, is little more than a "fancy spice box that is only opened to release its pleasing fragrance on Shabbat and Holidays." "American Jews," he concluded, "are only partial Jews, while Israeli Jews are total Jews."[1]

---

1   A. B. Yehoshua, "Appendix: A. B. Yehoshua's comments at the AJC Centennial Symposium" in *The A. B. Yehoshua Controversy: An Israel-Diaspora Dialogue on Jewishness, Israeliness, and Identity* (New York, NY: American Jewish Committee, 2006).

1

The reactions came swiftly. The eminent NBC News anchor Ted Koppel, who is Jewish, rebuked him for disregarding the major contributions of Diaspora Jews to the continuity and prosperity of the Jewish people. "There is something very special, universal and easily identifiable among all Jews," he said. "It is beyond territory; it is something we all have in common." Leon Wieseltier, the storied literary editor of the *New Republic*, also berated Yehoshua, reminding him that Judaism existed long before Israel: "There is Jewish religion, Jewish culture, Jewish literature, Jewish texts that have been with us for 3,000 years. Why do you insist on narrowing it down to Israeliness?"[2] Yehoshua was accused of being blind, among other things, to the continued dependence of Israel on the Diaspora's money and political power.

Much has changed in the last few decades, however. Israel's economy has grown quickly, with its per-capita GDP today on a par with the advanced economies of Europe and East Asia, and likely to surpass them. Its economic dependence on Diaspora Jews, as well as on the foreign aid from the United States government, has diminished dramatically, while its own economy and government budget have ballooned. At the same time, Israel's military power has outstripped that of all its enemies, and it has made peace with the most powerful countries in the Arab world, though it still faces major challenges to its security, including existential threats. Today, many young Diaspora Jews no longer see Israel as a country in need, surrounded by fearsome enemies, but rather as a land of opportunity. Writing in March 2021 in *Tablet*, Emily Benedek described Israel as "a unique place to unlock their human potential and create a robust future in a vital and growing society."[3]

2 Yitzhak Benhorin, "Author A. B. Yehoshua Vexes US Jews," *YNet News*, May 2, 2006, https://www.ynetnews.com/articles/0,7340,L-3246476,00.html.

3 Emily Benedek, "A Brighter Future," *Tablet*, March 23, 2021, https://www.tabletmag.com/sections/israel-middle-east/articles/a-brighter-future-emily-benedek-aliyah.

All of this stands in sharp contrast to what Jewish life looked like for many centuries prior to the establishment of Israel in 1948. The unpredictable nature of Jewish exilic life, which the literary critic Dan Miron calls "the surprise of chaos," led Jews to constantly scour for new strategies to ensure their survival.[4] They did so in a reality that seemed arbitrary, because chaos is by nature arbitrary. The Jewish exilic experience of chaos was best expressed by the well-known Yiddish writer, Sholem Aleichem, who wrote that many great hopes tend to explode into disappointment and calamity. "Everything built up in the air must eventually come crashing down," he wrote. "This is not a particularly welcome fact, but it is the truth, and everyone is fond of the truth."[5]

This book argues that the Israeli Century marks the end of a Jewish life "built up in the air," an end to the era of Jewish chaos.

In the absence of sovereignty, Jews have always sought political arrangements to protect them, whether in their homeland or among other nations. The Jews survived the loss of national sovereignty thousands of years ago and developed a unique identity as a "chosen people" stripped of independence. They did so, in part, by placing their faith in a unitary, non-territorial deity who controlled history, and in the timeless text of the Bible as their portable constitution. They developed a rich theology based around their communal life in the absence of sovereignty. They excelled at preserving their particularism in the Diaspora, whether during times of stability or when suffering the violent whims of others.

In the age of Enlightenment, when the state was no longer regarded as the divinely ordained personal property of its rulers, the survival of the Jews as a stateless people was often seen as either a perverse global conspiracy against the international order or,

---

4   Dan Miron, ed. *Sholem Aleichem: Stories of Chaos* (Jerusalem: Keter, 2010), 221–222 [Hebrew].
5   Sholom Aleichem, *Menahem-Mendel* (Tel Aviv: Olam Chadash, 2016), 8 [Hebrew].

alternatively, as a miracle. Some heralded the Jews' survival as a stateless nation as an *advantage* of modernity with its creativity, flexibility, and prosperity. Indeed, many Jews in the modern era championed their universality to present themselves as model citizens of the "neutral" constitutional state. But others saw the Jews' survival as a historical aberration that had to be ended. So even after they were systematically exterminated by the millions under the pretext of a "Final Solution" to this abnormality, some Jews continued to extol rootlessness as a transcendent and uniquely Jewish condition—and as the antithesis of the nationalistic blood-and-soil chauvinism that had engulfed Europe.

"Every generation of historians," writes the American-Jewish poet and literary critic Adam Kirsch, "draws a picture of the Jewish past that is bound up with what they think about the Jewish future."[6] Nowadays, the picture of the future of the Jewish people is becoming increasingly bound up with the prosperity and resilience of the Jewish state. We thus find ourselves in the Israeli Century, an era in which the majority of Jews will come to live in the historic Land of Israel and enjoy the protection of the State of Israel. Jewish sovereignty will overshadow—and even define—all other modes of Jewish life in the Diaspora.

From a strictly demographic standpoint, it has already happened. Today, nearly 7 million Jews live in Israel. The American Jewish population has been estimated at around 6 million. In the rest of the world, Jews number probably around 2 million. Conservatively, Israelis make up more than 45 percent of the global Jewish population today. However, this portion is likely to increase significantly, even without major immigrations to Israel, due to a radically different rate of natural growth. Of the thirty-four democracies on the

6   Adam Kirsch, "Why Jewish History is So Hard to Write," *The New Yorker*, March 26, 2018, https://www.newyorker.com/magazine/2018/03/26/why-jewish-history-is-so-hard-to-write.

Organisation for Economic Co-operation and Development, Israel has by far the highest birth rate (about 3.14 children per woman), far outstripping Jewish fertility rates in Diaspora countries.

This is not just because of the extreme fertility of the ultra-Orthodox, or Haredi, population or the relatively high fertility of Muslim women. In fact, Jewish Israeli women who describe themselves as non-Orthodox have a much higher fertility rate than that found in any other OECD country. Israel's exceptional fertility is driven by its national culture: "It is exceptional because strong pronatalist norms cut across all educational classes and levels of religiosity, and because fertility has been increasing alongside increasing age at first birth and education," say the authors of a 2018 study. "From an international perspective, these are atypical patterns."[7]

As a result, Israel will, over the course of the next decade or two, become home to an ever-growing majority of the world's Jews.

*　*　*

But if Israel's success and its centrality to the Jewish future are so overwhelmingly evident, why is there even a debate about the centrality of Israel in defining the future of Jewish life? Why did A. B. Yehoshua's comments trigger such outrage?

One example of the kind of alternative view of Jewish life that denies the reality of the Israeli Century is offered by the American-Jewish scholar Yuri Slezkine. He argues that we are actually in the *Jewish* Century, and life in the American diaspora best defines the emerging horizons of the Jewish people. America offers the Jews a chance to live in security, enjoying progress and prosperity, free of anti-Semitism. America, not Israel, is the fulfillment of Theodor

---

7   Alex Weinreb, Dov Chernichovsky, and Aviv Brill, "Israel's Exceptional Fertility," Taub Center for Social Policy, Jerusalem, December 23, 2018.

Herzl's promise of a secure homeland and a solution to the "Jewish Question." Slezkine writes:

> In the age of capital, they [the Jews] are the most creative entrepreneurs; in the age of alienation, they are the most experienced exiles; and in the age of expertise, they are the most proficient professionals. Some of the oldest Jewish specialties—trade, law, medicine, textual interpretation, and cultural mediation—have become the most fundamental (and the most Jewish) of all modern pursuits.[8]

The Jews, argues Slezkine, represent the greatest creative force in the modern world and enjoy a disproportionate influence given their share of the population. They have turned their rootlessness into their greatest advantage. They are "service nomads," he writes, a people "wedded to time, not land."[9] Their flexibility, creativity, and need to adapt quickly to changing situations are their defining traits in a globalized era of innovation and rapid upheavals. The Western Jew, in his view, has become a model of success and imitation. As a result, Jewish life in the West is far preferable to sovereign life in the odd, volatile, small, and internationally isolated country known as Israel.[10]

Slezkine's views are part of a strong, perhaps prevalent, trend within Diaspora Jewish thinking. It is not at all limited to anti- or non-Zionist Jews. It also includes a great many of those who publicly

---

8   Yuri Slezkine, *The Jewish Century* (Princeton: Princeton University Press, 2019), 2.
9   Slezkine, 9.
10   Slezkine, 364–365.

and privately support Israel, but nonetheless refuse to recognize the tectonic shift of Jewish history that has taken place.

It is one thing, especially for American Jews, to support Israel out of a sense of familial loyalty or a duty to care for Jews in need and under threat. It is another thing to come to terms with the fact that Israel has *displaced* the United States as the center of global Jewry and as the long-term definer of the Jewish people's interests and identity. Understanding what has really changed takes time, and above all, it takes an overwhelming preponderance of evidence.

* * *

The evidence, however, has become increasingly difficult to ignore. The transformation of Israel from a project of the Diaspora to something entirely different is reflected in the dramatic rise of the Jewish state in the last few decades as a major power, both on the world stage and in redefining every facet of Jewish life across the Diaspora. The immense impact of Israel derives from both its successes and challenges. This became evident once again in May 2021 when massive violence, the most intense in years, erupted between Israel and Hamas regime in the Gaza strip. This latest round of hostilities also ignited unprecedented violence between Israeli Arabs and Jews and inescapably engulfed Jews wherever they were.[11]

Israel's success, both within the Jewish world and globally, has taken on dimensions that cannot be overstated. It has become an important geopolitical actor and a role model with international influence, especially on issues of security, innovation, and economics.[12]

---

11   "The Gaza Conflict Is Stoking an 'Identity Crisis' for Some Young American Jews," *New York Times*, May 20, 2021.

12   Peter Berkowitz, "The Untold Story of Israeli Innovation," Real Clear Politics, March 18, 2018, https://www.realclearpolitics.com/articles/2018/03/13/the_untold_story_of_israeli_innovation_136508.html.

It is acting as a geopolitical "player" to a degree far beyond anything in the past, whether as a potential alternative to Russia in supplying natural gas to Europe, a counterweight to Turkey's ambitions in the Eastern Mediterranean, a silent partner in Azerbaijan's war against Armenia, or a naval adversary to Iranian efforts to ship illicit oil and operate intelligence-gathering vessels in the Red Sea. And this role has only increased since the signing of the peace agreements known as the Abraham Accords in 2020–2021, bringing the combined economic and military might of the Gulf States and Israel into direct alliance. Owing to its military, economic, and cultural strength and its Jewish-democratic character, Israel has become a key actor on the world stage and the supreme Middle Eastern power.

Israel also plays a critical role in almost every technological field. To take one crucial example, by 2021 Israel has become second only to the United States in the size of its global cybersecurity market share and in the number of companies operating. Israel accounts for a third of world's investment in cybersecurity, and a third of the cyber "unicorns"—private companies worth more than $1 billion—in the world. Another example is that of water technology, in which Israel has become a global leader in everything from desalination, to wastewater management, to water-saving agriculture, to urban water management, exporting its expertise to governments and municipalities around the world at a time of increasing droughts and shortages. Recent investments totaling many billions of dollars by global corporations like Google, Facebook, Microsoft, Intel, and Cisco further testify to the belief in the exceptional concentration of talent available in the Jewish state.

In this context it is important to point out just how far Israel has emerged from the state of fragile economic dependency that characterized its first half-century.

Two decades into the twenty-first century, Israel's dependence on Diaspora donations and foreign aid has become almost negligible. Whereas Jewish philanthropic gifts to Israel stand at between $1 billion and $2 billion, and the US government's military aid stands at under $4 billion, these are a small fraction of Israel's annual government budget, which stands at well over $100 billion. From a purely financial standpoint, American Jewry's *entire* Jewish philanthropic output, including gifts not just to Israel but also to their own communities, schools, and other organizations—all of which come to around $4 billion—is a drop in the bucket compared to the taxes collected by the government of the Jewish state. Israel has thus become a behemoth of Jewish financial resources, dwarfing those of the Diaspora.

A similar misconception surrounds the question of immigration between Israel and the Diaspora. Immigration to and from Israel has always been an important test for Zionism and its critics. *Aliyah* was taken to be the ultimate expression of the victory of Zionism, and emigration from Israel—*yerida* (literally, "descent")—was understood to signal its failure. In 1976, Israeli Prime Minister Yitzhak Rabin famously used the expression "the fallout of weaklings" to describe Israeli contempt for emigrants. Some even construed emigration as the end of Zionism itself.

Yet in recent years, especially due to Israel's economic growth relative to the rest of the West, fewer Israelis are looking to settle down abroad. Economic optimism and confidence in the future are the key to Israel's low emigration rate, which at the time of this writing is "at an almost historic low."[13] Some even question whether Israel still needs Jewish immigration, especially since it is already facing a population explosion that threatens its environment and

---

13 Sergio DellaPergola, "Israel Harel Doesn't Understand Demographics," *Haaretz*, January 22, 2017 [Hebrew]. See also Lior Datal, "Number of Israeli Migrants Drops By 30% In Recent Years: The Israeli Diaspora Abroad Is Not As Big As We Would Like To Think," *The Marker*, March 27, 2013.

citizens' quality of life.[14] Indeed, the changed attitudes toward immigration in and out of Israel are today symbolic of Israel's sovereign normality in the Israeli Century.

Israelis are inveterate world explorers, and the Israeli start-up scene contains thousands of globalized Israelis with worldwide reputations in fields ranging from science and academia to business and commerce. Yet even these globalized Israelis remain, for the most part, intensely patriotic. They typically endeavor to maintain strong ties to home even if they spend years abroad. Israel has also changed its attitude towards Israelis overseas. No longer does it deride them; instead, it upholds them as proof of the success of the Israeli Century and as an essential resource to boost the country's economy, develop its international standing, and "Israelize" the Diaspora.

In the last decade, Israelis abroad have developed new organizations—such as the Israeli-American Council (IAC)—that speak on behalf of the *Israeli* Diaspora and amplify their voice, often competing with the established American Jewish community for the megaphone. When President Trump attended the IAC's annual conference in 2019 and described American Jewish support for the Democratic Party as bordering on disloyalty to Israel, American Israelis applauded, but many American Jews were left perturbed—not just by the accusation, but also by a sense that a forum of Israeli-Americans suddenly had sufficient clout to upstage more traditional American Jewish institutions.

But this, too, is a product of the Israeli Century. It is in the State of Israel where Jews generally feel most rooted and confident in their national identity. It is the Jewish state that best enables them to realize their global abilities—*contra* Slezkine—without eroding their strong attachment to their heritage and unique culture. Israel has progressed quite far in its century-long project of fashioning the

---

14   Alon Tal, *The Land is Full* (New Haven: Yale University Press, 2016).

"new Jew," one who feels a deep commitment to his heritage and a natural bond to his historic homeland. Shielded by the power of the Israeli Century, Israeli Jews are channeling the global traits and talents accumulated by generations of Jews in the absence of sovereignty, into international success in a constantly growing number of fields.

And this is happening at the same time that Diaspora communities face seemingly insurmountable forces of assimilation, along with rising anti-Semitism, especially in the United States. The contrast between Israel's rise and the Diaspora's decline is one of the central stories of the Israeli Century.

In the Israeli Century, therefore, we are witnessing a turning point in the relationship between the Jewish Diaspora and the Jewish state. If in the past Israelis talked about the "rich uncle from America" and longed to emigrate in droves, today the Jewish conversation often centers around Israel's own prosperity and concomitant responsibility to help weak Jewish institutions across the Diaspora, including in the United States.

* * *

Israel's rise has reverberated across the world, spanning military, diplomatic, economic, technological, and cultural spheres. Western commentators often describe Israel as isolated and under constant threat of potential sanctions and boycotts, especially from within European countries. But despite the fact that Israel has many detractors, and despite the constant flood of anti-Israel votes in UN bodies, Israel is also becoming popular and even admired in many parts of the globe, including in India, China, Japan, and most surprisingly in the Arab world, where Israel is respected because of its technological achievements and its character as a progressive and open country. In this context as well, the Abraham Accords marked a watershed in the approach of Muslims and Arabs towards Jews, proving once and for all that there no longer exists a broad, intractable "Arab-Israeli conflict."[15] And while many enviously see Israel as a successful democratic nation-state, Israel has also become attractive to reactionaries in both eastern and western Europe who oppose liberal democracy, multiculturalism, and borderless globalization. In eastern Europe in particular, some leaders seek to emulate the Israeli model of a strong ethnic nation-state enjoying intense kinship ties with Diaspora communities.

The influence of Israeli power and wealth has gone beyond politics and technology into popular culture as well. The emergence of Israel as a creative force behind new films and television series has been widely discussed. No less important, however, are Israeli influences felt in fields as diverse as electronic and jazz music, architecture, fashion, and the culinary arts. Israel has begun to capture the imagination of world culture, expressed not only in the success of TV series like *Fauda* and actors like Gal Gadot, but also in the frequent appearance of Israeli characters in Western productions, as well as more prosaic developments, such as the relocation of the director Quentin Tarantino to Tel Aviv. Israel, it seems, is increasingly seen as an exotic focus of cultural curiosity.

The Israeli Century has even changed the way other religions have viewed themselves—especially within the Christian faith. This is most evident among Evangelicals, especially in the United States. For many of them, Israel's existence validates their Christian theology and faith in Scripture, serving as proof that God has accepted the Jewish people in their ancient homeland once again, as the prophets envisioned, and imposing on Christians a responsibility to support

---

15   James Sinkinson, "Israel Trounces BDS in the Marketplace, but Its Struggle in the Public Square Continues," *Israel Hayom*, March 31, 2021 [Hebrew]; Michael B. Oren, "The Death of the Arab-Israeli Conflict," *Tablet* January 13, 2021, https://www.tabletmag.com/sections/israel-middle-east/articles/death-of-arab-israeli-conflict.

them. The American televangelist Jerry Falwell described Israel's establishment as a "miracle" and "providential in every sense of the word.... The State of Israel, though small in geography and population, remains the focal point of history. All eyes are on Israel."[16]

The Catholic Church, too, which had previously rejected on theological grounds the Jewish claim to sovereignty in the Holy Land, has in recent years fundamentally revised its attitudes in the face of the ineluctable fact of Israeli sovereignty, recognizing (at least de facto) their sovereign rights. This was a dramatic development, because until recently the very existence of the State of Israel contradicted fundamental tenets of Catholic theology, which viewed the loss of the Israelites' sovereignty after the destruction of the Second Temple as divine proof that Christendom was the "true Israel."

Indeed, the Holy See's recognition of Jewish sovereignty in the Holy Land is, according to the Jesuit theologian Dennis McManus, "the most important historical drama that Christianity has undergone since the days of Luther."[17]

* * *

Yet it is not Israel's international influence, but rather the internal development of the sovereign Jewish state—the constant, churning inner turmoil over its political, religious, and economic future—that will most powerfully determine the culture and future of the Jewish people as a whole. Jews outside of Israel, especially in North America, still have an important role to play in fashioning the Jewish future. But this role is gradually diminishing and is increasingly dependent on their involvement in the Israeli drama. As Elliot

---

16 Jacques Berlinerblau, "On Philo-Semitism," *Occasional Papers on Jewish Civilization, Jewish Thought and Philosophy* (2007), 11.

17 Conversation between the author and McManus in Washington.

Cosgrove, Rabbi of Park Avenue Synagogue in New York, recently put it:

> These days, American Jews no longer debate who wrote the Bible. Instead, we argue about Israel. Israel is what brings us together and what tears us apart. We work to keep our relationship with Israel strong and are anxiety-ridden at signs of its weakening.... The labels that delineate our denominations are no longer based on belief or observance—Orthodox, Conservative, Reform, Reconstructionist—but on our views about Israel: AIPAC, ZOA, JVP, J-Street and the rest of the alphabet soup of Israel advocacy.[18]

The Diaspora's dependence on Israel is especially evident in the changes we have seen in Jewish creativity in the Diaspora. Israel has taken center stage as the place where Judaism is being revived in every branch of art and popular culture. It is witnessing a tremendous renaissance of not just Israeli but also identifiably Jewish art. It is the home of a flourishing modern Hebrew music industry, including traditional Jewish music. Israeli cinema and television are not just gaining a higher global profile; they are also increasingly expressive of the Jewish experience.

But it is seen most powerfully in the evolution of Jewish literature in the United States. The American-Jewish literature that thrived in the twentieth century—against the backdrop of the American-Jewish experience and the living memory of Europe and the Holocaust—is

18 Yossi Shain and Michal Schwartz, "The Jewsraeli Century," *Jewish Review of Books* (2019), https://jewishreviewofbooks.com/articles/5357/the-jewsraeli-century/.

a shadow of its former self. Contemporary American Jewish authors no longer write like Isaac Bashevis Singer, Philip Roth, and Saul Bellow, whose works were steeped in the American and European Jewish experience. Today's leading American-Jewish writers, such as Nathan Englander, Jonathan Safran Foer, Joshua Cohen, and Nicole Krauss, are unable to avoid writing novels that deal with Israel, Israeli life, and American-Israeli issues. Although many of their works reflect a certain ambivalence, and even harsh criticism, toward Israel, they nonetheless often depict American-Jewish life as lacking in focus and meaning, whereas life in Israel is seen, for better or worse, as a vibrant and central element of Jewish life that can no longer be ignored. The American-Israeli author Matti Friedman put it this way: "Jewish American writers of a few decades ago might have poked around the strange Jewish country in the Middle East, but they knew that the real literary action for them was back home. The novelists of 2017 don't seem so sure."[19] Nathan Englander, too, recently attested to Jewish-American writers' obsession with Israel: "I really do not know what got into our heads.... We are all friends, we all like it here in New York, and yet somehow Israel consumes us."[20]

But it is also telling that one can no longer speak of Jewish literature in the Israeli Century without giving serious attention to the works being produced in the Hebrew language.[21] Nowadays, Israeli-Jewish Hebrew literature exists alongside a Diaspora literature defined by its relationship with Israeli sovereignty. The latter is not written in Hebrew, nor is it written in the Jewish homeland, but its thrust is the story of the Israeli Century.

Israel remains the central point of reference for the Jewish

---

19 Shain and Schwartz, "The Jewsraeli Century."

20 Tzipi Smilovitz, "In Jerusalem I Knew I Might Die in a Terror Attack, and it Would at Least Be a Fitting Death in the Struggle for Peace," Ynet News, May 25, 2018 [Hebrew].

21 Hannan Hever, "A Map of Sand: From Hebrew Literature to Israeli Literature," *Theory and Criticism* 20 (2002), 165–190 [Hebrew].

cultural experience in every corner of the world. Its position also stems from the weakness of Diaspora Jewry in preserving Jewish communities and in shaping a clear vision for their future. Therefore, it is the strength and character of the State of Israel more than anything else that will determine the boundaries of Jewish identity, religion, and culture.

* * *

One of the most remarkable outcomes of the Israeli Century, however, has taken place completely outside the hearts and minds of Diaspora Jews. We have also witnessed an "Israelization" of anti-Semitism.

Around the world, Diaspora Jews are closely associated with the State of Israel, and this means that attitudes towards the Jewish state—as well as Israel's own actions and decisions—affect the lives of Jews worldwide. Take, for example, the wave of anti-Semitism that swept Argentina in the 1960s following the capture and arrest of the Nazi war criminal Adolf Eichmann by the Mossad. Indeed, criticism of Israel in Argentina has been a cover for what is in fact a long history of hostility toward Jews. Under Argentina's brutal military dictatorship in 1976–1983, increased talk of international Zionist conspiracies and of Jews as servants of Zionist and American imperialism led to the sanctioning of the torture, murder, and disappearance of hundreds of Argentinian Jews.[22]

The Israelization of anti-Semitism began in the Arab world and its Third World allies in the 1950s and 1960s, fueled in large part by the Soviet Union's anti-Western propaganda strategy. This intensified after the Six Day War in 1967 and came to a head in

---

22 Raanan Rein, *Argentina, Israel, and the Jews* (Bethesda, MD: University Press of Maryland, 2003).

the infamous UN General Assembly Resolution 3379, adopted on November 10, 1975, which proclaimed that "Zionism is racism." In a historic speech at the UN General Assembly, the Israeli ambassador to the United Nations, Chaim Herzog, tore up a copy of the resolution and accused the world body of racism and anti-Semitism towards the State of Israel. US Ambassador Daniel Patrick Moynihan said in response to the resolution: "The abomination of antisemitism has been given the appearance of international sanction. The General Assembly today grants symbolic amnesty—and more—to the murderers of the six million European Jews."[23]

In 1978, the French-Jewish philosopher Vladimir Jankélévitch recognized that anti-Zionism had become a magical formula enabling one to be "democratically anti-Semitic."[24] In recent decades, anti-Zionism has become the glue binding young Muslims of North African descent to "progressive" left-wing forces across Europe and North America. Together, they maintain that their "legitimate" hatred of Israel justifies protests and violence against the economic, political, and cultural elites of Europe and, of course, the Jews. Some have therefore sought to harm world Jewry on the grounds that they are the "soft underbelly of the security of the Jewish people."[25]

But in recent years there has been significant pushback as well. Since 2016, at a time when minorities are increasingly given credit to define their own oppression, governments and major institutions are adopting the International Holocaust Remembrance Alliance (IHRA) definition of anti-Semitism that includes hatred of Israel. In 2019, the

---

23 Daniel Patrick Moynihan's speech responding to United Nations Resolution 3379, November 10, 1975, https://www.americanrhetoric.com/speeches/danielpatrickmoynihanun3379.htm.

24 Sarah Fainberg, "Don't Hear O Israel!," *Jerusalem Post* August 26, 2014, https://www.jpost.com/Opinion/Dont-Hear-O-Israel-372426.

25 Yossi Shain and Barry Bristman, "The Jewish Security Dilemma," *Orbis* 46, no. 1 (2001), 47–71; Suzanne Fields, "The Israelization of Antisemitism," *Washington Post*, September 17, 2014; Sarah Fainberg, "Don't Hear O Israel!"; Alain Finkielkraut, "In the Name of the Other: Reflections on the Coming Anti-Semitism," *Azure* 18 (Autumn 2004), http://azure.org.il/article.php?id=211.

German Bundestag voted to define boycotting Israel as anti-Semitic because "it questions the right of the Jewish and democratic state of Israel to exist or Israel's right to defend itself." The French National Assembly adopted a similar resolution. And the United States went further when President Trump extended the 1964 Civil Rights Act to include Jews suffering anti-Israel boycotts. Here, too, Judaism and Jewishness cannot be separated from the reality of Israel.

In the face of anti-Semitism's metamorphosis into anti-Zionism, the Israelization of Diaspora Jews and Judaism has accelerated, especially in France and Britain. These countries contain the two largest Jewish communities in Europe, and in recent years most of their cultural, religious, and political life has become focused on Israel and its challenges. According to the French-Jewish sociologist Pierre Birnbaum, many Jews in France "pay attention each day to what is happening in Israel…and Israel has become very present for them."[26] They follow Israeli media, watch Israeli films, read Israeli literature, conform to Israeli religious patterns, and eat Israeli cuisine.[27] Indeed, the growing fear of radical Islam and terrorist attacks have brought tens of thousands of Jews to emigrate from France to Israel in the past decade. The Israelization of French Jews even came up in domestic political discourse in France during the 2017 national elections. Marine Le Pen, the leader of the far-right National Front party, questioned the attachment that many French Jews had to Israel. She called on them to "choose their nationality" and remain French.

British Jewry has also undergone a similar process in its communal, organizational and religious life.[28] The shift of Jewish voters

---

26   Benjamin Ivry, "Pierre Birnbaum on the 'Israeli-zation' of French Jews," *The Forward*, December 12, 2015, https://forward.com/culture/books/326515/pierre-birnbaum-on-the-destiny-of-french-jews/.

27   Yossi Shain and Sarah Fainberg, "The Israelization of Judaism and the Jews of France," *Jewish Review of Books* (Fall 2015), 10–12.

28   Toby Greene and Yossi Shain, "The Israelization of British Jewry: Balancing between Home and Homeland," *The British Journal of Politics and International Affairs* 18, no. 4 (2016), 848–865.

away from the Labour Party, which had been their overwhelming home since World War II, and toward the Conservative Party stems in part from Labour's increasing hostility towards Israel and the cover for anti-Semitism that this has provided. With the rise of Jeremy Corbyn as the head of Labour in 2015, the tension between British Jews and the Labour Party reached new heights. In July 2018, the three major Jewish newspapers in the UK published a joint editorial declaring that a Corbyn-led government was an "existential threat to Jewish life in this country."[29] When Corbyn was defeated in a landslide in 2019, Jews breathed a sigh of relief—though the question of anti-Semitism continues to dog British politics and the Labour Party.

The Israelization of Judaism in western Europe is not only evident from the issue of anti-Semitism, but also in the religious life of many western European Jews. European rabbis have willingly accepted the authority of rabbinical courts in Israel and overwhelmingly receive their rabbinic training in the Jewish state. In June 2018, the Knesset passed an amendment to the Rabbinical Courts Jurisdiction Law, allowing Israel's religious authorities to impose sanctions and a criminal record on recalcitrant husbands *in Europe* who refused to grant their wives a divorce. The Israeli legislation was actually initiated by rabbinical courts in Europe, which have no power to force husbands to grant a divorce.[30]

In Europe today, the Jewish Question—which has overshadowed Jewish life since the eighteenth century—has increasingly become the Israeli Question.

The Israelization of Diaspora Jewry is clear even from Israel's

---

29 "Three Jewish Papers Take the Unprecedented Step of Publishing the Same Page on Labour Antisemitism," *The Jewish Chronicle*, July 25, 2018, https://www.thejc.com/comment/leaders/three-jewish-papers-take-the-unprecedented-step-of-publishing-the-same-page-on-labour-antisemitism-1.467641.

30 Shachar Chai and Kobi Nachshoni, "Rabbinical Courts: Now with International Powers," *YNet News*, June 26, 2018 [Hebrew].

unpopularity in certain quarters, including some progressive Jews in the West and the ultra-Orthodox Jews who reject Zionism for theological reasons. In both cases, Israel has become a major focus of their Jewish existence. Many progressive Diaspora Jews, who deplore Israel's nationalist slide and the erosion of universal Jewish values, are angry at the Jewish state for betraying their vision of inclusivity in favor of populist politics. Yet however much they criticize their Israeli cousins, liberal Jews cannot easily disengage from Israel—especially if they want to preserve their Jewish identity. Community mobilization and institution-building based on some sort of relationship with Israel remain one of the great organizational principles for even the most liberal sections of the Diaspora.

Increasingly, even American Jews are questioning the viability of Diaspora Jewish life in the face of rising anti-Semitism. To what extent does the liberal reality in the West actually reduce their ever-present ancient Jewish anxieties? To what extent do they see Israel as a potential refuge during times of trouble?[31]

In October 2018, following the murder of Jewish worshippers at the Etz Chaim Synagogue in Pittsburgh, Pennsylvania, a debate broke out over what the attack meant for the future of Jews in the United States. One side of the debate argued that the synagogue massacre was an exception that did not reflect the "profound" acceptance of Jews and Judaism in America and should therefore not disrupt the normal, secure American-Jewish way of life.[32] Others warned against trivializing the massacre by chalking it up to a more "general hatred of religion, rather than specific hatred of Jews."[33]

---

31 Julie Cooper, "The Wisdom of the Ghetto Mentality," *Political Theology* 18, no. 1 (February 2017), 1–4.

32 Kirsch, "Why Jewish History is So Hard to Write."

33 Yair Rosenberg, "The Pittsburgh Shooter Didn't Hate 'Religion,' He Hated Jews. We Should Say So," *Washington Post*, November 2, 2018, https://www.washingtonpost.com/outlook/the-pittsburgh-shooter-didnt-hate-religion-he-hated-jews-we-should-say-so/2018/11/01/93343918-de05-11e8-b732-3c72cbf131f2_story.html.

One commentator, Carly Pildis, wrote that many American Jews, in an effort to detach themselves from the long, historical experience of Jewish persecution, were turning a blind eye to the intensifying anti-Semitic threats, "couch[ing] it in more gauzy and inclusive terms…which efface and erase us, while promoting causes and victim groups that they feel more comfortable with."[34]

Even Peter Beinart, a well-known spokesperson for cosmopolitan liberals in American Jewry, was struck overnight by a "ghetto mentality" when Donald Trump was elected President of the United States in November 2016. Beinart, an outspoken critic of the Israeli right and the American-Jewish establishment that he claims automatically supports it, wrote:

> I've never felt less American and more Jewish…. I've always assumed my country would be stable…. I've never experienced anything like the election of Donald Trump. I've never experienced anything so frightening or destabilizing. I'm experiencing political vertigo…. My grandmother…used to laugh at me when I boasted about America. She told me not to get too comfortable. She said a Jew must always know when to leave the sinking ship…. I still love America to my core. But I don't trust it in the same way…. I keep hearing my grandmother's voice in my ear.[35]

---

34 Carly Pildis, "Stop Erasing the Jewish Victims of Anti-Semitic Violence," *Tablet Magazine*, October 30, 2018, https://www.tabletmag.com/jewish-news-and-politics/273773/erasure-jewish-victims-anti-semitism.

35 Peter Beinart, "I Still Love America. But, after Trump's Victory, I Don't Trust It," *Haaretz*, November 9, 2016, https://www.haaretz.com/world-news/peter-beinart-i-still-love-america-but-after-trump-i-dont-trust-it-1.5459138.

A different but parallel phenomenon can be seen among the ultra-Orthodox. Although many American Haredim reject the idea of modern Jewish sovereignty in principle, many of them—like their peers in Israel—have accepted the fact of Israel's existence and are concerned for its security.[36] The exceptional story of the *aliyah* and enlistment of Chaim Meisels—the great-grandson of Rabbi Moshe Teitelbaum, rabbi of the Satmar dynasty and the anti-Zionist leader of one of the largest Hasidic movements at the time—received great acclaim in Israel and the Diaspora. Meisels, who became a combat officer, described how he left Brooklyn in secret and chose a different Jewish path from his family, "a Judaism in which standing up and defending the Jewish people's state is just as important and huge as studying Torah."[37]

In recent years, some in the ultra-Orthodox community have claimed that *they* are the most important voice in American Jewry. They argue that their commitment to Israel is stronger than that of the Reform and Conservative movements, whose members they accuse of abandoning Jewish identity. Daniel Goldman, former head of Gesher, an organization that aims to bridge gaps with Israeli society, argues that American Orthodox Jews are seeking to penetrate Israel under the guise of Zionism, with a view to *undermining* modern Judaism in both Israel and the Diaspora. According to Goldman, "The portrayal of the ultra-Orthodox as Israeli patriots, in contrast to the distancing of Jewish liberals, is designed to harm modernist movements in Israel and the Diaspora by casting doubt on their loyalty to the Jewish people and the Jewish State."[38]

To what extent will the Israelization of the ultra-Orthodox in Israel and the Diaspora ultimately lead to the *Haredization* of Israel?

---

36 Eliezer Don-Yehiya, "Orthodox Jewry in Israel and in North America," *Israel Studies* 10, no. 1 (Spring 2005), 180.

37 "How Satmar Rebbe's Grandson Became an IDF Officer," *YNet News*, September 11, 2017, https://www.ynetnews.com/articles/0,7340,L-5037640,00.html.

38 Conversation with the author.

Such an outcome would not only undermine Israel's free and open character but also threaten its continued connection with most of the Diaspora.

* * *

It would be a mistake to attempt to understand the Israeli Century based solely on current trends, however. The Israeli Century has emerged atop the foundations of centuries of Jewish collective memories. The quest for "Jewish" answers to questions of statecraft, including national-security dilemmas, is almost always guided by the "lessons of history," especially those learned from traumas inflicted on the Jewish people when they lacked sovereignty—chiefly the Holocaust—or, looking farther back in time, when biblical sovereignty was weak and beset by internal rivalries.

In the summer of 2018, Israeli Prime Minister Benjamin Netanyahu and his Polish counterpart Mateusz Morawiecki published a joint statement on Israeli-Polish ties. It provoked an uproar from Holocaust survivors, politicians, and scholars, who claimed that Israel was giving its stamp of approval to Poland's Holocaust revisionism.

The renowned Holocaust scholar Yehuda Bauer was furious, claiming that Israel had sold out memory of the Holocaust. He accused the Israeli government of agreeing to distort historical truth for the sake of political and economic interests, and Netanyahu of betrayal. In contrast, Israel's former Chief Rabbi Israel Meir Lau, a Holocaust survivor and chairman of the Yad Vashem Council, defended Netanyahu and said that he accepted the friendly tone of the agreement, which was drafted to help both nations move beyond a painful past: "There are two perspectives here that can't always be reconciled.... One is diplomatic-political which focuses on Israel-Poland relations today, in 2018, and the other is emotional and scientific, taken by scholars of Jewish history in World War II. The latter looks at the past—without taking into consideration the significance of the relations between the two countries, and the former focuses on the present and the future, with a more forgiving attitude toward the Poles as individuals."[39]

Israel uses its Jewish and international strength to implement the lessons of history as it sees them. Israel's national security doctrine holds that the country is permanently under existential threat and must always take its fate into its own hands. In his explosive book *Rise and Kill First*, the veteran journalist Ronen Bergman explores how the activist ideology of Zionism after the trauma of the Holocaust led Israel to adopt policies of "targeted killings" in its war on terror on a scale unparalleled in the free world. Israel makes prolific use of targeted killings, and maintains this strategy is morally and legally justified. To safeguard the future of the Jewish people, terrorist leaders must be eliminated, and "collateral damage" might be a "necessary evil."[40] Yet it is also due to the lessons of history that Israel has always seen itself as responsible for the security of Jewish communities abroad, even passing legislation to that effect. Indeed, the doctrine of Israel's spy agencies, especially the Mossad, doubling as "the Jewish people's intelligence services" predates the birth of the state and continues to this day.[41]

Israeli and Diaspora Jews often present themselves not only as a living reminder of the greatest crime against humanity ever committed, but also as a people who remain under threat of annihilation.

---

39   Inbar Tvizer and Kobi Nachshoni, "Holocaust Survivors Feel Betrayed by Polish-Israeli Statement," YNet News May 7, 2018, https://www.ynetnews.com/articles/0,7340,L-5304851,00.html.

40   Ronen Bergman, *Rise and Kill First: The Secret History of Israel's Targeted Assassinations* (New York: Random House, 2018).

41   Yossi Melman, "Spirit of the Age: Trump's Incitement and His Policies Provoked the Antisemitism That Led to the Massacre of Jews in Pittsburgh," *Maariv*, November 3, 2010 [Hebrew].

In contrast, critics of Israel, Jews and non-Jews alike, accuse Israel of developing an addiction to appealing to the Holocaust, distorting Israel's moral and political culture. The progressive American-Jewish scholar Ian Lustick wrote that the Israeli addiction to the "Holocaust syndrome" (what he calls "Holocaustia") encourages anti-Semitism and anti-Zionism, prevents Israeli leaders from moving towards a peace agreement with the Arabs, and could eventually lead to Israel's downfall.[42] Other scholars have strongly criticized this argument, however, calling it "a politically motivated, agenda-driven interpretation that is masked in scientific jargon."[43]

Still, many warn that Israel's "siege mentality" and frequent reference to existential threats have dulled its moral sensitivity on issues such as democracy and human rights. Israel stands accused of flouting international norms under the guise of being, as the political scientist Uriel Abulof has written, a "'victim community'... which leverages the Holocaust and turns Auschwitz into the ultimate card...in its relations with the world."[44]

In other words, although Israel is strengthened by its appeals to past traumas and especially the Holocaust as the basis for its moral legitimacy, it is also assailed precisely on those same moral and ethical grounds by those who seek to undermine its legitimacy.[45]

* * *

We should not underestimate the impact such seemingly

---

42   Ian Lustick, "The Holocaust in Israeli Political Culture: Four Constructions and Their Consequences," *Contemporary Jewry* 47 (2017), 127–170.

43   Dan Michman, Sergio DellaPergola, Paul Burstein, and Adam Ferziger, "A Reply to Ian Lustick's Article," *Contemporary Jewry* 37 (2017),171–181.

44   Uriel Abulof, *Living on the Edge: The Existential Uncertainty of Zionism* (Tel Aviv: Yediot Books, 2015), 282–285 [Hebrew].

45   Alan Dershowitz, *The Case for Israel* (New York: Wiley, 2003), 1.

abstract debates over memory, morality, and the character of the Jewish state will have on the future of Jewish life around the world.

True, the fact that most of world Jewry will soon live in Israel will create greater symbiosis between the Jewish state and the worldwide Jewish people. But this symbiosis will not necessarily herald greater cohesion among the Jews, or even among Israelis.

In June 2015, Israeli President Reuven Rivlin delivered his famous "Four Tribes" speech, in which he described the emergence of a new Israeli order comprising four tribes—three Jewish (secular, national-religious, Haredim) and one Arab. This tribal split, argued the president, is a result of cultural and demographic upheavals sweeping Israeli society.[46]

Some Diaspora Jewish leaders accept the primacy of the Israeli Century and demand that they be given a voice and status as a "fifth tribe"—the Jews of the Diaspora—out of a fear that they will become completely marginalized. Charles Bronfman, a prominent Diaspora leader and cofounder of Birthright Israel, recently issued a call to save the connection between Israel and the Diaspora. He urged the sides to engage in an essential and intensive dialogue to "ensure a future for everybody, a future for the people." Bronfman wrote that "while the four tribes living in Israel play a day-to-day role in the political life of Israel, the place of the fifth is missing."[47]

Ever since the establishment of Israel, its leaders have claimed an almost exclusive role as spokespersons for the entire Jewish people. As early as the controversy over Holocaust reparations in the 1950s, the Israeli government argued that sovereignty granted

---

46 President Reuven Rivlin, "Israeli Hope: Towards a New Israeli Order," address to the fifteenth annual Herzliya Conference, June 7, 2015, https://www.idc.ac.il/en/research/ips/Documents/4-Tribes/PresidentSPEECH2015.pdf.

47 Charles Bronfman, "Israel Comprises 43% of the Jewish People and Unfortunately, the Remaining 57% are Invisible," *Maariv*, June 4, 2018 [Hebrew].

it the prerogative to represent the whole Jewish people in negotiations with West Germany. Nahum Goldman, the acting chairman of
the World Jewish Congress and representative of the Diaspora-run
Claims Conference, opposed Israel's assertions. Yet Prime Minister
Ben-Gurion and Foreign Minister Moshe Sharett vehemently disagreed: "The State of Israel speaks for the Jewish people," Sharett
argued. "It is the only country the Jewish people has. That is a fact."[48]

Still, it remains in dispute whether Israel can indeed speak
on behalf of all Jews. On issues relating to Jews worldwide, such
as the struggle against anti-Semitism or the campaign to return
assets stolen from Jews during World War II, Israel often seems to
sit on the fence. Stuart Eizenstat, who led the negotiations for the
restitution of European Jewish property as President Clinton's
special envoy, wrote two decades ago that he saw himself as a
"Jewish diplomat," whose job was to deliver historic justice to
his brethren abandoned by the Americans during the war. He
was astonished to learn that Israel's response to his efforts was
at best passive and at worst hostile, acting out of its own *raison
d'état*.[49] Yet despite the accomplishments of Jewish Diaspora organizations in support of world Jewry, today nobody can seriously
compete with the State of Israel as the definitive spokesperson for
the Jewish people.

Over seven decades after the Holocaust, Diaspora Jews have
lost the ability to come together on nearly any subject affecting
their interests, or to raise up non-Israeli exemplars. Elie Wiesel,
the Nobel Peace Prize laureate, was seen as perhaps the preeminent
Diaspora Jew and the most articulate defender of the memory of the

---

48 Yehiam Weitz, "The Reparation Negotiations in Israeli Politics," in *The Reparations Controversy:
The Jewish State and German Money in the Shadow of the Holocaust 1951–1952*, ed. Yaakov Sharett
(Berlin: De Gruyter, 2011), 4.

49 Stuart E. Eizenstat, *Imperfect Justice: Looted Assets, Slave Labor, and the Unfinished Business of
World War II* (New York: Public Affairs, 2003).

Holocaust as a Jewish memory of universal moral significance. But since his death in 2016, it has become hard to point to any figures in the Diaspora who have attained anything resembling his stature.[50]

And even Wiesel was deeply connected to Israel, to the point of being denounced by the American scholar Samuel Huntington for his affinity with Israeli nationalism "at the expense of broader interests and American relations with long-standing allies."[51] For Wiesel, however, a profound connection to the Jewish state was central to his identity: "I support Israel—period. I identify with Israel—period. I never attack, never criticize Israel when I am not in Israel…. The role of a Jew is to be with our people."

Yet while Diaspora Jews struggle to find their voice, in Israel the discourse has become increasingly nationalistic and Orthodox. Some openly dismiss progressive and humanistic Diaspora Jews for their perceived naivety concerning Middle East affairs and the Israeli-Palestinian conflict. Many Orthodox Jews, both in Israel and around the world, argue that the continued existence of non-Orthodox Jews as a cultural-ethnic group in the Diaspora is uncertain as a result of intermarriage, abandonment of traditions, lack of Jewish education, and communal fraying. Their claims are not without foundation: even leaders of the Reform movement fear the devastating trends within their communities. Rabbi Ammiel Hirsch has said that "to feel connected to the Jewish people and attached to the Jewish state are not proof of ghetto Judaism. In fact, not to be committed to these values is evidence of Jewish decline…. Reform Judaism two generations from now will be a shadow of what it is today."[52]

---

50 In 2020, former UK Chief Rabbi Lord Jonathan Sacks passed away. Sacks was an intellectual giant who became a global voice for Orthodox Judaism. He was an eloquent fighter against anti-Semitism, and commanded a global following among Jews and non-Jews as a moral thinker.

51 Samuel Huntington, *Who Are We: America's Great Debate* (New York: Free Press, 2004), 293.

52 Ammiel Hirsch, "This is the Gravest Threat to the Future of Liberal Judaism," *Jewish Telegraphic Agency*, October 5, 2018, https://www.jta.org/2018/10/05/opinion/gravest-threat-future-liberal-judaism.

While Israelis are increasingly inclined to nurture a Judaism that emphasizes the national and religious aspects of Jewish peoplehood, many argue that Israel must not neglect the humanistic and cosmopolitan side of Judaism and must actively champion interfaith and intercultural dialogue. In a demonstration of support for liberal Judaism in the Diaspora, the former Knesset speaker Avraham Burg said on the eve of the Jewish New Year in 2017: "I won't celebrate this holiday with Netanyahu, with his traumas and Israeli paranoias that he invents or so skillfully represents. I'll be with [liberal philanthropist George] Soros, the Jews of the world and their struggle for open societies everywhere, for every human being." The State of Israel, according to Burg, opened up national horizons that had degenerated in the Jewish collective consciousness, "but almost completely blocked possibilities that characterized life in the Diaspora." Its isolationist instinct, based on the inherited beliefs in chosenness and eternal persecution, "has eroded the little that connected the Israeli Jew to more general spheres of humanity."[53]

This approach, however, remains on the liberal margins of Jewish discourse in Israel. The overwhelming majority of Israeli Jews and many of their Diaspora brethren see Israeli sovereignty as the key to the preservation of Judaism and of Jews. For them, the State of Israel is as Ben-Gurion envisaged: the guarantee for the successful *reconciliation* of Judaism's national-tribal and universalistic sides. After Israel's establishment, Ben-Gurion wrote:

> With the establishment of our political independence, we have become citizens of the world to a greater degree than we had been in the past. Nevertheless, as a scattered nation,

53   Avraham Burg, "Rosh Hashanah as the Battle of Netanyahu vs. Soros," *Haaretz*, September 21, 2017, ://www.haaretz.com/opinion/.premium-rosh-hashanah-as-the-battle-of-netanyahu-vs-soros-1.5452542.

dispersed to the ends of the earth and wondering from country to country, from nation to nation, we always had more of global sensibility than some other peoples. Our national independence has placed our global citizenship on a strong and stable foundation. This was not due to our previous lack of a homeland and sovereign political existence, but rather it is precisely because of the existence of our national and political sovereignty that we are awake to the problems of humanity, and are awake to its needs and uncertainties.[54]

There are still Jews in Israel and the Diaspora who dispute Israel's authority to rule on questions of "Jewish ethics," "Jewish interests," and "Jewish identity." The nationalist thinker Yoram Hazony published his book *The Jewish State: The Struggle For Israel's Soul* just a few months before the Second Intifada erupted in September 2000, and warned against what he called the "Israeli urge to suicide." Hazony cautioned against what he saw as a "post-Zionist" intellectual takeover of Israeli culture and academia that sought to abandon the entire idea of a Jewish state in favor of a more cosmopolitan "state of all its citizens." Zionism, the post-Zionists argued, was itself a distortion of Jewish universal ethics, which had long rejected the injustices and atrocities committed in the name of *realpolitik*.[55]

But the subsequent sea-change provoked by the Second Intifada's wave of suicide bombings in Israel, coinciding with the seismic global changes wrought by the 9/11 terror attacks, brought

---

54 Ben-Gurion, *Uniqueness and Destiny*, 42 [Hebrew].

55 Yoram Hazony, *The Jewish State: The Struggle for Israel's Soul* (New York: Basic Books, 2000). The phrase "Israeli urge to suicide" was taken from the title of a column in *Haaretz* by Aharon Meged of the same name.

an apparent end to the debate over Zionism in Israel, for it highlighted for most Israelis how critically important it was for them to have a strong and sovereign state of their own.

* * *

Today, many questions surrounding aims of the Jewish state and its relationship to both the Jewish people and Jewish history remain unanswered. What does it mean for a state to be "Jewish," in the battle between modernity and tradition? Who is a legitimate party to the debate, and who falls outside it?

The Israeli Supreme Court ruled in 2013—not for the first time—that the State of Israel is the nation-state of the Jewish people. The court rejected an appeal by a number of people requesting to register their nationality as "Israeli" rather than "Jewish." The Supreme Court judges ruled once again that in modern Israel, one must distinguish between "citizenship and nationality" and that "there is no place to unite the different nationalities and group them together legally under a new and inclusive 'Israeli nationality,' inasmuch as it is contrary to the Jewish and democratic character of the state."[56]

In 2018, the Knesset passed the "Basic Law: Israel—the Nation State of the Jewish People," which gave quasi-constitutional status to the earlier rulings without explicitly reaffirming the equal citizenship of Arab Israelis. Although defenders of the law insisted that such equality had already been granted in other "basic laws," and that this was meant as a corrective constitutional measure, it nonetheless provoked a storm in Israel and around the world over whether Israel is still fully democratic with regards to its minority groups, as Israel's Declaration of Independence stated it must be.

---

56 *Uzi Arnan* v. *Interior Ministry*, October 2, 2013.

In the nation-state of the Jewish people, Israeli Jews inhabit a dynamic spectrum between the progressivism of the "Start-Up Nation" and the regressive conservatism of a religious "Halakhic Nation," a country that simultaneously offers a haven for the LGBT community and places issues of marital status under the aegis of an Orthodox Chief Rabbinate. Yet a majority of Israelis still support an open, liberal democracy in a Jewish nation-state—granting equal citizenship for individuals and certain privileges for Jewish collective identity at the level of national expression, holidays, and symbolism.

Alongside Jewish debates in Israel over the nature of democracy, Israeli Arabs have a debate on a different axis. Some would seek not just full civic equality as individuals but also equal *national* recognition as an Arab minority, perhaps even with geographic autonomy. Others reject Israeli sovereignty altogether and even the notion of a Jewish people. Yet Israel's Arab community and other minority groups contain many who identify with the Jewish state and are loyal to it. To a large extent, they are even adopting the culture of Israel's Jewish majority. During the Covid-19 crisis of 2020, Arab-Jewish medical teams throughout the country battled the pandemic together. This important milestone also led to unprecedented political initiatives on the Israeli right to build political partnerships between Jewish and Arab parties.[57] Thus, when the May 2021 clashes between Arab and Jewish citizens of Israel erupted in the country's mixed Jewish-Arab communities, threatening to destroy all efforts to bridge the divide, many Israelis were gripped with shock and agony in the face of these events.

Despite these troubling developments and the growing

---

57 Addressing the Likud party secretariat, Prime Minister Benjamin Netanyahu said: "I believe in [Zionist leader Ze'ev] Jabotinsky's doctrine that all rights need to be given to every citizen in the State of Israel. We're reaching out to Arab voters—vote for us." See "Netanyahu Says He Wants to Break Joint List's Monopoly on Arab Israeli Vote," the *Times of Israel*, January 3, 2021.

warnings against Jewish-Israeli tribalism, Zionism is a phenomenal achievement, greater than any development in Jewish life in the Diaspora. In spite of the difficulties in bringing together so diverse a population, one must not overlook, as the historian Alexander Yakobson argued, "the size of the achievement inherent in the fact that a country made up of such a population has managed to survive, develop, establish a democratic regime, and avoid the ethnic bloody conflicts which characterize many multi-ethnic and multicultural societies." Even ideological critics of Zionism, Yakobson argues, accept the Zionist belief that, "ultimately, we are truly one nation."[58]

* * *

The magnitude of this achievement creates, however, a certain dissonance.

For a great many Jews and non-Jews around the world, the story of the Jewish people more or less begins two thousand years ago, with the destruction of the Second Temple in 70 CE and the beginning of the exile and Diaspora that would continue for two millennia. It was then that "Israelites" became "Jews," ancient biblical history transitioned into Jewish history, and the story of a people dispersed around the world, at times suffering and at others prospering, became a fixture of world history.

Seen through this lens, the establishment of Israel feels like a historical anomaly that adds to, but does not fundamentally alter, Jewish reality. Indeed, for the first few decades of Israel's existence, there was good reason to feel this way: only a small minority of world Jewry lived in Israel, and the Jewish state was both impoverished and tenuous, facing daunting strategic threats. Though this is

---

58 Alexander Yakobson, "Zionism and Multiculturalism," *Law & Business: IDC Law Review* 14 (2012), 1–45 [Hebrew].

today no longer the case, a great many people, critics and supporters alike, still try to see Israel through a lens defined, in large part, by this two-thousand-year view of Jewish history.

But the people that went into exile in the first and second centuries CE were in fact coming off a history of more than a thousand years before that of various forms of sovereign life in the Land of Israel, dating back to the Bible: from the conquests of Joshua, through the unified kingdom of David and Solomon, to the destruction and return in the sixth century BCE, to the Hasmonean kingdom and the reconstruction of the temple in Jerusalem at the time of Herod at the turn of the first millennium. Even when they didn't have full control over their foreign affairs, they nonetheless built a thick sovereign legal tradition that became only thicker after the Roman exile that ended their grasp on the land of their forefathers.

Taken in the context of *three* thousand, rather than two thousand, years of history, it becomes apparent that Judaism has always embodied a fierce tension between sovereign and anti-sovereign elements, between the urge of a nation to determine its fate in its land and a spiritual mission to survive and even thrive among the nations. Zionism emerged in the nineteenth century as a hybrid, drawing on the conceptual and political tools of the modern era of emergent sovereign nation-states, but also on centuries of messianic desire to restore the ancient kingdom, a desire that was canonized not only in the Bible but also in daily prayers and the refrain, recited every Passover, of "next year in Jerusalem."

The establishment and success of Israel was, therefore, not simply an appendix to Jewish history, but a kind of messianic revolution, channeling the perennial Jewish will to sovereign life. And with the progress of the Israeli Century, it has become increasingly clear that this upheaval of Jewish history represents nothing less than a *verdict*, a victory of the sovereign impulse ever-present in Judaism over the anti-sovereign impulse, one that shows every sign of being about as permanent as anything that happens in human history can ever be.

This is a difficult pill for many Diaspora Jews to swallow, especially in the United States, which for decades after the Holocaust enjoyed the status of being the epicenter of the Jewish world. This is the source of the dissonance, of the endless inner conflict that results from the issue of "Israel" within the Jewish community. It comes from a hesitation to upend one's *own* Jewish identity, grounded in a specific view of Jewish history, in the shadow of the verdict.

At the same time, when the facts increasingly do not fit the perception, one ought to revise the perception. It is Jewish history itself, as entrenched in the minds of Jews and non-Jews alike for generations, and the perception of Jewish identity as something essentially Diasporic, that must be reexamined if we are to understand the meaning of the Israeli Century.

In 1949, when the Israeli Century started to take shape, David Ben-Gurion recognized the historical cycle had been broken: "It is necessary to create a Hebrew character and style, which did not exist, which could not have existed, in the Diaspora, among a people without a homeland, without independence and national freedom. There is a need to revive and strengthen the relationship with the inspiring glory that is in our past, without enslavement to the fossilized legacy which has passed its time."[59]

Such a reexamination of Jewish history has already begun outside the Jewish conversation, in the field of political thought. Historians have long maintained that the connection between ethnicity and political sovereignty that forms the basis of the modern nation-state is a relatively new historical phenomenon, beginning with modernity or the French Revolution of 1789. It was in this spirit that many of the founders and historians of Zionism argued,

---

59 David Ben-Gurion, March 27, 1949.

as one scholar put it, that "only in the second half of the nineteenth century did the concept of political nationalism take hold among the Jews, one that explicitly demanded the establishment of a Jewish state on an ethnic basis."[60]

In recent decades, however, prominent scholars such as Steven Grosby, Anthony Smith, Azar Gat, and Aviel Roshwald have stressed the ancient roots of ethno-national states, including that of the Hebrew nation. They point out that many of the theoreticians of the modern nation-state leaned heavily on far more ancient teachings, not least on the Hebrew Bible itself. For these scholars, the history of the Jews, from early in the first millennium BCE to the Israeli Century, is a crucial test case for the nature and endurance of nation-states from ancient times to the present.

Yet even if we agree that ancient history can often be distorted to serve political ends as a "usable past," no serious scholar can deny the fact of ancient Hebrew sovereignty or the Jews' historical ties to the Land of Israel, which have been confirmed beyond question by a century of archeological excavation. Nor can anyone seriously question the endurance of a collective Jewish consciousness since antiquity, as evidenced across rabbinic texts through the ages. Over millennia, the Jews demonstrated extraordinary powers of continuity far from their homeland and a powerful devotion to their history once restored to that homeland.

It is not my aim to paint Zionism as an unalloyed success. Rather, my goal is to probe the primacy of the Israeli Century and ask: How can the State of Israel make itself the most effective tool for ensuring the continued existence and prosperity of the Jewish people, the Jewish religion, and Jewish culture for generations to come? And at the same time, how can the Diaspora internalize the

---

60   Assaf Malach, "A Look at Nationalism and the Jewish-Israeli Case," *Iyyunim Bitkumat Israel* 26 (2016), 157 [Hebrew].

true meaning of the Israeli Century against the long, strange trip of the Jews through history?

None of these questions, however, can be adequately answered without taking a fresh look at the three-thousand-year story of the Jews. The tale of Jewish history dating back to ancient times, we will discover, is one of a constant struggle between the need for a people to live a sovereign life in its land and the need of the same people to expand beyond—an empire, not of armies but of ideas, sharing its unique moral perspective with the world.

It is also a cautionary tale, in which the twin risks of chauvinistic parochialism on the one hand, and of self-effacing powerlessness on the other, come into full, often terrible, relief. For the five tribes of twenty-first-century Judaism to achieve a sense of community and coherence, rather than chaos, they will need to understand the nature of the Israeli Century and work towards building its future together.

Chapter I: The Jewish Paradigm and the End of History

The new clout wielded by the State of Israel and the declining influence of the Jewish Diaspora undermine the centuries-old idea that exile and dispersion are more critical to the Jewish people than independence and sovereignty. After the destruction of the Second Temple in 70 CE, the exile and Diaspora in Jewish life had a far-reaching impact on the nature of Jewish faith, memory, ethics, power, and the Jews' role in the world.

The ascent of the Israeli Century has rendered the "Jewish Question" increasingly less important, replacing it with the "Israeli Question." Israel and its behavior have important repercussions for the Jewish people and their place among nations, both in support for Jews as a flourishing and powerful tribe worthy of admiration and emulation and, conversely, hostility toward them over what is seen as their excessive power. With this transformation in mind, let us delve into the evolution of the relationship between Jewish sovereignty and diaspora to understand how the age-old debate manifests itself today.

The Theological Paradigm

The Jewish ethos of exile and return was shaped in the sixth century BCE, around the time of the destruction of the First Temple and the subsequent Babylonian exile. According to Judaism scholar Jacob Neusner this ethos has remained the "bread and butter" of Judaism ever since. Neusner argues that this is *the* Jewish paradigm; it is a theology that has developed over the generations, encompassing a narrative that swings between divine edicts condemning the Jews to exile and divine promises to restore them to their homeland.[61]

Historically, the cycle of exile and return was based on a "carrot and stick" relationship between God and his chosen people. The Jews believed that it was God's will to delay their sovereign return to the Land of Israel, and as such, they "made God the guarantor of their power."[62] God, for his part, used outside actors to penalize or reward the Jews, based on their willingness to obey and adhere to His commandments. In the Jewish ethos, the exile from their homeland is a disaster that they brought upon themselves. Their dispersion, however, is also an opportunity for renewal and moral growth in preparation for the ingathering of the exiles–the vision or yearning for a mass return to the Promised Land and the resumption of their independence.

The paradigm of exile and return is rooted in the destruction of the First Temple in 586 BCE and the Babylonian exile, which came to an end with the return to zion and the restoration of the Israelites' historic homeland, particularly during the period of Ezra and Nehemiah. This period is generally seen as coming full circle– the prophecies of redemption were fulfilled, and the Jewish people were granted sovereignty in their homeland.

This view, however, is not grounded in fact. Firstly, Judea did not become a sovereign entity again; it remained a tiny province of the Persian Empire, known as *Yehud Medinata*. The Jews merely enjoyed cultural and religious autonomy within a confined area and had no military force of their own. Their leaders were appointed by,

---

61 Jacob Neusner, *Self-Fulfilling Prophecy: Exile and Return in the History of Judaism* (Boston: Beacon Press, 1987).

62 Ruth Wisse, "The Brilliant Failure of Jewish Foreign Policy," *Azure* (Winter 2001).

and served, the Persians, and there was no symmetry between the reality of the Jews as a nation before exile and upon their return.

Secondly, many of the Judeans who went into exile (even prior to the destruction of the Temple in 586 BCE) never returned. The diaspora became an integral part of Jewish life and has been ever since.

Babylon's exiled elite managed to preserve and cultivate some of the institutions and authorities that existed prior to the fall of the Judean kingdom. First and foremost, they worked to maintain and safeguard a distinct tribal identity, managing the internal finances of their exiled community. They did so in the absence of sovereignty, thanks to the establishment of a new and revolutionary religious faith—the monotheistic belief in God as the "master of history" responsible for the conduct and fate of all peoples, including the people of Israel.

Central to this new Judaism was the concept of *sanctity* as a property of the Jewish collective, rather than of any territory, state, or ruler. This concept of the chosen people (or "the Holy Seed") is a notion that could only be meaningful in the context of a monotheistic religion, in which God controls history. He chose His people; it was He who led them into exile, and He who would ultimately restore them to their land. It was based on the thesis that the Jews established their collective consciousness, separating their community of exiles in Babylon from their alien environs.

Besides their faith in the God of history, Babylonian Jews developed customs that distinguished them from their neighbors, which facilitated the continued existence of Judaism, even without sovereign control in the Jewish homeland. They included, for example, a ban on mixed marriages, the laws of *kashrut* and "family purity," the sanctity of scriptures, communal worship, and the creation of houses of study. Thus, Jewish existence, disconnected from sovereign power, took root as a way of life outside the historic homeland.

Their ability to retain their cohesion and particularism greatly benefited from the Babylonian policy of keeping defeated and exiled communities together. This policy enabled the Babylonians to retain control over exiled elites and harnessed them for imperial projects. It stood in sharp contrast to the policy of Assyria 200 years earlier, which forced conquered peoples to integrate into the empire. However, true to the Jewish paradigm of loss, sovereignty, exile, and return, the Return to Zion was wrongly seen as the Jews coming full circle, even though they did not reestablish their political independence.

Indeed, in the Jewish tradition and the modern State of Israel, it is a matter of debate whether the Jews' attachments and commitments should be to the *Land* of Israel or the *State* of Israel. While some dispute the intrinsic connection between the Jewish people and the Land of Israel, others maintain that loyalty to the Land of Israel as the Holy Land far exceeds loyalty to the State of Israel and its laws.

The Babylonian Exile served to change the basis of Jewish identity, from being a political nation—the "Seed of Israel"—to a religious congregation, defined as the "the Holy Seed." It weakened the ethos of the Jews as an ancient ethnic community and thus created a conflict between two approaches: one prized the return to the Land of Israel as the fulfilment of the religious imperative to live in the Holy Land; the other emphasized political control in the homeland as the only guarantee of national survival.

The Return to Zion offered the Jewish people the option of life and eventually prosperity in the homeland without Jewish sovereignty. Yet, when the Temple was rebuilt by the returnees, Jerusalem remained under Persian rule. Historian Erich Gruen argues that the return itself was less important than the fact that most Judean exiles decided to remain and prosper in Babylon. He sees this episode as ground zero of the schizophrenic nature of the paradigm of exile and return.

Gruen cites two passages from the Hebrew Bible to illustrate the gulf between the contradictory concepts. One focuses on the trauma of the destruction of the temple, as expressed in Psalm 137: "By the rivers of Babylon, there we sat down, yea, we wept, when we remembered Zion…. How shall we sing the Lord's song in a foreign land?"[63]

The second is a pragmatic approach to a normal life in exile, as found in Jeremiah's prophecies:

> Thus saith the Lord of hosts, the God of Israel, unto all the captivity, whom I have caused to be carried away captive from Jerusalem unto Babylon: Build ye houses, and dwell in them, and plant gardens, and eat the fruit of them; take ye wives, and beget sons and daughters; and take wives for your sons, and give your daughters to husbands, that they may bear sons and daughters; and multiply ye there, and be not diminished. And seek the peace of the city whither I have caused you to be carried away captive, and pray unto the Lord for it; for in the peace thereof shall ye have peace.[64]

Indeed, the short Babylonian exile, the Return to Zion, and the Second Temple period ultimately reconciled the trauma of the loss of the Jewish homeland and normality in exile. Jews lived in *both* the Diaspora and their national home, as two complementary models that existed alongside each other and not at each other's expense. Jeremiah's prophecy of the Return to Zion can thus be seen as a

---

63   Psalm 137:1–4 (JPS Version). All subsequent quotations from the Hebrew Bible will be taken from the JPS Version.

64   Jeremiah 29:4–7.

"blueprint for diaspora existence, a guide for Jews who were developing strategies for survival and success in lands governed by Gentiles."[65]
In Jeremiah's words: "For thus saith the Lord: After seventy years are
accomplished for Babylon, I will remember you, and perform My
good word toward you, in causing you to return to this place. For I
know the thoughts that I think toward you, saith the Lord, thoughts
of peace, and not of evil, to give you a future and a hope."[66]

   To summarize Judaism's theological story, we can say that
Judaism in Babylon developed first and foremost as a substitute for sovereignty. Jerusalem continued to be a center for worship, even though
most Jewish people lived outside of the Land of Israel at the time.
This remained the situation after Israel was conquered and annexed
by Alexander the Great in 322 BCE, and under the subsequent rule of
the Egyptian Ptolemaic dynasty, which lasted until 198 BCE. During
this Hellenistic era, many of the Jews living in the Diaspora adopted a
cosmopolitan way of life that eroded their identity as a distinct nation
and religion. As the book of Maccabees recalls:

> In those days went there out of Israel wicked
> men, who persuaded many, saying, Let us go
> and make a covenant with the heathen that
> are round about us: for since we departed
> from them we have had much sorrow. So
> this device pleased them well. Then certain
> of the people were so forward herein, that

---

65   Erich S. Gruen, *Diaspora: Jews amidst Greeks and Romans* (Cambridge: Harvard University
Press, 2002), 135. The archaeologists Israel Finkelstein and Neil Asher Silberman argue that
we have virtually no biblical trace of the Babylonian exile, apart from the observation that the
people of Israel heeded Jeremiah's advice. "Both text and archaeology contradict the idea that
between the destruction of Jerusalem in 586 BCE and the return of the exiles after the proclamation of Cyrus in 538 BCE Judah was in total ruin and uninhabited," Finkelstein and Silberman,
The Bible Unearthed (Touchstone: New York, 2002), 307). This fact seems to strengthen the dualist
thesis (home and diaspora) of the late-First Temple and early-Second Temple eras.
66   Jeremiah 29:10–11.

> they went to the king, who gave them licence
> to do after the ordinances of the heathen:
> Whereupon they built a place of exercise at
> Jerusalem according to the customs of the
> heathen: and made themselves uncircum-
> cised, and forsook the holy covenant, and
> joined themselves to the heathen, and were
> sold to do mischief.[67]

It was during the Hasmonean period, at the end of the Seleucid and Ptolemaic empires, that the idea of achieving sovereignty became a realistic possibility for the first time since the United Monarchy (1050 BCE–950 BCE). The Hasmonean Kingdom achieved its sovereignty in a piecemeal fashion following the revolt of Judah the Maccabee against Antiochus IV Epiphanes, the Seleucid emperor, in 164 BCE. The Jews largely sustained independence from around 140 BCE until Jerusalem was conquered in 63 BCE by the Roman general Pompey. Later efforts to recapture sovereignty during the Roman period–the Great Revolt of 66–73 CE, and the Bar Kokhba rebellion of 132–135 CE–led to disaster, including the destruction of the Second Temple in Jerusalem in 70 CE. This in turn led to the institutionalization of rabbinical Judaism, ushering in a period in history dominated by a religious model of Judaism, which started to take shape during the Babylonian exile.

For centuries, this model held the community intact but also stigmatized the Jews for failing to reassert sovereignty in their ancient homeland. The Christians, who emerged from the Jews, interpreted the destruction of the Temple and the subsequent Jewish exile as evidence that Christianity was the one true faith and inheritor of God's promise.

---

67 1 Maccabees 1:11–15 (King James Version).

While Jews saw the fall of the First Temple as not only a disaster but also a fresh opportunity to renew and rejuvenate their religion,[68] the destruction of the Second Temple is represented as the Jewish people's greatest historical calamity. Following this catastrophe, the Jews gradually abandoned all thoughts of restoring political sovereignty in Israel while sustaining life in the Diaspora. The destruction of the Second Temple was the formative moment that shaped the sovereignty-dispersion paradigm as comprising two conflicting and irreconcilable foundations. The Jews saw the loss of their homeland and the subsequent Roman exile as divine punishment for their sins. They clung to their vision of returning to the Promised Land, but it would be a matter of divine grace, conditional on the nation's spiritual rebirth.[69]

Moreover, the Prophet Jeremiah's vision of the Return to Zion was fulfilled after two to three generations—in seventy years, to be precise. In contrast, after the loss of the Second Temple, the return from exile became a theological dream anchored in a vision of messianism and a series of religious prohibitions. First and foremost, Jews were prohibited from "storming the wall," i.e., returning to Jerusalem before the advent of the messiah. Second, according to a *midrash* (a biblical exegesis by ancient rabbis), God made the Jews swear not to provoke the Gentiles. Third, God made the Gentiles promise not persecute ingathering of the exiles the Jews "too much," because they were homeless and defenseless.

In the absence of a clear timeframe for the ingathering of the exiles following the destruction of the Second Temple, the Return to

---

68   Robin Cohen, "Rethinking 'Babylon': Iconoclastic Conceptions of Diasporic Experience," *New Community* 2, no. 1 (January 1995), 5–18.

69   The Musaf prayer recited during the three pilgrimage festivals contains a succinct summary of this thesis: "But because of our sins we have been exiled from our land and sent far from our soil.... Draw our scattered ones near from among the nations, and bring in our dispersions from the ends of the earth. Bring us to Zion your city in glad song, and to Jerusalem home of your sanctuary in eternal joy." For more see Hartman, *Israelis and the Jewish Tradition*.

Zion became a messianic vision and a matter of faith, not a practical plan of action. Christians adopted the Jewish theological view of the destruction of the Second Temple and the dispersion as divinely ordained; they also championed it as proof that the Jews were being punished for rejecting Jesus and the Gospels. It was precisely by virtue of this belief that the Catholic Church rejected the possibility of a resumption of Jewish sovereignty in the Holy Land in the early twentieth century. In 1904, when Theodor Herzl asked Pope Pius X to recognize Zionism, he replied, "The Jews have not recognized our Lord, therefore we cannot recognize the Jewish people... and so, if you come to Palestine and settle your people there, we shall have churches and priests ready to baptize all of you."[70]

Even after the establishment of the State of Israel, the Vatican remained hostile to the idea of Jewish sovereignty, especially in Jerusalem. Only in 1965 did the papacy begin to gradually reform its theology to come to terms with the Jews and their state, acknowledging the evils of antisemitism in the *Nostra Aetate* declaration of the Second Vatican Council. It took until 1993, after the Oslo Accords, for the Vatican to normalize diplomatic relations with the State of Israel. This emerging rapprochement included papal visits to Israel, climaxing in Pope Francis's visit to Jerusalem in 2014, when he paid respects at Herzl's tomb alongside President Shimon Peres and Prime Minister Benjamin Netanyahu. This visit was widely seen as recognition by the Catholic Church of the Jewish people's right to sovereignty in their homeland. In 2015, the Vatican issued a strict ban on attempts to convert Jews to Christianity. Pope Francis declared, "A [true] Christian can never be an anti-Semite, especially because of the Jewish roots of Christianity."[71]

---

70 *The Complete Diaries of Theodor Herzl: Vol. IV*, ed. Raphael Patai, trans. Harry Zohn, (New York: Thomas Yoseloff, 1960) 1602–04.

71 Hilla Zorthian, "Vatican Says Catholics Shouldn't Try to Convert Jews," *Time*, December 10, 2015.

Over history, the tendency in Western thought to conflate politics with national sovereignty led many to conclude that the Jewish exile thwarted the development of a "Jewish political tradition" in both theory and practice. In the same vein, many of the early Zionists argued that, from the destruction of the Second Temple till the birth of the Zionist movement, Judaism had remained, in effect, apolitical. Whereas anti-Zionists praised the Jews' apolitical nature as a moral virtue, Zionists pointed to Jewish powerlessness as the *reason* for the Jews' historical failures.[72] They depicted Hebrew as having been a "dead" language throughout the exile, linking its rebirth to the revival of Jewish sovereignty in the Land of Israel.

Indeed, since the Babylonian exile, language had not been a critical element of Jewish ethnicity. Hebrew was elevated to the status of a "holy tongue" and the Jews stopped using it in their everyday discourse for generations. They adopted many other languages and dialects, according to wherever they happened to be living.[73]

The philosopher Michael Walzer rejects the notion that Jewish politics went into abeyance when the Jews were stripped of sovereignty. Despite the absence of state power, he argues, Jews continued making political decisions for centuries. These dealt with the allocation of resources of power and influence. The Jews even developed systems of law, taxation, and education within their scattered autonomous communities.[74] Others echo Walzer in arguing that the Jews, perhaps more than any other group in history, developed and refined the idea of national-cultural autonomy. They even created, as Israeli philosopher and Bible scholar Yehezkel Kaufmann wrote, a model of a state-within-a-state without which they would have

---

72 Alan Dowty, *The Jewish State: A Century Later* (Berkley: University of California Press, 1998), 20.

73 Zvi Gitelman, "Language and Ethnic Identity: Yiddish in the Soviet Union," unpublished paper.

74 Michael Walzer, "Introduction: The Jewish Political Tradition," in *The Jewish Political Tradition: Authority (Vol. I)*, eds. Michael Walzer et al. (New Haven: Yale University Press, 2000), xxi–xxxi.

become extinct.[75] The scholar Yitzhak Be'er argues that Jewish community leaders always exercised "some degree of coercive power in order to maintain a minimum level of national-religious discipline and could always use excommunication and flogging to ensure religious discipline."[76]

In contrast, philosopher Aviezer Ravitzky argues that the Jews' millennia-long political exile caused a once creative tradition of religious jurisprudence to be disconnected from the historical reality of national and political rule. Jewish communities had their own internal procedures, which were often democratic, and they certainly had their own internal politics, including the rabbinical courts' exercise of authority over members of the community. However, since this was all done under the aegis of foreign sovereigns, even if the Jews enjoyed cultural autonomy, they certainly lacked the political might necessary for making life and death decisions for themselves.[77]

Whether or not we accept the argument that Jewish politics requires sovereignty, since the dawn of modernity the modern state has chipped away at Jewish autonomy in the Diaspora, imposing its civil religion of Enlightenment politics and philosophy. This erosion created a rupture between those who thought that Judaism could survive and flourish in this brave new world, and others who argued that its survival hinged on the restoration of Jewish political independence, including a reconfiguration of the relationship between its political and religious aspects.[78]

Only in the second half of the nineteenth century, when religious Zionism began to take shape, did Orthodox rabbis start to

---

75 Dowty, *The Jewish State: A Century Later*, 20.

76 Yitzhak Be'er, "The Foundations and Beginnings of the Organization of Jewish Communities in the Middle Ages: Part 1," *Zion* 9 (1949) [Hebrew].

77 Aviezer Ravitsky, "Values of Judaism and Democracy in Historical Memory" *Judaism and Democracy, Division and Unity [Annual Conference of the Lipschitz College's Center for the Study of Educational Thought in Jewish Philosophy]* (Jerusalem: 1995), 13–15 [Hebrew].

78 Alan Mittelman, *The Scepter Shall Not Depart from Judah* (Lanham, MD: Lexington Books).

explore solutions for a Return to Zion that reconciled Jewish theology with political realism. These early religious Zionists began challenging the long-standing consensus that this could only happen after the advent of the messiah. They "drew a clear distinction between the present and messianic time but did not draw a distinction between the Jewish religion and the Jewish nation."[79]

The Modern Paradigm between Political Power and Ethical Judaism

The conception of the Jewish people as a national tribe inhabiting a theological paradigm of exile and sovereignty as divine reward or punishment has been eroded in modern times with the declining role of religion in Europe. From the dawn of modernity, and at least from the time of Baruch (Benedict) Spinoza (1632–1677), the exile-sovereignty paradigm has been redrawn on more secular and rationalist lines.[80] Spinoza was the first to define the Jewish historical drama in purely political terms. He argued that the ancient Hebrews conceived of themselves as the chosen people as a means of legitimizing their Jewish theocracy. When this regime was overthrown with the fall of the Hasmonean dynasty and the destruction of the Second Temple, and Jews lost political control in their homeland, they also lost their tribal identity and *raison d'être*. Even the Hebrew Bible, which Spinoza regarded as a historical work that contained no philosophical truth, had lost its standing. Since the Jews were a political tribe, Spinoza believed that if one day they succeeded in reasserting their sovereignty, God would choose them anew.[81]

---

79   Yosef Salmon, "The 'New Jew' in Religious Zionist Thought," *Israel: Studies in Zionism and the State of Israel, History, Society, Culture* 17 (2010), 257.

80   Biale, *Not in the Heavens*, 97–104.

81   Baruch Spinoza, *Tractatus Theologico-Politicus, Part 3*.

As we shall see, many Zionists, including Herzl and Pinsker, were deeply influenced by Spinoza's idea of "the fate of the Jews as having to do not with divine promises [of redemption] but with power politics pure and simple."[82]

The decline of religion and rise of the Enlightenment in the modern era caused Gentiles to think about Jews—and Jews to think about themselves—in less theological terms. The debate in modern Europe went from being a theological question to simply "the Jewish Question" (or "the Jewish Problem"), connected to questions of citizenship, the economy, society, and race.

The dawn of modernity in the late eighteenth century and emancipation in the nineteenth century spurred a quest for answers about the place of Jewish identity and religious law in the modern nation-state. The "secular" Spinoza was excommunicated by the Amsterdam Jewish community and denounced as a traitor and heretic for saying that there was no place for the Jewish religion in the absence of sovereignty. A century later, Moses Mendelssohn, the greatest Jewish philosopher in the generation of Immanuel Kant, sought to defend the standing of Orthodox Judaism in the absence of Jewish sovereignty. Whereas Spinoza saw Judaism's system of religious commandments as an antiquated instrument for enforcing ancient its sovereignty, Mendelssohn championed it as the most appropriate ethical philosophy for the modern state. He rejected the messianic dimension of the exile-return paradigm in favor of a more rational and pragmatic view but still wanted to preserve Judaism's religious commandments outside the framework of Jewish self-government. For him, they were ceremonial laws that would direct the inquisitive mind toward a rational divine truth in the modern era. The commandments themselves did not *reveal* this divine truth, but

---

82 Steven B. Smith, *Reading Leo Strauss: Politics, Philosophy, Judaism* (Chicago: University of Chicago Press, 2006), 78.

they guided human thought in its pursuit. They were not merely intended to be enforced within a Jewish sovereign polity, but were better understood as part of a rational, universalist philosophy. David Biale, a professor of Jewish history, writes that Moses Mendelssohn was not opposed to the reestablishment of Jewish sovereignty but hoped to ensure Judaism's survival as a religion that could flourish in the private sphere, far from the powers of the state.[83]

Theodor Herzl and other secular Zionists had no time for messianic or theological visions of Jewish sovereignty. What they wanted was a territory where the Jews could achieve statehood and thus terminate the eternal paradigm of exile and return. Other opponents of the messianic dimension of the exile and return paradigm, however, opposed the establishment of a single, exclusive Jewish center, favoring multiple homelands where the Jews could become free, equal, integrated, and patriotic citizens of the countries they already inhabited.

In nineteenth Germany, Reform Jews made Berlin their Jerusalem. They declared that they were not a nation but rather belonged to the nations of the countries where they were already citizens. No longer were the Jews members of a cultural-linguistic ethnic group, but merely adherents of a particular religious faith. Later, in the early twentieth century, many Jews also came to see the United States of America as their homeland. Their American dream was embodied in what they called *"Die Goldene Medina"*–Yiddish for "the golden country." This belief hastened the Americanization of the Jewish faith and almost completely transformed the traditional conversation about the exile-sovereignty cycle.

Having struck roots in the soil of America, Reform Jews rejected the tribalistic notions of a "Jewish race" and "Holy Seed." They repudiated Jewish religious law and dismissed nationalism. Instead,

---

83 Biale, *Not in the Heavens*, 103.

they espoused universalist principles of morality, and declared their commitment to the "habits of modern civilization" and the "universal culture of heart and intellect" in the Pittsburgh Platform of 1885. Here, Reform Jews turned America into the Jewish homeland and proclaimed that they considered themselves "no longer a nation, but a religious community and therefore expect neither a return to Palestine... nor the restoration of any of the laws concerning the Jewish state."[84]

After the rise of Nazism, the Reform Jews walked back their harsh anti-Zionism in the 1937 Columbus Platform. While not exactly Zionist, they did "affirm the obligation of all Jewry to aid in [Palestine's] upbuilding as a Jewish homeland by endeavoring to make it not only a haven of refuge for the oppressed but also a center of Jewish culture and spiritual life."[85]

Consequently, the dawn of the Israeli Century forced Reform Judaism to undergo a dramatic turnaround. In 1999, the movement's representative body, the Union of American Hebrew Congregations, issued a "new" Pittsburgh Platform. Reform rabbis now declared that they viewed Zionism as a critical component of Judaism. The Reform movement has invested efforts to establish a legitimate and legal foothold in Israel in recent decades. This not only demonstrates Israel's predominance over other options for Jewish life, but also shows how Reform Judaism now sees having a presence in Israel and official Israeli recognition as critical to the existence of the dwindling Reform communities in the US.

The Zionist Paradigm and the Negation of the Exile

Since the late nineteenth century, the modern debate over the Jewish paradigm has included questions about the extent to which sovereign

84 Jonathan D. Sarna, *American Judaism: A History* (New Haven: Yale University Press, 2004), 149.

85 "Reform Judaism: The Columbus Platform," Jewish Virtual Library, https://www.jewishvirtuallibrary.org/the-columbus-platform-1937.

power is essential for the survival and vitality of the Jewish people and what the *purpose* of survival under sovereignty might be.[86] Jewish socialists in eastern Europe, including the Bundists and Yiddishists, adopted the Marxist thesis that nationalism and modern states were bourgeois fictions cooked up to oppress the proletariat. However, they also sought to maintain their Jewish ethno-communal identity as a cultural tribe. This created tension, both in theory and practice, between the Jewish socialists on one side and the Russian communists and proletariat on the other. Vladimir Lenin, the leader of the Russian Revolution, criticized the Bund and wondered incredulously how its members could cling to a particularist diasporic identity in his revolutionary, universalist, utopian world.

The political Zionists' retort to all these diasporic solutions was unequivocal; they wanted to "negate" the exile. Ever since Pinsker and Herzl argued that "if the Jews wanted to live, they had to deviate from the custom of their forefathers to live amongst other nations and to establish a state of their own,"[87] this concept has defined the Jewish national consciousness. Israeli historian Amnon Raz-Krakotzkin writes that, in Zionist historical consciousness, the negation of the exile "fuses a continuum between the ancient past— in which there existed an entity defined as a sovereign nation—and the present, which *perceives itself* as the renewal of that same entity." The negation of the exile, he adds, gained a "status of a paradigm that directs all the streams of Zionism that accept it as a given."[88]

Herzl acknowledged the historical uniqueness of the Land of Israel but was initially open to creating a safe haven for the Jews elsewhere. After his death in 1904, the English Zionist Israel Zangwill

---

86   Abulof, *Living on the Edge*, 211–225 [Hebrew].

87   Anita Shapira, *Jews, Zionists and What's Between Them* (Tel Aviv: Am Oved, 2007), 64 [Hebrew].

88   Amnon Raz-Krakotzkin, "Exile Within Sovereignty Critique of 'The Negation of Exile' in Israeli Culture," in *The Scaffolding of Sovereignty*, eds. Zvi Ben-Dor Benite et al. (New York: Columbia University Press, 2018), 393–4. Emphasis in the original.

scoured the world to find a land where the Jews could settle and live in peace. At the turn of the twentieth century, the concept of the negation of the exile became a cornerstone of the dispute between the advocates of sovereignty and the "autonomist" followers of the renowned historian Simon Dubnow, who articulated a vision of a "Jewish world-nation" or "diaspora nation."[89] He argued that, despite the difficulties experienced by the Jews since the fall of the Second Temple and the anti-Semitism in the Russian empire, there was hope for its blossoming, even without a state of its own. Dubnow sought progress and believed that humanity was marching toward a more humanistic future. He also thought that the destruction of the Second Temple—the "providence of history" (as distinct from divine providence)—had tasked the Jews with a mighty mission: to prove to the world that life as a diaspora, without political sovereignty, was not only possible but the morally and intellectually superior way of life. States, territories, and armies were merely "external attributes of national power" and "superfluous" luxuries. "Go out into the world to prove that a people can continue to live without these attributes," he proclaimed, "solely and alone through strength of spirit welding its widely scattered particles into one firm organism!"[90]

Indeed, at the turn of the twentieth century, Dubnow's idea of a diaspora nation seemed to be a realistic alternative to Herzl's vision of a modern Jewish nation-state and the thrust of the Zionist movement's aspirations.

Other prominent Jewish thinkers, including Hermann Cohen and Franz Rosenzweig, have also sought to defend the Diaspora model as the realization of a moral and universalist vision. Taking their cue from Moses Mendelssohn, they assigned the Jewish people an important role in "the redemption of the whole of humanity,"

89 Shapira, *Jews, Zionists and What's Between Them*, 64 [Hebrew].

90 Michael Selzer, "Politics and Human Perfectibility: A Jewish Perspective," *Cross Currents* 21, no. 1 (Winter 1971), 106–107.

precisely because the Jews had rejected the restrictive and corrupting temptation of state power. They railed against the Zionist yearning for a state and held that the loss of ancient sovereignty was a divine blessing, which transformed the Jews from being a provincial national tribe into a universal religion that existed like "dew from the Lord" among the nations.[91]

In this view, the Jews in exile had a role that was both moral and eternal. Even after the Holocaust and the birth of the State of Israel, there were those who continued to advocate for the vision of a "Diaspora nation" as a response to, and a substitute for, a Jewish sovereign state. Even today, there are supporters among Israel's critics, who claim that the Jewish state is a living testament to the corrupting nature of state power.

The political scientist Michael Barnett explores the universalist theology of American Jews, who draw inspiration from Dubnow's Diaspora-nation thesis. He is sympathetic toward their efforts to champion the cosmopolitan belief in "repairing the world" (*tikkun olam*) but cautions against the dangers inherent in Jewish naivety. Paraphrasing Christian theologian Reinhold Neibuhr, Barnett notes that nations that wish to survive "cannot be expected to take universalism to its logical conclusion because it would entail their erasure and extinction, which, of course, runs against their survival instinct."[92]

Indeed, Zionism's founders distinguished between the negation of the exile and the negation of the exilic way of life and mentality. The negation of the exile states that it is impossible for Jews to live and flourish *as Jews* outside of their homeland and without sovereignty. The negation of the exilic mentality, however, calls on Jews to overcome the characteristics they had absorbed as a stateless people—passivity, victimhood, anxiety, fear, and extreme humility.

---

91   David Hazony, "Eliezer Berkovits, Theologian of Zionism," *Azure* 17 (Spring 2005).

92   Michael N. Barnett, *The Star and The Stripes: The History of the Foreign Policies of American Jews* (Princeton: Princeton University Press, 2016), 273.

This mentality took the opposite view from those who claimed that it was life in the Diaspora that had given Jews higher ethical standards and made Judaism humanistic. They argued that, in the absence of political and state power, it was quite impossible for Jews to make moral decisions. Without political power, the Jews had adopted slave-like ethics of submission, which led them in critical times to believe that martyrdom—and not the healthy human instinct to fight for one's life—was proof of their adherence to Judaism.

For Zionists, this was a destructive pathology. They accused exilic Jews of preferring "passive heroism" to the "active heroism" that could only ever be realized by living in, or fighting for, a sovereign state.[93]

Religious Zionism: The Messiah and the Donkey

To quote historian David Vital, the principle of the negation of the exile differentiated Zionism "totally and completely from every other significant movement in the modern Jewish world."[94] Advocates of Dubnow's Diaspora-nation vision insisted that the Hebrew Bible's redactors had never given much importance to political sovereignty as a way of life, since it was God who fought Israel's battles and made the Israelites win or lose.

The Zionists, on the other hand, insisted—like Spinoza—that the Bible was the ultimate book of Jewish sovereignty.[95] David Ben-Gurion, who hoped to inspire Israelis to put the state's interests first, realized that he would have to change the historical convention whereby the Babylonian exile and Return to Zion were the starting

---

93   Yael Zerubavel, *Recovered Roots: Collective Memory and the Making of Israeli National Tradition* (Chicago: The University of Chicago Press, 1995), 19.

94   Abulof, *On the Edge of the Abyss*, 332, note 118 [Hebrew].

95   Michael Walzer, *In God's Shadow: Politics in the Hebrew Bible* (New Haven, CT: Yale University Press, 2012), 125.

points of the Jewish paradigm. For him, the supreme Jewish ethos was to be found in the long period of Hebrew sovereignty in the First Temple era, especially under David and Solomon's glorious reigns, and during the golden era of sovereignty under the Hasmoneans during the Second Temple period. He maintained that the theological paradigm had only spelled doom for people who had waited for generation after generation for the messiah to arrive.

Ben-Gurion embraced a vision of modern nationalism with roots in the Bible to inspire Jews about the drama of Jewish revival and to entrench his vision of statism (*mamlakhtiyut*) as Israel's civil religion. He became determined to impress statism on Israel's citizens, using it to depict the Zionist enterprise as a direct continuation of Jewish independence in biblical times, in a manner completely disconnected from the millennia-long exile and the supposedly apolitical rabbinical tradition of the Diaspora.

Mamlakhtiyut became a catchall doctrine that supported the recovery of Jewish sovereignty and nationhood as the ultimate creed of the future. This creed was also built on an aggressive policy of forcing the Hebrew language on new immigrants as their day-to-day language, erasing the foreign languages they came with.

Hebrew had always been the language of holy texts, liturgy, and of course, the Hebrew Bible. In the nineteenth century, it was considered a dead language and few could use it as a spoken vernacular. In the 1911 edition of the *Encyclopædia Britannica*, German orientalist Theodor Nöldeke wrote an entry on ancient Semitic languages. Of Hebrew, he wrote: "The dream of some Zionists that Hebrew—a would-be Hebrew, that is to say—will again become a living, popular language in Palestine, has still less prospect of realisation than their vision of a restored Jewish empire in the Holy Land."[96]

---

96   Ilker Aytürk, "Revisiting the Language Factor in Zionism: The Hebrew Language Council from 1904 to 1914," *Bulletin of the School of Oriental and African Studies, University of London* 73, no. 1 (2010), 47.

In the Israeli Century, Hebrew has become the hegemonic and unchallenged language of Jews in Israel, whose grandparents arrived speaking Yiddish, Ladino, Judeo-Arabic, and more.[97]

Ben-Gurion's biblical heroes were kings, judges, military leaders, and courageous prophets, and he believed the Diaspora had distanced Judaism from them. He saw these figures as role models for Israel's youth and reserved special praise for Joshua Bin-Nun, who conquered the Promised Land. Ben-Gurion's own admirers described him as the heir to these biblical leaders; Moshe Dayan went as far as to compare him to Moses.[98]

Those who advocated the negation of the Diaspora, which became a core plank of Zionist ideology, saw the lack of sovereignty as not only a recipe for national disaster, but also a psychopathological flaw and an addiction to weakness. Secular Zionists were utopian thinkers for whom the dream of building up the Land of Israel had nothing to do with God's plans.

They had some religious Zionist allies who also opposed the passive messianism and anti-Zionism of their Orthodox peers. The first religious Zionist thinker was Rabbi Zvi Hirsch Kalischer, who was active in Germany in the 1860s. Three decades before Herzl founded political Zionism, Kalischer praised Jews who were ready to sail to Palestine and settle there, calling them "messiahs." He had reservations about "the traditional messianic idea of divine intervention in the course of history by a superhuman person" and argued that redemption would come "only through those simple Jews who close their businesses in the Diaspora and ascend to the Land of Israel."[99] The scholar Yosef Salmon has written that for Kalischer,

---

97   Eliana Shohamy, "At What Cost? Methods of Language Revival and Protection," *Sustaining Linguistic Diversity: Endangered and Minority Languages and Language Varieties* (2008), 205.

98   Charles S. Liebman and Eliezer Don-Yehiya, *Civil Religion in Israel: Traditional Judaism and Political Culture in the Jewish State* (Berkeley: University of California Press, 1983), 94–95.

99   Aytürk, "Revisiting the Language Factor in Zionism."

"the content of redemption is transferred from the building of the Temple…and international recognition of the God of Israel, to political liberty."[100] At the turn of the twentieth century, Rabbi Samuel Mohilever, one of the great leaders of Religious Zionism, went as far as to argue that "the Holy One, blessed be He, would rather have his children live in His Land, even though they do not observe the Torah properly, than have them live outside the Land and observe the Torah as is proper."[101]

For nineteenth century religious Zionists, the commandment to settle and rule the Land of Israel took precedence over all other laws. Some claim that this approach was rooted in the philosophy of Rabbi Judah Halevi, who had already articulated a vision of national redemption in the twelfth century. Halevi saw the Jews' political impotence and settled Diaspora existence as a historic failure, but he believed it was one that could be rectified. The success of Christianity and Islam at Judaism's expense, Halevi contended, was only an interim stage in the dialectic of Jewish history on the path to redemption and the restoration of the glory of the Judaism of the Bible. This revival would occur only when the Jews actively worked to renew a settlement in the Land of Israel. Halevi pointed to a historical irony—by embracing monotheism, Christians and Muslims were helping to disseminate the greatness of Judaism and God's supremacy.

However, for the Jews to implement God's historic plan to rehabilitate them in their homeland, they would first have to settle there. In his famous elegiac, "My Heart is in the East," Halevi stressed the need to relinquish the ease of life in the Diaspora and settle in the Land of Israel: "A light thing would it seem to me to leave all the good things of Spain / Seeing how precious in mine eyes to behold

---

100   Ibid.

101   Yosef Salmon, "The Messianic Idea and the Jewish State," *Iggud: Selected Essays in Jewish Studies* 34 (1994), 125–136 [Hebrew].

the dust of the desolate sanctuary." Redemption would come, Halevi maintained, when the people of Israel returned to their land—this would be the messianic moment. He set a personal example and, without waiting for the messiah, moved to the Land of Israel himself at the age of sixty.[102] Today's religious Zionists consider Judah Halevi a pioneer.

In Israel's early days, the religious Zionists' redemptive program included some of the socialist values that defined the labor movement's ideology. Some religious kibbutzniks were particularly prominent and embraced the *Torah Va'Avodah* (Torah and Labor) as a way of bridging the secular and religious elements of Israeli society. Religious Zionism took a major historical turn, however, when it fused the theological paradigm of exile and return with the activist spirit that characterized the modern Jewish paradigm.

Despite his fervently Orthodox background, Rabbi Abraham Isaac Kook became the nemesis of anti-Zionist Haredim when he claimed that Zionism would not only guarantee the Jews a sovereign refuge but liberate them from the chains of their Diaspora mentality and lead to universal redemption. His son, Rabbi Zvi Yehuda Kook, who headed the famous Mercaz HaRav Yeshiva and became the spiritual leader of the religious Zionists following the Six-Day War, also harbored a deep contempt for what he saw as the "quietism of the ghetto." Like his father, he saw Zionism as a movement to resurrect the Jewish people. He called its secular leaders "holy Jews." He believed religious Jews who held a ghetto mentality "lack[ed] the spiritual vitality to implement Judaism's greatest dream." Rabbi Zvi Yehuda Kook regarded the Jewish state as true revelation of the divine spirit; the same goes for the Israeli army

---

102 Hartman, *Israelis and the Jewish Tradition*.

and the secular kibbutzniks—they were the pioneering, fighting avant-garde who were unwittingly working in the service of God's redemptive plan.[103]

Whereas Ben-Gurion harnessed the traditions of Jewish independence to foster secular statism as a civil religion, religious Zionists regarded their secular peers as fulfilling God's master plan for the Jewish people's revival in their own land. This thesis was reinforced by the conquest of the Old City of Jerusalem, the West Bank, and Gaza in the Six-Day War of 1967. About a decade earlier, Rabbi Joseph B. Soloveitchik, the most important voice of modern Orthodox Judaism in America, penned his monumental Zionist address "Kol Dodi Dofek." He reminded his fellow religious Jews in the United States that, while they were devoting their time to studying Torah, they were failing to heed the calls of the divine creator. Both Rabbi Abraham Isaac Kook and his son urged their disciples to join the Zionist pioneers and put an end to the historic cycle of exile and return.

There had always been profound disagreement between different streams within secular Zionism, going back to the period of the pre-state Yishuv. Socialist and liberal Zionists clashed on the centrality of the sovereign state as the basis for creating a new, modern Jew. Liberal Zionists saw the state as a refuge; their vision was to promote a secular, free-market democracy that provided maximum security. Socialist Zionists, the dominant force up until 1977, also emphasized security but argued that the Jewish state would *reform* Jews who had since become "infected" with the passive ethos of the Diaspora and its religious tradition and debased themselves by not working their own land. They hoped to forge a new Jew and Judaism to build

---

103   Yossi Klein Halevi, *Like Dreamers: The Story of the Israeli Paratroopers Who Reunited Jerusalem and Divided a Nation* (New York: Harper, 2013), 21–25.

a model society based on a return to agriculture, cooperative living, equality, and a renunciation of the "Golden Calf" of capitalism.

The socialist, liberal, and religious streams in Zionism were bitter ideological and political rivals but cooperated to fortify the nascent state. In June 1967, on the eve of the Six-Day War, when Israel's existence hung in the balance, Prime Minister Levi Eshkol invited right-wing opposition leader Menachem Begin and his Herut Party to join his government in a united front before Israel launched its preemptive strike against the Arabs. However, this cooperation gradually frayed, as profound divisions came to the fore following the 1967 war, and as Israel faced fateful questions about the status of the territories it had occupied and was beginning to settle.

The drama of settlement in Judea and Samaria (or the West Bank) is one element, and one cause, of a long series of tectonic shifts in Israel's society and economy over the past fifty years. These shifts have included huge demographic growth among Israeli Jews; revolutionary swings in the fabric of society and its basic, formative values; a shift in the balance of power between various ethnic sectors; and total reorganization of Israel's politics and national institutions.

All of these trends gained momentum following the political upheaval of 1977, when the Likud Party rose to power under Menachem Begin. This turnaround transformed the Israeli economy, which went from being neo-socialist to ultra-capitalist. However, it is Israel's geopolitical position and the question of its relationship with its Arab citizens that has most impeded efforts to achieve a clear consensus among Zionists on the future of the Israeli Century.

Until the 1970s, the religious Zionist community in Israel was a meager minority compared to the pioneering force of Labor Zionism. It was seen as a bookish and limp vestige of the past. However, since then it has gradually assumed a place of pride in the shaping of the Israeli Century. The national religious movement interprets the resumption of Jewish sovereignty as the start of a redemptive, messianic process based upon a holy trinity—the people of Israel, the Torah of Israel, and the Land of Israel. For all intents and purposes, Religious Zionism became the main force conflating modern Judaism with sovereign Judaism. Similarly, it also became the flag-bearer of the principle of the negation of the exile. Whereas the ultra-Orthodox reject Israeli Independence Day as blasphemy by upstaging God, and secular Zionists champion it as a "celebration of human effort," religious Zionists mark it as "one of the most sacred moments of the year."[104] This is the day that God made, but they are party to.

Religious Zionists also occasionally show disdain for Diaspora life. In politics and society, the national-religious camp sees itself as the new, vibrant, driving force of Jewish tribal nationalism. It has produced both pioneering settlers and dangerous messianic ultra-nationalists, for whom the purpose of Jewish sovereignty is not to create a modern, liberal democracy, but a state founded on the values of religious Jewish ultra-nationalism.

Yet despite the serious and fundamental differences (including over the occupied territories) between the Zionist factions, many believe that the most acute challenge in the Israeli Century is the empowerment of the ultra-Orthodox (Haredi) communities, who reject modernity and Israeli sovereignty in principle.

Since the dawn of the modern era and the birth of Zionism, the Haredim have steadfastly clung to the sovereignty-Diaspora paradigm as a theological tenet. At the turn of the twentieth century, the Haredim were a minority fighting both secular and religious Zionism, as well other factions that they deemed "assimilationist." As early as 1919, the heads of the Edah HaChareidis, an ultra-Orthodox sect based in Jerusalem, condemned Zionism as the "kingdom

---

104   Halevi, *Like Dreamers*, 32.

of evil."[105] Today, the enormous birth rates in the Haredi community are pushing Israeli society towards a fateful fork in the road: Will it continue on a path of modernity, or will the rise of anti-modern religious extremists force it into retreat?

Preempting the Messiah and Denying the Israeli Century

While Israelis and Diaspora Jews argue over what form Judaism and the Jewish nation should take in Israel, some still refuse to accept that we are living in the Israeli Century, and that the classic Jewish paradigm of return and exile has ended. They believe that Israelis are provincial and tribal, blinded by power and nationalistic arrogance, and are profoundly mistaken about Diaspora Jewry's strength, vitality, and sense of mission. Some dismiss Israel as unstable and fragile, while upholding life in the Diaspora as vibrant and increasingly sophisticated. Gidi Grinstein argues that, the revival of Jewish communities in places such as Russia, Poland, and Germany, undermines the Zionist argument that Jews have no future outside of Israel.[106] In my view, this position is fundamentally mistaken.

Many Jews and non-Jews alike, supporters and detractors of Israel, still find it difficult to part with the image of the "Diaspora nation" as the universal prototype of a Jewish prosperity without sovereignty. Internationalists, including some in Israel, regard Jewish nationalism as petty and narrow, in contrast to their vision of Jewish peoplehood as transnational cosmopolitan, the engine of relentless human progress. Throughout history, Diaspora Jews have been

---

105   The US-based, ultra-Orthodox Satmar community sees American independence as a "kingdom of grace." While waiting for the messiah to come, they established a settlement north of New York City, Kiryas Joel, which has a population of over 20,000 and enjoys a kind of cultural autonomy. The American-Jewish scholar David Myers argues that Kiryas Joel is the most successful semi-sovereign effort of our times outside of Israel.

106   Gidi Grinstein, *Flexigidity: The Secret of Jewish Adaptability* (Israel: Gidi Grinstein, 2013).

repeatedly denounced by both the left and the right as "rootless cosmopolitans" or traitors loyal only to their ancient tribe. Yet some still extol the virtues of a stateless Judaism, adrift in a free world. They celebrate the achievements of individual Jews in the Diaspora in the arts, sciences, and academia, while disparaging the Jewish state as too tribal and mediocre.[107]

Until the modern era, Jews lived in scattered religious communities and spoke different languages and dialects. Their interactions with their non-Jewish surroundings were diverse, swinging between prosperity and atrophy. Time after time, and sometimes in no time at all, the Jews were thrust from being a segregated, despised, persecuted, and massacred minority to enjoying relative tolerance and openness that they integrated into their local cultures.

Even in the wake of horrible catastrophes over the centuries, Jews held faith in the possibility of renewal. They worked to rebuild their lives in the aftermath of wars and persecution, always rationalizing that such upheavals were providential signs of change and redemption. Through all of it, they also preserved a messianic yearning for Zion.

Their dreams of redemption were not just symbolic—they sometimes led to "messianic activism," resulting in small waves of migration to Israel. From the thirteenth century until the nineteen century, Jewish migration to Palestine (*aliyot*) was inspired by kabbalistic-eschatological calculations. Mystical Jews believed that God would not tolerate foreign conquerors of the Holy Land, since the Almighty was awaiting the Israelites' return. Generation after generation, prominent Jews made the voyage to settle there and kept the old flame of Jewish nationalism alive with their messianic *aliyot*. Arie Morgenstern has written that the *aliyot* "were of enduring significance, partly because of the renown of those who took part, partly

---

107 Cohen, "Rethinking 'Babylon,'" 5–18.

because of their regular appearance over the centuries, and partly because of the variety of diaspora communities which participated." These waves of immigration "were in no way marginal to the Jewish tradition, but in fact became an axis of Jewish spiritual life…[they show] the depth and force of the Jewish people's connection to its ancestral homeland, a connection that was carried into the late nineteenth and twentieth centuries, when modern Zionism found a new way of giving it a voice."[108]

Centuries before modern Zionism, the *aliyot* brought thousands to settle in Palestine, which led to a renaissance in places like Safed in Galilee and Jerusalem. But these experiences represented a small fraction of Jewish life and often ended in disillusionment and religious persecution. The bigger story of Jewish communities prior to modernity was outside Israel, in the Diaspora.

Wherever they were, and whatever period they lived in, the Jews around the globe remained trapped by the model of a powerless "global Diaspora" that thrived and collapsed time after time, and yet it's virtues remain attractive, even to this day when the State of Israel is the epicenter of Jewish life.

Some continue to believe, even after the Holocaust, that Jewish internationalists are far superior to those grounded in sovereignty. In this context, it is worth mentioning how ideas that inform globalization, celebrating borderless communities while disdaining those who turn inward and tend to stagnate, often also look to "the success of Jewish intermediaries" in pre-Reformation Spain, who, it is said, played a key role on the frontier of Christian and Islamic civilizations as a model to be imitated.

Of course, this rosy picture is misleading. Consider the upheavals experienced by the Jews of Spain during the wars between the Muslim and Christian kingdoms from the eleventh to fifteenth

---

108   Arie Morgenstern, *Azure* (Winter 2002), 76.

centuries. They were persecuted under the Catholic Visigoths but enjoyed a revival under Muslim rule following the conquest of the Iberian Peninsula. This period of prosperity, during the Golden Age of 1020–1150, came to an end with the tragic saga of the Christians' final defeat of the Muslims (the Reconquista) and expulsion of the Jews.

Throughout history, Jews have found themselves caught between rival camps, even if they sometimes served as a bridge between civilizations. Such was the case in Spain, where they initially rebuilt their communities in areas where the Christians reasserted their rule. They even enjoyed an interlude of relative well-being under their rulers, who needed their services and money.

In the end, however, the Jews fell victim to the religious zeal of the Catholic monarchs Queen Isabella of Castile and her husband, King Ferdinand of Aragon. They suffered pogroms, forced conversions, and finally, a mass expulsion from Spain in 1492.

However, during the periods they did flourish, Jews were a well-heeled minority who managed become major financial and cultural players, involved in the state apparatus, and sometimes even representing it overseas. During their heyday in Muslim Spain, they learned Arabic and integrated into their surroundings, harmoniously fusing Jewish and Arab cultures.

Israel Levin, a scholar of medieval poetry, notes that a highly influential class of wealthy Jews emerged, who enjoyed close ties with rulers and governing officials. They had state titles and occupied important offices. For the first time, leadership of the Jewish community passed from religious elders and scholars to the wealthy class, who lived like Muslim nobility. According to Levin, this wealthy Jewish elite "dictated the values of ethics and society, and the Jews' great cultural centers evolved under their aegis. Similarly, to the Arab elite, the Jewish ministers also maintained magnificent courts. The ministers attracted groups of intellectuals, artists, and poets, who showered them with benefits and supported them generously."[109]

Historian Benzion Netanyahu (the late father of Israel's former prime minister) documented how the merciless expulsion of Spanish Jewry was a product of Ferdinand and Isabella's religious and economic campaigns against rival Spanish elites. Catholic monarchs cunningly deceived the Jews; they relied on their economic power during the financial crisis following the war with the Moors in Granada, yet worked to destroy the Jewish community simultaneously.

Don Isaac Abarbanel was perhaps the most influential Jew of the late Middle Ages. In 1484, only eight years before the Alhambra Decree, he was enlisted as the Spanish royal court's chief economic advisor. Concurrently, Catholic monarchs began separating the Jews from the rest of society on religious and racial grounds. According to Benzion Netanyahu, Spain was the first country to raise the notion that Jews were not only a separate religion, but a separate race.[110]

Abarbanel assisted the Spanish monarchy in its war against feudal lords who sought to erode the crown's power. He operated at a time when the Catholics were treating the Jews and the *conversos* (Jews who had converted to Christianity under duress) as bargaining chips against the economic aristocracy. The feudal lords demanded greater political and economic rights and viewed the Jews' economic position as a threat. They eventually agreed to compromise with the Catholics, at the cost of subjugating the Jews. Thus began the Spanish Inquisition, which investigated the new converts' loyalty to the crown, and issued the decree to expel all the Jews, whose assets the Spanish feudal elite coveted. Thus ended the history of the Jews

---

109   Israel Levin ed., *The Poetry of the Golden Age: Shlomo Ibn Gabirol* (Tel Aviv: Tel Aviv University, 2007), x–xi [Hebrew].

110   Benzion Netanyahu, *Don Isaac Abravanel: Statesman and Philosopher*, 5th ed. (Ithaca, NY: Cornell University Press, 1998).

in Spain, "the only country in the Middle Ages where Jews were converted to Christianity on a mass scale."[111]

Bizarrely, this clique of Jewish elites has recently been presented as a historic model for internationalism, with lessons for contemporary globalization. In his book *Borderless Economics: Chinese Sea Turtles, Indian Fridges and the New Fruits of Global Capitalism*, Robert Guest argues that Spanish Jews perfectly illustrate the idea that a borderless economy can provide countries with far greater benefits than traditional sovereign arrangements. According to Guest, the Jewish historical experience of being a "transnational nation" and a bridge between civilizations can provide inspiration for the international, globalized economy of the twenty-first century.

Others argue that the existence of "cosmopolitan" Judaism in medieval Spain proves that present-day Jews have no need for sovereign territory. They describe Jewish history as comprising multiple, positive, coexisting Diaspora experiences, with no preference for any geographic center. For example, Córdoba in Spain was good as Worms in Germany, and both were as good as New York or Jerusalem.[112] However, these assertions are made with utter disregard for the fact that the Spanish Golden Age was brought to a most cruel and bitter end.

Even after the 1492 Alhambra Decree, also known as the Edict of Expulsion, the Spanish aristocracy did not stop abusing the Jews who had served them so loyally. In the sixteenth century, after Spain conquered the port cities of North Africa, its soldiers pillaged and raped the local Jews and recruited them as mediators with the Muslims immediately afterward. This was how the Jewish community in the city of Oran in Algeria began. It existed for some 160 years under the protection of the Spanish crown and built up a regional trade

---

111 Ibid., 42.
112 Robert Guest, *Borderless Economics* (New York: Palgrave Macmillan, 2011), 7.

network for it. French historian Jean-Frédéric Schaub has written that despite their loyalty to the king and their residence in Christian quarters, the Jews of Oran were completely dependent upon the good will of the aristocracy, even in a time of "remarkable stability."

In April 1669, their world turned upside down overnight. Religious hatred against the Jews led to Queen-Regent Mariana of Spain, the widow of Felipe IV, to expel the Jews of Oran. Their desperate pleas fell on deaf ears; they were expelled within eight days, and their synagogues were converted to churches.[113]

It is difficult, therefore, to find a place anywhere in the world where temporary prosperity for the Jews was not followed by downfall, despair, and disaster. Contemporary North America and Australia are possible exceptions as countries that embody the dual vision of a liberal nation, which allows and even encourages the presence of thriving diasporas in their midst as part of their pluralist creed.

Three decades ago Zionist historian Yosef Gorny wrote:

> Jewish society in Israel represents the greatest collective achievement in the history of the Jewish people in the modern era, perhaps even of all time. On the other hand, the status of the Jews in the United States represents the greatest success of individuals in the history of the Jews during the exile.... Both communities have powerful positions in the intra-Jewish framework and in the international system. However, the power of the Jewish population in Israel stems from its

---

113   Jean-Frédéric Schaub, *The Jews of the King of Spain: Oran 1509–1669* (Tel Aviv: Tel Aviv University, 1999), 20–21 [Hebrew translation of French original].

> political sovereignty, whereas the strength of
> the Jews in the United States is linked to their
> rights as citizens of their country…. Despite
> and also because of this difference, a close
> relationship based on mutual dependence
> has developed between these two commu-
> nities. After all, Jewish Israeli sovereignty…
> requires the constant political and financial
> support of American Jews, while the liberty
> and freedom of American Jews…requires a
> connection to the State of Israel as a source
> of life.[114]

Gorny could not have predicted just how much American
Jews' dependence on Israel *as Jews* would grow, and how Israel's dependence on American Jewry would diminish. In 1986, there were
5.8 million Jews in the United States and approximately 3.5 million
Jews in Israel. In 2020, the US Jewish population stands at around
5.5 million, compared to 6.8 million in Israel. This significant trend
is only intensifying. The sharp, rapid growth in Israel's Jewish population and its growing strength relative to American Jewry stems in
part from the dramatic changes that have taken place in the United
States, where the communal-ethnic structure of American Jewry is
being eroded.

Despite the prosperity of the State of Israel, not everybody
accepts the advantages of sovereignty as manifestations of Jewish
achievement. Indeed, some still believe that the emphasis on the
politics of sovereignty reflects contemporary Jewish *weakness*. At its
core, this position is anti-sovereign, pro-Diaspora, and transnational.

---

114   Yosef Gorny, *The Search for National Identity* (Tel Aviv: Am Oved, 1990), 14 [Hebrew] (emphasis in the original).

In his 1992 book *Tribes: How Race, Religion, and Identity Determine Success*, American journalist Joel Kotkin described the Jews as the archetypal example of a global tribe, lacking a national-territorial focus. While they had a strong inner sense of their unique historical and ethnic identity, they had no commitment to a specific territory. In fact, they typically *preferred* mobility—sometimes the result of persecution or expulsion—out of an awareness of their extraordinary ability to function and prosper in a transnational economy. As a global tribe, the Jews are well known for their contributions to the growth of their "host countries" and the development of global cities and regions where they promote and encourage technological and cultural innovation.

Kotkin argued that the State of Israel had only slightly modified the overall qualities of the global, universal, and anti-local Jewish tribe. He believed that emigration by Israelis, Israel's dependence on Diaspora money, and the attraction of life in the Diaspora for most of its citizens reveals "the bankruptcy of some of the most fundamental portions of traditional Zionist dogma."[115]

In my opinion, Kotkin was completely mistaken. The global Jewish tribe is in fact increasingly dependent on the military power of the sovereign State of Israel and on its national, cultural, and economic achievements.

Since its establishment, Israel has become *the* home for Diaspora communities in distress, including Holocaust survivors, Jews from Muslim lands, the former Soviet Union, and Ethiopia, and those facing increasing anti-Semitism in Western countries. A majority of Jews who are *not* in distress see Israel as a central component in the preservation of their communal identity and heritage. Those who reside in North America, Europe, and Latin America

---

115   Joel Kotkin, *Tribes: How Race, Religion, and Identity Determine Success in the New Global Economy* (New York: Random House, 1992), 16–17, 65.

regard Israel as not only their potential home but also as the most important element in the shaping of their Judaism, and recognize its unparalleled and essential contribution to the safeguarding of the Jews as a people with a long and rich religious heritage.

Yet, even among Jews who are sympathetic to Zionism and acknowledge the strength of the Israeli Century, some still deny or refuse to recognize Israel's dominance in Judaism and Jewish life. Political scientist Alan Wolfe wrote in his book, *At Home in Exile: Why Diaspora Is Good for the Jews,* that Jews in the non-sovereign Diaspora have stronger roots than the evil forces that afflict them. He maintains that the Jewish Diaspora has given them—and humanity as a whole—a wonderful heritage.

Jews who understood the limits of their status as a minority group, developed empathy toward other minorities and promoted a universalist ethical agenda that championed human rights and *tikkun olam* ("repairing the world") regardless of nationality, race, or religion. Wolfe attacks the more particularistic and chauvinist attitudes heard in the US and Israel, which stress the importance of the Jewish tribe and sovereignty over a Judaism that is more liberal and universalist.

He sees himself as following in the footsteps of historian Simon Dubnow and joins self-identifying liberal Zionists in claiming that liberal American Judaism is of critical importance to Israel's future because it could prevent it from descending further down a nationalist spiral. Wolfe believes that only the experience and mentality of a liberal Diaspora can ensure the victory of the universalist exile tradition and its commitment to social justice. However, this is difficult, if not impossible, to achieve in a sovereign national state, whose citizens hold a narrow and dangerous worldview centered on a false dichotomy between friend and foe—in other words, the theology of the chosen people and of Jewish supremacy.[116]

---

116 Alan Wolfe, *At Home in Exile: Why Diaspora is Good for the Jews* (Boston: Beacon Press, 2014).

This approach is typical of many Jewish progressives in the Diaspora, but most concede the difficulties and failures of attempts to nurture and preserve viable alternatives in the Israeli Century. Political theorist Julie Cooper contends that "diasporic thinkers," who advocate living in the Diaspora and avoid defining the Jewish people based on national-political or ethnic-cultural belonging, have emptied the Diaspora concept of all political content and turned it into a meaningless identity label.

Even more drastic are the attempts by intellectuals like radical philosopher Judith Butler to water down the concept of Jewishness to a question of individual ethics devoid of any communal or political significance. Cooper writes that Butler uses the term "Jewishness" instead of "Judaism" to escape not only a *halakhic* debate, but also national or religious categories. She prefers to speak of the Jews as a social group sharing similar psychological characteristics. According to Butler, Jews are not a politically defined community. Their Diasporic character is, rather, a symbolic geographic feature indicative of Judaism's evolution from a tribal religion to an amorphous identity. All of this serves her criticism of the State of Israel and its alleged "crimes" against the Palestinians.[117]

Pulitzer Prize-winning playwright David Mamet criticizes progressive Jews ostensibly troubled by Israel's mistakes and failures. In a sarcastic and trenchant critique, he writes: "Many Jews are confused about or opposed to the existence of the Jewish State, and, in their ignorance or muddle-headedness, wish it away. Much of this disaffection is laziness, for if Israel were gone, these anti-Zionist souls believe they might dwell in an unmitigated state of assimilation, any pressures of which might conceivably be combated by an effortless supineness." Mamet argues that many liberal Jews "simply expand… the neurosis of Diaspora thinking," despite enjoying the benefits of

---

117   Julie E. Cooper, "A Diasporic Critique of Diasporism," *Political Theory* 43 (2015), 80–110.

America's liberty, security, and success. They seek to assuage their sense of alienation by becoming "citizens of the world." Yet this attempt only worsens their neuroses and creates a fantasy akin to "one who believes in the benevolence of Nature. [And] anyone ever lost in the wild knows that Nature wants you dead."[118]

The pro-Diaspora approach got an intellectual boost with the fall of the Soviet Union. The 1990s saw the collapse of Communism and the apparent victory of liberalism, an event that economist Francis Fukuyama famously called "the end of history." With peace in the Middle East in the wake of the 1993 Oslo Accords, and with global-ization and transnationalism seemingly triumphant, national borders were increasingly seen as an anachronism. Over the course of this short period, some believed that Israel was wielding an excessive and unnecessary degree of power and called upon the country to be like all other liberal democracies by embracing globalization and renouncing nationalism. One of these optimists was *New York Times* columnist Thomas Friedman, who urged countries in his bestseller *The Lexus and the Olive Tree* to downplay their patriotic national agendas in favor of the "real concerns" of their citizens.[119] Israel's foreign minister, Shlomo Ben Ami, offered similar arguments at the time.

During this period, as the Soviet Union and its propaganda machine that had encouraged global anti-Semitism for decades dis-integrated, there was an awakening and revival of Jewish communi-ties all over the world, including in eastern Europe. As this region enjoyed a democratic rebirth, and Israel and American Jewry grew in strength, many were full of hope for a worldwide Jewish renaissance. Jewish organizations in the United States were particularly outspo-ken at the time, encouraging these new democracies to help renew

---

118   David Mamet, *The Secret Knowledge: On The Dismantling of American Culture* (New York: Sentinel, 2012), 132–133.

119   Thomas L. Friedman, *The Lexus and The Olive Tree: Understanding Globalization* (New York: Farrar, Straus, Giroux, 1999), 280–282.

Jewish life while taking responsibility for past crimes and injustices, including during the Holocaust.

The eastern European Jewish revival was intertwined with the prevalent spirit of democratization and liberalism, and it received prominence thanks to American hegemony, which amplified the voice of American Jewry in the 1990s. It was then that Jewish organizations reached their peak of influence and sought to portray themselves as the moral guiding light of the new global era.

This was the context for the author Larry Tye's 2001 book *Home Lands: Portraits of the New Jewish Diaspora*, in which he heralded the reemergence of vibrant Jewish life around the world. Liberated of anti-Semitism, it belied the contention that Diaspora Jewry was somehow in retreat as Israel became ascendant. Tye admitted that Israel was indeed a central player in the Jewish world, but he predicted that the vision of open borders in a post-national and globalized world would increase the power of Jewish communities everywhere, including in eastern Europe, as powerful alternatives to Israel. The two worlds—Israel and the Diaspora—could therefore reinforce each other: Israel would strengthen the Jewish presence across the globe, and Diaspora Jews could contribute toward a pluralism that would nurture not only the Jewish people but everyone.[120]

French-Jewish historian Diana Pinto also argued that the realization of the concepts of multinationalism, universalism, and pluralism in Europe meant that European Jewry was also experiencing a revival and had an important role to play in the European Union. It had become, Pinto contended, the "third pillar" of world Jewry.[121]

Yet these utopian visions were swiftly felled in the face of massive exodus of Jews from eastern Europe after the collapse of

---

120   Larry Tye, *Home Lands: Portraits of the New Jewish Diaspora* (New York: Henry Holt and Co., 2001).

121   Diana Pinto, "The Third Pillar? Toward a European Jewish Identity," Central European University. Budapest, Jewish Studies Lecture Series (March 1999).

the Soviet Union and with rising anti-Semitism in the western parts of the continent. In fact, Jews throughout Europe began feeling an increasing sense of emergency soon after the Second Intifada in September 2000 and the terrorist attacks on United States on September 11, 2001. Within a few months, the semblance of Jewish popularity worldwide was replaced by an eruption of global hatred.

Of course, Jewish internationalists did not give up. Until recently, especially amid the premature euphoria surrounding the Arab Spring, they believed that the imminent democratization of the Arab world would enable the Jews to establish "renewed Jewish communities [even in Arab countries] without the need to present Israeli sovereignty as the most recognized, prominent and leading Jewish symbol in the world."[122] These optimistic predictions turned out to be fantasies, crushed by resurgent nationalism in eastern Europe, Islamist chaos in the Middle East, violent right- and left-wing radicalism in the US and elsewhere, and the retreat of liberalism around the globe.

Supporters of the internationalist Jewish model include ardent post-Zionists who argue that the concept of a world Jewish collective is a fiction. They reject both Jewish nationalism *and* the idea that Jewish communities are exilic or diasporic. They even deny the existence of ethno-national bonds between Jews and oppose Israel's Law of Return, which gives automatic Israeli citizenship to any Jew who immigrates to Israel. Post-Zionist intellectuals decry the Zionist concept of "the negation of the Exile" and criticize the notion that Israel is a haven for Jews.

The reality of Diaspora life, they claim, is not only as safe and secure as it is in the State of Israel but also is more meaningful in terms of the quality of Judaism and its universal values. Some have

---

122 Joelle Fiss, *Tiptoeing on Minefields: How to Improve the Flow of Ideas Between Israel and the Diaspora without it Necessarily Exploding in Your Face,* (New York: McNally Jackson Books, 2012).

argued that Israel's attempt to territorially delineate Judaism, as if it offered a superior form of Jewish life, is no more than a distortion of Judaism itself, which is a moral way of life that manifests itself through sensitivity towards the weak and the stranger at its core. The Zionist ethos of negating the exile, therefore, means opting for the wanton belligerence that produced the Palestinian tragedy, which in itself is a tragedy for the Jews.[123]

In recent years, however, many post-Zionist voices have been marginalized, out of despair or defeat; others have backtracked, seeing Israel's robustness. In Israeli academic and cultural circles, post-Zionism has been in full retreat since the dream of an enlightened New Middle East imploded. Moreover, for decades, many warned that Israel's Jewish majority was facing a "demographic threat" because of emigration and low fertility rates relative to the Palestinians. However, the dramatic rise in Jewish fertility and negligible emigration rates belie this thesis. Although post-Zionism still has a place in progressive Jewish discourse in the Diaspora and on the Israeli Left, it has been dwarfed by the strength of the discourse concerning sovereignty, and the Israelization of Judaism. There are always extreme anti-Zionist voices who wish to "halt the usurpation of the designation of Jewishness by the artificially implanted state that calls itself 'The State of Israel.'"[124] The vast majority of Israeli Jews dismiss such fringe groups as irrelevant. They also reject extreme "secular Zionism" divorced from traditional Jewish beliefs and practices.

The Jewish State's Fading Allure?

A century after historian Simon Dubnow proclaimed his vision of the Jews as a "diaspora nation," and nearly eighty years after he

123   Anita Shapira, "The Debate over the 'New Historians' in Israel," in *Handbook Of Israel: Major Debates: Volume 2*, eds. Eliezer Ben-Rafael et al. (Oldenbourg: De Gruyter, 2016), 896–897.
124   "Jewish Anti-Zionist Congress Declaration," Jewish Anti-Zionist Congress (July 2019).

perished in the Holocaust, few advocates remain for the Diaspora nation as a supreme ideal. Today, the principal issue is whether the predominance of the Israeli Century allows for the sovereign State of Israel to coexist peacefully with liberal American Jewry. Have these two models, which for years were touted as complementary and mutually reinforcing, now become contradictory or even adversarial? Many liberal American Jews warn that they are being alienated by an Israel whose foreign policy is jeopardizing their way of life and existence as Jews and excluding them by embracing an increasingly tribal and Orthodox identity. In the twenty-first century, many liberal American Jews are growing tired of Israel. However the question remains: If these two factions are drifting apart, is it due to Israel's behavior or the reality of Jewish life in America? The answers given to such questions are usually a reflection of their advocates' political leanings.

In 2010, Peter Beinart, a former editor of the *New Republic* and columnist for the Israeli liberal newspaper *Haaretz,* ignited the debate among American Jews about Israel's place in their lives. He published an article titled "The Failure of the American Jewish Establishment" in the *New York Review of Books*, which he followed up with his 2012 book, *The Crisis of Zionism*. Beinart criticized traditional American-Jewish elites in Washington, DC, for being out of touch with what younger Jews thought about Israel's character and policies. These liberal Jews, Beinart argued, feel an instinctive affinity with Israel, but less than their parents and grandparents do. They would no longer obediently fall in line with Israeli policies, especially regarding occupation, and were repulsed by its increasingly tribal and nationalistic particularism.

Indeed, Beinart argues, young American Jews are more critical and committed to universal values and human rights than their parents are. He believes that the unreserved support for a hawkish country expressed by traditional establishment voices, such as the pro-Israel lobby AIPAC and the Conference of Presidents of Major Jewish Organizations, is pushing young American Jews away from Israel. "For several decades, the Jewish establishment has asked American Jews to check their liberalism at Zionism's door," writes Beinart, "and now, to their horror, they are finding that many young Jews have checked their Zionism instead."[125]

When Beinart disclosed that Shin Bet internal security officials had detained him when he landed at Ben Gurion Airport and subjected him to prolonged questioning about his political views in August 2018, an international public storm broke out over Israel's democracy—or lack thereof. Soon after the incident, Prime Minister Benjamin Netanyahu and Shin Bet issued an apology. On July 8, 2020, Peter Beinart declared in the *New York Times*, "I no longer believe in the Jewish State." He argued that "Israel has all but made its decision: one country that includes millions of Palestinians who lack basic rights. Now liberal Zionists must make our decision, too. It's time to abandon the traditional two-state solution and embrace the goal of equal rights for Jews and Palestinians. It's time to imagine a Jewish home that is not a Jewish state."

Beinart's claim that Israel's "anti-liberal" behavior is pushing American Jews away is not universally accepted. His critics maintain that the reason for this alienation, if it exists, lies not in major political questions but internal trends within American Jewry, including intermarriage and assimilation. The current generation of American Jews is moving away from Israel because its community is changing. In many respects, it is in gradual decline and is less willing and able to stand in solidarity with Jews in Israel and around the world.

The tensions and fluctuations in the relationship between Israel and American Jewry have concerned pollsters and pundits since the

---

125   Peter Beinart, "The Failure of the American Jewish Establishment," *New York Review of Books*, June 10, 2010, https://www.nybooks.com/articles/2010/06/10/failure-american-jewish-establishment/.

early 1980s. At first, some pointed to cracks in the alliance during the First Lebanon War of 1982 and the First Intifada, the Palestinian uprising of 1987–1991. Then others highlighted the renewed romance between liberal Jews in America and Israel during the peace process of the 1990s. Later, still others stressed the enormous shock that American Jews felt when Prime Minister Yitzhak Rabin was assassinated in November 1995, Benjamin Netanyahu rose to power in 1996, and after he was replaced by Ehud Barak in 1999, the Oslo process collapsed in 2000. The sense of fraternity between American Jewry and Israel was bolstered during the bloody period of the Second Intifada, and Jewish solidarity received another boost following the 9/11 terrorist attacks. It was at this time that David Harris, the director of the American Jewish Committee (AJC), wrote that many Jews felt they had been mugged: "It wasn't that everything that happened in the '90s vanished.... It's just that we were reminded that life as a Jew is a bit more complicated, and that progress is not necessarily as linear as we lulled ourselves into believing during the golden decade."[126] However, when their sense of security increased again, and the Israeli Right gained political and cultural dominance, liberal American Jews increasingly came to see the country as a burden rather than a source of pride.

The shifts in American Jews' attachments to Israel can also be explained in the context of the crisis of liberal American Judaism and the decline of non-Orthodox denominations, above all the Conservative Movement. Some argue that the dwindling of Jewish ethnicity in the United States is a product of post-ethnic Judaism. Researcher Shaul Magid has advanced a somewhat optimistic theory of post-ethnic American Jewry, arguing that American Jews can survive and even thrive without the "ethnic anchor of Jewish

---

126   Yossi Shain, "The Jewish Question: The Old and the New," in *The Maze of Fear: Security and Migration after 9/11*, ed. John Tirman (New York: The New Press, 2004), 196.

identity," without dependence on Zionism, and even without the Holocaust. New forms of Judaism, emerging outside of traditional institutions, will eventually create a new American Jew who is an integral part of society.[127]

Magid's critics, however, argue that post-ethnic Judaism is a fiction and that no commitment to liberal-cosmopolitan values, such as *tikkun olam*, can substitute for particularistic Jewish ties. On the contrary, the belief that "anything goes" and that Judaism is but one option within a broad spectrum of lifestyles in the free world will destroy the Jewish community.

Paradoxically, during the heyday of globalization, when the story of the Jews as a "diaspora nation" became the template for thinking about transnationalism, Israeli Jews have become strongly attached to their tribe and independent state. The family remains the most central institution in the State of Israel, whose people, no matter how cosmopolitan, rebuff the vision of borderless internationalism, dismiss global humanism as naïve, and see no substitute for the nation-state.

Yet Israelis are not a provincial people—they are curious and adventurous. They roam the world while retaining a clear sense of belonging and patriotic ties with their nation. Sociologists have observed that Israeli tourists travel the world in packs and lend each other support. Even Israeli high-tech professionals and entrepreneurs—the most internationalist sector of Israeli society—make exemplary use of their ties and social networks with fellow Israelis.[128]

For more than seventy years, the State of Israel and Diaspora Jewish politics have focused primarily on buttressing Israel's

---

127 Shaul Magid, *American Post-Judaism: Identity and Renewal in a Postethnic Society* (Bloomington IN: Indiana University Press, 2013).

128 Yossi Dashti, Dafna Schwartz, and Ayala M. Pines, "High Technology Entrepreneurs, Their Social Networks and Success in Global Markets: The Case of Israelis in the US Market," *Current Topics in Management* 13 (2008): 132–143.

sovereignty, especially in terms of defense and demographics. This has included the absorption of Jewish immigrants and the settlement of the country's lands. This important chapter of bolstering the reborn Jewish state is not yet over and will likely continue to unfold for years to come. But Israel's security and demographic challenges are no less monumental than questions concerning its character—they will be settled by the intra-Israeli struggle over the nature of the country's society and state.

The world has changed dramatically since the emergence of Zionism. Israeli columnist Shmuel Rosner writes that there is one thing that Zionists and anti-Zionists agree on: "Israel is a fact and the central force in the Jewish world today. In other words, even if the debate over whether the existence of Israel is good for Judaism has not been decided in principle, it has, at least for now, been settled in practice."[129]

The truth that the existence of a Jewish state creates a powerful magnet of attention and identity among Jews is not just a function of the unusual circumstances of the last century, however. It reflects something far more ancient, buried deep in Jewish history and psyche. No matter how far back you go, whenever the Jews enjoyed national sovereignty, this always overshadowed Jewish life and created the fundamental context of Jewish self-definition everywhere. When they didn't have a state of their own, its absence never stopped exerting its pressure across time, on both their political realities and their constantly changing sense of self, community, and religion.

---

129   Rosner, *The Jews: Seven Frequently Asked Questions*, 92 [Hebrew]

Chapter II: From Tribe to Sovereign Nation

The original Hebrews, the biblical children of Israel, were nomadic tribespeople. Having found a homeland, they united to form a kingdom, secured independence, and became a nation.[130] The ancient kingdom eventually split into Israel and Judah; these entities were sometimes at odds and, at other times, in cahoots. Nevertheless, they always saw themselves as belonging to one nation: the House of Jacob. Israeli philosopher Yeshayahu Leibowitz once likened the division between Israel and Judah to the Cold War-era division between East and West Germany, or the ongoing division between North and South Korea.[131]

The northern Kingdom of Israel was conquered by the Assyrian Empire in 721 BCE. Most of its population—the "Ten Lost Tribes of Israel"—disappeared. Judah survived as a sovereign country in the central and southern parts of the Land of Israel, centered around Jerusalem and the Temple of Solomon. But in the sixth century BCE, Judah was conquered by the Babylonians. Its king and elites were exiled. After they could return, Judah gained cultural autonomy, but after more than 500 years, its people were forced into protracted exile under the Romans—an exile we now know as the Jewish Diaspora. Nevertheless, the Jews survived as a people, even without

---

130   Azar Gat, *Nations: The Long History and Deep Roots of Political Ethnicity and Nationalism* (New York: Cambridge University Press, 2013), 90. Gat writes that even those who assert that nationhood is a modern construct tend to agree that the Israelite people is an exceptional example of an "ancient nation."

131   Yeshayahu Leibowitz, *Nation, Land, State: Judaism Then and Now* (Jerusalem: Keter, 1992), 68 [Hebrew].

territorial sovereignty or a central place of worship, because they had developed ethno-religious codes, which determined kinship boundaries and communal membership.[132] The Jews, therefore, experienced a different fate from other peoples of the ancient Near East who were conquered, exiled, and ceased to exist.

This transition from a national tribe to a religious congregation did not begin with the Roman exile, however. In fact, its origins go all the way back to the sixth century BCE, during the six decades of the Babylonian captivity after the destruction of the First Temple. Then, and later after the Return to Zion, Judeans made revolutionary changes to how the Jewish collective was defined; these changes laid the foundations of the tensions about sovereignty felt across the Jewish world today.

What were the implications of the transition from the territorial nationhood of antiquity to the new reality of dispersion? How did the leadership in exile in Babylon shape this dramatic change? How did the distance from their homeland and the loss of national sovereignty paradoxically *strengthen* the Jews' distinct cultural and communal identity? How did Judaism morph from a sacrificial cult into a text-based religion, and what role did concepts such as "the chosen people" and "Holy Seed" play in its preservation? These are some of the questions we shall address in this chapter.

The Jews' exile in Babylon was relatively brief, lasting from about 598–538 BCE, but it engendered a transformation of Jewish peoplehood into one based on theology rather than sovereignty and territory. This process continued during and after the migration to the Land of Israel (the Return to Zion), sanctioned by the Persian Empire under Cyrus the Great after conquering Babylon in 539 BCE.

---

132 To this day, according to a ruling by the Israeli Supreme Court and the 1970 amendment to the Law of Return, it is not possible under Israeli law to be both an ethnic Jew and to have adopted another religion. Although many and perhaps most Jews are not religious, they will always be considered Jews even by the ultra-Orthodox as long as they do not convert to another faith.

Many Judeans chose to remain in the Diaspora, and in 450 BCE, the Persians dispatched Ezra and Nehemiah, both Babylon-born descendants of exiles, to govern Judah on the empire's behalf. Their crowning achievement was to produce the final redaction of the Five Books of Moses and sanctify them as "the Torah," the canonical text of the Jewish nation. This was their way of securing exclusive control over religion in Judah, where most common people had remained while the elites were in exile, and some had turned to idolatry.

Bible scholar Yehezkel Kaufmann argued that the final redaction of the Torah at the time of Ezra was, in its essence, an "exilic project" that ran counter to the original spirit of Israelite national sovereignty. Devotion to the Torah as the focus of the community eroded ethnicity as the defining trait of the ancient Hebrew tribe. The final redaction of the Torah was therefore a "tragic paradox"—on one hand, it preserved the uniqueness of the people of Israel and spared them the fate of nations who were wiped out when they lost their sovereignty; on the other, it fostered a sense of religious community at the expense of the ethnic national sovereignty needed to navigate a dangerous ancient world.[133]

From "Seed of Israel" to "Holy Seed"

In the biblical story, ancient Israelite tribes began as clans of nomads and shepherds who sojourned together in Egypt and spent a generation wandering in the Sinai desert before they ultimately conquered and settled in Canaan, where they lived together among the nations that had previously been there. They had a language and culture of their own, but despite the existence of the tabernacle as a primary focus of worship, later replaced by the Temple of Solomon

---

133 Ehud Luz, "Judaism, Nationalism and Humanism in the Work of Yehezkel Kaufmann," *Jerusalem Studies in Jewish Thought* 1 (1982), 290 [Hebrew].

in Jerusalem, the people did not yet have a universally accepted faith in the one true God. They regarded their land as family estates, to be passed down generationally through the tribe. The Israelites considered themselves the only true "citizens" of Canaan and saw the other nations as socially inferior, as they held no title to the land. Some of these peoples were absorbed into the Israelites; others were not. Hebrew prophets emphasized the need to treat outsiders humanely but did not advocate for integrating them into the Israelite nation. Nevertheless, according to the Bible, these foreigners played a prominent role in the royal armies of David and Solomon. Both kings took Gentile wives. During the First Temple era, writes historian Shalom Ratzaby, "the *ger* [foreigner] was someone who came to live in the Land of Israel and, in the course of time, became culturally and religiously assimilated, adopting the God of Israel and his laws."[134]

Judah was ruled between 640–609 BCE by King Josiah, a boy-king who saved the Judean nation after the defeat of the northern kingdom. Josiah carried out coercive religious reforms, crushing the worship of idols and other ancient gods, and bolstering the monarchy's political and economic standing. He did not make do with removing the statues of only pagan gods; he also banned a series of shrines to Jehovah, the Israelite God.[135] With the help of the family of Shaphan the Scribe, who educated the king, and High Priest Hilkiah, Josiah mandated the worship of the one God as the national deity who would unify a nation facing daunting geopolitical challenges. He imposed repentance as a means of nation-building and strove to unite refugees from the fallen northern kingdom of Israel and coopt them into his realm.

Josiah's crowning achievement was the renovation and purification of the Temple of Solomon and the chance discovery of

134   Shalom Ratzaby, "Historical introduction," in *Jewish Identities: Fifty Intellectuals Answer Ben-Gurion*, ed. Eliezer Ben-Rafael (Leiden and Boston: Brill, 2002), 126.

135   Yigal Bin-Nun, *A Brief History of YHWH* (Tel Aviv: Resling, 2016), 37 [Hebrew].

a "Book of the Law," believed to be Deuteronomy, under a pile of rubble. Historian Simon Schama describes this apparent coincidence as the most sophisticated of all efforts to reform the identity and religion of the Children of Israel in the image of Jehovah as the one true God. Judean sovereignty thus became inexplicably tied to the Holy Torah.[136]

Biblical scholar Yigal Bin-Nun argues that it was Shaphan the Scribe who implemented this critical theological and political turnaround when he staged the discovery of the book during the renovation of the Temple and represented it as ancient and therefore binding. An analysis of Deuteronomy, he argues, indicates that Shaphan and his associates in Judean nobility composed the book and formulated the principles for the worship of Jehovah to strengthen their own standing vis-à-vis the monarchy and the priesthood. Yet the concept of "one God" in Josiah's time was fundamentally different from the monotheistic faith that was to be born in Babylon, which saw Jehovah as an abstract universal deity, not the personal god of the Judean nation.[137]

Josiah aimed to exploit the decline of Assyria and the international upheavals that were shaking the Near East to expand his realm northward and build a new, enlarged version of the Kingdom of David. But the collapse of the Assyrian Empire did not leave a vacuum—Pharaoh Necho II of Egypt conquered Judah and Syria and killed Josiah at Megiddo. Archaeologists Israel Finkelstein and Neil Asher Silberman say that his demise struck the death knell for Judean sovereignty in the coastal plain and the hills and constituted "a national trauma that would never be healed."[138]

Pharaoh Necho also did not survive for long in the region. In

---

136   Simon Schama, *The Story of the Jews: Finding the Words (1000 BCE–1495)* (London: The Bodley Head, 2013), 68.

137   Bin-Nun, *A Brief History of YHWH*, 375–376 [Hebrew].

138   Finkelstein and Silberman, *David and Solomon*, 207.

605 BCE, he was routed by King Nebuchadnezzar of Babylon on the banks of the Euphrates. This defeat was welcomed with a vengeful glee by the prophet Jeremiah: "For the Lord God of hosts shall have on that day a day of vengeance, that He may avenge Him of His adversaries; and the sword shall devour and be satiate and shall be made drunk with their blood; for the Lord God of hosts hath a sacrifice in the north country by the river Euphrates."[139]

During Necho's brief reign, he had transformed Judah into an Egyptian protectorate and appointed Jehoiakim as its puppet ruler, as II Kings relates: "And Pharaoh Necho made Eliakim the son of Josiah king in the room of Josiah his father, and changed his name to Jehoiakim."[140]

Henceforth, Babylon was to become the dominant force in the region. But under King Jehoiakim, its leadership had failed to correctly appraise the relative military power and determination of Nebuchadnezzar and his Egyptian adversaries, propelling them into a hopeless rebellion against the Babylonians. The outcome–after an attempt by King Jehoiachin to save Jerusalem by surrendering to Babylon–was the eventual destruction of Jerusalem and the First Temple in 586 BCE and the banishment of the Judean elites to Babylon, which lasted until 538 BCE. The prophet Ezekiel–himself an exile–referred to the rebellion as not just a breach of the Judeans' oath of allegiance to Nebuchadnezzar, but also as a betrayal of God that would bring the Judean monarchy down after a long list of idolatrous sins, including burying kings and admitting prostitutes next to the Temple.

There is virtually no dispute among historians that the exile from Judah took place during Babylonian rule. In fact, there is abundant evidence of this historical saga. Textual sources from the ancient Near East corroborate the biblical account, as do archaeological

139   Jeremiah 46:10.
140   II Kings 23:34.

findings and the fact that a well-established and thriving Jewish community existed in Babylon and became the most important Jewish cultural center in the ancient world.

The Judean exiles' success in preserving and even enhancing their ethnic and cultural identity in Mesopotamia was by no means a foregone conclusion. It shows that, despite the dispersion and the troubled conditions of exile, the Judean elite maintained impressive internal cohesion and formulated effective societal mechanisms for raising funds and exercising communal control.

The fall of Jerusalem to the Babylonians in 598 BCE struck a lethal blow to the prestige and power of the Judean royal household. Many of King Jehoiachin's subjects were grateful for his surrender to Babylon, as it initially spared Jerusalem and the Temple from destruction, but he paid a heavy personal price for the adventurism of his late father, Jehoiakim, who had remained loyal to Egypt, despite being warned of its treachery. Nebuchadnezzar banished Jehoiachin, together with his mother, princes, eunuchs, "and all the men of might, even seven thousand, and the craftsmen and the smiths a thousand, all of them strong and apt for war, even them the king of Babylon brought captive to Babylon."[141] Many of the exiles in Babylon accepted Jehoiachin as the legitimate heir of the House of David, and the royal household enjoyed a special status in the Babylonian court. Nevertheless, Jehoiachin's prolonged imprisonment, even in relatively benign conditions, undermined his status and prevented the crown exercising its traditional powers.[142]

Eleven years elapsed between Jehoiachin's exile and the destruction of Jerusalem and its Temple in 587–586 BCE. In this short

---

141 II Kings 24:16 (JPS Version).

142 Finkelstein and Silberman note: "The prophet Ezekiel, who belonged to the exiled community, reckoned the dates of his oracles by the years of Jehoiachin's exile…apparently an alternative royal dating formula that suggests continuing allegiance to the exiled king." Finkelstein and Silberman, *David and Solomon*, 212.

period, the people of Judah suffered fresh waves of exile; tens of thousands seem to have been deported. Exiled families settled "by the rivers of Babylon,"[143] where they rebuilt their community and developed identities that would help them survive as a people. Bible scholar Yair Hoffman wrote that the Jehoiachin exile had two main centers: a community hub in the Babylonian capital, and another in Tel Aviv (not to be confused with the Israeli city) in the frontier territory near the city of Nippur: "The exiles' ability in Babylon to successfully preserve their Jewish identity, their national ethos, and the foundations of their monotheistic faith was only possible because this wave was preceded by the Jehoiachin exile." This new wave of exiles was absorbed by the older one and learned from its survival tactics. "Were it not for this legacy," Hoffman wrote, "it is unlikely that Cyrus would have seen a reason to publish his declaration, which set in motion the Return to Zion and construction of the Second Temple."[144]

Yet, even without independence, the Judean elites in Babylon worked to preserve the cohesion of their community and led it by devising theological alternatives to the now-defunct monarchy. They embraced an innovative means of organization and control, backed by an effective array of social sanctions through, as Hoffman explains, "writings based partly on the traditional texts of the Kingdom of Judah and partly on new concepts and prophecies," which transformed the Judean monarchy's ideology "from a political platform into a religious ideal."[145]

The exiles' achievements are particularly impressive when contrasted with the disintegration of the Kingdom of Israel 150 years earlier in 722 BCE after the Assyrian conquest. Other ancient nations

---

143 Psalms 137:1.

144 Yair Hoffman, *The Good Figs: The Jehoyachin Exile and Its Heritage* (Tel Aviv: Tel Aviv University, 2018), 9 [Hebrew].

145 Ibid., 196 [Hebrew].

also proved unable to survive defeat and vanished from the pages of history. Yet the Judeans in Babylon fared considerably better, as their leadership grabbed history by the horns. How did they achieve this? The answer lies in contemporary theories about Diaspora politics in the age of the modern state, which may shed light on their little-understood lives.[146]

The Politics of Exile and the Emergence of a Diaspora Nation

The global debate about refugees and diasporas has become increasingly popular in recent decades. The story of the Babylonian Captivity and the Return to Zion is widely seen as a formative model in the discussion about sovereign versus diaspora ways of life. Throughout history, this drama has been the archetype in inspiring struggles for religious rights, national liberation, return, and independence. Many Irish refugees from the Great Famine of the 1840s saw their escape to America in these terms. To this day, the term "Babylonian Exile" remains a powerful metaphor in the political thought of oppressed peoples. It has become part of the ethos of millions of Africans and African Americans when referring to their trauma of oppression, exile, and enslavement. Diaspora scholar Robin Cohen argues that in the globalized era of the late twentieth century, the term "Babylonian Exile" also came to refer to the possibility of prosperity in the *absence* of national independence and of human adaptability without the constraints of "the corrupting" power of sovereignty.[147]

Recent references to the Babylonian Exile in diaspora studies have been largely symbolic; academics use the concept of the

---

146   Yossi Shain, *The Frontier of Loyalty: Political Exiles in the Age of the Nation-State* (Ann Arbor: University of Michigan Press, revised edition 2005).

147   Cohen, "Rethinking 'Babylon,'" 5–18.

"Babylonian model," despite the paucity of knowledge about the lives of the Judean community in Babylon 2,500 years ago. Even with recent discovery of clay tablets that mention Jewish settlement of "Al-Yahudu," historians are still groping in the dark.[148] Neither has the saga of the Babylonian Captivity and the Return to Zion been discussed in the context of recent analyses of the politics of exile.

Nevertheless, we can draw some analogies about the past based on contemporary theories about the modern era. Instead of using the Babylonian Exile to make inferences about today's diasporas, we shall try to understand the distant past through the prism of what has happened since.

The story of the Babylonian captives, we can reasonably assume, shares similarities with those of political exiles in the modern world. Around the globe, they are affected by a range of factors, including the relationship between their homelands and host societies and the international status of their non-sovereign communal organizations.

Think, for example, about the Dalai Lama and his Tibetan government-in-exile in northern India. He and his exiled court have survived for over sixty years outside of Tibet, after the Chinese conquered it and suppressed its culture. However, it remains to be seen as to whether this Tibetan government-in-exile can survive a change of such mythological leadership.

The status of exiled elites is a function of their ability to maintain unity in dispersion, issues of citizenship and identity connected to national borders, and more. Researchers agree that the Jews in Babylon were led by a prominent core headed by both royal and priestly families. This nucleus dominated the society of craftsmen and functionaries. Their survival capacity was enhanced by their relative homogeneity, which served to unify them in the face of hostility

---

148   Nir Hasson, "Ancient Tablets Disclose Jewish Exiles' Life in Babylonia," *Haaretz*, January 29, 2015, https://www.haaretz.com/archaeology/.premium-exiles-life-in-babylonia-revealed-1.5367088.

emanating from their homeland. In Judah, the common folk almost certainly saw them as a clique of failed leaders who bore responsibility for the catastrophe of the loss of national independence.

Exile presented the remnants of the Judean monarchy with the complex challenge of preserving its status among a split nation in search of an identity, hope, and new legitimate authorities, both in and out of the homeland. It was in this context that members of the priesthood, who were not tarnished with the military failure blamed on the monarchy, emerged as an alternative source of authority and leadership. Yet the question remains: Why, in the absence of Temple worship, was it the *priests* who managed to fill the power vacuum and ensure collective continuity?

Exiled peoples are thrust into a reality of political fragmentation. Intense disputes *between* political exiles over strategy, tactics, resources, and leadership frequently divert their attention away from working toward the common goal of maintaining unity in a foreign land and realizing their dream of return. Instead, they often engage in intense arguments over the identity of the authentic representative of the collective interest. Prominent figures and rival organizations trumpet competing historical, legal, or moral claims to represent the national will.

Those who remain in the homeland also vie for the recognition and loyalty of potential allies, both within the nation and outside of it. Most of the disputes between and within exile groups, as well as between exiled communities and compatriots still in the homeland, boil down to issues of leadership, ideology, and tactics. This happened during the exile of Vladimir Lenin, who fought from afar against both tsarist rule and his Menshevik rivals.

Moreover, disputes amongst exiled leaders are often continuations of political arguments that *predate* the exile and are intensified when transplanted into a foreign environment. Pre-exile organizations are burdened by prejudices, antagonisms, and resentments connected to their failure to secure victory in the homeland.

Harking back 2,500 years, this is exactly how the conflict between the Judean priesthood and monarchy intensified in Babylon. The priests emerged as the dominant force, redefining Judaism as a religion that could exist independently of territorial control, and the vestiges of the monarchy fell into desuetude.

The ability of exiled communities to remain united depends largely on the extent of their communal cohesion before the exile. In the modern era, those who lack an advanced sense of political unity at home and a unified and effective leadership abroad have struggled to maintain their cohesion in exile.

In my book *The Frontier of Loyalty*, I demonstrate how it becomes more difficult to preserve pre-exilic symbols of unity or develop new ones in foreign lands the longer the estrangement from the homeland lasts. The forces that unite the leaders themselves are usually weak, and their ability to exercise authority depends mainly on the consent of their subjects and on the wishes of their hosts. Often, however, the hosts themselves are those responsible for the exile—as with the Jews in Babylon.

The creation of a leadership vacuum with the loss of sovereignty, and the exiles' dependence on the host state or other international patrons, thus tends to weaken their internal cohesion. They often struggle to sustain the old mechanisms of sovereign rule and develop new political ideas that might help them realize their future national ambitions.

Time is of the essence for exiles. Uncertain as to when they might return, they cannot preserve the status quo or make plans because the natural urge to live normal lives in their current residence is a powerful force.

This is what happened to many of the governments-in-exile in the twentieth century; they simply fizzled out.[149] Today, for example, while Tibetan Buddhists wonder what will happen after their spiritual leader dies, the Dalai Lama talks about his reincarnation.

Babylonian Jewry largely succeeded in maintaining communal cohesion despite the leadership rift between the monarchy and the priesthood, which had begun back in Judah. Recent archaeological discoveries indicate that Nebuchadnezzar was relatively tolerant of the first generation of exiles and hoped they could boost the Babylonian economy.[150]

As a rule, the tension between an exiled community's fear of assimilation and its desire for normalcy demands a high degree of creativity from the leadership. In Babylon, for example, the Judean elite were exposed to an imperial civilization, and some of them adopted local names along with their Hebrew ones. Historian Joseph Klausner argued that these name changes were proof of assimilation. However, Ben-Zion Lurie challenged this on the grounds that every generation of Jews has public figures who are loyal to their Judaism but bear non-Hebrew names.[151]

Many of the captives began worshipping the Babylonian gods under pressure from local authorities. These deities had ostensibly proven their superiority over the Hebrew God when Jerusalem was conquered and the Temple went up in flames.

Other exiles fused the two religions and cultures. They accepted Babylonian idols while retaining their belief in the God of Israel, in what E. J. Bickerman calls "double insurance against evil."[152] But

---

149   Yossi Shain ed., *Governments in Exile in Contemporary World Politics* (New York: Routledge, 1991).

150   Daniel Eisenbud, "Ancient Tablets Reveal Daily Life of Exiled Jews in Babylon 2,500 Years Ago," *Jerusalem Post*, March 2, 2015, https://www.jpost.com/Not-Just-News/Ancient-tablets-reveal-daily-life-of-exiled-Jews-in-Babylon-2500-years-ago-389864.

151   Ben-Zion Lurie, "In Exile in Babylon," *Beit Mikra* 34, no. 1 (1989), 6 [Hebrew].

152   E.J. Bickerman, "The Generation of Ezra and Nehemiah," *Proceedings of the American Academy for Jewish Research* 15 (1978), 1–28.

those faithful to the Hebrew God and those who spoke for them, including the prophets Ezekiel and Isaiah, cultivated a monotheistic theology in which Jehovah's power was not measured by any single event, as dramatic it may have been. Instead, Jehovah was the master of all of history. It was he who had determined the fall of Jerusalem and he who would bring about the fall of Babylon at the hands of the Persians just fifty years later, which would lead to the Return to Zion.

To recap, a Judean elite-in-exile community was born under the Babylonians in the sixth century BCE, and later developed under Persian rule. Lacking sovereign power, it transformed Jews both in and out of the homeland from being a feeble nation that had collapsed under the onslaught of mightier forces into a religious community—the "chosen people"—which saw itself as implementing the plans of the God of history. Monotheistic Judaism was now a reality.

Many exiled elites have limited abilities to control events and remain effective from afar in their occupied homeland and among their potential supporters in the diaspora. This often leads to internal ideological or intergenerational tensions that might endanger the organization and the leadership of the exiled community. As a result, leaders tend to become more rigid in their ideologies and avoid compromise when they fear it might jeopardize their reputation after returning to the homeland. This is why Lenin, Ayatollah Khomeini, and other exiled leaders of the twentieth century remained ideologically inflexible.

On the other hand, a leadership-in-exile can boost its credibility and prestige by maintaining unity among its peoples and international supporters. The leaders of Babylonian Jewry were empowered by Persian conquest of Babylon ahead of their return to Judah. Eighty years after the Edict of Cyrus allowed them to return home, Ezra and Nehemiah, third-generation exiles, lobbied the Persians to more actively support the Return to Zion and were thus appointed to leadership positions in Judah, long after their forefathers were forced out.

After the return, the descendants of the people who had remained in Judah were reluctant to contribute to the initiatives of the returning exiles and the construction of a new temple. They feared it and this new Judaism would crush the existing centers of worship, including the Samaritan sanctuary on Mount Gerizim. For their part, the returning captives were not only unconcerned that the common folk might reject them because of their long absence, they also treated the "inferior" Judeans with condescension. The distance from the homeland had so strengthened their own collective identity that they no longer regarded those who had remained as true Jews. One of the principal bones of contention between the returnees and those who remained concerned the boundaries of the Jewish community—who was "one of ours" and who was a Gentile. The Babylonian governors had allowed those who remained to settle on the exiles' lands; it was too difficult to dispossess them after fifty years had passed. While the remainers maintained that the captivity was a punishment for sins against God—sins for which the exiles had also forfeited their right to their lands—the returnees peddled the narrative of an "empty land" as propaganda against those who had stayed behind.[153]

Moreover, the dispute over conversion to Judaism, which remains an explosive issue in the Israeli Century, was, in effect, born in the confrontation over whether Samaritans should take part in the construction of the Second Temple.

Samaritans had long been seen (and saw themselves) as a sect within the Israelite people, but once the return from Babylon began under the leadership of Zerubbabel, they were marked as outsiders

---

153 Bin Nun, *A Brief History of YHWH*, 377 [Hebrew].

and eventually excluded from the nation altogether. Judeans did not regard Samaritans as idol worshipers; however, the returners insisted on the purity of the Jewish pedigree and called for them to undergo a conversion that included not only recognizing the God of Israel but also accepting all the commandments. For the returnees, the Samaritans were beyond the pale; for the remainers, their faith in God was enough to keep them in the tribe. When Ezra and Nehemiah returned to Judah around 450 BCE and imposed the new Jewish concepts and the Holy Seed doctrine, the Samaritans were forcibly ejected from the Jewish world. In the fifth century BCE, they were called "enemies of Judah and Benjamin." As historian Shalom Ratzaby explains: "Whereas in the past residence in the Land of Israel and cultural and religious assimilation had been sufficient to make a person a Jew, now, with the perception of Judaism as a religion, this was no longer the case."[154]

As we shall see, living in Israel in the Israeli Century effectively bestows, over time, the right to join the Jewish nation (and in the second generation, even the Jewish religion) without a halakhic conversion and even without state approval. Indeed, many immigrants from the former Soviet Union who are not Jews according to halakha and have not undergone formal conversions have become deeply integrated into Israel's Jewish society. They serve in its military, enroll their children into the state school system, and adopt traditional Jewish rituals. They have undergone what we might call "sociological conversion," which proves that—despite the monopoly of the Orthodox rabbinate over certain aspects of life in Israel—it is possible to become Jewish for all practical purposes without undergoing a religious conversion (barring the sensitive issues of marriage and burial).[155]

---

154 Shalom Ratzaby, "Historical introduction," 131.

155 Asher Cohen, *Non-Jewish Jews: Israeli Jewish Identity and the Challenge of Expanding the Jewish Nation* (Jerusalem: Shalom Hartman Institute, 2005) [Hebrew].

Ideologies and religions tend to become rigid and dogmatic in periods of exile. Political groups who wish to position themselves as future alternatives in the homeland must bolster their organizational and ideological foundations precisely when it is most difficult to advance national political goals. In situations of protracted exile, which are often defined by political impotence, this ideological focus is a necessary means of preserving communal loyalty and internal hierarchies. Exiled leaders must therefore formulate a set of ethical and political principles that will be broadly accepted by present and future adherents.

This was the strength of Ayatollah Khomeini. From his seat of exile in Iraq, he successfully subverted the corrupt rule of the shah and built the ideological and religious infrastructure that allowed him to triumphantly return to Iran in 1979 and transform it into a Shi'ite theocracy by steering the Islamic Revolution.[156]

In the absence of concrete political achievements, adherence to ideology should serve as a social glue. Nevertheless, it is difficult to maintain bonds of loyalty and ideological vitality under the hostile conditions of foreign rule.

Sometimes it is the *ease* of the foreign environment that most damages the exiles' cohesion and determination to return. When they despair of ever going home, they demand to fit into their host country. The passage of time and this spirit of defeatism provoke rivalries within exiled communities, which can render their leaders irrelevant. As new generations assimilate into the host country and become disillusioned with the old, exiled leaders, the *ancien régime* loses its grip, and its time runs out. This, for example, is what happened to Cuban exiles in Miami, whose struggle against Fidel Castro in the early 1960s waned over time. The same goes for the shah

---

156   Yossi Shain, *The Frontier of Loyalty: Political Exiles in The Age of The Nation-State* (Ann Arbor: University of Michigan Press, 2005), 64–65.

of Iran and his heirs, who went into exile following the Islamic Revolution of 1979, and have since become irrelevant.

In the context of the Babylonian Captivity, King Jehoiachin was imprisoned and released only after thirty-seven years in exile. Humiliated and enfeebled, he could no longer justify his claim to the throne. Thus ended the reign of the Davidic dynasty and the ethos of Jewry as a sovereign nation. This ethos wouldn't reappear until four centuries later, at the time of the Hasmonean dynasty.

Religious leadership tends to flourish most in the *absence* of sovereign and military power. It centralizes authority by emphasizing the need to fatalistically accept God's plan, while creating a new, prophetic morality based on redemption and abstention from the corrupt and valueless reality of worldly politics.

Sociologist Max Weber saw Babylonian Jewry as a classic example of how a community of believers could emerge as an alternative to political sovereignty. It was the priesthood that succeeded in seizing the leadership by legislating on questions of sanctity, worship, and communal self-segregation and by turning religious practice into a substitute for the collapsed monarchy.[157]

The priests' laws in Babylon focused on keeping the Jewish tribe distinct by insulating it from the outside world. They created a complex apparatus of laws of purity and impurity, including dietary laws (*kashrut*), and the novel prohibition on intermarriage. The inability to perform sacrificial rites outside of Jerusalem was a serious challenge for the exiled community and its leaders. Like other nations in the ancient Near East, they worshipped their god and cleansed their sins by performing animal sacrifices. This left the Judeans feeling frustrated and jealous at the sight of Babylon's mighty imperial temples. The priests feared that their people would

---

157   Max Weber, *Economy and Society: Volume 1*, Guenther Roth and Claus Wittich eds. (Berkeley: University of California Press, 1978), 590–591.

erect altars in Babylon to worship the God of Israel or local deities, and they began championing the power of prayer as the primary channel for human connection with the divine.[158]

Unable to perform sacrificial rites, the Jews embraced an innovative approach to worship that centered on communal prayer using a canonical text. These prayers, in turn, came to be regarded as sacred. The launch of this text-based worship was a historic step that heralded this scattered nation's reconfiguration as the "People of the Book." It was also the starting point of a new historical narrative that rationalized the Jewish people's existence and gave them a future horizon. The maintenance of control by the priests, the creation of a communal vision for the future, and the strict observance of a halakhic way of life were all meant to preserve the internal unity and exclusivity of the exiles' community in Babylon.

The transition from national sovereignty to a religion that sanctified the written word was made possible by the invention of new writing technologies, including parchment. The scribes in priestly families quite likely grounded and solidified social control through their mastery of the secrets of literacy. They adopted the Aramaic alphabet as a substitute for Paleo-Hebrew script, the local variant of the Phoenician alphabet, because Aramaic was the *lingua franca* of the Persian Empire. Parchment—which Jews have used since time immemorial for writing Torah scrolls—also seems to have been a Persian innovation.[159]

Some sociologists maintain that non-sovereign social enforcement mechanisms are especially effective among primary groups, such as families and tribes, who are united by intimate, emotional,

---

158   Hoffman, *Good Figs*, 467–485 [Hebrew].

159   So wrote the Greek historian and physician Ctesias, who served in the royal court of the Achaemenid King Artaxerxes II. For more see Arnaldo Momigliano, *The Classical Foundations of Modern Historiography* (Berkeley, California: University of California Press, 1990).

and spontaneous bonds.[160] The Babylonian captives were organized into kin groups, tribes, and families—all involved first-degree relations, which reduced the need to rely on formal mechanisms of social control. The exiles were adept at using these enforcement mechanisms over their families and clans, despite lacking the power of formal political rule.

Another element that facilitated the Jewish exiles' communal cohesion was their geographic isolation from the rest of Babylonian society; evidence suggests that they lived in a few locations reserved exclusively for Jewish settlement. Whether this geographic isolation was dictated by Babylonian authorities or a natural choice by the exiles (just as ethnic groups have always sought to keep to themselves), it made a critical contribution to the cultural survival of the Jewish community in exile.

Recently unearthed cuneiform tablets from the early days of the Babylonian Captivity indicate that the Jews maintained a cohesive settlement bloc between the Euphrates and Tigris rivers. One of the villages identified in the tablets was "Al-Yahudu," the name that Babylonian sources used for Jerusalem.[161]

The tablets also contain long lists of Judean names that have survived to this day or been revived by historically conscious Zionists, such as Sha'altiel, Netanyahu, and Gedalyahu. They also reveal how the Jews led their day-to-day lives in an orderly, bureaucratic fashion, with the issuance of business permits, deal-making, financial transactions, bills of debt, and so forth. "This is 'Babylon's Jerusalem,'" maintains archeologist Wayne Horowitz, "just as New York is the 'new York.'"[162]

---

160 Yonatan Shapiro and Uri Ben-Eliezer, *Elements of Sociology* (Tel Aviv: Am Oved, 1989), 66–67, 94–96 [Hebrew].

161 Wayne Horowitz et al., *By the Rivers of Babylon: Cuneiform Documents from the Beginning of the Babylonian Diaspora* (Jerusalem: Bible Lands Museum, 2015) [Hebrew].

162 Hasson, "Ancient Tablets Disclose Jewish Exiles' Life in Babylonia," *Haaretz*.

In August 2018, an extraordinary meeting of the Israeli Cabinet was held at the Bible Lands Museum in Jerusalem. Ministers were shown a clay tablet from 511 BCE, bearing the family name of Prime Minister Benjamin Netanyahu. It was a bill of debt of a Jew named Benayahu ben Netanyahu, and it was loaned to the prime minister's office at Netanyahu's request so he could show it to world leaders as historical evidence of the continuity of the Jewish people since the Babylonian Captivity. In fact, the prime minister's father, Benzion Netanyahu, was born as Benzion Mileikowsky and Hebraized his original name to Netanyahu ("gift of God" in Hebrew) in honor of his father, Nathan.[163] Which of the exiles could have imagined that their financial documents would be translated into Hebrew 2,500 years later by Jews living in a State of Israel?

It seems, therefore, that the launch of a new set of rules, laws of purity and impurity, and the practice of public prayer created a symbolic, spatial, and personal buffer between the Judean exiles and the environment they chose to see as foreign. One core expression of this strategy was the relocation of sanctity from a physical space—the Holy Land or the "Holy City"—to a *demographic* space, redefining the *people* as a "Holy Seed."

We do not know when or where the idea of the "chosen people" originated, but nationalism historian Anthony Smith presumes that it came from an earlier concept of the Holy Seed, which the Babylonian captives translated into a ban on mixed marriages to ensure the community's survival in the absence of sovereignty.

It is quite possible that the concept of the "God of history" and further motifs and customs, including the laws of purity, reached the exiles via Persia's Zoroastrian influence, as Yigal Bin-Nun argues.

---

163 "Museum Loans Prime Minister 2,600-Year-Old 'Netanyahu Tablet,'" the *Times of Israel*, August 22, 2018, https://www.timesofisrael.com/museum-loans-prime-minister-2600-year-old-netanyahu-tablet/.

But it is likely that this uniquely Jewish set of religious ethics was a product of coupling of the idea of a supreme deity with Jewish practices expressing their "chosenness," such as the hostility to intermarriage with foreign women. If there is a single and special God, why should he not choose a single and special nation? Smith demonstrates how the idea that God chose the Jews, which was cultivated in exile, has since become a prototype for how modern nations regard themselves as chosen or otherwise special. It is by virtue of this trait that nations can claim the right to self-determination, sovereignty, and a privileged role among other nations.[164]

As we have seen, the consolidation of Judaism's supraterritorial monotheism was preceded by two stages. First, each nation had its own god, and each god had its own territory; this was also true of the Kingdom of Judah. The second stage evolved in Babylon, when sanctity was detached from territory and transferred to the tribe, via the idea of the Holy Seed. From being a tribal nation, Jewishness was now defined by *Judaism*, a monotheistic religion whose role was to provide a means of relief to a tribe severed from its old center of politics and worship, to which they might never return. It is from this means of relief that there emerged a deep and seemingly insoluble bond between Jewishness and exile.

The Return to Zion

In the Israeli ethos, the Return to Zion symbolizes national revival. The establishment of the State of Israel is therefore sometimes depicted as a repeat of the ancient wave of immigration under Ezra and Nehemiah, which initiated the Jewish paradigm of exile and

---

164   Anthony D. Smith, "Culture, Community and Territory: The Politics of Ethnicity and Nationalism," *International Affairs* 72, no. 3 (1996), 445–458.

return.[165] In modern Hebrew, the term for immigration to Israel is *aliyah*, which literally means "ascent." It is borrowed from the historical context of the Return to Zion. In the famous Edict of Cyrus, the Persian emperor decreed: "Whosoever there is among you of all His people—his God be with him—let him go up to Jerusalem, which is in Judah, and build the house of the Lord, the God of Israel."[166] This became a mantra for world leaders who supported Zionism, such as Lord Arthur Balfour and President Harry S. Truman, both of whom adopted the terminology of the Babylonian Exile and the Return to Zion as the historical rationale for their backing for Jewish sovereignty in the twentieth century. President Truman said of himself, "I am Cyrus, I am Cyrus," when he officially recognized the State of Israel moments after Ben-Gurion declared independence on May 14, 1948. Truman did so to the dismay of his close associates, including Secretary of State George Marshall. For his part, Ben-Gurion called Cyrus's edict the first Balfour Declaration in Jewish history.[167]

In 2017, when President Donald Trump formally recognized Jerusalem as Israel's capital and moved the US embassy there, he was dubbed by some "the modern-day Cyrus." Prime Minister Netanyahu told Trump that his declaration would be remembered in the same vein as the historic proclamations by Balfour and Cyrus. It is interesting to see how the State of Israel and the Israeli Right, as proud as they are of their political sovereignty, still use historical language that relates to Gentile nations as "saviors" or "foes."

---

165   The late novelist Amos Oz and his daughter Fania Oz-Salzberger wrote that in Babylon the Jews "excellently performed the first, but not the last, great reboot of their history [and] when they returned to their ancestral land from the Babylonian Exile, they demonstrated a vigorous ability to act and a powerful national consciousness under a determined political leadership, much like their symbolic successors 2,500 years later, the Zionists, who dreamed and realized the second Return to Zion." In "Amos Oz and his Daughter's Response to the Question of Who Is a Jew," *Haaretz*, February 6, 2014 [Hebrew].

166   Ezra 1:3.

167   David Ben-Gurion, *Rebirth and Destiny of Israel* (Thomas Yoseloff: London, 1959).

Yet to tell the story of the Zionist drama and the Israeli Century as the direct continuation of the Edict of Cyrus and the Return to Zion is to overlook that the returning exiles did not demand sovereign self-rule from the Persians, nor did they receive it. Under the Achaemenid dynasty, the Return was connected to the Persians' efforts to use the Judean elite to bolster the economic and geopolitical status of their empire in the Near East. The sociologist Max Weber, who distinguished between government by common interests and government by authority, wrote that its power is expressed by its ability to shape its subjects' culture and consciousness.[168]

This distinction will help us grasp the goals of the two migrations from Babylon that constituted the Return to Zion—the early returns headed by Zerubbabel (the grandson of King Jehoiachin) and Joshua (the son of Jozadak the High Priest) at the end of the sixth century BCE, and the second wave led by Ezra and Nehemiah in the mid-fifth century BCE. Each expressed a different stage in the building of the Achaemenid imperial network, a process that paralleled the building of Jewish consciousness.

These two migrations formed a project undertaken by the descendants of the exiled Judeans to conquer the minds of the inhabitants of what was now the province of Yehud, under the patronage of the conquering empire and for its benefit. The Persians supported Ezra and Nehemiah's aspirations to unify the Jewish people; they encouraged them in their bid to codify a constitution and an agreed leadership and build a Jewish identity around the idea of the Holy Seed. In so doing, they aimed to set an address that would facilitate tax collection and coerce Judah's Jews to be loyal to the empire.

Cyrus conquered Babylon in 539 BCE; this was also the official date of the foundation of the Persian Empire, which seized

---

168 Max Weber, *Economy and Society: Volume 2*, eds. Guenther Roth and Claus Wittich (Berkeley: University of California Press, 1978), 943.

Judah shortly thereafter without a fight. Cyrus was a benevolent and enlightened ruler who promoted freedom of worship of the ethnic and national groups across his empire. His policies were remarkably tolerant and stemmed from a basic respect for individuals, ethnic groups, other faiths, and ancient kingdoms.

Cyrus's tolerance is commonly seen as the antithesis of the callousness of the Assyrians, who oppressed the nations that they conquered and forced them to abandon their religions and accept their own pagan pantheon.[169] Cyrus gave the nations that he conquered autonomy in exchange for their loyalty, and his historical reputation is linked principally to his decision to allow exiles, most notably Judeans, to return to their homelands.[170] United Nations headquarters in New York displays a replica of a clay tablet bearing the Edict of Cyrus as an ancient testimony to the sanctity of human rights. In 2019, US Secretary of State Mike Pompeo celebrated Cyrus's legacy by tweeting: "Today in 539 BC, Cyrus the Great entered Babylon and freed the Jewish people from captivity. His respect for human rights and religious freedom inspired America's founding fathers. The U.S. stands with the Iranian people, who are blocked by the regime from celebrating his legacy."[171]

However, despite all the humanistic praise heaped upon this Persian king and hero of the Jews, Cyrus was no liberal. He was a pragmatic emperor who ruled with a firm hand. He could be alternately cruel and generous, but always acted with a view to securing his own power and wealth. He ruled his empire with a system of

---

169   J. B. Bury et al., eds., *The Cambridge Ancient History: Volume 4—The Persian Empire and the West* (Cambridge: Cambridge University Press, 1926), 187.

170   R. J. van der Spek, "Cyrus the Great, Exiles and Foreign Gods: A Comparison of Assyrian and Persian Policies on Subject Nation," in *Extraction & Control: Studies in Honor of Matthew W. Stolper*, eds. Michael Kozuh et al. (Illinois: The Oriental Institute of the University of Chicago, 2014), 233–263.

171   Tweeted by @SecPompeo, October 26, 2019, https://twitter.com/secpompeo/status/1189 199170537689088?lang=en.

indirect government over conquered nations through vassal kings and bestowed cultural autonomy in exchange for allegiance to Persia. According to Dutch historian Bert van der Spek, "Cyrus appears to have been less an organizer than a conqueror."[172] Like the rulers of other ancient empires, he fostered local monarchic dynasties, governors, and priesthoods without forcing an ideology on them and with mutual consent, lest they rebel or seek independence. And yet, despite his reputation as the liberator of exiles, the policy of allowing them to return home was selectively enforced. This is why his edict was so remarkable.

At the time of the first wave of the return, in 536 BCE, Judah was a backwater province. Its inhabitants were poor and dependent upon the budget allocations and infrastructure of the Persian imperial power, for whom ruling Judah promised limited economic gain. However, the Land of Israel was a vital buffer zone against Egypt, and in the first phase of what would be known as the Second Temple era, Persia's policy was based on its desire to make the most of the geopolitical situation at the minimum cost.[173]

Although Cyrus allowed the reestablishment of a center of worship in Jerusalem in the Zerubbabel migration, the reconstruction of the Temple and the revival of its rituals progressed slowly due to shortages of timber and stone. Zerubbabel may have had dreams about restoring the old kingdom, but the Temple was dedicated twenty years after work on it had begun, and even then, it was only a modest structure. In the words of historian Heinrich Graetz: "The people burst forth into a loud transport of joy. Yet there mingled

---

172   Van der Spek, "Cyrus the Great, Exiles and Foreign Gods," 256.

173   The historian Samuel L. Adams has estimated that in the years 539–450 BCE, the population of Judah numbered only some 13,500 souls, among them about 4,000 returnees—many of whom even went back to Babylon. See Samuel L. Adams, *Social and Economic Life in Second Temple Judea* (Louisville: Westminster John Knox Press, 2014), 17.

with the jubilant notes the voice of regret that the new Temple was smaller and less magnificent than the old."[174]

The significant turning point in the Persians' policy came only two generations later, when the Persian Empire spread across the East and when they appointed Ezra and Nehemiah as officials of the imperial regime in 450 BCE. The pair arrived in Judah with the second migration, equipped with broad powers, including a military force to rebuild Jerusalem and its city walls. Nehemiah, in particular, was a social reformer, according to historian Joseph Klausner who wrote: "The entire advanced national democracy that governed the Land of Israel from the time of Nehemiah until the time of Herod and which transformed the nation into 'the People of the Book'... was largely anchored in the great economic policies of Nehemiah the governor."[175]

What explained the shift in Persian policy from the minimal investment in Judah during the reign of Cyrus and his successors to the substantial investment of manpower and resources decades later? Should this change be attributed to the heightened tension between the Persian and Egyptian empires or was it the result of the close personal ties between the Persian potentates and Ezra and Nehemiah, who had served as cupbearer to King Artaxerxes I of Persia?

As far as Ezra and Nehemiah are concerned, all we can say is that they were sent to Judah by Persian conquerors because of an extraordinary confluence of economic and political interests with the two men's tribal and national interests. In their status, personalities, and commitments, the pair embodied a classic example of dual loyalty to their nation and to the Persians.

---

174   Heinrich Graetz, trans., *History of the Jews: Vol. I* (Philadelphia: Jewish Publication Society of America, 1956), 357.

175   Josef Klausner, "Nehemiah's Social Revolution" in *The Hebrew State: Anthology of Sources and Thoughts*, ed. S. Levy (Tel Aviv: Baterem, Tel Aviv, 1946), 174–175 [Hebrew].

The Economic Reason for Persia's "Tolerance"

The Persian Empire wished to maximize its tax revenues in Judah and deployed Nehemiah to raise significant income from the Temple in Jerusalem and turn it into an important tax-collection center. In fact, Ezra received broad authority from the Persians to appoint Jewish judges and religious officials not only in Judea but also the surrounding region, which would enable him to encourage Jewish loyalty across the Near East to their Persian masters. The strategic change of direction in Achaemenid policy in the province led to broad reforms in collection methods and was apparently connected to the emergence of a money-based economy in the mid-sixth century, as indicated by archaeological findings.[176]

Israeli academic Erez Casif argues that, until coinage use was widespread, places of worship, including the Temple in Jerusalem, were small, low-key institutions whose primary function was to provide the local regime with symbolic justification. Governments were generally controlled by royal families or dynasties whose ability to rule was directly correlated to their coercive powers. Places of worship also supplied material backing for priests, who served as functionaries in the local or imperial government and whose job was to collect tributes, offerings, tithes, and various kinds of agricultural produce.

This was how the Judean priesthood under Ezra became both an arm of the central government and an independent force with symbolic capital. The ability to transport agricultural produce over great distances was very limited in the sixth century BCE, because of its short shelf life, or "camel's-back life."

Moreover, wealthy Persia had no need for most of Judah's produce. The local nature of the collection apparatus, therefore,

---

176   Yehoshua Zlotnik, "The Minting of Local Coins in the Land of Israel in the Persian Period—Does It Reflect Political Situations?," lecture before the Israeli Numismatist Society, February 12, 2007 [Hebrew].

provided no incentive for imperial investment in Judah. Control over the center of worship was deemed unimportant and left in the hands of local religious elites to run for their own benefit. But the picture changed when Ezra and Nehemiah arrived armed with wide powers and semi-sovereign authority. They instituted a new money-based collection system with the goal of enriching the imperial Persian treasury.

Nehemiah's project to fortify Jerusalem, renovate the Temple, and introduce other reforms was connected to the new economic reality, with coinage at its center. According to historian Yehoshua Zlotnik, the use of coins in the Persian era started off as a tool of political import and was a statement of sovereignty or autonomy.[177] In time, it spread to all levels of society. Clearly, transporting a chest of gold coins on the back of an ass was simpler than, and possibly equivalent to, ten caravans of camels bearing dates and wine. Against this background, the Temple treasurer became the second most important man in the priestly hierarchy, after the high priest. (The Hebrew for "treasurer" is "*gizbar*." This term entered the language via Aramaic and appears only once in the Bible, in Ezra 1:8: "Even those did Cyrus king of Persia bring forth by the hand of Mithredath the treasurer....")

To ensure the loyalty of the rural population, Ezra and Nehemiah forgave the farmers' debts to the landed gentry. The next step in securing control of the finances was to establish a collection process based on a religious commandment of paying one-third of a shekel to the Temple. This tax was imposed on every household in the land.[178] Zlotnik writes that Ezra and Nehemiah's reforms were designed to encourage the use of coins, thereby transforming the economy in theory and practice from a barter system into a monetary one.[179]

---

177   Ibid. [Hebrew].

178   Nehemiah 10:33.

179   Zlotnik, "The Minting of Local Coins in the Land of Israel" [Hebrew].

By drawing on the tradition of pilgrimages to the Temple, Ezra and Nehemiah were able to incentivize and encourage the use of coins as a religious precept. Coins also served as a substitute for and supplement to the offering of tithes, making access to coinage mandatory for each Judean household. The cancellation of the debts of the poor may have also contributed to the transition to a monetary economy, in that it obligated the wealthy and the priests to begin using coins instead of barter trade. In addition, the enforced concentration of one tenth of the population of Judah in Jerusalem was aimed at restricting the rural-agricultural population and boosting the urban one, whose ability to barter had become limited and who had, therefore, become more dependent on the monetary economy.

The Shaping of Communal Boundaries Under Persian Rule

When Ezra and Nehemiah arrived in Judah some eighty years after the Edict of Cyrus, they did not come merely to serve as tax collectors. They also had a distinctly Jewish mission—to rebuild a strong community and shape its identity around the rituals of the Temple. Their goal was to establish and unify the Jewish nation by setting its borders and returning it to the Torah, as recorded in the Talmud: "Some of the Torah laws were forgotten from the Jewish people in Eretz Yisrael, Ezra ascended from Babylonia and reestablished the forgotten law."[180] Since their standing in the Persian royal court was firm, and the Persian emperor granted Ezra "all his request,"[181] according to the Bible, Ezra and Nehemiah were given the opportunity

---

180 Babylonian Talmud, Sukkah 20a:70, trans. William Davidson, available from the Sefaria Library at Sefaria.org. See Mordechai Zer-Kavod, "Ezra the Scribe, the 'Founder' of the Torah," *House of Scripture: A Journal for the Study of the Bible and Its World* 7, no. 3 (Tevet, 5723), 3–11 [Hebrew].

181 Ezra 7:6.

to realize their vision of reconsolidating the Hebrew nation by redrawing the boundaries of national and cultural belonging, despite the absence of sovereignty. As Ezra said: "For we are bondmen; yet our God hath not forsaken us in our bondage, but hath extended mercy unto us in the sight of the kings of Persia, to give us a reviving, to set up the house of our God, and to repair the ruins thereof, and to give us a fence in Judah and in Jerusalem."[182]

Ezra and Nehemiah were keen to revive an ethno-national Jewish identity that was distinct from all other nations in the region. They took vigorous action against the expansive interpretations of identity that prevailed at the time and sought to fuse definitions of religious and national belonging. To do so, they marshalled the power of monotheism and sacred texts and emphasized that it was not enough to simply live in the homeland; henceforth, adherence to the Jewish religion and its commandments would define Jewish belonging. Some of these commandments were linked to the purity of the Holy Seed. Since then, Jews have fought over what this doctrine means and who has the right to delineate the boundaries of the nation and its faith.

Throughout Jewish history, the question of the Holy Seed has tied into the debate over whether belonging and identifying with the Jewish people is more important than accepting the yoke of the Torah and its commandments. Recall that the arrival of Ezra and Nehemiah and their retinues in Judah sparked apprehension from the local populace, especially the priestly elite, who stood to lose their status. They related to Babylonian captives who had returned to Judah decades earlier as part of the Zerubbabel migration and realized that the new Persian bureaucracy headed by Ezra and Nehemiah would likely deprive them of their privileged and lucrative position.

---

182 Ezra 9:9.

The two leaders, in turn, also fully grasped the challenge to their government. To entrench their status and remove any threat of noncooperation or rebellion, they threatened to order the expulsion of the foreign wives of the former elites. Their decree would signal to the local priestly elite that they would be considered as living in sin if they refused to accept this new authority. The fact that the Bible suggests that Ezra and Nehemiah intended to banish only a few dozen women seems to indicate that they sought a controlled purification process through which to maintain their domination over a small, rebellious clique among the Judean upper classes. This group of potential troublemakers included not only priests, but also wealthy merchants, amongst whom the practice of taking foreign wives was quite widespread.

The polemics over the issue of the Holy Seed and the boundaries of the community and its connection to the Land of Israel dragged on for generations after the Second Temple period. After Herod's Temple was destroyed in 70 CE, triggering the great dispersal of the Jews, the dispute took the form of a clash between the Babylonian Talmud and the Jerusalem Talmud on the question of the efficacy and use of conversion. According to the Jerusalem Talmud, as law professor Arye Edrei explains, if "a convert is separated from his Gentile family and his children are brought up in a Jewish family framework and a Jewish atmosphere, and even if the convert himself began his path as a Jew not for Judaism's sake but because of love and marriage, he will be as Jewish as the Jews around him, and his sons will certainly be brought up as Jews and will be Jewish in all respects." Converts who lived in the Land of Israel stood a better chance of fostering an affinity for the Jewish people and religion than converts who lived elsewhere "in an atmosphere that is foreign and alien to Judaism." For this reason, "The Land of Israel is preferable as [it] purifies the converts and ensures that they integrate and merge in all respects into the way of life of the Jewish people, and will ultimately do so for the sake of Heaven." The Babylonian Talmud, meanwhile, written outside the Jewish homeland, is more hardline because life as a minority forced the Jews to police their identity more strictly.[183]

In the Israeli Century there have also been fierce disputes between the various streams of Judaism over conversion. What is the most important element of conversion? Who should have the authority to convert (i.e., which rabbis are legitimate)? Where does the center of gravity in Jewish identity lie—simply identifying with the Jewish people, its legacy, and destiny, immigrating to Israel, or strictly observing the Torah and its commandments?

In Israel, ultra-Orthodox rabbis and politicians who insist that religious criteria are paramount are at loggerheads with the rabbis of the religious Zionist movement, who see commitment to the state and its land as key. Religious Zionists agree that conversion is a religious procedure but believe that one who lives in Israel and acts in accordance with its national interests, even without devoutly obeying religious law, is a better Jew than a pious Jew living in the Diaspora. They contend that the commandment to the Land of Israel takes precedence over all others, as Rabbi Shlomo Goren preached. Goren, who served as Israel's chief rabbi after establishing the IDF Chaplaincy Corps, taught that the foundation for Torah observance was essential to the Jewish people's national existence, and that immigrating to the Land of Israel, identifying with its national rebirth, and fighting for its defense made one a member of the Jewish people.

Rabbi Goren's thinking has been accepted by much of Israeli society with respect to the many Israelis from the former Soviet Union who serve in the IDF but are not Jewish under the religious

---

183   Arye Edrei, "The Historical and Ideological Roots of the Polemic on Conversion (*Giyur*) in Israel," *Hebrew Annual of Jewish Law* 27 (2013), 44–45 [Hebrew].

definition. Most Israelis believe that people who are naturalized under the Law of Return can become Israeli Jews when they identify with the state's symbols, celebrate its festivals, speak its language, and are prepared to shed blood for its sake, although they may not be recognized as Jewish by the state rabbinate. For all intents and purposes, Israeli patriotism is deemed a sufficient conversion procedure to the dismay of hardline Orthodox rabbis.

In January 2020, when Israel's Sephardic Chief Rabbi Yitzhak Yosef called Russian immigrants "communist, religious-hating Gentiles," he sparked a huge backlash. Many Israeli leaders, including the prime minister, condemned his remarks as "anti-Semitic."

Many people maintain, therefore, that in the Israeli Century, the Jewish nation-state is the only state under whose aegis the Jewish people can be preserved. Assimilation and the loss of Jewish identity is a problem for the Diaspora, especially the liberal Jewish population of North America who, according to polling data, face extinction because of intermarriage.

In Israel, meanwhile, there are very few mixed marriages, so Jewish public discourse assumes that Israeli society is a success story when it comes to the preservation of a Jewish identity.[184] Jews comprise its vast majority, so even when Israeli Jews intermarry, their partners will most likely be brought into the Jewish fold, rather than taking them out of it. Unlike in the Diaspora, it is widely presumed that in a sovereign Israel, communal boundaries are protected by the institutionalized distinction between Jews and non-Jews and that Muslim and Christian minorities are equally protective of their own closed communities, faiths, and cultures.

In 1958, Ben-Gurion asked a broad panel of Jewish intellectuals in Israel and in the Diaspora to write back to him with their opinion

---

184 Aharon Ariel Lavi, "We and Us: Jewish identity in the Diaspora and in Israel," *Hashiloach* 9 (April 2018): 107 [Hebrew].

on the question: "Who is a Jew?" His objective was to establish clear criteria for registration of the children of mixed marriages in Israel's population registry. The Israeli premier wrote that, in Israel, "We are not a minority subject to the pressure of a foreign culture, and there is no fear that the Jews will become assimilated among the non-Jews as there is in several prosperous free states."[185] However, in contrast to the view that Israel protects Jews and their identity, there are those—largely from the ultra-Orthodox sector—who argue that it is precisely in Israel, with its stress on territory and security as supreme values, where assimilated Jews are being raised without a clear affinity to their ancient national heritage.

New Holy Text, New Holy Tribe

Ezra and Nehemiah used more than just sanctions to draw the boundaries of Jewish identity. To bring the inhabitants of Judah on board, they undertook swift action to impart a religious consciousness based on the new monotheistic faith shaped in Babylon and the acceptance of scripture. They launched the new template for Jewish identity with ceremonial fanfare, summoning the whole nation to Jerusalem's Water Gate for a festive public reading of Deuteronomy, as redacted by Ezra. Simon Schama writes that this rehearsed an ancient custom of oral recitals: "The Hebrew for reading presupposes vocalizations before an audience: the word *qra* means literally 'to cry out,' and *miqra* derived from it is the noun form of a gathering of listeners and readers. That same reading obligation would become *the* characteristic practice of Jewish observance outside the Temple, the impact of its vocalization not even dependent on literacy.... Ezra's elevation above the rapt multitude is not just a reiteration of that first Mosaic transcription but a self-conscious re-enactment

---

185   Ben-Rafael ed., *Jewish Identities: Fifty Intellectuals Answer Ben-Gurion*, 146.

of it."[186] The local priests at this event were not familiar with the new version, and according to the Bible, protested being suddenly told that–having been unaware of God's law–they were actually sinners.[187]

The sanctification of the new version of the Torah was aided by its use at the core of ritual worship. Only a few Jews had the privilege of access to the text. Most remained illiterate farmers; this situation endured for centuries, at least until the destruction of the Second Temple in 70 CE.

The people saw the reading of the Torah as an almost magical rite. The written word and the physical scroll became an organic, sacred whole around which the Jews developed a system of worship. They became intrinsic representations of God on Earth. The concept of one God, one people, and one text–the beating heart of the Jewish national ethos–evolved to establish the political authority of the new priesthood and set the boundaries of a national and religious identity for the entire nation. Schama writes: "The scroll itself must have been significant too: the compact roll of portable memory, something that had a chance of being carried through the fires of disaster."[188] One might see it as the ancient equivalent of a USB flash drive.

Ezra was the sanctifier of the Torah, or the Five Books of Moses, which tells the story of the Jewish people from their earliest forefathers, through the exodus from Egypt to the brink of entering Canaan. Although his centrality in Judaism faded over the generations and centuries, we still see it hinted at in a vestigial form–in the fast of the Tenth of Tevet, which commemorates (among other

---

186   Schama, *The Story of the Jews*, 33.

187   Unlike Kaufman and Baron, who contend that the Torah preceded the destruction and the exile, we consider that the version redacted by Ezra was *not* the one that the Judean priests were familiar with, which is why they were so confounded.

188   Schama, *The Story of the Jews*, 33.

things) his death. No other classical figure's death is similarly recognized; to this day, traditional Jews refer to him as "Ezra the Scribe"—an appellation shared by no other ancient figure—presumably for his role in redacting the Torah.

However, in its stories, there are only hints of Jewish sovereign rule over the Promised Land. God's covenant with the patriarch Abraham was meant to turn the people of Israel into a "great nation… from the river of Egypt unto the great river, the river Euphrates."[189] This vision was realized in the time of Ezra and Nehemiah, when the Jewish people were scattered across the whole Near East, from the Nile to the Euphrates, with a renascent center of worship in Jerusalem but no sovereign control in Judah.

The question of sovereignty, therefore, lost its power following the destruction of Solomon's Temple and the Babylonian Captivity. The homeland remained significant as the central place of worship, with a Temple run by priests rather than kings.

But as real-world political issues, Jewish sovereignty and its religious rationale were of secondary importance in the period of Ezra and Nehemiah. The matter would reappear once again in the Hellenistic period, during the second century BCE, when the possibility of independent Jewish self-rule suddenly waxed as the power of the Seleucid Empire waned. It was at this time that the Hasmonean Kingdom arose as a kind of Jewish theocracy that united the powers of the priesthood and the monarchy—crowns that members of the Hasmonean dynasty bore at the same time.[190]

During the early Second Temple period, the high priests won

---

189   Genesis 12:2–15:18. The United Monarchy nurtured the perception that the eastern bank of the Jordan River formed part of the Promised Land, falling within the idealized borders from the Euphrates to the Nile. See Moshe Weinfeld, "The Extent of the Promised Land–Two Different Views," *Cathedra* 47 (1988): 10 [Hebrew].

190   "The Concept of Three Ketarim: Their Place in Jewish Political Thought and Implications for Studying Jewish Constitutional History," in *Kinship and Consent: The Jewish Political Tradition and Its Contemporary Uses (Second Edition)*, ed. Daniel Elazar (New Brunswick, NJ: Transaction, 1997), 47–76.

the battle for communal leadership and gradually expanded their sphere of authority. As historian Uriel Rappaport explains, they "subsumed the governor's powers and the image of rulers of other temple-states in the Near East, who functioned simultaneously as high priests and district governors."[191]

Indeed, in the absence of sovereignty, ritual sacrifice and worship became the defining feature of Jewish autonomy, and the dream of a kingdom never fully returned. Even when the Maccabees restored sovereignty, they were wary of claiming the throne.

---

191   Uriel Rappaport, "On the 'Hellenization' of the Hasmoneans," *Tarbitz* (1990), 496 [Hebrew].

Chapter III: The Rise and Fall of Jewish Sovereignty During the Second Temple Era

The ancient Near East was a place of empires, independent countries, and rival city-states. In most of the independent states, sovereign power was vested in a monarch who claimed that his rule was sanctioned by idols or, in the case of the Jews, the one God. The king's will was the law of the land, although people's assemblies, advisory councils, other traditional institutions sometimes functioned alongside the monarch. The king set policy in all spheres, and it was he who decided when to go to war. The city-states, like the ancient Greek *polis*, were ruled by their citizens, who served as legislators.

However, the modern concept of popular sovereignty that underpins the constitutional state is fundamentally different from the equivalent in Athenian democracy. There, the (male) *demos* ruled directly and not through a system of elected representatives; this was a phenomenon that evolved in Europe in the late Middle Ages and early modern era. Moreover, although the citizens of the Greek *polis* saw their gods as the source of justice, they never made an ideology out of obedience to them as the supposed source of social order.[192] Interestingly, when Alexander the Great conquered the Greek city-states in the fourth century BCE, he demanded that they recognize him as divine, even though they were used to popular rule.[193]

---

192   Josiah Ober, *The Rise and Fall of Classical Greece* (Princeton: Princeton University Press, 2015), 60.

193   Ibid., 299.

In ancient monarchies like those of the late Middle Ages, and even today, states and nations were defined by the personal rule of their kings. Royal houses also purported to enjoy an intimate relationship with their nations' gods. This was also the case in pre-exilic Judah, where King Josiah strove to create a symbiosis between loyalty to himself, as the heir to the dynasty's founder, King David, and the worship of Jehovah as the one true God. The ancient Hebrew kings had to come, as the Bible says, from within the people—"one from among thy brethren."[194]

The king was also limited in his powers and prohibited from arbitrarily appointing the priests responsible for religious rites, whose job it was to "guard the traditional laws of the nation and teach them to the king."[195] When Josiah set out to purify Judean rituals and ban other ritual practices with the aid of the scribes, priests, and other officials, his aim was to magnify God's name to boost his own and strengthen the standing of his monarchy.[196]

The identification of the ancient Judean kingdom with religion lay at the core of its monarchy's claim to legitimacy. The monarchy represented itself (not entirely incorrectly) as the physical manifestation of the existence of a Judean nation. The collapse of the monarchy and the Babylonian Captivity left an acute power vacuum that threatened the survival of this tribal nation.

Stripped of the sovereign state that had overseen their religious rituals, the Jewish people needed an alternative organization to provide leadership and ideology for preservation of their religious and national identity. Devotion to the one God, therefore, became an increasingly vital means of defining the national collective.

The demise of the House of David transformed the nature of

---

194 Deuteronomy 17:15.

195 Yoram Hazony, *The Virtue of Nationalism* (New York: Basic Books, 2018), 18.

196 Henry Wassermann, *People, Nation, Fatherland: Observations on the Emergence, Growth and Demise of Nationalism-Generating Concepts* (Raanana: Open University, 2007), 55–54 [Hebrew].

the people of Israel. They went from being a sovereign nation with a territorial-political focus to an exiled nation defined by religious laws but bereft of sovereign political power. This led to the collapse of the Jews' status among nations and role as players on the regional geopolitical stage.

The Jewish explanation for the fall of the monarchy was the kings' betrayal of their covenant with God. The prophet Ezekiel accused the kings of engaging in sacred prostitution inside the Temple and having themselves buried there, thus breaking their vows of loyalty and devotion. This "desecration of God's name" led God to strip the monarchy of his divine protection. Channeling God, Ezekiel thunders:

> Son of man, this is the place of My throne, and the place of the soles of My feet, where I will dwell in the midst of the children of Israel for ever; and the house of Israel shall no more defile My holy name, neither they, nor their kings, by their harlotry, and by the carcasses of their kings in their high places; in their setting of their threshold by My threshold, and their door-post beside My door-post, and there was but the wall between Me and them; and they have defiled My holy name by their abominations which they have committed; wherefore I have consumed them in Mine anger. Now let them put away their harlotry, and the carcasses of their kings, far from Me, and I will dwell in the midst of them forever.[197]

---

197   Ezekiel 43:7–9.

Ezekiel prophesied that the kings of Israel, whose sins provoked the destruction of the First Temple, would play no role in any future temple. Instead, the people of Israel would be led by a *nasi*—a tribal leader functioning under the aegis of a foreign king (or in modern Hebrew, a president).[198] Accordingly, after the Babylonian Exile, the Jews strove to preserve their community by defining it as a religious collective charged with a unique divine mission.[199]

As soon as Nehemiah arrived in Judah as the representative of the Achaemenid crown, there emerged a stratum of religious leaders whose power was independent of territorial control. It was headed by the high priests, who retained their powers to govern the sacrificial rites and worship in the rebuilt Temple.[200] This priestly aristocracy remained in leadership for centuries, until the end of the Second Temple era.

Yet there also emerged another elite, whose knowledge of the Torah bestowed upon them a broad legitimacy as "possessors of the Law." Tensions between the old aristocracy and the newer elite of scribes and sages increased, sometimes to the point of open hostility. As the popularity of the scholarly laymen rose, so did resentment over the priests' corruption of sacrificial rites and economic exploitation of their status.

During the Second Temple period, the Jews of Judea were the subjects of passing empires—the Persians, the Macedonians, the Ptolemaic Kingdom, the Hellenistic Seleucids, and, starting from the late Hasmonean period, the Romans. Under these empires, Jewish life focused on the ritual and worship shaped during the time of Ezra and Nehemiah, and the Jews rarely challenged their imperial overlords.

---

198 See also Ganzel, "The Status of Office Holders in the Future Temple in the Prophecy of Ezekiel," 18–19, 25 [Hebrew].

199 Malach, "A Look at Nationalism and the Jewish-Israeli Case," 170 [Hebrew].

200 Rappaport, "On the Hellenization of the Hasmoneans," 496 [Hebrew].

Historian Seth Schwartz has written that life in Judea was characterized by a constant tension between the forces who wished to preserve Jewish exclusivity and the sectors who pushed for greater integration into the imperial, mostly Hellenistic, culture.[201] The fragile equilibrium between isolation and integration was upset when King Antiochus IV Epiphanes terminated the priesthood of Onias III (175–172 BCE). The Seleucid king's violent conduct, together with the internal currents pushing for increased integration, effectively provoked the collapse of Jewish autonomy under imperial rule.

Hasmonean Sovereignty and the Transformation of Judaism

The story of the Hasmonean's rise to power began when the Seleucids ousted High Priest Onias III and appointed his brother, Jason, as his successor. With the agreement of Antiochus IV, he implemented reforms in the government and social order in Jerusalem, including the construction of a gymnasium in a bid to transform the city into a Greek-style metropolis under Seleucid rule, like Tyre and Sidon. But Jason was an unstable ruler, and Antiochus IV doubted his loyalty during the Seleucids' war against Egypt. The Seleucids appointed a new puppet ruler, Menelaus, who was not a member of the high-priestly family. "A new page was thus opened in the history of the relations between the Seleucid kingdom and the Jewish people," wrote historian Menahem Stern. "The high priest, who previously had represented the Jewish nation before the king, now became the representative of the king in Judah, something of a commissioner of Antiochus and his right-hand man in executing his policy among the Jews."[202]

---

201   Seth Schwartz, *Imperialism and Jewish Society: 200 B.C.E. to 640 C.E.* (Princeton: Princeton University Press, 2001).

202   Menahem Stern, "The Hasmonean Revolt and Its Place in the History of Jewish Society and Religion," *Journal of World History* 11, no. 1 (1968), 95 [Hebrew].

Antiochus's persecution of the Jews and decrees outlawing the Jewish religion in 168–167 BCE soon provoked the Hasmonean revolt. It began locally in Modi'in before snowballing into a popular uprising, culminating with the ultimate establishment of the Hasmonean Kingdom as a sovereign Jewish entity in the Land of Israel. At the outset, the new rulers refrained from declaring themselves kings, and Simon was proclaimed the *nasi*–the chief or prince–just as Ezekiel had prophesied. Stern wrote that the rebellion saved the Jews from extinction, explaining: "It is doubtful whether the spiritual or material resources of...Jewish groups [in the Diaspora] were adequate to enable them to maintain the character of Judaism and the revealed monotheistic religion in the event of the destruction or the effacement of the nature of the Palestinian center."[203]

However, in the centuries that followed the destruction of the Second Temple by the Romans in 70 CE, Talmudic sages downplayed the wars of the Maccabees and the Hasmonean Kingdom in favor of a vision of messianic redemption, according to which a struggle for sovereignty–preempting the messiah–was a real threat to the existence of the Jewish people. This could well be the principal reason why the Books of the Maccabees were not included in the Hebrew Bible: the failure of the Great Rebellion and the Bar Kokhba revolt against the Romans had pushed the Jewish people to the brink of extinction. Many survivors scattered to the winds, so the sages focused on preserving the Jewish religion.

The festival of Chanukah was celebrated to mark a divine miracle–a jar of oil that lasted for eight days–and not as a military victory.[204] It was, ironically, the Crusaders who next made use of the

---

203 Ibid., 99.

204 Scholars disagree on the extent to which the Talmudic sages wished to conceal the Maccabees' heroism, but it is clear that until the nineteenth century, Jewish tradition placed no emphasis on the Hasmonean struggle for sovereignty. On this, see Vered Noam, "The Miracle of the Cruse of Oil: The Metamorphosis of a Legend," *Hebrew Union College Annual* 73 (2003): 191–226.

ethos of the Hasmoneans' heroism. Christian art in the Middle Ages glorified the Maccabees, depicting them as medieval knights, while the Ashkenazi Jews in Germany preferred to place their emphasis on the suffering of the persecuted and martyred Jews.[205]

Jewish attitudes towards the Hasmoneans changed only at the dawn of the Zionist era, when the Maccabees assumed epic status as part of the revival of the idea of Jewish sovereignty. Henceforth, they were to be seen as patriotic warriors who fought against oppression and achieved national independence. This interpretation was manifested in the Zionists' choice to rebrand Chanukah as a celebration of heroism and the struggle for Jewish sovereignty, thus fostering the idea of a national revival in the Land of Israel and the Diaspora.

Chanukah, in its nationalist form, was first celebrated in the school of the settlement of Rishon Lezion in Palestine in 1899. The practice spread, and from early in the settlement era, schools began organizing trips to Modi'in.

The pre-state Zionist education system began marking the festival in the newfound context of the Hasmonean spirit of heroism. In keeping with this trend, Jews founded the Maccabi Sports Association in Constantinople in 1895 and brought it to Europe, championing "muscular Judaism" over what they saw as a limp and passive Diaspora.[206]

When American-born theologian David Hartman moved to Israel in 1971, he was surprised to discover that Chanukah was celebrated not as a symbol of the Jewish struggle against Hellenism (as it was in America), but as a festival that enabled Israelis to define themselves as the modern Maccabees. He was also astonished to find a Chanukah educational program that included a discussion between a military analyst and military historian comparing Napoleon's battles

205 Haim Grossman, "Judas Maccabaeus and Modern Visual Representations," *Jerusalem Studies in Jewish Folklore* 22 (2003), 126–127 [Hebrew].

206 Ibid., 130 [Hebrew].

with the surprise attacks of Judah the Maccabee. The Chanukah he knew in the United States—with its focus on the spiritual significance of the purification of the Temple—had given way to a narrative about fighting role-models who inspire modern Israeli Jews.[207]

Indeed, in the twentieth century, from the start of the Zionist struggle for independence, Israelis saw their soldiers as the new Maccabees, who reestablished and continue to defend Jewish sovereignty. In a pamphlet that was disseminated to all IDF officers in the 1950s, Ben-Gurion wrote: "The Hasmonean era will forever stand as one of the most wondrous political, military, and spiritual trials in our history."[208]

But the Zionist ethos stressed that the story of Chanukah was no miracle. The mantra "no miracle befell us, no jar of oil did we find" was drilled into every child in Israel's state school system, emphasizing a vision of being proactive as a nation and striving sovereignty without relying on God's help.

The traces of the Hasmonean ethos are still evident in the modern State of Israel. In a Bible study circle at his residence in 2017, Prime Minister Benjamin Netanyahu said: "The Hasmoneans ruled here for 70 to 80 years, and that was the longest period so far of Jewish political independence. I have set myself the target of reaching the 100th year. We'll pass that and keep on going. But the important thing is to get there. It will be a milestone marking a significant period of time."[209]

Can the Hasmonean Century be compared with the Israeli Century? Are there any useful lessons to draw from it for the modern State of Israel, regarding the centrality of sovereignty in the Jewish

---

207 David Hartman, *Conflicting Visions: Spiritual Possibilities of Modern Israel* (New York: Schocken Books, 1990), 70.

208 Ben-Gurion, *Uniqueness and Destiny*, 22 [Hebrew].

209 Israel Cohen, "If We Must Learn from the Hasmoneans," *Haaretz*, October 13, 2017 [Hebrew].

experience? Indeed, there are stark similarities between the hallmarks of political sovereignty in antiquity and in the present day, even though the concept of sovereignty is commonly thought to be a product of the modern era, with its roots in the seventeenth century.

In the ancient world, state sovereignty entailed several features, including control over ritual worship; self-determination; dominance over co-nationals living in the dispersion; exclusive territorial control including the ability to impose an identity, to control the population, and to decide who may enter and leave; defining the nation's language and culture; control over the status of foreigners and the delineation of the borders of belonging, including with regards to rebellious opposition groups; authoritative control over the allocation of resources, including the minting of coins and the establishment of taxation systems that also apply to nationals abroad; independence in diplomatic relations; and the power to define the difference between friend and foe.

State sovereignty is also a function of international status. Nation-states since antiquity have aimed to bolster their status by means of building a formidable historical narrative and ethos as a means of earning the respect of other nations. According to one scholar, "This is why the nations of the East attempted to show the Greeks that they also had roots in the distant past. In the case of the Jews, this was done by translating biblical history for the perusal of the civilized nations in a language that they knew–Greek."[210]

All the above components of sovereignty existed to a large degree during Hasmonean rule. In the era of the Israeli Century, they represent a history from which Israelis can learn about their own country and its position within the Jewish world and among the nations, and can serve as a springboard for further arguments.

---

210 Bezalel Bar-Kochva, "Judaism and Hellenism: Between Scholarship and Polemics," *Tarbiz* 63, no. (1994), 457 [Hebrew].

During the Second Temple period, the Temple in Jerusalem was the focus of attention for Jews in Judea and the Diaspora and a point of interest for foreign powers, who treated it as an imperial tax-collection asset. Starting with the Persians, conquering empires granted the Jews of Judea broad cultural autonomy and even encouraged them to live according to their own national and religious laws. The enforcement of the laws of the Torah, as something of a constitution, was a matter of consensus among Jews and was supported by various imperial powers, which granted the priesthood and the Jewish bureaucracy in the Temple broad authority to maintain order and collect taxes on their behalf. Imperial support for autonomous Judean institutions, including Temple rites and Torah recitals, decisively contributed to shaping a distinct Jewish identity based on one God, one Torah, and one temple.[211]

While Jews lived in the Land of Israel, many of their brethren lived in the dispersion in Babylon, Egypt, and the Hellenistic world. In the time of Alexander the Great, the Jewish Diaspora flourished. Many Jews were attracted to the commercial centers of the Mediterranean and to new cities, such as Alexandria and Antioch. Jews worked in commerce and agriculture, and many were also employed as mercenaries, frontier marksmen, and even as soldiers in the Greek armies.[212] Historian Simon Schama writes: "It is a fact—though to modern instincts a surprising one—that to much of the ancient world west of Babylon, the Jews would have been most familiar as spears for hire."[213]

Diaspora Jews, mainly in the Hellenistic world, struggled to settle on agreed-upon leadership and adopted various cultures and

---

211 Schwartz, *Imperialism and Jewish Society*, 40–44.
212 Erich S. Gruen, *Diaspora*.
213 Simon Schama, *The Story of the Jews: Finding the Words*, 93.

practices in the observance of their faith.[214] Yet, despite their remoteness from the homeland and different approaches to Jewish practice, they preserved their culture and adherence to monotheism and the laws of the Torah. They established houses of worship outside of Judea, but after the Temple in Jerusalem was rebuilt toward the end of the sixth century BCE, the latter was restored to dominance as the world center of Jewish worship.[215]

The Temple continued to serve as the tax and tribute collection center for the imperial powers and the priesthood. Historian Bezalel Bar-Kochva writes: "Each year, deposits were amassed there, not only from Judea and the Land of Israel...[but] also from Jews of the more distant diaspora who had faith in their Temple. In addition, for many years the Temple accumulated half-shekel contributions sent by the Jews in the Diaspora." The Seleucid government demanded constant reports on the Temple's coffers so that it could "evaluate the economic capability of the inhabitants and set the various types of tax rates accordingly, and in order to locate tax evaders and expose political organizations."[216]

Recall that ever since the Persian era, and in the absence of a monarchy, the high priests in Judea enjoyed their major status in government and among the people, and vis-à-vis imperial powers. The title of high priest had always been passed from father to son.[217] During the second phase of the Return to Zion, Nehemiah acted to cleanse and strengthen the priesthood, which he saw as the nation's

---

214 Schwartz, *Imperialism and Jewish Society*, 74.

215 In the words of the Hellenistic-Jewish philosopher Philo of Alexandria: "Concerning the holy city I must now say what is necessary. It, as I have already stated, is my native country, and the metropolis, not only of the one country of Judaea, but also of many, by reason of the colonies which it has sent out from time to time into the bordering districts." See "On the Virtues and on the Ambassadors. Addressed to Gaius," in Philo, "Against Flaccus" in *The Works of Philo Judaeus: Vol IV*, trans. C. D. Yonge (London: Henry G. Bohn, 1855), 60.

216 Bezalel Bar-Kochva, "The Religious Persecution by Antiochus Epiphanes as Historical Reality," *Tarbiz* 84, no. 3, 322–333 [Hebrew].

217 Menachem Mor, "The High Priest in Judah in the Persian Era," *Beit Mikra Journal on Studies of the Bible and its World* (1977), 57–67 [Hebrew].

guardian and a model for shaping its identity. One of his moves was to oust Jehoiada from his position as high priest because he had married a Samaritan woman, the daughter of the Achaemenid official Sanballat the Horonite.

Uriel Rappaport notes that the high priests' responsibility for collecting taxes and managing the city marketplace was a sign that they had assumed the privileges of local governors, "similar to what happened in other temple-states in the region where the high priests were also the heads of the government."[218]

Yet, as early as this Persian era, the position of the priesthood had begun to erode, as literacy and Torah scholarship spread. The democratization of knowledge in the Jewish world of the Second Temple era started a process that culminated with rabbinical, text-based Judaism supplanting priestly, rite-based Judaism after the Temple was destroyed.

The priests formed a wealthy, elitist class that became known as the Sadducees (*Tz'dukim*), named after Zadok (*Tzadok*), the high priest during David and Solomon's reigns. However, in both Judea and the Diaspora, the numbers of learned students of the Torah grew, and they challenged the Sadducees' claim to exclusive control over Jewish national identity and ownership of Torah knowledge. The process that began with Ezra's public reading of the Torah in the fifth century BCE gnawed away at the priestly monopoly over religious life.

The priests, of course, concentrated on Temple rituals,[219] and although their caste remained large during the Second Temple era, "the study of Torah and the development of halakha, which shaped the character of life, worship, government and law in the State of Judea, gradually attracted the cream of the nation's spiritual powers,"

---

218   Rappaport, "On the Hellenization of the Hasmoneans," 496 [Hebrew].

219   Zvi Eckstein and Maristella Bottichini, *The Chosen Few: How Education Shaped Jewish History, 70–1492* (Princeton, NJ: Princeton University Press, 2012).

as Menahem Stern observed. "Alongside the priests, and even to a greater degree than them, the outstanding Torah scholars in this period are the sages who sprang from various classes of the Jewish population of Palestine and the dispersion."[220]

Seleucid rule further undermined the status of the priests and the Temple, ultimately provoking the Hasmonean revolt against Antiochus Epiphanes's forced conversions. Scholars of the period disagree over the motives behind the uprising by the sons of Mattathias; some even challenge the very claim that Antiochus imposed enforced conversions upon the Jews. According to historian Bezalel Bar-Kochva, "The enforced conversions and acts of mass religious coercion were totally foreign to the policies of the Hellenistic kings in general and the Seleucids in particular, and they have no parallels in the long history of the Hellenistic world."[221]

Josephus Falavius, who according to historian Jonathan Price, "was on the Temple Mount a lot," recounts that the Seleucid monarch Antiochus III, the father of the wicked Antiochus Epiphanes IV, had issued a proclamation forbidding Gentiles to enter the Temple's Holy of Holies, which was also forbidden to Jews.[222] Some historians, like Sylvie Honigman, argue that the Seleucids' religious persecutions and the rebellion by Judah the Maccabee were an invention by the writers of the Book of the Maccabees, who wanted to glorify the Hasmonean dynasty. According to this theory, the narrative was written to legitimize the Hasmonean rulers as the defenders of the faith and the saviors of the Temple; this was the basis for their right to the priesthood and to rule the Temple and its treasures. Honigman believes the authors of 1 Maccabees and 2 Maccabees served the

---

220   Stern, "The Hasmonean Revolt," 103.

221   Bar-Kochva, "The Religious Persecution by Antiochus Epiphanes," 330 [Hebrew].

222   Ilan Ben Zion, "Ancient Temple Mount 'Warning' Stone is 'Closest Thing We Have to the Temple,'" *Times of Israel*, October 22, 2015, https://www.timesofisrael.com/ancient-temple-mount-warning-stone-is-closest-thing-we-have-to-the-temple/.

Hasmonean dynasty by hiding that the aim of the uprising was to acquire money and power, including control over the Temple treasury, as well to lift the burden of taxation. The Hasmoneans, therefore, invented a tale of religious persecution to smear their domestic political enemies for allegedly seeking to Hellenize the Jewish community.[223] They wanted to justify the rebellion as a response to religious oppression, as "to rebel for religious reasons, according to Babylonian writings, bestowed a special prestige upon its leaders and apparent approval from above for the founding dynasty."[224] Bezalel Bar-Kochva severely criticizes this historiography as "erroneous and misleading." He agrees that the conduct of Antiochus Epiphanes was excessive for the Hellenistic world, but explains this by saying that he was mentally ill, and his megalomania led him to deviate from the norms of religious autonomy. The twentieth century also witnessed "monumental and dramatic developments and events that did not fit into the humane and cultural image of certain nations." But besides the pathological explanation, Bar-Kochva maintains that Antiochus acted against Jewish religious leaders because he saw them as the key political force behind the instability in Judea and its incipient appetite for sedition. He was no stranger to issuing anti-religious decrees and plundering temples, and in this instance, he was assisted and even pushed into action by extremist Jewish Hellenizers.[225]

Once established, the Hasmonean dynasty chose to bolster its position as a priestly institution rather than grounding its right to rule in political, non-religious terms. "The emphasis on the religious side of Judaism, and the departure from political boundaries for the sake of religious identity, were a phenomenon unique to the Hasmoneans," writes historian Eyal Regev. "They show that they

---

223 Sylvie Honigman, *Tales of High Priests and Tales: The Books of the Maccabees and the Judean Rebellion* (Oakland, CA: University of California Press, 2014).

224 Bar-Kochva, "The Religious Persecution by Antiochus Epiphanes," 298 [Hebrew].

225 Ibid., 331–343 [Hebrew].

wanted to lead the entire Jewish nation, not only the Jews under their rule in the Land of Israel, and they did so by virtue of being high priests."[226] It would have been typical in the Hellenistic world to place an emphasis on the monarchy, but the Hasmoneans' choice to emphasize the priesthood was rooted in their fear of creating the impression of an illegitimate usurpation of power.

The Hasmoneans, after all, were not scions of the traditional House of David. Although they came from an important priestly family and traced their lineage back to Jehoiarib, some of their rivals cast doubt on whether they had any connection to the Sadducee families. Furthermore, the Hasmoneans were initially apprehensive about declaring themselves kings—since the destruction of the First Temple, Jews had seen the monarchy as a myth or a distant dream, and for most of the Second Temple period, the priests had served as the nation's leaders.

The sovereign Hasmonean dynasty was proclaimed with a kind of declaration of independence during the time of Simon Thassi, the last living son of Mattathias. Historian Uriel Rappaport calls this "a sophisticated Jewish constitutional creation," designed to legitimize the dynasty in the absence of clear historical justifications or agreed-upon dynastic ties. The declaration is described in 1 Maccabees as a demand for the nation's loyalty to Simon as the *nasi* and high priest following the war of liberation from Seleucid rule.

This demand was anchored in the Hasmoneans' demonstration of courage and sacrifice in the rebellion. They had conquered and fortified Jerusalem and had liberated the Temple. They had consolidated Jewish control over wide swaths of the Land of Israel and imposed a central government over the resident Gentiles. They had restored honor and glory to a nation that had been subjugated by

---

226 Eyal Regev, "Hever ha-Yehudim and the Political Ideology of the Hasmoneans," *Tarbiz* 70, no. 3 (2012), 334–335, 346 [Hebrew].

conquerors and had formed an impressive and effective government. They had also attained international recognition by establishing ties with Rome.

Each of these achievements gave Simon the status of an absolute monarch. As 1 Maccabees records:

> The Jewish people and their priests had decided the following: Simon shall be their leader and high priest forever until a trustworthy prophet arises. He shall act as governor over them, and shall have charge of the sanctuary, to make regulations concerning its functions and concerning the country, its weapons and strongholds. He shall be obeyed by all. All contracts in the country shall be written in his name, and he shall be clothed in purple and gold.

> It shall not be lawful for any of the people or priests to nullify any of these decisions, or to contradict the orders given by him, or to convene an assembly in the country without his consent, to be clothed in purple or wear a gold buckle. Whoever acts otherwise or violates any of these prescriptions shall be liable to punishment.[227]

Despite being an absolute ruler, Simon Thassi (c.220–c.135 BCE) refrained from crowning himself for fear of not winning

---

227   1 Maccabees:14 (New American Bible Revised Edition).

widespread consent; he appointed himself only as high priest and head of state.[228]

Unlike Seleucid coins, which bore the king's name and royal title, Hasmonean coins bore only the name of the high priest alongside the words "Council of the Jews" as an acknowledgement that the nation was a partner in the government and as a statement of national self-government.[229] Historian Eyal Regev says that the name of the Hasmonean ruler and the words "Council of the Jews" indicate that the Hasmoneans saw themselves as democratic rulers, governing not only in the name of the Jewish people but *with* it: "Such a partnership was unique in the Hellenistic world [because] for the Hasmoneans it was important to demonstrate the religious aspect of their leadership, and by mentioning the Council of the Jews they were underlining that they were the religious leaders of the Jews [worldwide]."[230]

Many Diaspora Jews joined in, or were recruited for, the campaign to renew Jewish sovereignty. They were asked by the Hasmoneans to continue paying a half-shekel tribute to the Temple, and many obliged. Historians observe that they developed the infrastructure to encourage mass pilgrimages to Jerusalem, for which there is archaeological evidence. The Hasmoneans are believed to have dug the open pools unearthed by archaeologists in Jerusalem to supply the needs of the pilgrims who came to the Temple from all over the Land of Israel and the Diaspora in the Hasmonean period and later, during the time of Herod. They were used both for storing water and ritual immersion. Pilgrims also made large contributions to the Temple, over and above their regular taxes.[231]

---

228 Rappaport, "On the Hellenization of the Hasmoneans," 498 [Hebrew].

229 Regev, "Hever ha-Yehudim and the Political Ideology of the Hasmoneans," 341 [Hebrew].

230 Ibid., [Hebrew].

231 David Gurevich, "The Water Pools and the Pilgrimage to Jerusalem in the Late Second Temple Period," *Palestine Exploration Quarterly* 149, no. 2 (2017), 103–134.

The Hasmoneans led the people of Israel in extensive conquests, from the Galilee to the Negev, into Transjordan, and toward the shore of the Mediterranean Sea. They founded settlements in the conquered territories and forced many of the inhabitants to convert to Judaism. They, thereby, sought to strengthen their national and territorial sovereignty in the Land of Israel, but by expanding their borders, converting their neighbors, and adopting Hellenistic affectations, did so at the expense of the punctilious observance of Jewish purity.

John Hyrcanus, the son of Simon Thassi and nephew of Judah Maccabee, conquered Edom, Transjordan, and Samaria and converted the Edomites as part of his policy of annexing territory and expanding the Jewish people. Flavius Josephus, the first century Roman-Jewish historian, wrote that Hyrcanus "permitted them to stay in that country, if they would circumcise their genitals, and make use of the laws of the Jews; and they were so desirous of living in the country of their forefathers, that they submitted to the use of circumcision, and of the rest of the Jewish ways of living; at which time therefore this befell them, that they were hereafter no other than Jews."[232] Hyrcanus's heir, Aristobulus I, similarly converted the Itureans in the north, albeit less successfully. Alexander Jannaeus did the same to the peoples of Transjordan and the coastal cities.

This campaign stood in stark contrast to the period of Ezra and Nehemiah, when conversion was performed sparingly, with a view to preserving the purity of the chosen people. The Hasmoneans pushed the concept of a Holy Seed based upon blood ties, kinship, and lineage aside.

According to historians, as part of the re-politicization of Judaism, the Hasmoneans fostered deep ties with the Jews of the Diaspora, encouraging them to maintain an affinity with their

---

232 Flavius Josephus, *Antiquities of the Jews, Book XIII*, chapter 9, trans. William Whitson.

historical homeland and declaring themselves to be the leaders and spokespeople of all Jews, wherever they may be. They were also responsible for allocating large amounts of money that Jews all over the world had contributed.[233] But they stressed the paramount importance of Jewish sovereignty in the formation of a collective national identity centered around the nation-state and the Temple. Jewish sovereignty in Jerusalem, whose population increased dramatically under the Hasmoneans, became a principal ethos during this period.

In 1952, celebrated historian Joseph Klausner wrote that the Hasmonean Kingdom would have collapsed "if not for the contributions of the Jews in the diaspora...despite the large amounts of booty taken in their victorious wars." He equated this situation with the young state of Israel being similarly dependent on fundraising from a generous Diaspora.[234]

But the Hasmoneans' success in securing sovereignty and political control made them arrogant and forgetful of the traditional and popular foundation that underpinned their legitimacy. In Simon Thassi's time, they sought to downplay the monarchical values typical of Hellenistic kingdoms in favor of religious and national values, but with time, they neglected the basis of their support within the council of the Jews.[235] They began to not only unravel the religious tradition, but they also ignored the exclusive right of the House of David to the monarchy—the reason that Simon refrained from crowning himself in the first place.

Even during John Hyrcanus's long rule, which consolidated and expanded Hasmonean sovereignty, he kept his priestly title and was careful not to declare himself king. But his son and heir,

---

233 Eyal Regev, "The Self-Image of the Hasmoneans as Religious Leaders," *Zion* 77 (2012), 21–22 [Hebrew].

234 Joseph Klausner, "The State of Israel and the Jewish Diaspora," *Mozna'im* 4 (1955), 201 [Hebrew].

235 Regev, "Hever ha-Yehudim and the Political Ideology of the Hasmoneans," 346 [Hebrew].

Judah Aristobulus, who ruled for only one year, cast off these shackles, had himself crowned with Hellenistic fanfare, and unleashed a reign of arbitrary terror against Jews and Gentiles alike. The pace of Hellenization and the arrogance of power only increased during the three decades of the reign of Alexander Jannaeus, who consolidated the monarchy.[236]

The Hasmonean Kingdom, therefore, grasped for monopolistic control over the Temple and its treasure while basing itself on the Israelite monarchy of the First Temple period.[237] It reached the pinnacle of its material and institutional power during the reign of Alexander Jannaeus and enriched itself in wars and the plunder of Greek cities along the Mediterranean coast and on the edge of the Negev Desert. The consolidation of a dynastic monarchy that enjoyed a monopoly over military power, including mercenaries, led the Hasmoneans to gradually abandon their pretenses of piety and adopt a fully Hellenistic model for their kingdom, going as far as to crown a queen—Salome (Shlomzion) Alexandra. This was almost unheard of in Jewish history.

In Alexander Jannaeus' time, a three-way spiritual rift had opened between the king, the Sadducees (the priests) and the Pharisees (the Torah scholars). Queen Salome, Jannaeus' widow and successor, tried to mend this rift. But, as a woman, she was deemed an illegitimate heir. Her reign was considered one Hellenistic influence too far and provoked a bloody conflict.

In his account of the Hellenization of the Hasmoneans, Uriel Rappaport writes: "Simon's successors could not fulfill a fundamental condition required of the kings of Judah—descent from the House of David. They were not willing…to suffice with what the people's assembly had granted them, which was less than the authority of

---

236 Rappaport, "On the Hellenization of the Hasmoneans," 499 [Hebrew].

237 The author discussed this subject with Bezalel Bar-Kochva, who made a significant contribution to this chapter.

contemporary foreign rulers." The Hasmoneans overreached; they grasped for a similar status to other ancient kings, and in so doing, they unleashed a civil war.[238]

The Hasmonean dynasty and the state it ruled atrophied after Salome's death. The decline was a product of internecine intrigues inside the royal family between the legal heir, Hyrcanus II, and the pretender, Aristobulus II, who had forcibly seized control of the priesthood and crown. The decline also stemmed from conflicts of interests and struggles over the division of authority between different elements of the Hasmonean state, including the mercenary armed forces, the royal guard, the council of the Jews, and the ruling elite. The internal quarrels concerned legal and halakhic disputes, often over pedanticism, and involved popular, hostile rumormongering both between and within rival factions.

In the Israeli Century too, clashes like these lead people to declare that they are willing to die or kill, and that Israeli society risks sliding into civil war. This happened more than once in the Hasmonean Kingdom, where a protracted rift emerged between the patrician Sadducees and the plebian Pharisees, and fringe sects, like those documented in the Dead Sea scrolls.

Hasmonean monarchs, for their own part, flip-flopped on matters of faith and their interests. They frequently switched allies, acting on the whims and fears that often afflict kings.[239]

Nonetheless, the main reason for the decline and fall of the Hasmonean Kingdom was the rise of Roman Republic. The conquests of the Roman general Pompey in Asia Minor and Syria sealed their fate. When Pompey intervened on the side of Hyrcanus II and sent Aristobulus II into exile in Rome, he effectively settled not only

---

238 Rappaport, "On the Hellenization of the Hasmoneans," 501 [Hebrew].

239 Bezalel Bar-Kochva, "Relations between the Judean Desert Sect and the Rulers of the Hasmonean State: From Simon ben Mattathias to Alexander Jannaeus (142–76 BCE)," manuscript sent to the author, August 2018. For future publication in *Tarbiz* [Hebrew].

the question of precedence between the brothers, but also the status of Jewish rulers under Roman suzerainty and of the Jewish people in their land.

Herod, King of the Jews

Jewish life in the centuries after the Babylonian Exile revolved around the center of worship in Jerusalem. The sanctity of the rituals and the sacrifices erected barriers between Jews and non-Jews. The creation of this holy space ensured the Jews' ethno-religious separation from other nations, which in turn preserved their identity. The absence of a sovereign monarchy and the Jewish dispersion naturally undermined their ancient national identity. But as a religious and ritual identity, Judaism was preserved under foreign imperial rule. Diaspora communities enjoyed tremendous growth, especially after the period of Alexander the Great.[240]

The Jewish dispersion across the Greek and Roman worlds grew in the third and second centuries BCE for economic and political reasons. It was during this period that the Bible was translated into Greek, an effort that ended in Alexandria in about 200 BCE. It became known as the Septuagint, the Translation of the Seventy. From then on, the Bible was no longer just a source of communal and spiritual identity for Jews, including those who lived far from the Temple in Jerusalem. It was also how the God of Israel gained acceptance by large swaths of humanity.[241]

Historian Paula Fredriksen contends that the Jewish invention of a God who created the universe, singled out the Jewish people, established social ethics, and laid down laws that governed

---

240 Jacob Neusner, "Exile and Return as the History of Judaism," in *Exile: Old Testament, Jewish and Christian Conceptions*, ed. James M. Scott (New York: Brill, 1997), 33–35.

241 Israel Finkelstein and Neil Asher Silberman, *The Bible Unearthed: Archaeology's New Vision of Ancient Israel and the Origin of Its Sacred Texts* (New York: Simon & Schuster, 2002).

personal, family, and communal conduct became the foundation stone of Western civilization: "No Septuagint, no Christianity. No Christianity, no Western civilization."[242]

As Jews settled into largely "normal" lives in the Diaspora during the Hellenistic and Roman eras, their existence came to provide an alternative model to the thesis of exile as a national disaster. In the Israeli Century, Zionism saw the exile as necessarily ruinous, but in antiquity, there arose an alternative theory, which celebrated the vibrancy of Jewish life without sovereignty. It maintained, in the words of historian Erich Gruen, that the homeland of the People of the Book "resides in the text–not just the canonical Scriptures but an array of Jewish writings that help to define the nation and give voice to its sense of identity.... [The Jews'] 'portable Temple' serves the purpose. A geographic restoration is therefore superfluous, even subversive. To aspire to it deflects the focus from what really counts: the embrace of the text, its ongoing commentary, and its continuous reinterpretation. Diaspora, in short, is no burden, indeed a virtue in the spread of the word."[243]

In recent decades, anti-Zionists have made an ideology of championing the paradigm of dispersion as "normal" instead of as a failure of national self-determination. This is the argument that Jewish-American Jonathan and Daniel Boyarin advance in their book *Powers of Diaspora*, in which they describe Israel's focus on sovereign might as the thrust of its national existence as a diversion from Judaism's true, universalist foundations. They argue that Israel seeks to imprison Judaism in an exclusivist state and stifle the diversity of Jewish life–the broadest cultural mosaic in human existence. They also believe that "the only moral path would be the renunciation of Jewish hegemony qua Jewish hegemony" and that Jewish identity

---

242   Paula Fredriksen, "Everywhere at Home," *The New Republic*, July 8 and 15, 2002.

243   Gruen, *Diaspora*, 232.

should be reformulated "not as a proud resting place (hence not as a form of...nativism) but as a perpetual, creative, diasporic tension."[244]

During the Hasmonean period, nationality and sovereignty played a decisive role in the life of the Jewish people and the shaping of their identity and weakened the centrality of the Diaspora. Of course, not everyone was happy about this, and internal opposition was brutally suppressed. Many Jews disputed the Hasmonean monarchy's airs and graces and right to bear the crown.

Within Pharisee circles, there was opposition to the politicization of Jewishness and perhaps even a willingness to waive the nation's political freedom in favor of preserving the Torah and its laws. The Hasmoneans launched a bloody crackdown on Pharisee uprisings. However, as historian Gedaliah Alon argues, Pharisee opposition to the Hasmoneans by no means implied support for Roman rule as a means of achieving the quiet to study Torah. Instead, it remained an internal Jewish dispute.[245]

During Pompey's occupation in the first century BCE, the Jews attempted to revolt against the Romans whenever factional disputes in Rome or imperial setbacks seemed to provide a golden opportunity to seize power in Jerusalem. However, Rome responded with an iron fist and brought the remnants of the Hasmonean dynasty to its knees by appointing High Priest Hyrcanus II as ethnarch of Judea. Never again would Judea have a sovereign king.

The Roman Republic, and later the Roman Empire, aimed to maintain stability and quiet in the territories it conquered. It left almost all internal matters to client rulers, who did not govern "by right but by special consent which could be withdrawn at any

---

244   Daniel Boyarin and Jonathan Boyarin, "Diaspora: Generational Ground of Jewish Identity," *Critical Inquiry* 19, no. 4 (1993), 693–725.

245   Gedaliah Alon, "The Pharisees' Attitudes to Roman Rule and the Herodian House," *Zion* 3, no. 4 (1938), 3. [Hebrew].

moment."[246] They were expected to remain obedient and loyal to Rome, particularly in matters of foreign relations and security. Judea became, therefore, a semi-sovereign client state, or a partially independent satellite state.

Rome initially appointed Antipater the Idumaean, a Hasmonean-era official, as chief minister of Judea. On his death, and after much intrigue, Rome appointed his son Herod as the client king. The story of Herod is one of an effective and powerful autocracy that enjoyed Roman patronage but no popular legitimacy. To make up for this, Herod embraced cruelty and violence and sought to foster a basis of support among the Jews of the Diaspora. He turned the Diaspora into a source of governmental, religious, and ethnic authority for his reign to balance out opposition within his client kingdom. Herod deemed himself not merely king of Judea, but "King of the Jews."

Herod, born an Edomite, was a friend and ally of the Romans. He governed Judea as an absolute ruler and erased all traces of the Hasmonean-era national sovereignty. He removed the words "Council of the Jews" from the coins he minted. He had no need of public backing, because his authority was external.[247] He bolstered his position by building a magnificent royal court with eunuchs, slaves, and feasts for his Hellenistic cronies.

Herod overhauled the nature of Judean society and government, replacing the old pro-Hasmonean nobility with a new, collaborationist aristocracy. Herod's regime brushed aside the local Jews' exclusive claims to political leadership and made room for non-Jewish populations in his royal court.[248] He also acted to neutralize the

---

246   Benjamin Isaac, *The Limits of Empire: The Roman Army in the East*, 2nd ed. (Oxford: Oxford University Press, 1993), 119.

247   Getzel Kressel, "Herod, Example of Depraved Machiavellianism," *Mozna'im* 37, no. 2 (1962), 124–129 [Hebrew].

248   Uriel Rappaport, *Judea and Rome: From the Decline of the Hasmonean State to Yehudah HaNasi* (Tel Aviv: Open University, 1998), 132 [Hebrew].

old powers of the Pharisees and the Sadducees, both of which would be excluded from his pro-Roman administration.

The fact that Herod, an Edomite convert, became a fully-fledged Hellenist, and spoke for Roman interests while brutally suppressing the Hasmonean-era elite made him *persona non grata* for broad swaths of the Judean population. They simply regarded him as an alien imposition.[249] "Although at the outset the Pharisees did not come out stridently against Herod, they were enemies of his regime and resisted him and his successors until they lost their kingdom," explained Gedaliah Alon. "Many Pharisees refused to swear an oath of allegiance to Herod and rejected his claim to the throne because he was not ethnically Jewish."[250]

Herod diluted Judea's character as a particularistic Jewish nation-state. "When Herod was faced with the question of whether to maintain the interests of the Jewish people in their own land or to do Rome's bidding," wrote historian Avraham Schalit, "he unfailingly did the latter."[251]

Herod married the Hasmonean princess Mariamne in a bid to foster a degree of traditional legitimacy, but he based his rule on his ability to impose his authority and mobilize his loyalists. Above all, he seems to have based his claim to legitimacy on massive support from Jews in the Diaspora. They held the key to consolidating his position as the "King of the Jews," whose realm was not limited to a specific territory. Thus, Herod effectively changed the nature of Judaism from being a territorial, sovereignty-based religion to a less rigid and more multifaceted faith, which repressed isolationist tendencies.

---

249 Ibid., 99 [Hebrew].

250 Alon, "The Pharisees' Attitudes to Roman Rule and the Herodian House," 300–332 [Hebrew].

251 Avraham Shalit, *King Herod: Portrait of a Ruler* (Jerusalem: Bialik Institute, 1960), 97 [Hebrew].

Historian Seth Schwartz argues that the most egregious fact of Herod's rule was that five of the seven high priests he appointed were not from Judea. One was brought in from Babylon, another grew up in the Galilee, and two were from Egypt. Another high priest, a scion of the Hasmoneans whom Herod chose because of marital ties, drowned under mysterious circumstances. Nevertheless, Herod built up Judea as the homeland of all Jews and Jerusalem as a world city. Pliny the Elder hailed Jerusalem as "by far the most famous city of the East."[252]

Herod leveraged his ties with Rome to advance the status and the rights of Diaspora Jews as an autonomous religious community. He heaped gifts upon Hellenistic cities outside of Judea, to induce them to treat their Jewish inhabitants with generosity. He commissioned magnificent construction projects, most notably the port at Caesarea and the renovation of the Temple, which he upgraded from the modest edifice built during the Return to Zion into a monumental feat of architecture.

Part of his rationale was to make it easier for Diaspora Jews to visit their homeland and dramatically enhance their role and influence there. The Herodian state effectively became a semi-sovereign entity that sought to sideline the forces of isolationism—namely Hasmonean holdovers, who wished to preserve Jewry as an exclusivist sovereign nation.

Yet, in the Jewish consciousness, Herod's kingdom has never been perceived as an ideal to be restored. As classical historian Jonathan Price notes, Herod was never seen as a rightful heir to King David, and his kingdom was never seen as a harbinger of the messianic age, even though many believed it was close and numerous self-proclaimed messiahs and prophets were calling for the restoration of an independent Jewish kingdom. "Herod had liquidated

252 Schwartz, *Imperialism and Jewish Society*, 47.

or neutralized the remains of the Hasmonean house," Price writes. "Herod was rather remembered in the Jewish tradition for what he was: a client-king dependent totally on Rome, brutal toward his own subjects and generous to outsiders, unable to control his wives or scheming sons. His Jewishness was persistently (if unfairly) doubted, the loss of his kingdom was not mourned, and he was unstintingly praised only for his magnificent Temple, the inner precincts of which he himself could not enter."[253]

Two thousand years later, David Ben-Gurion declared the independence of a Jewish state and downplayed the importance of the Diaspora. Like the Hasmoneans, he believed that the driving force behind Jewish history was the result of the actions of Jews in the Land of Israel, while the Diaspora played second fiddle.

Nevertheless, like the Hasmoneans and Herod, Ben-Gurion saw the Diaspora as a significant source of economic support and assistance for Israel's sovereign diplomacy, as well as a reservoir of immigrants and reinforcements. For him, immigration to Israel was the mark of genuine commitment to Zionism, and Jews who chose to live in the Diaspora were not true Zionists. However, he grasped that the support of Western Jewry was inescapably important for his small country and compromised on his attitude towards American Jews, refraining from demanding that they acknowledge Israel as the center of Jewish life. In an important gesture, he gave his approval to American Jews' universalism and *de facto* recognized the existence of "two Jewries," in Israel and the United States.

Unlike Ben-Gurion and the Hasmoneans, Herod gave the Diaspora priority, with a view to weakening the more exclusivist forces of Jewish nationalism. As the king of a Roman client state who was seen by Judeans as a foreign implant, Herod courted and

---

253 Jonathan Price, "The Herodian House after Herod," in *Herod the Great: The King's Final Journey*, eds. S. Rozenberg and D. Mevorah (Jerusalem: Israel Museum, 2013), 7.

promoted Diaspora Jews as part of an effort to curb nationalism at home, solidify his rule, and integrate Judea into the Roman world. His co-option of the Diaspora was based on the unwritten understanding that he would help them abroad if they helped him at home.

Menahem Stern argued that Herod's efforts to encourage Diaspora Jews to move to Judea, where he elevated their social status and gave them government posts, left a deep mark on Jewish society during the period of the Talmud and Mishnah.[254]

Seventy years after the founding of the State of Israel, as the Jewish state's dependence upon the Diaspora fades and liberal elements in American Jewry decry the forces of nationalism and orthodoxy in Israel, the gap between the independent Jewish state and progressive elements of the Diaspora is only widening. Yet the Diaspora Jews have great difficulty maintaining an ethno-cultural identity without maintaining ties to Israel and its affairs. While many are being "Israelized" and see their identity validated by the Jewish state, key elements in the Israeli political scene regard the universalist Diaspora Jews as foes.

In the Zionist ethos, lack of Jewish sovereignty and continued life in the Diaspora are pathological. Ben-Gurion saw defenseless and rootless Jews as mere objects and playthings in the hands of foreign political forces.[255] Only a sovereign Jewish state could rehabilitate the nation and make it the master of its own fate.

For the State of Israel's founding father, the Hasmoneans' struggle and their state served as a historical parallel for the Zionist rebirth and the formation of the Israel Defense Forces and played an important role in engendering the inspirational story of a "victory of the few over the many" in the 1948–1949 War of Independence.

---

254 Dov Gera, "Studies in the Second Temple Period," *Jewish Studies* 32 (1992), 76–77 [Hebrew].

255 David Ohana, *The Origins of Israeli Mythology: Neither Canaanites nor Crusaders* (New York: Cambridge University Press, 2012).

In the Israeli Century, the Hasmonean state is remembered as a model of national honor based on power, whereas the honor of Diaspora Jews had always been based on navigating foreign systems and, in the worst case, martyrdom. The Jews amassed power after Judah the Maccabee waged a guerrilla war for national liberation and proceeded to transform his band of rebels into a well-equipped army that proved itself in combat, and which continued, after Judah's death, to serve the rule of his brothers, Jonathan and Simon. It was the military power of the Hasmoneans that made Jewish independence possible, combined as it was with the diplomatic tools available to the real state of a real nation. Ben-Gurion drew parallels between the Maccabees' battles and the achievements of the Israeli military in 1948–1949 and of Israeli diplomacy.

But the Roman conquests in Syria and Asia Minor brought an end to the Hebrew Hasmonean state. Under Herod, Judea became a Roman client-state. Herod was not permitted to conduct independent foreign and defense policies, and his loyalty to his Roman patrons was so complete that he used his armed forces for their benefit, often brutally and against real or imaginary opposition. Herod's impressive strength as a vassal earned him great respect in Rome, but it also led the empire to tire of his adventurism, including his invasion of the neighboring kingdom of Nabatea (with its capital in Petra) without the emperor's permission.

Herod's reign of terror in Judea, his loosening grip over traditional Jewish institutions, and the burden of his excessive taxation generated unrest, which exploded into huge protests after his death. This rage was sparked by the execution of Yehuda Ben Tzippori and Mattityahu Ben Margalit, the two sages who smashed the emblem of the Roman eagle that Herod had placed over the Temple.

In his will, Herod left instructions for the division of his realm between his sons, a step that in effect terminated his unitary kingdom.[256] His heirs struggled to impose their authority or maintain stability in the areas they ruled. The eruption of violence that spread in the protests against their father's legacy of oppression eventually persuaded the imperial authorities in Rome to impose direct rule over Judea and demote Herod's sons from kings back down to ethnarchs.

Rome's move was also part of a change in its imperial strategy in the Near East. In the first century CE, the Roman Empire gradually reshuffled from a system of client-states to one of provinces ruled by Roman governors. While Emperor Augustus was considering whether to allow the implementation of Herod's will and divide his kingdom between his sons, the violence in Judea "burst into a full-scale uprising in all of the major centers of Jewish population… [and releasing] religious energies and political aspirations that had been forcibly submerged but not extinguished during his reign."[257] The uprisings and instability snowballed into the Great Revolt of 66 CE and the destruction of the Temple.

Agrippa I, Lobbyist King

Despite the instability that prevailed in the six decades between Herod's death in 4 CE and the destruction of the Temple in 70 CE, the Jews also enjoyed a tantalizing glimpse of sovereignty during the brief reign of Agrippa I, Herod's grandson, and a scion of the Hasmoneans on his mother's side. Menahem Stern called these years "the final period of glory before the destruction."[258] Agrippa tried to restore Jewish sovereignty in the style of the Hasmonean

---

256 Herod did so not only for fear of wars of succession between his surviving sons, but also because he was an egomaniac. See Price "The Herodian House after Herod," 5.

257 Ibid., 6.

258 Menahem Stern, "The Kingdom of Agrippa I," in *Studies in the History of Second Temple-Era Israel*, eds. Menahem Stern et al. (Jerusalem: Ben-Zvi Institute, 1996) [Hebrew].

state, but with the consent and patronage of Rome. He believed he could walk the tightrope between sovereign independence and imperial patronage, and he made this dichotomous vision into a reality because he was so deeply embedded in Roman culture and politics. He also thought he could be a true Jew speaking for his people, acting to achieve their independence without being considered a traitor to Roman interests.

Like the princes of other client states, the young Agrippa was educated in the finest Roman households and was a friend of the future emperors Caligula and Claudius. But he was also a hostage, held in Rome as collateral in case Herod's family tried to breach its oath of allegiance to the emperor. Agrippa was particularly close to Claudius and played a role in his rise to power after Caligula was assassinated. Eventually, Claudius crowned him king of the Jews, and Agrippa worked to replace Herod's Roman kingdom with something more particularly Jewish. He achieved the impressive success of restoring a semi-sovereign Jewish monarchy by persuading his counterparts in Rome and by building a base of support within his people, both in the Land of Israel and in the Diaspora.

Unlike Herod, who was a foreign implant, Agrippa became "a Jewish king in all respects and a representative of the Jewish interests in the entire Land of Israel."[259] His attempt to build a political system culturally and nationally detached from Rome, yet dependent on it, was a tough juggling act. It all hinged on one man, whose brief reign combined a vision of Jewish sovereignty, an impressive degree of ethno-religious cohesion within the Jewish people, and personal connections with the ruling elite in Rome.

Agrippa's rule was based on what is now called *shtadlanut*, a kind of stateless diplomacy—international relations for a non-sovereign nation. The need to base statecraft on lobbying a foreign power

---

259 Ibid. [Hebrew].

was a consequence of the Jews' abnormal status and lack of power. Agrippa was a lobbyist (*shtadlan* in Hebrew), guided by the fact that his nation could not take its fate into its own hands and must navigate a network of asymmetrical patron-client relationships, where it was always at the bottom.

The lobbyist, in the context of Jewish history and particularly in the late Middle Ages and the modern era, is not a diplomat or statesman; he lacks the capacity to negotiate or to make and receive reciprocal concessions in the international arena. The *shtadlan*, according to international relations scholar Aharon Kleiman, had access to the powerful, but no real power of his own. His culture was close to that of his Gentile patron, and he could speak to him in his own tongue. He was able to penetrate the innermost ruling circles by virtue of his wealth or much-needed profession, mainly medicine. His intimate relations with rulers were grounded in a sophisticated ability to satisfy their immediate interests without possessing any institutional legitimacy or reciprocal strength. He had no troops, but he did have a talent for creating an impression of unwavering personal loyalty to the ruler. That loyalty, however, also made him a hostage. At the first hint of suspicion that he was not delivering the goods, or was unfaithful, he was finished.

Jewish lobbyists throughout the generations have always been suspected of dual loyalty by both their Gentile patrons and Jewish brethren. They have always operated under the risk of being accused of betrayal. Unlike official diplomats in antiquity and in modern times, the *shtadlan* enjoyed no immunity or any true legal status; he hoped to play for time and catch favorable winds until the messiah finally came, and his people's dreams would finally be realized.

"Jewish diplomacy," scholars contend, became possible only after the Jews began to unite, to speak in one broad collective voice as citizens of modern states, and became part of democratic politics. Only then could they amass power and be seen as effective pressure groups in the international arena. This is what happened at the time of the Damascus blood libel in 1840, when European Jewish leaders organized to obtain international support for their persecuted brethren in Syria.

The idea that Jews were capable of exerting influence to further their people's interests without sovereignty became stronger at the end of the nineteenth century. During World War I, it was commonly believed that Zionist activism in Europe and America was influencing the great powers' decisions regarding war and peace. The Jews remained devoid of any real power, however and failed to organize as a collective or even define what they wanted. Historian David Vital has argued that, although the wartime activities of luminaries like the Rothschilds and American-German banker Jacob Schiff evoked images of power, the catastrophes that continued to befall the Jews proved that these were illusions.[260]

Since the establishment of the State of Israel, the achievements of Israeli diplomacy and American-Jewish pressure groups are no longer perceived as the groveling of the *shtadlan* but rather as a legitimate, and very powerful, part of the democratic and diplomatic game. This is true, despite efforts to smear American Jews as unpatriotic and other vestigial prejudices from the era of the *shtadlan*.

The *shtadlan* was an integral part of the politics of antiquity, even if not recognized as such at the time. Many played a critical role in the Jewish world and were dependent on imperial patrons to whom they could appeal and remind them of the Jews' contributions to their empires. Even in the absence of sovereignty, imperial emissaries of Jewish origin could persuade foreign potentates that Jews could get things done for them, so their activity was diplomatic in the sense that it involved a measure of pressure and influence.

---

260   Aharon Klieman, "Shtadlanut as Statecraft by the Stateless," *Israel Journal of Foreign Affairs* 2, no. 3 (2008), 99–113.

Nevertheless, without a powerful sovereign state, the Jews remained at the mercy of the whims of their allies, who could perform a sudden and calamitous about-face at any point.

Thanks to his successful lobbying and friendly ties with the Roman Empire's ruling families, Agrippa I enjoyed the status of an actual king, in a departure from the Roman practice in conquered lands. His Hasmonean origins won him public plaudits, and his desire to prove to his people that he was one of them and that his interests were ultimately Jewish rather than Roman earned him the esteem and support of the Jews of Judea. The *shtadlan* king largely succeeded in establishing Jewish sovereignty, which expanded past the borders of Herod's kingdom, by bringing sects and groups that had not been prepared to cast their lot with his tyrannical and cruel grandfather on board.

The story of Agrippa's brief reign is the story of the Jews' last golden age before the destruction of the Temple.[261] It involved the most serious effort by the Roman Empire to balance its own needs with the desire of the Jewish people to maintain an autonomous presence in its homeland. Agrippa had an exceptional personality, which enabled him to feel at home in the imperial court, not unlike Moses in the court of Pharaoh.

After Claudius became emperor, Agrippa leveraged his friendship with him, and the new emperor expanded his kingdom even further, making him king over the entire Land of Israel. Agrippa annexed large swaths of territory in the Galilee and Transjordan to Judea, and he became the ruler of most of the Jews in the Land of Israel. Claudius also abolished the former provincial regime, which had existed for thirty-five years, and restored almost the entire territorial reach of Herod's Judea.

With great pomp and circumstance, Claudius and Agrippa

---

261   Stern, "The Kingdom of Agrippa I," 6 [Hebrew].

signed a pact, inscribed on copper plates in the capitol. Agrippa was in fact a "born-again" Jew who piously observed the laws of family purity. In the words of Menachem Stern: "He did everything to behave himself as a Jew in all respects in the areas of Jewish settlement in his kingdom and used all means in his attempts to win the hearts of the Jews. He donated a gold chain he had received as a gift from the emperor to the Temple, he offered up many sacrifices of gratitude, personally paid the sacrificial fees for the ascetic Nazarites, and thus won the hearts of the people. He kept this up until his last day, and echoes of his popularity are clear from the Talmudic sources that depict Agrippa I as the only Jewish ruler accepted by the whole people."[262]

In the Israeli Century, as Jewish security and diplomacy centers on the State of Israel and is backed by its military might, the traditional role of the *shtadlan* is disappearing, apart from in some weak Jewish communities dependent on autocratic rulers, such as those in Russia and Iran. Even pro-Israel pressure groups—the strategic asset that assumed the mythological aura of "the Israel lobby"—are gradually losing their standing. Since Israel is not a client-state, not even of America,[263] and maintains that it alone speaks for the Jews, it is rendering the traditional role of the *shtadlan* obsolete.

The Fall of the Temple, and the Rise and Fall of Bar Kokhba

Agrippa's lobbyist juggling and success in establishing monarchical sovereignty, even fleetingly, sparked messianic hopes for the restoration of the Davidic monarchy, but his sudden demise in 44 CE

---

262   Ibid. [Hebrew].

263   Nevertheless, Israeli leaders cannot let go of these historical analogies. When US President Donald Trump recognized Jerusalem as Israel's capital in December 2017, Israel's leaders lionized him as a kind of modern Cyrus.

created a power vacuum that pushed the Romans to reinstall direct rule over Judea. This only intensified the local population's frustration and appetite for rebellion, until the dams burst.

In the years between Agrippa's death and the Great Revolt, Judea suffered a severe economic crisis, partly due to a drought and famine in the fourth and fifth decades of the first century CE. Judea had also been preyed on by roaming marauders. Without a government able to provide security, there emerged a groundswell of spiritualist, anti-imperialist, anarchist, and messianic sentiment, centered on a belief in the imminent end of days and redemption.

These movements, including the new Christian Jews, challenged the Sadducee elite and the Pharisee sages, who had proved incapable of providing salvation. This tense transitional situation was a hothouse for independent cults to pop up and proclaim their own religious practices and laws.[264] Especially prominent were the Essenes, who numbered some 4,000 members; the early-Christian Therapeutae; and the Sicarii underground, who embraced violence and political assassinations. It was in this context that Jesus's apostles proposed their radical new doctrine, which subverted the Sadducees' and Pharisees' social and religious hegemony.[265] These circumstances and others ultimately triggered the Great Revolt.[266]

Throughout history, messianism has always cropped up in politics and theology in the wake of great tragedies or euphoric victories.

---

264   The political, cultural, and sociological changes that led the Judaism of antiquity to its rabbinical form during the Mishnaic and Talmudic periods gained momentum and force during the period of the sages. See Itamar Gruenwald, "Review: The Problem of Jewish Sectarianism in the Second Temple Period," *Cathedra* 92 (1999), 177–184 [Hebrew].

265   Daniel Schwartz, "Scribes and Pharisees, Hypocrites?: Who are the 'Scribes' in the New Testament?," in Daniel Schwartz (ed.) *Studies in the Jewish Background of Christianity* (Tubingen: Mohr Siebeck), 89-101.

266   Richard A. Horsley, "Popular Messianic Movements around the Time of Jesus," *The Catholic Biblical Quarterly* 46 (1984), 474.

It involves a certain belief in the divine "with or without a human savior figure."[267]

People commonly attribute remarkable historic developments to supernatural forces. Rabbi Joseph B. Soloveitchik was the spiritual leader of the modern Orthodox movement in the United States in the generation of the establishment of the State of Israel. In his sermon *Kol Dodi Dofek* ("Listen, My Beloved Knocks"), he described the rise of Israel after the Holocaust as a manifest expression of divine providence, which could not be explained rationally but revealed the hand of God and signs of an impending redemption. Secular Zionists, according to Soloveitchik, were the flag-bearers of this messianic redemption:

> Eight years ago, in the midst of a night of the terrors of Majdanek, Treblinka, and Buchenwald; in a night of gas chambers and crematoria; in a night of total divine self-concealment; in a night ruled by the devil of doubt and destruction who sought to sweep the Lover from her own tent into the Catholic Church; in a night of continuous searching for the Beloved—on that very night the Beloved appeared. The Almighty, who was hiding in His splendid sanctum, suddenly appeared and began to beckon at the tent of the Lover, who tossed and turned on her bed beset by convulsions and the agonies of hell. Because of the beating and

267   Aviezer Ravitzky, *Messianism, Zionism, and Jewish Religious Radicalism* (Tel Aviv: Am Oved, 1993), 113 [Hebrew].

knocking at the door of the mournful Lover,
the State of Israel was born.[268]

Israel's establishment was indeed a historic moment, so dramatic that even many anti-Zionist Haredim were swept away with excitement and spoke as if the redemption were imminent. For ultra-Orthodox Jews sympathetic to Zionism, the secular Zionists who founded Israel were instruments of the first stage of the redemption. Israel's establishment had ensured the rescue of hundreds of thousands of Jews, said one ultra-Orthodox political leader, but it was only an interim stage—"the beginning of the beginning of redemption"—pending the rise of a Torah-based state in the Land of Israel.

These ultra-Orthodox voices, traumatized by the Holocaust, fleetingly saw Israel as a kind of messianic miracle. But their initial emotional reaction had completely dissipated by the 1970s, undercut by growing solidarity within the ultra-Orthodox world and anti-Zionist fanaticism. They prioritized the rehabilitation of the lost world of Torah study, which became an expression of their hostility to secular Zionism.

Messianic rhetoric is often a symptom of individual or national pessimism in the wake of disaster or defeat, or a sign of elation or emotional intoxication in times of prosperity and victory. Messianic thought involves different concepts of time, which is not necessarily linear or heading toward a better future; it might express a yearning for the restoration of the glorious past.

Prophets have preached different visions of the end of days, from the apocalypse to salvation. The historical recurrence of messiahs, true or false, is a function of humans' worldly and spiritual needs. Messianic sentiments have been symptoms and causes of dramatic social and cultural change. Bar Kokhba, who led a rebellion in

---

268   Joseph B. Soloveitchik, "Kol Dodi Dofek," Sefaria.org.

Judea against Rome in 132–135 CE, was hailed as the messiah by the greatest rabbinic sage of the time, Rabbi Akiva, and had coins made declaring himself as such.

Sometimes, structural changes are the work of charismatic figures who are self-declared messiahs. In the past, political and social actors promoted other characters as the messiah. For example, in the seventeenth century, Nathan of Gaza promoted Sabbatai Zevi, who lived from 1626–1676, as the messiah. Zevi had a huge influence on world Jewry at the time, to the extent that the renowned scholar of the Kabbalah, Gershom Scholem, wrote that Sabbatai Zevi was, in effect, a herald of the modern era, given his focus on Jewish national liberation.[269]

Currently, the Chabad Hasidic movement does the same for the late Lubavitcher Rebbe Menachem Mendel Schneerson, who passed away in 1994. Even before his death, "The Rebbe" was hailed by many of his followers as a messiah waiting to reveal himself. They also claim that "all Jewish souls are connected to the Rebbe."

Adam Ferziger has written that the rise of Schneerson as messiah and the evolution of his movement into a global phenomenon can be understood as a counter response to the advent of the powerful State of Israel. In a review essay of the Hebrew version of *The Israeli Century*, Ferziger maintained that my characterization of "an Israelization of Judaism" should have given more attention to the fast-growing global Chabad-style school of Judaism: it "epitomizes the opposite phenomenon from Shain's Israelization scenario. According to the Lubavitch worldview, the sovereign state has no inherent significance, and while there is a considerable Chabad presence in Israel, this is purely due to the critical mass of Jews who reside there."[270]

---

269   Gershom Scholem, *Sabbatai Sevi: The Mystical Messiah* (Princeton, NJ: Princeton University Press, 1973).

270   Adam S. Ferziger, "Israelization and Lived Religion: Conflicting Accounts of Contemporary Judaism," *Contemporary Jewry* (June 2020).

The late Rabbi Elazar Shach, a powerful leader in ultra-Orthodox Lithuanian communities, declared that Chabad was a "cult" that offered only "total heresy." He called Schneerson "a false messiah" and compared him to Sabbatai Zevi. Those who see Rabbi Schneerson as a messiah, he added, "will burn in hell."

Jewish messianism is almost always connected to a vision of worldly and spiritual national sovereignty and began with the restoration of the House of David. In the Hasmonean period, pretenders to the throne who could not prove a link to their Davidic lineage were perceived as illegitimate. Since the end of the Second Temple period, and especially since the nineteenth century, the revival of Jewish sovereignty has been a bone of contention between forces actively pushing to hasten the messianic age and those who preferred to pray for the Ingathering of the Exiles and the establishment of Jewish sovereignty in the Land of Israel.

In the modern era, as European Jews enjoyed the fruits of the emancipation and as Reform Judaism took hold, yet another school emerged. It separated messianism from the nationalist, territorial narrative of Jewish peoplehood, and reinterpreted messianism through the lens of universal ethics and the Jewish aspiration to "repair the world."

German-Jewish philosopher Hermann Cohen (1842–1918) was a prominent advocate of the view that Israelite prophets made the biggest historical contribution to the formation of universal ethics. The teachings of the prophets, according to him, promoted a messiah that is not just a national savior but an advocate of perfect unity of all mankind. Such "ethical idealism," he believed, was possible in a "German-Jewish symbiosis" between "the nation of Kant" and "the people of the book." Cohen opposed Zionism because it linked the Jews' future to national sovereignty with its vanities and rivalries; which "would only affirm what the anti-Semites has believed all along."[271] He saw the prophets' messianic hope as the thrust of the Jewish faith—a hope that he interpreted through a liberal lens as a march towards higher morality.[272] Indeed, one of the most striking changes to the Jewish liturgy introduced by the Reform movement was the removal of references to the restoration of both the monarchy and the Temple service in the messianic era.

In the Israeli Century, the messianism-sovereignty argument continues to play a key role in the public discourse in Israel and the Diaspora, over the questions of the nature and essence of the state, its borders, community relations, and ties between the Jewish people and the Christian world. As religious scholar Tomer Persico wrote: "There is nothing that is more familiar to Israelis than the influence of messianic religiosity over politics. Whereas the Zionist movement attempted to secularize the messianic Jewish ethos and to subject it to the *realpolitik* of building a modern state, religious Zionism...was already acting out of a distinctly messianic motive...as part of the plan for redemption."[273]

Among Israeli religious nationalists, there is a prevailing sense that we are in the grips of a redemptive historical process, and liberal and far-Left concerns about the corrupting nature of Israel's occupation of the West Bank and annexation of East Jerusalem are expressive of a defeatist, Diasporic mentality. But rather than deny the incipient redemption, are these liberal voices correct in warning that the embrace of a "false messianism" will lead Israel once more to perdition?

---

271   Cited in Steven B. Smith, "Leo Strauss: Between Athens and Jerusalem," *The Review of Politics* 53, no. 1 (1991), 86–87.

272   Julius Guttman, *Philosophies of Judaism: The History of Jewish Philosophy from Biblical Times to Franz Rosenzweig* (New York: Schocken Books, 1973).

273   Tomer Persico, "Messianic Solidarity," *Haaretz*, December 15, 2017 [Hebrew].

Messianism and the Destruction of the Second Temple

When the Jews had an independent polity during the First Temple and Hasmonean eras, and even during their limited sovereignty under Rome and Agrippa, they had control over their own lives and identity. Their rulers generally knew how to handle foreigners and deal deftly with rebel factions and sects. The Pharisees and Sadducees maintained a duopoly on religious and social control under the Hasmoneans, who largely succeeded in uniting or neutralizing more minor sects, and messianic ideas about the end of days were suppressed. Judaism might have had a messianic phase after the first stage of the Return to Zion in the days of Zerubbabel, the grandson of Judea's last king, Jehoiachin, who the prophet Amos said would restore the House of David.[274] But historians have not found a single clear expression of aspirations of sovereignty associated with messianic redemption during the Persian and Hellenistic eras. Indeed, until the first century CE and the rise of Christianity, few spoke of the "messiah" or "son of David."[275]

Jesus and his disciples were no more than a minor stream in Judaism, which was not perceived as a threat to the hegemony of its established form. Bible scholar David G. Horell writes that Jewish Christians "remained loyal Jews, worshipping at the temple according to the established Jewish pattern and apparently faithful in their adherence to Torah." He notes that the Gospel of Matthew stresses that "believers in Jesus are not to abandon any parts of the law; on the contrary, they are to fulfil it perfectly, in intention as well as action."[276]

---

274 Amos 9:14.

275 Horsley, "Popular Messianic Movements around the Time of Jesus," 471.

276 D. G. Horrell, "Early Jewish Christianity," in *The Early Christian World: Vol. I*, ed. P. F. Esler (London: Routledge 2000), 136–145.

Many of the leaders of the Great Revolt, which ended with the razing of Jerusalem and the Temple in 70 CE, anchored themselves in a messianic vision, and some faction leaders who fought the Romans claimed to be messiahs, including Menahem ben Judah, the leader of the knife-wielding Sicarii. Rebel leader Simon bar Giora was also seen as a messiah by his followers. Uriel Rappaport writes: "If it had not been for this messianic faith, it is doubtful that [their followers] would have dared to rebel against the Roman rule."[277]

Some Jews who fought for liberation from the Romans and their Herodian vassals demanded the installation of a legitimate monarchy, similar to that of the Hasmoneans. Some also believed that active rebellion against the Romans would pave the way for the messiah; others preferred to passively anticipate the messianic age. They left the timing to God and disapproved of anti-Roman actions.

Yet messianic expectations failed to materialize in the Great Revolt, and indeed collapsed in the face of the superior Roman forces. Nevertheless, even after the fiasco of the uprising, hopes for renewed Jewish sovereignty refused to die. In fact, in the hundred generations since the destruction of the Second Temple, hopes of renewed sovereignty have been fused with messianic dreams. Israeli philosopher Aviezer Ravitzky writes: "The dream was flawless: The day would come and the whole People of Israel…would be ingathered as one man and would return to its whole land and constitute its life in accordance with God's perfect Torah. The nation would be liberated from enslavement to [other] kingdoms and all of the families of the soil would be blessed in it and its seed."[278]

After crushing the rebellion, the Romans launched a heavy-handed crackdown. They crippled a large agricultural sector of the Judean economy with a wave of land appropriations and tax

---

277   Uriel Rappaport, "The War of Destruction," in Rappaport, *Judea and Rome*, 68–69 [Hebrew].

278   Aviezer Ravitzky, *Messianism, Zionism, and Jewish Religious Radicalism* (Tel Aviv: Am Oved, 1993), 11 [Hebrew].

rises, including a poll tax known as "the Jewish tax." Chaos and despair spread throughout Judea due to the devastation, massacres, and expulsions, although the latter were limited. Poverty and famine proved fertile soil for banditry and black marketeering by Jewish criminals. Refugees flowed from Judea to the Galilee, and many others fled the homeland altogether.[279] According to Josephus, Titus proclaimed: "Are not your people dead? is not your holy house gone? is not your city in my power?"[280] It was a powerful and succinct expression the miserable reality for the Jews of the time.

Without their place of worship and their priestly nobility, which had served as the national, spiritual, and symbolic center of gravity before the Great Revolt, the Pharisee leadership rebuilt itself at Yavne, a coastal town near modern-day Tel Aviv. In the words of the writer Avraham Aderet: "The way of Yavne gave the agonized people a new reason to adhere to Jewish life, and armed it with faith, solace and hope in its struggle to hold on to the Land of Israel and live there in the style of the Diaspora."[281] Sages would journey from Yavne to Judea and the Galilee to entrench their status and preserve Jewish cohesion within a framework of cultural-religious autonomy.

It was during this period that the idea took hold that "the measure of a man's place on the ladder of social class was his study and knowledge of the Torah."[282] Through the institution of the Sanhedrin and headed by Rabbi Yohanan Ben Zakkai and later Rabbi Gamliel, Torah sages laid the foundations for what would become an autonomous Jewish community. They enlisted loyalists and built

---

279   Yehudah Neeman, "The Poverty in the Galilee in the Days after the Destruction of the Second Temple," *Beit HaMikra* 4 (1989), 366–380 [Hebrew].

280   William Whitson trans., *The Wars of the Jews*, chapter 6, available online on the Gutenberg Project.

281   Avraham Aderet, *From Destruction to Revival: The Way of Yavne in Rebuilding the Nation* (Jerusalem: Magnes, 1990), 462 [Hebrew].

282   Aharon Oppenheimer, "The Jewish Community in Galilee during the Period of Yavneh and the Bar Kokhba Revolt," *Cathedra* 4 (1977), 53–66 [Hebrew].

support among the Jews of the Diaspora. Yavne became the hub of Jewish culture and law; there, the Jewish calendar was set, halakha was debated, and Diaspora rabbis were ordained.

During this era, the sages tightened the restrictions demanding strict separation between Jews and Gentiles. This trend was very similar to the religious isolation fostered during the Babylonian Exile. In both cases—one in exile, the other in the homeland—Jews adopted a rigid, tribal religiosity as a substitute for national cohesion in a sovereign state.

According to Israeli philosopher Yirmiyahu Yovel during the period of ancient Jewish sovereignty "there were many Jews who disavowed religious authority or transgressed against its laws without being considered enemies; or who took issue (like the Sadducees) with the Oral Law and with the very principle of theocracy, and yet were legitimate, even influential, citizens of the polity."[283]

Despite the immense religious and social changes in the Land of Israel after the destruction of the Second Temple and the trauma of the Great Revolt, the Jews' rebellious, nationalistic zeal was not extinguished during the Yavne era. Yavne's rabbinical leadership was not happy to settle for an autonomous center of learning as a substitute for sovereignty. To claim otherwise is to deny that, between the destruction of the Temple in 70 CE and the Bar Kokhba rebellion sixty years later, the Jews still fervently wished to liberate Jerusalem. The Yavne sages, who later moved to Lod and Beitar, laid the ideological and practical foundations for further revolutionary activity. They maintained national cohesion around their leadership, and nurtured hopes to cast off the yoke of foreign rule and swiftly rebuild the Temple.[284]

---

283 Yirmiyahu Yovel, *Spinoza and Other Heretics: The Marrano of Reason—Vol. I* (Princeton, NJ: Princeton University Press, 1989), 181.

284 Israel Ben-Shalom, "The Support of the Sages for Bar-Kokhba's Revolt," *Cathedra* 29 (1983), 13 [Hebrew].

More than anything else, this rebellious spirit was fostered by ongoing oppression from the Romans, and in 115–117 CE, Jews in the Diaspora revolted against Roman Emperor Trajan, in a reaction to anti-Jewish atrocities and the increasing insecurity of life, both in the Land of Israel and abroad. In fact, as early as the reign of Agrippa I, three decades before the Great Revolt, the Jews of Alexandria, the largest community of its kind in the Hellenistic diaspora, already suffered pogroms. For roughly 400 years, Alexandria had been home to an illustrious Jewish community numbering an estimated 200,000 souls—4 percent of the population of Egypt. It was a vibrant community with extensive connections to the local government. Alexandria's synagogues bore dedications to their major patrons. Judah ben Ilai, a second century rabbi, marveled at Alexandria's Great Synagogue saying, "He who has not seen it has not seen glory."[285]

The Jews identified deeply with Alexandria; they called themselves Alexandrians and enjoyed a special status in the city as part of wider society. However, their non-Jewish neighbors expected them to worship the city's pagan gods and compromise on their identity, and there is evidence that the Jews feared the ramifications. These fears proved justified in 38 CE, when they fell prey to a violent pogrom.

The Jews feared that the status of the Roman governor of Egypt, Aulus Avilius Flaccus, in the imperial court would be undermined when Caligula became emperor after Tiberius's death in 37 CE. Egyptian and Greek residents of Alexandria, who were at odds with the Jews, assured Flaccus that they would promote his cause in Rome if he clamped down on the Jewish judges in the courts.

This crisis prompted King Agrippa to visit Alexandria in a bid to help the local Jews. Known to be close to Caligula, Agrippa marched through the streets of the city with a guard of honor, and

---

285 Schama, *The Story of the Jews: Finding the Words*, 100.

the Jews rejoiced. But as soon as he left, the locals launched violent attacks against them and their institutions, accusing them of dual loyalties. Agrippa's visit had also aroused Flaccus's suspicion; he declared the Jews to be foreigners in Alexandria, effectively making them legitimate targets. Mobs set upon the Jews, claiming that they had disobeyed the emperor's orders to place his image in all places of worship in the empire.[286] The great philosopher Philo described the rape of Jewish women and how Jews were forced to eat pork in public—just two of many atrocities committed upon this community:

> They were dragged away as captives, not only in the market-place, but even in the middle of the theatre, and dragged upon the stage on any false accusation that might be brought against them with the most painful and intolerable insults.... And if they appeared to belong to our nation, then those who, instead of spectators, became tyrants and masters, laid cruel commands on them, bringing them swine's flesh, and enjoining them to eat it. Accordingly, all who were wrought on by fear of punishment to eat it were released without suffering any ill treatment; but those who were more obstinate were given up to the tormentors to suffer intolerable tortures, which is the clearest of all possible proofs that they had committed

---

286 Gruen, *Diaspora*.

no offence whatever beyond what I have
mentioned.[287]

The Paradox of Living in the Diaspora and Dual Loyalty

Alexandria's Jews lived in constant friction with their neighbors after the events of 38 CE. In the year 41, after Caligula died,
Claudius became emperor. Known to be an old friend of Agrippa,
Claudius responded firmly to quell the unrest in Alexandria among
Jews, Greeks, and Egyptians. He restored the Jews' ancestral traditions in the city while reaffirming the sovereignty of a Jewish king
in Judea.

But Claudius's kindness was limited. While restoring the Jews'
rights, he also ordered them to stop seeking further privileges and
warned them not enlarge their community by bringing more Jews
from Egypt or Syria. If they did, he would develop "greater suspicions" about the Jewish people throughout the Roman empire.[288]

The status and the rights of the Jews in the city were maintained
for a further two decades, but their world was turned upside down
after the Great Revolt broke out in Judea in 66 CE. The shockwaves
from the dramatic events in the Land of Israel created palpable apprehension among the Gentiles of Alexandria. Lest they be tainted
by the stigma of disloyalty to Rome, they joined the Roman legions
in massacring the Jews of the city and accused them of conflicting
religious and civil loyalties. They were accused of being loyal to the
Temple in Jerusalem instead of to the imperial religion, due to their
half-shekel contributions and excessive solidarity with their rebellious brethren in Judea.[289] The smear of dual loyalties and heresy

---

287   Philo, "Against Flaccus," 80.
288   Slingerland, "Suetonius 'Cladius'," 311.
289   Gruen, *Diaspora*.

were to become major elements in Christianity and Islam after the destruction of the Second Temple.

In the modern era, the dual loyalty issue has passed from the religious sphere to political and social spheres. Jews have been asked repeatedly to prove their loyalty to their countries of residence and have frequently been the victims of violent discourse and anti-Semitism on account of their allegedly treasonous instincts, both as a group and as individuals.

The nationalist ideological movements of the nineteenth century intensified the Jewish loyalty dilemma. Jews were accused of dividing, polluting, and economically exploiting their host nations. Jewish socialists were accused of fomenting class warfare and a dangerous strain of internationalism, while Jewish financiers were attacked from the other direction. "The Jews, whatever is said of them, have a country—the London stock exchange," said the nationalist French historian, Jules Michelet. "They are active everywhere, but are rooted in the country of gold."[290]

The high-water mark of these accusation that Jews were traitors to their countries came with the trial of Alfred Dreyfus, a Jewish officer in the French military. In 1894, he was arrested, framed, and found guilty of treason and spying for Germany. He was publicly stripped of his rank and sent to Devil's Island penal colony. Dreyfus was exonerated in 1906 and reinstated into the army at the rank of major after a tortuous process, and the affair catalyzed the emergence of Theodor Herzl's brand of political Zionism. "The only visible result was that it gave birth to the Zionist movement," wrote Hannah Arendt, "the only political answer Jews have ever found to anti-Semitism and the only ideology in which they have ever taken

---

290 Brian Barry, *Culture and Equality* (Boston: Harvard University Press, 2001), 85–86.

seriously a hostility that would place them in the center of world events."[291]

Nevertheless, many Jews, including Herzl, were initially cautious and assumed that the Dreyfus affair had *led* to an outbreak of anti-Semitism, not that anti-Semitism was behind the libelous charges. The editor of a French-Jewish weekly wrote at the time: "If the impossible comes to pass and the guilt of the accused officer is proven by absolutely ironclad facts, all the Jews will be ready to condemn him.... It would be a disgrace to accuse all the Jews of France, who during the generation of emancipation have given more than enough guarantees [of their loyalty]."[292]

However, the French public was incited by military officers and the Catholic press, both inside France and abroad. They used the Dreyfus trial to stir the masses and draw a line between loyal Frenchmen and traitors, including the non-Jews who supported Dreyfus. Right wing elements decried Dreyfus as a national traitor, and some socialist activists called him a class traitor. Catholics inflated the loyalty issue to accuse the Jews of being agents of Germany, stoking Jew hatred with French antipathy for the Germans.

Hannah Arendt believed the Dreyfus affair had shown the world that "that in every Jewish nobleman and multimillionaire there still remained something of the old-time pariah, who has no country, for whom human rights do not exist, and whom society would gladly exclude from its privileges."[293]

The Jews of England, in contrast, were not subject to local anti-Semitism at the time. They saw themselves as a religious

---

291   Hannah Arendt, *The Origins of Totalitarianism* (San Diego: Harcourt Brace Jovanovich, 1979), 120.

292   Gideon Kouts, "He Is Innocent! Or Is He? The Response of the Jewish Press in Europe and Eretz Yisrael to the Initial Phase of the Dreyfus Affair," *Kesher* 33 (2003), 41–53 [Hebrew].

293   Arendt, *The Origins of Totalitarianism*, 117.

community, not a national one, and emphasized that that their civil obligations took precedence over those that were communal. The attitude to political Zionism was tepid, and at times hostile, even among British supporters of the Hibbat Zion movement, who preferred to settle Eastern European Jews in Palestine but otherwise distanced themselves from the project.

On the eve of World War I, Lucien Wolf, an English-Jewish journalist and official at the Board of Deputies of British Jews, condemned the idea that Jews should have to emigrate to a country of their own. According to historian Aviva Herskovits, he feared that the idea of a Jewish nationality might provoke questions about dual loyalties and jeopardize the status of Jews in their countries of residence. This could be especially detrimental to the achievements of the Jewish community of England.[294] Wolf opposed the Balfour Declaration, as did Jewish cabinet minister Edwin Montagu, who argued that Zionism was a political belief that no patriotic citizen of the United Kingdom could tolerate:

> If a Jewish Englishman sets his eyes on the Mount of Olives and longs for the day when he will shake British soil from his shoes and go back to agricultural pursuits in Palestine, he has always seemed to me to have acknowledged aims inconsistent with British citizenship and to have admitted that he is unfit for a share in public life in Great Britain, or to be treated as an Englishman.... It seems to be inconceivable that Zionism should be officially recognised by the British Government,

---

294   Aviva Herskovits, "The Goals of the Jewish Agency for Palestine—A Reappraisal," Zion (1995), 431 [Hebrew].

and that Mr. Balfour should be authorized to
say that Palestine was to be reconstituted as
the 'national home of the Jewish people.'[295]

During World War I, while Jews fought and killed each other in
rival armies, German and Russian, they were scapegoated as traitors
by both sides. Hundreds of thousands of Jews, among them Zionists,
fought in the Russian Army, demonstrating loyalty to the Czarist
regime for which they died. Yet the Russian forces adopted the
"scorched earth" policy of looting and destroying numerous Jewish
communities before abandoning them to the German enemy, while
leaders of the Russian military, which fought poorly, were quick to
label Jewish soldiers as a fifth column and as spies. Many Jews were
summarily executed.[296] Similarly, German Jews fought side by side
with Gentiles in defense of their fatherland just to be accused of
profiteering and stabbing Germany in the back.[297]

In the Interwar Period, American Jews had to deal with the dual-loyalty charge, especially after accusations of harboring sympathy
for the communist enemy. In 1934, Mordecai Kaplan, the founder
of the Reconstructionist Movement, came out strongly against
the idea of the Jews as the "chosen people" in his influential book
*Judaism as a Civilization: Toward a Reconstruction of American-Jewish
Life*. He saw it as incompatible with the civil status of American
Jewry. Kaplan, who described Judaism as a civilization rather than a
people, demanded that the term "chosen people" be expunged from
the prayer book. He believed that it implied that Jewish interests

---

295 "Anti-Semitism: Montagu Memo on the Anti-Semitism of the British Government,"
Jewish Virtual Library, https://www.jewishvirtuallibrary.org/montagu-memo-on-british-govern-
ment-s-anti-semitism.

296 Michael Stanislawski, "Why Did Russian Jews Support the Bolshevik Revolution?," *Tablet
Magazine*, October 25, 2017.

297 David Mikics, "The Jews Who Stabbed Germany in the Back," *Tablet Magazine*, November
9, 2017.

took precedence over the American national interest, and was thus preventing American Jews from identifying fully with the United States and validated accusations of dual loyalty.[298]

Today, almost a century later, the mere notion of Jewish-American distinctiveness is often contested, and the idea that Jews were elected by the Almighty for an ethical mission is often repudiated as an assertion of ethnic supremacy. As Jews are lumped in with other whites, their "privilege" also seems to negate their claim of thousands of years of oppression through anti-Semitism. The writer Judith Colp Rubin recently lamented that, while in the past the idea of Judaism as an ethical culture was celebrated, intended to replace an American Judaism "trapped in ritual and theology [with] a universal religion steeped in morality," today American Jews are often described as "white aggressors." Moreover, attacks on Israeli nationalism are now "cornerstones of progressive 'intersectional' ideology."[299]

Since the establishment of the State of Israel, allegations of dual loyalty have concerned Diaspora Jews' connections to and solidarity with Israel. In the Israeli Century, Jews cannot easily shirk the question of mutual Jewish responsibility and ties to Israel, even if they want to. This is because Israel has, through power, politics, and legislation, indirectly or forcibly associated them with itself, and it also sees itself as responsible for the security and well-being of Jews worldwide. The Israeli penal code includes a unique clause—the so-called "Jewish security" clause—by which Israel claims an extraterritorial power to enforce its criminal law beyond its borders against persons who commit "offences against the state or the Jewish people." The clause states that it will also apply in cases of offenses committed abroad against "the life of a Jew, his body, his health, his

---

298   Arnold M. Eisen, *The Chosen People in America: A Study in Jewish Religious Ideology* (Bloomington, IN: Indiana University Press, 1983).

299   Judith Colp Rubin, "My Alma Mater's Jewish Problem," *Commentary*, February 2020.

liberty or his property, because he is a Jew, or against a Jewish insti-
tution, per se." This legislation broadened the link between Diaspora
Jews and Israel, making it their country even more explicitly than the
Law of Return does, which gives all Jews the right to immigrate to
Israel and become citizens.[300]

As in the days of Agrippa I and the pogroms in Alexandria, so
in the Israeli Century do suspicions that Diaspora Jews harbor dual
loyalties often focus on their commitment to the Jewish homeland
at the expense of their civic loyalty to the societies and countries
in which they live. The explosiveness of the dual-loyalty question
loomed large in 1987, when Jonathan Pollard, a Jewish US Navy intelligence analyst, was convicted of aggravated espionage on Israel's
behalf and was sentenced to life in prison. It seemed that this was not
just a criminal case against an individual—Pollard's guilt impugned
all American Jews by association. Commenting on the subsequent
panic that seized the American Jewish community, Israeli political
scientist Shlomo Avineri said:

> In the Pollard case, something more pro-
> found is now surfacing: a degree of nervous-
> ness, insecurity and even cringing on the part
> of the American Jewish community which
> runs counter to the conventional wisdom of
> American Jewry feeling free, secure and un-
> molested in an open and pluralistic society....

---

300 When the bill was proposed for a first reading, Minister Dan Meridor said: "We accept
Prof. Feller's proposal...to assume responsibility as a Jewish state to defend Jewish lives, if Jews
are attacked for being Jews. We can certainly ask whether other countries follow similar customs,
maybe they don't, but there is no state like ours, which is according to a different basic law—
paragraph 7a of Basic Law: The Knesset—is the state of the Jewish people. When a Jew is pursued
anywhere on earth for being Jewish, not for committing a crime, I think we need to be able
to apply...the State of Israel's criminal law on their attackers, as we see fit," Knesset Protocols
124:15 (1994), session 371, 2297–2799 [Hebrew].
See also Zeev Segal and Yossi Shain, "Defender of the Jews, Wherever They May Be," *Haaretz*
September 6, 2002, https://www.haaretz.com/1.5136673.

> But the truth of the matter is simple: you,
> in America, are no different from French,
> German, Polish, Soviet and Egyptian Jews.
> Your exile is different–comfortable, padded
> with success and renown. It is an exile none-
> theless…. America, it now evidently appears,
> may not be your promised land.[301]

In the 1990s, as globalization peaked, multiple citizenship became increasingly accepted and considered an expression of the new transnational world. While ethnicity and dispersion were celebrated as expressions of multiculturalism, links between ethnic diasporas and homelands were seen as natural and even welcome. To many, dual loyalty seemed to have become an archaic concept, but it reared its ugly head again after the 9/11 terror attacks and the subsequent American military campaigns in Iraq and Afghanistan. People complained about the supposedly excessive power of the "Jewish lobby," which stood accused of urging retaliation against the Arabs to promote Israel's interests at the expense of US foreign-policy goals. "The damn war in Iraq is because of you. Israel and the Jews are dragging us," said General William Odom, a former US national security advisor. "In my opinion, Israel has no right to exist."[302] A bestselling book by Stephen Walt and John Mearsheimer also turned "the Israel lobby" into a synonym for treachery, harming relations between the United States and the Muslim world.[303]

Of course, the robust situation of Diaspora Jews in the Israeli Century differs greatly from those at the start of the protracted exile

---

301   Alan Dershowitz, *Chutzpah* (New York: Simon & Schuster, 1991), 7.

302   Yossi Shain, "Israel Should Not Rely on Republicans' Sympathy," *YNet News*, July 11, 2014, https://www.ynetnews.com/articles/0,7340,L-4589006,00.html.

303   John J. Mearsheimer and Stephen M. Walt, *The Israeli Lobby and U.S. Foreign Policy* (New York: Farrar, Straus and Giroux, 2007).

following the destruction of the Second Temple. Historian Erich Gruen argues that the Greek riots against the Jews of Alexandria in 66 CE were a direct response to the Great Revolt in the Land of Israel. Attacks on Jews because of their links to the homeland spread to other communities in the Mediterranean basin and eventually triggered the Diaspora insurrection of 115–117 CE, which started in Egypt and Cyprus and spread to Mesopotamia. The rebels fought to preserve their Jewish identity in both the homeland and the Diaspora and inflicted heavy damage on their neighbors and the Roman governmental system. They were harshly suppressed by Roman general Lusius Quietus, whom Trajan appointed governor of Judea as a reward.[304] The result of the uprisings was the almost total annihilation of Jewish communities in the Roman world and a mass exodus of refugees to Babylon, the only Diaspora community free from Roman rule.[305]

The sages of Talmudic and Mishnaic times downplayed the Jewish Diaspora Revolt of AD 116–117, aiming to conciliate their imperial overlords until quiet was restored. But these rebellions attested to active warlike operations being possible beyond the borders of the Land of Israel, contradicting the Zionist idea that Diaspora Jews were always impotent in the face of oppression and sufficed with prayer and supplication. Historian Aya Barsky-Elyashiv has written that the uprisings prove that, even in difficult times, the Jews are capable of demonstrating "warrior-like, active loyalty to their faith and to their brethren in the Land of Israel."[306]

---

304   Jacob Kaplan, "Evidence of the Trajanic Period at Jaffa," *Eretz-Israel: Archaeological, Historical and Geographical Studies* 15 (1981), 412–416 [Hebrew].

305   Third-century Roman historian Cassius Dio observed that the rebellion in Cyprus was led by a Jew called Artemion, and that "two hundred and forty thousand perished [at the hands of the Jews], and for this reason no Jew may set foot on that island, but even if one of them is driven upon its shores by a storm he is put to death," Earnest Cary trans., *Roman History: Vol. VIII* (New York: G. P. Putnam's Sons, 1925), 423.

306   Aya Barsky-Elyashiv, "Martyrdom in the Land of Israel in Antiquity" (PhD thesis, Tel Aviv University, 2007), 172–182 [Hebrew].

In the decades following the Great Revolt and the Diaspora uprising, Jews of the Land of Israel were in an extremely bad condition, physically and religiously. The Romans had launched a vicious crackdown on them, which included a ban on circumcision, the forced Hellenization of Tiberias and Sepphoris, and the construction of a pagan city, Aelia Capitolina, on the ruins of Jerusalem.[307] These were the critical factors that eventually led to the Bar Kokhba revolt, a "war of liberation for Israel and Jerusalem," in the words of historian Israel Ben Shalom. This insurrection represented the only hope of shaking off the intolerable Roman oppression. Bar Kokhba united most of the Jews against the Roman regime, briefly reinstated their sovereignty, and restored the dignity of his nation. "Was it not only natural," Ben Shalom wrote, "that the rebels should extol the deeds of their Hasmonean-era forefathers and derive confidence in their victory from the victory of the Hasmoneans?"[308]

According to Cassius Dio, the Bar Kokhba revolt severely damaged the confidence and honor of the Roman Empire and even threatened its stability. It inflicted heavy casualties upon the Romans, who feared that it might spread beyond the borders of Palestine. To suppress it, the Romans had to bring in large forces from Britain, and when it was crushed, they celebrated its victory as one of the Roman Empire's finest achievements.

The Bar Kokhba revolt clearly left a profound impression on the Roman psyche.[309] As we shall see, the ethos of the brief sovereignty achieved in Bar Kokhba's time had a significant effect on

---

307 Joseph Geiger, "The Ban on Circumcision and the Bar-Kokhba Revolt," *Zion* 41, no. 3–4 (1976), 139–147 [Hebrew]. There is a debate among academics as to whether the Bar Kokhba revolt was also triggered by Hadrian's prohibition on circumcision, and whether this prohibition even existed.

308 Israel Bar-Shalom, "The Support of the Sages for Bar-Kokhba's Revolt," *Cathedra* 29 (1983), 27–28 [Hebrew].

309 Werner Eck, "The Bar Kokhba Revolt: The Roman Point of View," *The Journal of Roman Studies* 89 (1999), 76–89.

Christianity's claim to be the divine successor of the Jews as the chosen people and on medieval Jewish-Christian disputations about the nature of the messiah.

From Rabbi Yohanan Ben Zakkai and Bar Kokhba to Ben-Gurion

Israeli society is deeply influenced by the dissonance between some groups' focus on Jewish strength and others' focus on apocalyptic anxieties. The arguments over the nature of Jewish power and vulnerability often draw on messianic discourse and build on the nation's experiences since the Second Temple era that have shaped the Jewish collective conscience for millennia.

Simon Bar Kokhba, the leader of the revolt of 132 CE, has similarly been treated to polar interpretations. Was he a great hero, or the instigator of the Jewish people's greatest-ever national disaster? Israelis are arguably afflicted with, and warned against, the dangers of Bar Kokhba syndrome—a complex of arrogance and overestimation of power, which can backfire spectacularly. In Israel's early days, Bar Kokhba's mythical heroism shaped the self-image of the *sabra*, the native-born Israeli. Lag Ba'Omer, the campfire holiday associated with Bar Kokhba, became the definitive celebration of native Israeliness. But after the initial debacles of the 1973 Yom Kippur War and the 1982 First Lebanon War, that ethos turned into a controversial and emotional debate about the limits of Israeli power.[310]

The well-known rabbinic legend of Rabbi Yohanan Ben Zakkai represents the antithesis of Bar Kokhba. Ben Zakkai was said to oppose the Great Revolt and the Jewish zealots and surrendered to

---

310   Oz Almog writes that Lag Ba'Omer became "the holiday most loved by the young Israeli natives, the time when everyone sat in circles around the fires...[and] recalled the rebel leader, the hero of the Jewish people's mythical war, whose descendant the Sabra was," *The Sabra: The Creation of the New Jew* (Berkeley, CA: University of California Press, 2000), 244.

Vespasian in the hope of saving his people and the Temple from destruction. As a reward, the Romans allowed him to establish a rabbinic center in Yavneh, which would come to be viewed as the foundation of the rabbinic movement. Ben Zakkai failed to save the Temple, but tradition says that he did save the Jewish people because Yavne became the spiritual successor to the center of worship in Jerusalem.

In the early 1980s, the former commander of IDF military intelligence and international relations scholar Yehoshafat Harkabi, argued that Ben Zakkai's surrender was an example of shrewd political realism and should serve as a lesson and alternative to the delusionary myth of the heroism of the Bar Kokhba revolt, which destroyed Judea and brought its people to the brink of annihilation. "With the exception of the Holocaust of European Jewry by the Nazis," he argued, "it would seem that there was never such a catastrophe like that of Bar Kokhba, one in which so many Jews were killed at once." Bar Kokhba's defeat at the hands of the Roman superpower was predictable, and the rebel leaders' risks were both unrealistic and unreasonable.[311]

Harkabi's thesis caused a commotion in Israel. He hoped to use a case study from Jewish history to draw analogies to post-Yom Kippur War Israel and challenge what he saw as its rigidity toward the Arab world and power drunkenness. He warned Israelis against fostering of the myth of "the few against the many," which he argued was giving moral sanction to the religious Zionist thesis that Israel enjoyed divine providence and was on course for redemption.[312] He also contrasted Bar Kokhba's fatal revolt with Ben Zakkai's surrender, as an example of "responsible" Jewish conduct in the face of Rome's overwhelming might.

311 Yehoshafat Harkabi, *The Bar Kokhba Syndrome: Risk and Realism in International Politics* (Chappaqua, NY: Rossel Books, 1983), 48.

312 Ibid.

Historian Gedaliah Alon disputed the story of Ben Zakkai's surrender as a case study of the virtues of political realism, as if it enabled the Jewish revival in Israel and the Diaspora. It was a baseless myth, he wrote—Ben Zakkai and his disciples did not go to Yavne because they had won a reprieve from Vespasian, but because they were part of the deluge of refugees out of Jerusalem.[313]

Former IDF chief of staff, and well-known historian and archaeologist, Yigael Yadin accused Harkabi of basing his interpretation of the Bar Kokhba revolt on a selective, biased, and moralistic approach to history. He alleged that Harkabi was misleading readers in a bid to criticize Israeli policies as leading to disaster and was using historical analogies in an unscientific and invalid manner. If there were any room to draw analogies from the Bar Kokhba revolt, Yadin wrote, it would be to David Ben-Gurion's declaration of the State of Israel on May 14, 1948. Many in Israel and abroad feared that he might plunge the Jews into existential danger just a few years after the Holocaust. Senior Truman administration officials also believed that the nascent Jewish state would collapse in the face of invading Arab armies. Yet Ben-Gurion's decision, Yadin argued, was a courageous act of leadership that changed the course of Jewish history.[314] Ben-Gurion thanked President Truman for extending recognition to the new Jewish state against the advice of his senior officials, saying it gave him an "immortal place in Jewish history."[315]

Zeev Sharef was the cabinet secretary of the People's Administration, Israel's pre-state national executive, and personally witnessed the debates before its declaration of independence. In his book *Three Days*, he described the drama and uncertainty that

---

313   Gedaliah Alon, "How Yabneh Became R' Johanan ben Zakkai's Residence," *Zion* 3, no. 3 (1938), 20 [Hebrew].

314   "The Bar-Kokhba Revolt and Its Consequences (Conversation with Yigael Yadin)," *Mibifnim* 46 (1983) [Hebrew].

315   "Harry Truman and the Recognition of Israel," AJC, https://www.ajc.org/harry-truman-and-the-recognition-of-israel.

gripped Jewish leadership before the declaration, during the deliberations in Tel Aviv. He wrote that the decision to go ahead with
the declaration was made only two days in advance and passed with
a minimal vote of six members to four—and this was only because
Ben-Gurion placed pressure on his *de facto* foreign minister, Moshe
Shertok (later Sharett).[316] Ben-Gurion pushed for a vote while point-
ing a historical gun at his colleagues' heads.

The cabinet debate of May 12, 1948, lasted thirteen hours.
Its members heard a report by Moshe Shertok about his meeting
in Washington with US Secretary of State George C. Marshall, who
had warned that declaring a state at such an early stage would ignite
a war and end in a fiasco. Marshall proposed that the Jewish leaders
agree to a three-month truce and the imposition of a UN trusteeship
system instead of a state. Golda Myerson (Meir), who participated
as an observer, reported that it was clear from her talks with King
Abdullah of Jordan that he would go to war. He had no choice, she
argued, as he was being dragged along by the British and the Arab
states.[317] "We can't afford to zigzag," she said. "There should have
been an executive committee of the U.N. to oversee the partition
but it has been silenced and is no more. We are forced to declare the
state ourselves."[318]

Cabinet members also heard from Yisrael Galili and Yigael
Yadin, two senior officers in the Haganah, the pre-state Jewish military force, on the army's capability to resist an Arab invasion. They
did not give the declaration of a state their full backing. "If I might
summarize cautiously," Yadin said, "I would say that right now the
chances are very even. To be honest, I would say that they have a
great advantage, if that entire force comes and wages war against

---

316 Ariel Feldstein, "Three Days in Iyyar 5708: A New Study in Light of the Evidence," *Iyyunim Bitkumat Yisrael* 8 (1998), 361 [Hebrew].

317 Feldstein, "Three Days in Iyyar 5708," 359 [Hebrew].

318 Nakdimon, "What Happened Here" [Hebrew].

us."[319] Do we really know whether Bar Kokhba thought his chances were any better?

Debates about the limits of power, national honor, and decision-making in the times of existential threats are not exclusive to Jews. The reservoirs of memories of nations, religions, states, and even individuals are always key to their attitudes toward, and relations with, others. To a large extent, these memories dominate international conduct, and they determine whether certain acts will be carried out and others will not. The memories of one group can be adopted by another, or forced upon another, or adapted to suit the needs of others. Since historic traumas and triumphs are also tools in the building and exploitation of myths, the way they are remembered, nurtured, and preserved has a decisive influence upon the formulation and understanding of policies. The memories that shape the identity and determine the acts of groups are liable to come back and haunt them, or be used against them, if their members deviate from the ethical codes that have made those memories sacred or are accused of desecrating them. Memories of certain players in historical status of evildoers, victims, or liberators can shape certain issues and negotiations between nations.

In 2018, President Emmanuel Macron of France sparked a row when he enshrined General Henry Philippe Pétain as a hero of World War I. Pétain had been notorious since World War II in collective French and Jewish memories for having surrendered to the Germans and delivering the country's Jews to the Nazis. He was sentenced to death for treason after World War II, but De Gaulle commuted his sentence to life imprisonment.

On the hundredth anniversary of the end of World War I, Macron decided to intercede in France's collective memory by giving Pétain a place of honor in history, and proved that definitions of

---

319   Feldstein, "Three Days in Iyyar 5708," 359 [Hebrew].

the national good, including questions of surrender and victory, can change as time passes. Some argue that the Vichy regime's surrender saved France from devastation, although De Gaulle denounced it as treason at the time. Leaders can thus be seen as saviors or traitors for the very same actions.[320]

Collective memories are part of the strategic reservoir at the disposal of international players. Certain salient recollections–of heroic struggles, of defeats and suffering, of victories and accomplishments of the human will–can bestow legitimacy on actions in the international arena, even if they are not completely in accordance with the international ethical codes.

To a certain extent, defining memories provide an added value of legitimacy to the conduct of players on the world scene. But those of past suffering do not justify questionable conduct in the present; indeed, they can diminish the value of collective memories.

International players are always plugged into memory reservoirs, whether consciously or unconsciously, to justify their actions and weaken their rivals. Both open societies and authoritarian regimes can draw from the same well, while competing with each other's interpretations of events and actions.

In open societies, nobody has a monopoly on the interpretation of memories and their translation into action; they make room for revisionist historians, who touch a nerve when addressing formative, identity-shaping events, whether in the recent or distant past. International actors do not enjoy unlimited flexibility, since memories can be rigid and unbending in the contemporary political climate. Yet the process of change is neither linear nor uniform–it is dynamic. Memories comes in waves and cycles. They can slip back into history or be reawakened by younger generations.

---

320   "Macron's Plan to Pay Tribute to Nazi Collaborator Pétain Stirs Anger," *The Guardian*, November 7, 2018.

After the Bar Kokhba revolt, Jews became a minority in the Land of Israel. Refugees from Judea flocked to the Galilee, where they attempted to rebuild their leadership institutions and reconstitute the Sanhedrin, the top rabbinical council, in Usha. They began by collating the writings of the *Tannaim*—first and second century sages—which served as the basis for the final redaction of the Mishnah a generation later by Rabbi Judah HaNasi.

According to Aharon Oppenheimer: "This project was executed at a time when the results of the revolt were still evident, and could not have been done without the combination of the heritage of the center in Yavne and the Jewish infrastructure in the Galilee."[321]

But due to tough conditions from the end of the second century CE, the Land of Israel lost precedence over the Diaspora and the center of Jewish life shifted to Babylon, to which many Jews—included leading sages—had emigrated. Babylon hosted a flourishing Jewish center, which replaced the Land of Israel as the leading influence over Diaspora Jewry. The Jews established great religious academies in Sura, Nehardea, and Pumbedita, where the Babylonian Talmud was compiled.[322] Babylonian Jewry, which traced itself back to the destruction of the First Temple, soon became the largest Jewish community in the world.[323]

The Aftermath of the Bar Kokhba Revolt

As noted earlier, Rabbi Akiva, one of the most important sages of the Mishnaic period, believed that Bar Kokhba was the messiah. But as time passed, and Jews moved further away from the Land of Israel,

---

321   Oppenheimer, "The Jewish Community in Galilee during the Period of Yavneh and the Bar Kokhba Revolt," 65–66 [Hebrew].

322   Joel Florsheim, "The Establishment and Early Development of the Babylonian Academies, Sura And Pumbeditha," *Zion* 29, no. 3–4 (1974), 183–197 [Hebrew].

323   Shmuel Safrai, "Review: Yavneh and Babylonia: Two New Books in the Study of the Mishnaic and Talmudic Periods," *Jewish Studies* (1991), 121 [Hebrew].

later sages denounced him as a false messiah. He was mocked as "Bar Koziba"—a play on words that meant "Son of a Lie." Maimonides named him and Jesus Christ as false messiahs.

In the twelfth and thirteenth centuries, Jewish commentators depicted him as a criminal rather than a hero and blamed the exile under Emperor Hadrian as a response to his folly. Christians also labeled Bar Kokhba a false messiah and saw his defeat by the Romans as validating Jesus's status as the redeemer.[324] Only in the late nineteenth century was he rehabilitated by Zionist historians, and only when Israel was founded did the story of his heroism become a subject of research animated by Jewish nationalist sentiments.[325]

Scholars disagree over the demographic and social processes that gripped the Jewish world in the post-Bar Kokhba period. What they do agree on is that a significant section of the Jewish elite was exiled by the Romans, and many of them were sold into slavery. However, many remained in the Land of Israel, mostly in the Galilee, including refugees from Judea.

As a result of the Bar Kokhba revolt, Rome renamed the country Syria-Palaestina, expropriated the land around Jerusalem, dispossessed the Jews, and slapped poll and land taxes on them, aggravating the poverty in Judea. The Jews lacked political power, but the Romans granted them a certain internal autonomy and recognized the *Nasi*, the head of the community, as their representative vis-à-vis the imperial rule and as the supreme Jewish authority throughout the empire.

Jews of the Land of Israel survived and found ways to renew their national existence. Archaeologist Michael Avi-Yonah wrote:

---

324   Ram Ben Shalom argues that Bar Kokhba was a major preoccupation for the Jewish and Christian worlds of the Middle Ages, and in disputations between Jews and Christians, the question of the messianic credentials of Jesus and Bar Kokhba were debated together. See Ram Ben Shalom, "Bar Kokhba: How did the Man of Disaster Become a Big Hero?," https://www.openu.ac.il/adcan/adcan46/p22-26.pdf [Hebrew].

325   Ibid.

"The nation that had been defeated in battle, was able to hold on to the land; to expunge as far as it possible the errors of the war; to preserve its human and economic strength; to adapt its laws to the needs of the hour. The defeated nation once again became a political player in its land, and began to build up strength for the third round of combat against the foreign rulers."[326]

Indeed, only two or three generations after the Bar Kokhba revolt, they had rehabilitated themselves—this time as a nation that had lost its sovereignty. Banished from Judea, they settled in the Galilee as farmers and petty merchants. Their national and communal leaders were the rabbinical sages, who laid down the law and shaped the identity of their scattered nation, including as arbiters of the laws of conversion.

The painful transition from national sovereignty to the rebuilding of cultural autonomy was accompanied by an intense emphasis on building an education system based on the duty to study. Shortly before the destruction of the Temple, High Priest Joshua ben Gamla had decreed that every Jewish father must send his sons to study the Torah from the ages of six or seven, and that communities must provide the teachers and impose a tax for this purpose.

In their book *The Chosen Few: How Education Shaped Jewish History*, Zvi Eckstein and Maristella Botticini describe a blossoming of Jewish literacy. The robust enforcement of the ben Gamla decree by the Pharisee elite headed by Judah HaNasi, they write, altered the nature of the Jews and Judaism. They went from being members of an illiterate nation that made sacrifices to their God, to the most educated community in antiquity, at a time when elsewhere only the aristocracy was educated.

Institutionally, therefore, the legacy of the Pharisee sages

---

326   Michael Avi-Yonah, *In the Days of Rome and Byzantium* (Jerusalem: Bialik Institute, 1980), 4 [Hebrew].

gradually came to dominate Judaism. The unrivaled leader of the era was Judah HaNasi, who by the turn of the third century, had redacted the corpus of Jewish law into the six tractates of the Mishnah with his colleagues.[327]

At first, Jewish Diaspora communities, including the large one in Babylon, accepted the authority of the rabbis in the Land of Israel. However, in time, the erudition of Diaspora rabbis came to exceed that of those in the homeland, and the Babylonian sages gained recognition as the supreme arbiters of Jewish law.[328]

Economic decline and poverty had had a detrimental effect on Torah scholarship in the Land of Israel. The Babylonian Talmud, redacted between 450–550 CE, soon achieved precedence over the Jerusalem Talmud, completed a century before.

The situation of the Jews in Judea and the Galilee also worsened steadily as time went on. Rampant disease and persecution spurred emigration to Mesopotamia, as Jews sought a better livelihood opportunities. Some succumbed to religious and economic pressures and converted to Christianity. The poor also felt unable to meet the high expense of compulsory schooling for small children, and many of the converts to other faiths no doubt saw them as less demanding.[329]

Rabbinic Judaism revolutionized Jewish identity, using literacy to bolster its religious aspects over ethnic ones, but it could not prevent a demographic collapse in the Land of Israel, brought on by harsh living conditions. The data on Jewish demographics is not precise, but it appears that in the five centuries between the Bar Kokhba revolt and the rise of Islam in the seventh century, the

---

327   Abraham Goldberg, "Purpose and Method In Rabbi Judah Hannasi's Compilation of the Mishna," *Tarbiz* 28 (1959), 260–269 [Hebrew].

328   Avi-Yonah, *In the Days of Rome and Byzantium*, 106 [Hebrew].

329   Zvi Eckstein and Maristella Botticini, *The Chosen Few: How Education Shaped Jewish History, 70–1492* (Princeton, NJ: Princeton University Press, 2014).

number of Jews dropped by 66 percent, from 3.3 million to 1.2 million, because of persecution, conversion, and declining birthrates. Historian Rivka Shpak-Lissak states that, in the first century CE, there were some two million Jews in the Land of Israel; by the time the Arabs conquered it in the seventh century, fewer than 200,000 farmers and merchants remained.[330]

330   Rivka Shpak-Lissak, *When and How the Jewish Majority in the Land of Israel Was Eliminated* (Thorofare, NJ: Edwards Brothers Malloy, 2015).

Chapter IV: Jewish Life in the Shadow of Christianity and Islam

One of the most widespread theories in the debate about Jewish history is that ever since the Bar Kokhba Revolt national sovereignty was only ever a secondary element of Jewish national identity, such that the loss of sovereignty did not erase that identity. Rather, in the words of Israeli novelist A. B. Yehoshua, "The homeland component of the Jewish-Israeli national identity…lost its primary and key role to the religious-divine component."[331] According to Yehoshua, the Jews paid lip service to their longing to return ("If I forget thee, Jerusalem") but stubbornly insisted on living outside the Land of Israel, even though many of them could have settled there if they had wanted to. In their souls, argues Yehoshua, the Jews were "a diaspora nation" (as Simon Dubnow articulated in the late nineteenth century) who did not respect other nations' claims of exclusive belonging to their own homelands.

But these theories fail the test of history. The Jews have always sought territorial stability, whether in the Land of Israel or as an autonomous minority elsewhere. They have always aspired to have a presence in the Land of Israel, whether enjoying stability or suffering oppression in exile.

During the Second Temple era and the momentary glimpse of sovereignty under Bar Kochba, aspirations for political independence

331 A.B. Yehoshua, "Time to Say Goodbye to the Two-state Solution. Here's the Alternative," *Haaretz*, April 19, 2018, https://www.haaretz.com/israel-news/.premium.MAGAZINE-time-to-nix-the-two-state-solution-and-stop-israel-s-apartheid-1.6011274.

defined their national identity. Even after the destruction of the Temple and the defeat of the Bar Kochba revolt, survivors fought to hold onto their land. The Jews' national yearning for sovereignty was never extinguished, despite their traumatic loss of sovereignty, the razing of their capital, the despoliation of their religious and cultural treasures, and the harsh economic conditions in the Galilee under Roman occupation, which all made an active independence struggle impossible.

After the demise of their presence in the Land of Israel and until the dawn of the Israeli Century, the Jews were scattered across the globe, yet still managed to maintain their ethno-religious separateness. Gentiles all knew who was a Jew. What has become known as "the Jewish bookshelf"—the Hebrew Bible, the Talmud, the prayer books, and other religious writings—proved to be a powerful glue and palliative for a people who had lost their land.

Religious observance, based on halakha, made national life possible for a nation without territory; it also spurred the consolidation of a messianic theology that promised the renewal of sovereignty at the End of Days. For Jews in exile, Torah study and religious law were not intended to supersede the homeland but were simply a brilliant solution for national cohesion in the absence of territorial self-rule.

Indeed, prominent scholars of the roots of nationalism have marveled that even when there were no practical prospects for ingathering the Jewish exiles or rebuilding their home country, they still succeeded in maintaining their particularism and identity by clinging to their distinctiveness as a religious tribe and because of the Gentiles' commitment to exclude them.

However, once Jews met modernity, and modernity met the Jews, many did not wish to keep their cultural and religious distinctiveness or carry the burden that came with it. Astonishingly, when conditions ripened in the modern era, the Jewish national project awoke both modern Zionists and Orthodox Jews, who successfully gathered their brethren from all corners of the earth back to their homeland. They achieved this despite persecution and hardship and the accrual of multiple new traditions and ethnic identities over the generations.

Anthony Smith, a British scholar of nationalism, compares the history of Jewish nationalism with that of other nations and concludes that what was most remarkable about the Jews was their continued devotion to their homeland, not their failure to return. Many other nations stripped of their land and ruled by outsiders fought for political liberation, but they did so without having to contend with dispersion, which smashes communities and blurs identities. The Jews, however, first had to return to their homeland and only then fight for liberation.

When compared to other peoples who lost their independence and were exiled—like Armenians and Greeks—the Jews' devotion to their homeland was exceptional because of the length of their absence and breadth of their dispersion across the globe in hostile settings. Smith argues that Armenians and Greeks learned how to cling to their religion and texts to preserve their national identity from the Jews and were inspired by their determined struggle to return to their homeland and restore their independence. These nations adopted their own "chosen people" ethos and acted to fuse their religion with their national identity as a means to preserving their sense of nationhood.[332]

Substitution Theory and the Jew as Witness

For the first 300 years after Jesus, under the heel of Rome, the early Christians succeeded in establishing the church as an institution

---

332   Anthony D. Smith, "Zionism and Diaspora Nationalism," *Israel Affairs* 2, no. 2 (1995), 1–19.

with its own laws, courts, authorities, and internal hierarchy—and all as a subversive movement in an empire that failed to see them as a meaningful threat.

But Christianity eventually transformed Rome. In the fourth century, Constantine the Great converted to Christianity and Emperor Theodosius made it the imperial faith. The Roman Empire redefined its mission based on its new theology. Rome—soon reincarnated as the Byzantine Empire—became a Christian domain. Thus, for the first time ever, Christianity wielded imperial power, which it exerted forcefully to impose its religious hegemony across the empire.

In demanding a monopoly on monotheism in the Eastern Roman Empire, the Byzantines treated the Jews as an enemy. Indeed, the Jews had never stopped rebelling against imperial rule, but Christian hegemony dashed their dreams of self-rule.[333] After the Byzantine Church ordered the closure of the Sanhedrin in the Land of Israel in 363, many fled to the great Jewish community of Babylon, far from Christendom and under Sassanid Persian rule.

After the rise of Christianity in the first century, Jesus's successors scorned the Jews as Christ-killers and their faith as obsolete. They recast the Land of Israel as the cradle of Christianity and the Holy Land, and it became a flashpoint between the two religions.

Eventually, church doctrine declared that Christianity had superseded Judaism. The disappearance of Jewish sovereignty was taken as proof of the church's replacement theology—that Judaism had laid the groundwork for Christianity but had completed its role with the advent of Christ. Christians were the "new Israel," replacing the Jews as a chosen people united not by ethnicity or territory but by faith in Christ and the promise of universal salvation.

---

333   Michael Avi Yonah, *Understanding the Jewish World from Roman to Byzantine Times* (Jerusalem: Carta Jerusalem, 2015).

Nevertheless, early Christian dogma assigned the Jews an important role in the ultimate redemption of humanity—they would find God's favor again at the End of Days.[334] In other words, the Jews' existence confirmed the truth of the Gospels—although God had abandoned the Jewish people, He would choose them again when, like all followers of Christ, they accept His messiah.

By the end of the fourth century, the great Christian theologian Augustine had already cemented the notion that the Jews' very existence had an important function in the unfolding of the redemption. At the End of Days, the surviving Jews would embrace Christianity, and the universal reign of the church would be complete. It was therefore forbidden to kill Jews, for as Psalms 59 said: "Slay them not, lest my people forget." This was Augustine's doctrine of "Jewish witness"— the Jews' purpose was to bear witness to the truth of Christianity.

Indeed, in the Middle Ages, medieval popes adopted Augustine's thesis and reminded their flocks of the commandment "slay them not" to restrain the rampant anti-Jewish hostility in the church and among the faithful. Historian Shlomo Simonsohn argued that the popes were "the most moderate of all the main forces in the Catholic Church when it came to attitudes to Jews," and that even the most hostile of them "paid lip service to the Augustinian principle...until the Counter-Reformation of the mid-16th century."[335] Alongside the popes' efforts to impose restraint, the Church increasingly came to see the Jews as guilty for the crucifixion and accused them of blindly refusing to acknowledge the prophecies littered throughout the Hebrew Bible heralding the advent of Christ. They had become the allies of Satan.

---

334 Jeremy Cohen, *Living Letters of the Law: Ideas of the Jew in Medieval Christianity* (Berkeley and Los Angeles, CA: University of California Press, 1999), 363.

335 Jeremy Cohen and Yaakov Shavit, "Interview with Professor Shlomo Simonson," *Zemanim* 115 (2011), 96 [Hebrew].

In the seventh century, after Muhammad conquered the city of Medina and founded Islam, Muslim armies rode out of the Arabian Peninsula and conquered Syria, Egypt, North Africa, and the Land of Israel (640–41 CE), which was divided into two Byzantine provinces, Palaestina Prima and Palaestina Secunda.

The conquest of the Land of Israel was not a methodical operation. It was executed by raids of Bedouin tribes who often fought among themselves while defeating the Byzantine armies. Thousands of Jews and Christians were slaughtered in these raids but were not immediately forced to convert to Islam. The coastal towns retained their Hellenistic and even cosmopolitan culture, as noted by ninth-century Arab writers. One observed that "the coastal towns are inhabited by a mixture of communities and nations: Jews and Samaritans, Persians and Greeks, and also some Arabs."[336]

In the early days of the Muslim conquest, most Jews in the Land of Israel worked as farmers or artisans; but in time, their security and prosperity worsened and their community thinned out dramatically. The Land of Israel fell off the economic map of the Mediterranean basin.[337] As noted historian S. D. Goitein observed: "The Jewish people…so to say, died as an agricultural people during the seventh and eighth centuries, but unlike other ancient populations, returned to life as a nation of merchants and artisans."[338]

Operating out of their base in North Africa, the Muslim armies built an alliance with Berber converts to Islam, conquered Spain and Portugal, and invaded France. By the ninth century, they had also conquered Sicily, and Arab raiders plundered even the outskirts of Rome.

---

336   Moshe Sharon, "The Cities of the Land of Israel under Islamic Rule," *Cathedra* 40 (July 1986), 40, 90 [Hebrew].

337   Ibid., 120 [Hebrew].

338   S. D. Goitein, *Jews and Arabs: their Contacts Through the Ages* (New York: Schocken Books 1967), 7.

The meteoric rise of Islam meant that, between the eighth and thirteenth centuries, most of Jewry came to live under its sword. However, the Jews maintained their distinct identity and close cooperation between scattered communities on matters of religion and custom. They proved that, wherever political conditions allowed, they could maintain a vibrant diaspora life, build communal institutions, and develop an independent culture, often in collaboration with their host nations, to whom they remained loyal. This occurred in the periods of the *Geonim* (the heads of the great Talmudic academies) in Babylon, of Jewish autonomy in Egypt, and in the Golden Age in Spain.

In the wake of the Arab invasions, the Christians began organizing the Crusades, with the goal of reconquering the Holy Land. These campaigns briefly blocked the spread of Islam, but the Christian armies were ultimately defeated and driven out of Jerusalem. The Muslim advance continued, leading to the fall of the Byzantine Empire and the conquest of its capital, Constantinople.[339]

The Crusades, which began in 1096, were a dramatic turning point in Jewish history. The marauding crusader mobs rained destruction on Jewish communities of the Rhineland and Palestine, proving to them the precariousness of their existence and their vulnerability to arbitrary upheavals. Nevertheless, the great suffering of the Jews in the Middle Ages was not chronicled as a continuum of defining events. Only in hindsight is it clear that the attacks on the Jews in the twelfth century were the opening salvo for the near destruction of European Jewry—they were prelude to the mass expulsions of the Middle Ages, the pogroms, and of course the Holocaust.[340]

During the Crusades, and the epic battles between Islam

---

339 Bernard Lewis, *What Went Wrong? Western Impact and Middle Eastern Response* (New York: Oxford University Press, 2002), 3–19.

340 Daniel J. Lasker, "The Impact of the Crusades on the Jewish Christian Debate," *Jewish History* 13, no. 2 (1999), 23–36.

and Christianity for dominion over Jerusalem and the Holy Land, Augustine's dictum "slay them not" was eroded. Although the papacy generally tried to protect the Jews from crusader violence, its influence over the clergy in Europe was limited.

Moreover, in the frenzy of the Crusades, the papacy ignored or overlooked attacks on Jews, who became the most "accessible enemies of Christ," as historian Jeremy Cohen put it.[341] Christians depicted the Jews as demons, the spawn of Satan, and pagans who no longer had a place in Christendom; they, therefore, could be killed with impunity.

Augustine's doctrine of "the Jew as witness" gave way to a belief that they had concluded their role in history. Jeremy Cohen explains that the collapse in Judaism's global status stemmed mainly from the clash between Muslims and Christians over whose founding prophet was superior. Moreover, in view of Christianity's "new commitment to rational argument in matters theological," Christian theologians dismissed Talmudic Judaism as irrational and insisted that the Jews had nothing more to contribute to their understanding of God's law.[342]

By the twelfth century, the Church deemed the Jews yet another heretical sect and no longer treated them as "witnesses" to the historical truth of Christianity. Quite the contrary—the Catholic Church condemned the Talmud as part of a broader doctrine that accused the Jews of betraying their own biblical tradition and thereby forfeiting the right to be protected as "witnesses," as Augustine had preached. Thirteenth-century pontiff Pope Gregory IX contended that the Jews' fixation on the Talmud, which disparaged Christianity and denied the Gospels and their prophecies about Christ, condemned them to betray Jesus. Everything, therefore, was to be done

---

341   Jeremy Cohen, *Sanctifying the Name of God: Jewish Martyrs and Jewish Memories of the First Crusade* (Philadelphia: Philadelphia University Press, 2004), 15.

342   Cohen, *Living Letters of the Law*, 16.

to crush Judaism and convert Jews to Christianity. Gregory authorized Talmud burnings, which became a spectacle across Europe.[343]

Jews in the Islamic caliphates were much better off than their brethren in Christian Europe, where Jew-hatred was deeply ingrained in the minds of the Christian faithful and Church teachings. In contrast, pluralism and religious heterogeneity were the hallmarks of the Islamic world; there, Jews were not firmly separated from everyone else, as they were in Christendom.[344]

At the same time, the Muslim caliphates considered both Jews and Christians as *dhimmis*: monotheistic minorities considered second-class, yet protected, persons. The eighth-century Pact of Umar imposed harsh restrictions on non-Muslims, intending to stigmatize and humiliate them. Over the years, the Jews were subjected to special per-capita taxes, forced to wear specific clothing, forbidden to build synagogues, and barred from praying in public. However, the Pact of Umar, which was adapted over the years to different rulers' needs, also committed Muslim caliphs to protecting the Jews' lives, safety, and religious freedom. Some scholars have maintained that the harsher terms of the pact were never fully enforced and did not reflect the tolerant reality of the Muslim caliphates; some have even inaccurately idealized Jewish life under Islam.

The Jewish predicament in the Muslim world was complex. At times, they lived comfortable and even privileged lives, but they also were subject to the arbitrary whims of Muslim rulers. Physical attacks, blood libels, and expulsions were an integral part of their lives until (and including) the twentieth century.

Of particular note are the harsh anti-Jewish policies of the

---

343 Pope Gregory IX wrote to the zealous King Louis IX in June 1242 ordering him to burn copies of the Talmud in Paris because "no punishment would be sufficiently great or worthy of the crime" of the Jews' heresy. Schama, *The Story of the Jews: Finding the Words*, 351.

344 Mark R. Cohen, "Islam and the Jews: Myth, Counter-Myth, History," *The Jerusalem Quarterly* 38 (1986), 133.

Fatimid caliph al-Hakim in Egypt and Palestine in the eleventh century, the forced conversion of Jews in Yemen in the twelfth century, and their forcible transfer in Morocco to *mellah* ghettoes beginning in 1438.[345] Whereas in Egypt, the persecution began with attacks on Christian churches before spreading to synagogues, the assault on the Jews of Yemen was intended from the outset to destroy their community.[346] Responding to a desperate cry from the Yemenite Jewish community, the great philosopher Maimonides wrote that the Ishmaelites were persecuting the Jews and degrading them as no other people had done before. As the historian Bernard Lewis once put it, the Jews' situation under Islam was "never as bad as in Christendom at its worst, nor ever as good as in Christendom at its best."[347]

The shifts in the Jewish condition were themselves a product of tectonic shifts in the Islamic world and especially the deterioration that began after the rise of the Mamluks in the thirteenth century. It was then that Islam had abandoned the Hellenistic Mediterranean heritage of reason, innovation, and a certain degree of "democracy." This decline led to "irrationality, benighted mysticism, superstitions, corrupt and despotic government, isolationism, and ignorance," all of which deeply influenced Middle Eastern Jews before they came to Israel.[348]

In the twelfth and thirteenth centuries, in the shadow of the clash between Islam and Christianity, Jews began thinking about the advent of their messiah and the renewal of their sovereignty. Spanish-Jewish philosopher and poet Judah Halevi, who sailed to

---

345   Eliezer Bashan, "New Evidence of the Injury to Moroccan Jewry's Religious Life in the Last Third of the Nineteenth Century," *Pe'amim* 63 (1994), 7–65 [Hebrew].

346   Mark R. Cohen, "Review of 'Palestinian Jewry in Early Islamic and Crusader Times', by S. D. Goitein," *Tarbiz* 53, no. 1 (1983–1984), 149–154 [Hebrew].

347   Bernard Lewis, *Semites and Antisemites* (New York: Norton, 1986), 121.

348   Miriam Frenkel, "The Medieval History of the Jews in Islamic Lands—Landmarks and Prospects," *Peamim* 92 (2002), 23–62 [Hebrew].

the Holy Land while it was still in crusader hands, proposed a re-sounding theological interpretation of the war of the two faiths. The failure of both Christianity and Islam to impose their exclusive hegemony on the world proved that Judaism remained the one true faith. He was not the only Jew saying so at the time, and the late Middle Ages saw the circulation of similar polemics, which argued that Christianity and Islam's failure to suppress Judaism proved its superiority.

One notable writer in this vein was Rabbi Meir ben Simeon of Narbonne, who argued in his 1270 treatise "Obligatory War" (*Milhemet Mitzvah*) that while two "rotten" religions were attacking each other, the Jews had been given the role of holding them to account. It was, therefore, possible to categorically state that Judaism alone was "the true religion," which in the course of time would "triumph over all of them as it gets stronger at the time of redemption," because as Psalms says, "Truth will spring up from the ground."[349]

In 1140, at the height of the Crusades, Judah Halevi wrote the *Book of the Kuzari*, which is considered a canonical text on Judaism's status vis-à-vis Christianity and Islam to this day, and a calling for a Jewish national awakening. It opens with a description of a recurring dream dreamt by the king of the Khazars, a pagan monarch who is considering converting to Judaism. "Thy way of thinking is indeed pleasing to the Creator," the king is told in his dream, "but not thy way of acting."[350] The king summons a Muslim, a Christian, and a philosopher, but after understanding that they do not have the answer, he turns to a rabbi, who convinces the king that Judaism holds the true answer to his questions. The king and his people then convert to Judaism.

---

349 Lasker, "The Impact of the Crusades on the Jewish-Christian Debate," 26–27.

350 Judah Halevi, *Judah Hallevi's Kitab al Khazari* (London: G. Routledge, 1905), trans. Hartwig Hirschfeld, 34.

The *Book of the Kuzari* was written as a defense of Judaism, an abased faith at a time when Islam and Christianity claimed absolute supremacy and brutally trampled the Jews, both politically and religiously. Defying this pretension, Halevi sought to tell a different story about history, one that would bolster the Jews' self-confidence and restore their long-lost national honor. Although Christianity and Islam claimed to have superseded Judaism, the Jews remained the chosen people and retained God's particular favor. Judaism, therefore, had a higher status than Islam and Christianity, and only the Jews could reach the level of the divine. The *Book of the Kuzari* makes a case for the superiority of Judaism, as the fictional Khazar king embraces it, and establishes a mighty Jewish kingdom between the Caspian Sea and the Black Sea.

Halevi emphasized that Judaism was not merely a matter of Talmudic halakha, but was primarily the political doctrine of a nation committed to its sacred homeland, the Land of Israel. In Halevi's account, Christianity, Islam, and Greek philosophy fail to answer the riddle in the Khazar king's dream. But the king, who wants to know what to believe *and* how to act, sees that the answer lies in Judaism, which had been national and political in its past. For precisely this reason, the *Book of the Kuzari* stresses that there is only a limited possibility for converts to join the Jewish people, unlike the proselytizing faiths of Christianity and Islam, which will take everyone and anyone. Belonging to the Holy Seed is not a matter of belief alone but rather a matter of nationality, bestowed selectively upon the seed of Seth, via Noah, Abraham, Isaac, Jacob, and all of Jacob's sons. Halevi called on the Jews to return to their homeland, in a campaign for spiritual, national, territorial, and political revival in which they would establish their superiority and precedence before the deity in the sight of all mankind.[351]

---

351 Lippman Bodoff, "Was Yehudah Halevi Racist?," *Judaism* 38, no. 2 (1989), 174–184.

In the Israeli Century, religious Zionism has adopted Halevi's theology and views him as the movement's earliest precursor. David Hartman writes that Judah Halevi was "the prototypical philosopher of modern religious Jewry and one of the most beloved spiritual forebears of modern Zionism."[352]

The story of the Khazars' conversion to Judaism in the ninth century has attracted a great deal of interest and inspired numerous studies over the years. The subject was widely publicized in 1976, when Arthur Koestler claimed in *The Thirteenth Tribe* that the Jews of eastern Europe were the descendants of the Khazar converts, not of the ancient Israelites.[353] More recently, controversial Israeli historian Shlomo Sand has argued that what he called "the Zionist enigma" was based upon the "the mythology of an eternal 'ethnic' time."[354] Sand writes that Zionist historians have refrained from dealing with the true Khazar origins of eastern European Jewry to avoid undermining the myth of the ingathering of the exiles and the return to the Land of Israel.

The thesis that the Jewish nation is an "invention" has gained currency in recent years among detractors of Zionism, who have deployed it to deny Israel's right to exist as a Jewish state. Some people have even tried appealing to genetics to substantiate their claim that the Jews are foreign to the Land of Israel. One of Sand's claims is that, although there is no historical evidence that Jews migrated eastward from western Germany (*Ashkenaz* in Hebrew), Zionist historians identified the Jews of eastern Europe as "Ashkenazim" to back up a fictitious story of an "exiled, wandering nation" without facing up to the fact that

---

352   David Hartman, *Israelis and the Jewish Tradition: An Ancient People Debates its Future* (New Haven : Yale University Press, 2000), 27.

353   Arthur Koestler, *The Thirteenth Tribe: The Khazar Empire and Its Heritage* (London: Hutchinson, 1976).

354   Shlomo Sand, *The Invention of the Jewish People* (London: Verso, 2009), 250.

these Jews are "the offspring of tough horsemen from the Volga-Don steppes."[355]

Contrary to Sand's explosive allegations, there is extensive evidence of a mass eastward migration of Jews from Bohemia and Germany in the thirteenth and fourteenth centuries, in the wake of Crusade-era massacres and expulsions. This was shown by historian Bernard D. Weinryb.[356]

There is even a debate as to whether there was ever a massive conversion among the Khazars. Researcher Shaul Stampfer found that there is no historical proof of a mass conversion of the Khazars. Moreover, there is also no evidence of a mass exodus of Khazars following the fall of their kingdom in the tenth century, or for a mass influx of Khazars into Poland and the Russian Empire, where most of the world's Jews lived in the nineteenth century. The entire story, he claims, borders on fantasy.

Stampfer dryly notes that the study of Khazar history, like the study of Jewish history, should stick to facts and not be swayed by political or personal agendas, and that "sober studies by historians do not always make for great reading and that the story of a Khazar king who became a pious and believing Jew was a splendid story."[357]

The Wandering Jew

In the early Islamic era, at the end of the period of the Geonim, so named for the heads of the major Babylonian Talmudic academies, many of the world's Jews lived in Mesopotamia, far away from Christendom. There, they prospered spiritually and materially

---

355 Ibid., 253.

356 Bernard D. Weinryb, *The Jews of Poland: A Social and Economic History of the Jewish Community in Poland 1100–1800* (New York: The Jewish Publication Society of America, 1972), 27–29.

357 Shaul Stampfer, "Did the Khazars Convert to Judaism," *Jewish Social Studies*, 19, no. 3 (2013), 1–72.

and created what became an alternative model to Jewish sovereignty. They cooperated closely with their Muslim overlords, until their world was turned upside down at the dawn of the twelfth century with the Crusades. They became a humiliated minority, forced to wear yellow badges and chains as a sign of their inferiority.

Baghdad was the seat of the Exilarch, the leader of the Jewish community in Babylon. In 1170, Jewish traveler Benjamin of Tudela reported it was also home to 40,000 Jews, twenty-eight synagogues, and ten *yeshivot*. It was only after the Mongol invasion of 1258, when Baghdad was almost entirely razed, that Jewish refugees began to stream out of Babylon and into the wider world, and so the curtain fell on the great Babylonian diaspora. Spain was a prime destination.

In Europe, the Jews were largely a sideshow to the titanic clash between Christendom and Islam. In Muslim Spain they rebuilt a magnificent center of Diaspora life, which remains, for some, a model for a successful minority existence.[358] But in the late eleventh century, the Christians began to recover their strength and they eventually drove the Muslims out of Spain. This, with the concomitant Inquisition and eventual expulsion of Jews from the Iberian Peninsula, spelled the end of the Golden Age. By 1492, almost 800 years after the Muslim conquest, the Reconquista was complete, and the path was clear for the Christians to invade North Africa and Asia.

In the early sixteenth century, opposition was growing to the papal monopoly over power, fueled by anger over the corruption of the clergy and the Vatican's use of piety for financial gains. There was anger over the papacy's sale of indulgences to fund Rome's opulent extravagance and the construction of St. Peter's Basilica, the largest cathedral in the world.

Martin Luther, a German monk, sparked the Protestant Reformation with a daring act of rebellion. On the morning of

358   Robert Guest, *Borderless Economics* (New York: Palgrave MacMillan, 2011), 7.

October 31, 1517, he nailed his "Ninety-Five Theses" to the door of All Saints' Church in Wittenberg and accused Archbishop Albrecht of Mainz of selling indulgences for personal profit.

By 1560, after a millennium of Catholic hegemony, Europe's religious unity was shattered, and for the first time, believers had a choice between churches. In a wave of conversions, more than half of Europe embraced Protestantism, and the Catholic Church found itself competing with Lutheranism, Calvinism, Anglicanism, and other sects.[359]

Luther was no liberal. On the contrary, he was a Christian fundamentalist who insisted on building a congregation of the faithful around a stringent interpretation of holy scripture, with a diminished role for the church as the mediator between believers and God. At the outset of his revolutionary journey, Luther demonstrated empathy toward the Jews and believed, in the words of historian Jacob Katz, "his purification of Christianity would remove the obstacles to the conversion of the Jews."[360] He asserted that the Jews were even closer to Jesus than the Christians, who were therefore obliged "to deal kindly with the Jews and to instruct them in the scriptures; in such a case we would expect them to join us."[361]

But in having failed to proselytize the Jews, Luther became their bitter enemy. He developed a venomous anti-Semitic theology, which was imbibed by his masses of followers, including the noblemen and princes who had seized power in the new Germany. In his screed "On the Jews and Their Lies," he wrote that the Jews were "our plague, our pestilence, our misfortune.... [Christians] are at fault in not slaying them. Rather we allow them to live freely

---

359   Eugene F. Rice Jr., *The Foundations of Early Modern Europe 146–1559* (New York: W. W. Norton & Co., 1970), 146.

360   Jacob Katz, *Exclusiveness and Tolerance: Studies in Jewish-Gentile Relations in Medieval and Modern Times* (London: Oxford University Press, 1980), 138.

361   Avi Beker, *The Chosen: The History of an Idea, the Anatomy of an Obsession* (New York: Palgrave Macmillan, 2008), 44.

in our midst despite all their murdering, cursing, blaspheming, lying, defaming."[362] He taunted them: "Listen, Jew, are you aware that Jerusalem and your sovereignty, together with your temple and priesthood, have been destroyed for over 1,460 years?"[363]

Little is known about Europe and its Jews during the Dark Ages, from the fourth to ninth centuries. But by the Middle Ages, their world in western Europe was characterized by a persistent fear of an outburst of Christian rage. They were segregated from the world around them and lived in constant fear of expulsion. The Jews were expelled from England in 1290, from France in 1394, and most famously, from Spain in 1492. In Germany, where there was no central political authority, they were a regular target for persecution, banishments, and economic restrictions. Confined to crowded ghettos on the outskirts of cities, they lived as self-contained religious communities, estranged from their surroundings.[364]

Luther's pathological hatred for Jews led to the growth and refinement of anti-Jewish doctrines across Europe in the early seventeenth century, centering around the myth of the "Wandering Jew"–a rootless, inimical, treacherous, and subversive figure who hid among the Christians and spread like a plague across the continent.[365] The motif of the Wandering Jew had preoccupied Christianity since its inception, shifting shape throughout history. Its outlines had formed as early as the fourth century, when Augustine of Hippo preached that the Jews were historically cursed because they were guilty of crucifying Jesus Christ and rejecting his gospels. Augustine likened the Jews to Cain and the Christians to Abel, contending they carried a mark that distinguished them from other humans and were doomed

---

362 Ibid., 44.

363 Egil Grislis, "Martin Luther and the Jews," *Consensus* 27:1 (2001), 66.

364 Katz, *Exclusiveness and Tolerance.*

365 Luther's anti-Semitism would later have an enormous influence on romantic German nationalism and Nazi dogma.

to eternal wandering as a sign that they had rejected their brother and crucified him.[366]

Christianity also linked the curse of the Wandering Jew to morality and finance. Church elders considered trade for the sake of profit as a base and deplorable occupation and merchants as despicable sinners. The very concept of buying cheap and selling dear was considered fraudulent. Jewish traveling merchants, who came to Europe after the fall of the Roman Empire and traded throughout the Carolingian Empire, were condemned as rootless, homeless sinners.

During the Reformation in the sixteenth and seventeenth centuries, as Luther's anti-Semitic tract resonated in Christian ears, the myth of the Wandering Jew became an integral part of European culture and seeped into the mass consciousness, as well as into literature and art. In 1602, an anonymous pamphlet was published in Germany, titled "A Brief Description and Narration Regarding a Jew Named Ahasuerus." It added a new and seemingly topical layer to the story of Jesus's abandonment on his way to his crucifixion on Golgotha. The original Christian version of the story was that Jesus was betrayed by a Roman by the name of Cartaphilus who refused to help him along the Via Dolorosa and was therefore condemned to eternal wandering. The German pamphlet replaced Cartaphilus with a Jewish cobbler named Ahasuerus (apparently named for the Persian king from the Book of Esther).

The story of the Wandering Jew was printed and disseminated across Europe. By the beginning of the seventeenth century, the myth was deemed a reality, with multiple reports of sightings of Ahasuerus in Hamburg, Bavaria, Prague, Brussels, Munich, and Newcastle. Ahasuerus had supposedly even reached America, where he was reported to have been spotted by Mormons as late as the

---

366 Cohen, *The Friars and the Jews.*

nineteenth century.[367] As a major factor in the formation of the stereotype of Jews as rootless and disloyal, the myth inspired a long list of books and plays, some of which led to the expulsion of the Jews from Danzig in 1616, demands for their expulsion from Hamburg, and harsh sanctions against them elsewhere in Germany.[368]

Jewish life was harsh and precarious in early modern Europe, but there were islands of relative normalcy. In early seventeenth century Prague, for example, the Jews were on reasonable terms with the Christians, and they even intermingled. They lived in the same neighborhoods, traded with each other, and even held impassioned theological debates in public, including in synagogues. This era is sometimes called the Golden Age of Bohemian Jewry. The dominant figure in communal life and its philosophical leading light was Rabbi Judah Loew (1520–1609), also known as the "Maharal."

At the time, minorities in Prague were developing their own national consciousnesses. Lutheran Germans, Polish Catholics, Czechs, Italians, and Jews all felt like distinct ethnic groups. According to the Maharal, "Every nation has its own religion, and its religion made it that nation." There was also room for Jews, who were "Israel by religion."[369]

The Maharal expounded a unique conception of Jewish peoplehood without a polity, whereby life in the Diaspora was a breach of the natural and cosmic international order. Like Judah Halevi, who influenced him, the Maharal believed that there had

---

367   The myth of the Jew as the eternal sinner fated to wander the earth until the second coming of Christ penetrated the core of European folklore, featuring in dozens of works of art and literature. It was eternalized in poems by Schubart, Schreiber, Schlegel, and Goethe, and in the stories of Hans Christian Andersen. It appeared in a novel by Franzhorn and a tragedy by Klinemann. See Joseph Jacobs, "Wandering Jew," *Jewish Encyclopedia: Vol. 12*, http://www.jewishencyclopedia.com/articles/14773-wandering-jew.

368   On the character of Ahasuerus and his historical significance, see R. Edelman, "Ahasuerus, The Wandering Jew: Origin and Background," *Proceedings of the World Congress of Jewish Studies* 2 (1965), 111–114.

369   Maharal of Prague, Be'er HaGolah, chapter 7 [Hebrew].

to be cohesion between a nation, its religion, and its territory. He, therefore, adopted a philosophical-theological approach that saw human history as subject to a natural law in which nations existed as organic units within the system of divine creation. Each nation had a natural place in which it could exert its independence, and it was therefore inconceivable for any nation to live in unnatural bondage to another nation. The Jewish people also deserved to fit into this pattern, as it was God who corrected aberrations in the cosmic order. It was God who would steer the redemption and restore the People of Israel to their land.

The Maharal took a passive and mystical approach to the restoration of Jewish independence in the Land of Israel. Indeed, in the Israeli Century, national-religious disciples of Rabbi Kook cite his faith in a cosmic national order, as well as Judah Halevi's arguments in the *Book of the Kuzari*, as proof that Jewish tradition, and not secular European nationalism, was the engine of the Zionist revolution.[370] Remember that even in Prague, Jews who wished to show national pride and demanded equality were told sternly by judicial authorities that they were not equal to Christians and should not demand to be, because "by law, the Jews were to be considered 'a despised and degraded nation…and thus it should be forever. For these Jews are a nation of wanderers."[371]

The story of the Wandering Jew, which played an important theological role for Christians in the early modern era, became an integral part of "atheistic" anti-Semitism in the nineteenth century. Modern anti-Semites saw not only a dangerous enemy of the nation-state, but also a member of an inferior, demonic race that had to be exterminated. German poet Heinrich Heine (1797–1856), a Jewish convert to Christianity, lived years after the apex of the myth

---

370   Avi Sagi, "Exile, Strangers, and Sovereignty: Reflections on Biblical Tradition," *Democratic Culture* 16 (2015), 225–226 [Hebrew].

371   Maharal of Prague, Be'er HaGolah, chapter 7 [Hebrew].

of the Wandering Jew. In his poem "Sabbath Princess," he depicted the Jewish man cursed to transform into a wild dog: "Dog with
doglike thoughts and worries / Slogging on year after year / Through
the daily muck and mire / And the urchins' mocking jeer." This curse
is only lifted once a week, allowing the Jew to briefly assume human
form on Friday night to celebrate the Sabbath.[372]

The Wandering Jew underwent another metamorphosis in the
twentieth century, when the debate passed from the Christian world
to the Jewish-Israeli one. After the Holocaust, and in the State of
Israel's early years, Jewish intellectuals in Europe and the United
States tried to transform the Wandering Jew into an idealized, universalistic motif, redefining him as the consummate cosmopolitan. Thinkers like George Steiner, Hannah Arendt, and Zygmunt
Bauman extolled the universal ethical responsibility of Jews, who
could shake off the chains of nationalism and see the world through
humanistic eyes. The Wandering Jew became a cosmopolitan moral
prophet—an intellectual unbound by the shackles of statehood and
its constrictive territoriality, free from belligerent national chauvinism. For Zionists, of course, the return to Israel meant the myth
could be retired, and in their art and philosophy, the Wandering Jew
gave way to the Pioneering Jew. Indeed, the attraction of the modern
Wandering Jew has been fading in the Israeli Century, and with it,
the sway of anti-Zionist intellectuals who championed it.

In the first decades of Israel's existence, it was common for
Israelis to fear having to wander again and feel contempt for Jews
who insisted on remaining in exile—and Israelis who chose to go into
exile. This attitude has changed over time, with the consolidation of
Israel's national security and transnational, technological economy.

---

372   Amos Elon, *The Pity of It All: A Portrait of the German-Jewish Epoch, 1743–1933* (New York:
Picador, 2002), 30.

Israelis who venture out into the wider world are no longer held in contempt by their fellow citizens.

Today, the Wandering Israeli is a symbol of the country's strength and worldwide patriotism. Young Israelis taking post-military treks abroad and start-up entrepreneurs building business bridges across the globe are evidence of how a sovereign Israel has empowered Jews, giving them a concrete sense of home and the knowledge that someone will come to their defense wherever they may be. Firmly anchored in a country of their own, Israelis travel the world with pride, making a mockery of centuries-old Christian hatred and of cosmopolitan Jews. They are proof that it is possible to be both deep-rooted and intensely global at the same time. Israelis are also proud that their country goes to extraordinary lengths to rescue and help both Israelis and Diaspora Jews in distress overseas—and bring the Wandering Jew home.

The Hebraist Roots of Modern Political Philosophy

While Jews after the Reformation continued to suffer from the Christian belief that they must be condemned to eternal wandering, their own ancient texts were increasingly studied to understand the meaning of national sovereignty in an emerging new international order. Hostility toward the old order spurred major European thinkers to develop new political theories to rationalize and justify the territorial nature of independent political entities emerging across the continent. In so doing, they started discussing the Jews not only as a malignant theological phenomenon, but as a historical model and religious minority that presented a challenge to Christian-majority sovereign states.[373]

---

373   The advent of modernity was obviously not a single revolutionary event, and it took time for Europe to relinquish the chains of religion, which continued to play a central role in politics well into the twentieth century. Even today, Europe has its own political questions about religion—mainly in regard to the growth of Islam.

The Reformation was followed by the Thirty Years' War (1618–1648)–a predominantly religious war between Protestants and Catholics, which tore the Holy Roman Empire asunder. This new socio-political reality led to the Treaty of Westphalia of 1648.

The war had profoundly affected the structure of Jewish communities and their position in Europe. Countless Jews were uprooted; they became refugees fleeing persecution, disease, and the atrocities of war. Others migrated in search of new opportunities that were opening across the continent. The Thirty Years' War dramatically transformed Jewish demography and geography, as historian Yosef Kaplan documents.[374]

The Treaty of Westphalia created new territorial states and a continental order that was the antithesis of the universalist Catholic vision. The European peace debated at Westphalia was indeed a Christian peace, but surprisingly, its architects showed an interest in the model of Jewish sovereignty in antiquity. As Reformation ripped through Christendom, it had brought with it a "Hebraist" theological-philosophical debate that made the heritage of the Hebrew Bible an important ideological pillar of post-Catholic Europe. In later years, the contribution that ancient Hebrew statehood made to the Reformation would become a key factor in the emergence of modern nationalist movements and nation-states throughout the nineteenth century.

Prominent Protestant theologians and thinkers between the sixteenth and eighteenth centuries studied Hebrew, familiarized themselves with rabbinic and Talmudic literature, and based some of their doctrines on the Hebrew kingdoms of David and Solomon, which became their template for modern European regimes. Among Europe's Hebraist thinkers were Switzerland's Cornelius Bertram,

---

374 Yosef Kaplan, "Amsterdam and Ashkenazic Migration in the Seventeenth Century," *Studia Rosenthaliana* 23 (1989), 22–44.

who published his treatise *De Republica Hebraeorum* in 1641;[375] England's Thomas Hobbes, perhaps the greatest political theorist of the early modern age; the legal theorist John Selden; France's Jean Bodin, an architect of modern political theory; Flanders's Hugo Grotius, the father of international law; and James Harrington, another Englishman, who was the first to argue for the restoration of Jewish territorial sovereignty.

The mid-seventeenth century was also the age of Oliver Cromwell, the autocratic ruler of Interregnum England, who believed that the readmission of the Jews was a theological imperative that would herald the reappearance of Christ. In 1649, with Puritan rule at its height, two English Baptists in Amsterdam, Johanna and Ebenezer Cartwright, petitioned the English government "that this Nation of England, with the inhabitants of the Netherlands, shall be the first and the readiest to transport Izraell's [*sic*] sons and daughters in their ships to the land promised to their forefathers...for an everlasting Inheritance."[376] They also called for the annulment of the Edict of Expulsion of 1290, which had been in force in England for over 300 years, since the days of King Edward I. According to historian Barbara Tuchman, the Puritan movement's deep interest in the return of the Jews to Palestine and England was not out of love for the Jews but their faith in the divine promise that their dispersal to all lands and restoration to Palestine, would hasten the Second Coming of Christ.[377]

The Bible and its Hebrew spirit had a sweeping influence on the Puritans, and Cromwell, as a zealous Puritan, wanted to not only convert Amsterdam's Jewish merchants but also to use them in

---

375   The treatise cited the Hebrew Bible as the most important source of inspiration for the establishment of good sovereign regimes. See Yoram Hazony, "Judaism and the Modern State," *Azure* (2005), 33–51.

376   Barbara Tuchman, *Bible and Sword: England and Palestine from the Bronze Age to Balfour* (New York: Random House, 2014), 106.

377   Ibid.

England's economic competition with the Dutch Republic, which spiraled into war in 1652. He permitted Jews to enter England without official legislation, contrary to a court decision which approved their entry in small numbers and in accordance with strict financial criteria. In 1653, he convened the so-called "Barebone's Parliament" to draft a new constitution for England inspired by the New Testament. However, his effort failed, and some condemned Cromwell for attempting to "Judaize" English law.[378]

Central to the Jews' return to England was the role of Menasseh Ben Israel, a renowned Amsterdam rabbi whose book, *El Conciliador,* aimed to prove the logical consistency of the Hebrew Bible and became a bestseller in Europe. Ben Israel argued that there was no friction between the Jewish faith in the Ingathering of Exiles in the Holy Land and his petition to readmit the Jews to England. He also pushed for translations of the Bible to be printed, and distributed them across Europe. Joseph Athias, a well-known Jewish printer in Amsterdam, boasted that he had printed one million copies of the Hebrew Bible in English and "not a single farm worker or maidservant in England or Scotland was without a copy."

Cromwell invited Menasseh Ben Israel to participate in the debate over the possible readmission of the Jews to England. He gave the Puritans scriptural justification for the policy, showing that the worldwide dispersal of the Jews was part of the process of Redemption. Today, Ben Israel is considered the founder of English Jewry.

Fania Oz-Salzberger contends that biblical Israel was the source of the concept of the rule of law within fixed borders, as well as constitutional principles concerning the decentralization of power, as advocated by prominent Western political theorists in the seventeenth century. "Jewish texts were not accidental sources for the subtle discussion of liberty engaged in by seventeenth-century

---

378   Ibid., 122.

thinkers," she writes. "There were several important ideas about the nature of freedom, which early modern Europe learned from the Bible and its Jewish interpreters, and from them alone."[379] Other scholars have similarly emphasized that the ancient Hebrew republic was a powerful source of inspiration for liberal political thought, which posited that human reason was the source of sovereign authority in God's design. This position flew in the face of absolute monarchs claiming the divine right of kings.[380]

During the seventeenth and eighteenth centuries, political philosophy focused on territorial (i.e., national) sovereignty, and the ethos of the ancient Jewish republic gained prominence in devising an international order of peaceful Christian states. It was in this context that there emerged serious intellectual thought about restoring Jewish sovereignty.

The prevailing belief in Europe was that the Jews' religious and cultural particularism prevented them from being integrated in their lands of residence because they would presumably upset the religious balance of the emerging republics. English thinker James Harrington, therefore, made a radical proposal in his utopian 1656 work *The Commonwealth of Oceana*: the Jews should be accorded territory to establish their own independent state. Inspired by the French philosopher Jean Bodin, the father of the concept of "modern sovereignty," Harrington credited the Jews with political wisdom, which they had acquired in antiquity, preserved throughout their endless exile, and could revisit to resurrect an independent polity. Since he believed their integration into the Commonwealth of England was undesirable, and their religious devotion threatened Anglican unity, Harrington proposed that the Jews be granted territory to form a sovereign polity and govern their own affairs. He saw their ability

---

379   Fania Oz-Salzberger, "The Jewish Roots of Western Freedom," *Azure* 13 (2002), 91–92.

380   Eric Nelson, *The Hebrew Republic: Jewish Sources and the Transformation of European Political Thought* (Cambridge, MA: Harvard University Press, 2010), 134.

to maintain their particularism as a mark of their national resilience and entitlement to sovereignty.

Harrington can be considered an early pioneer of political thinking about Jewish sovereignty, although his vision of statehood was quite different from that of Spinoza (and later Herzl), whose aim was to advance Jewish interests.[381] For him, the purpose of a Jewish state was to provide the Jews the means to foster their separate and unique religious identity, just as England would do for Anglicanism. In the spirit of the age, Harrington saw the state as primarily a vehicle for nurturing a coherent and collective religious identity, which is why he scorned states with minorities and supported restoring Jewish independence. He distributed his book to members of Parliament in 1656, the same year that Cromwell decided to allow Jews to settle in England again. Presumably, Harrington wanted to warn the English against making their country a multicultural state of minorities.[382] Notwithstanding the Hebraist zeal of Harrington and others, it would take another two centuries before the restoration of Jewish sovereignty became a subject of serious debate in Europe.

Sabbatai Zevi: False Messiah

As major thinkers embraced the heritage of the ancient Hebrew state as a model for Europe after the Thirty Years' War, the Jewish world was engulfed by a wave of messianism in the seventeenth century. Reports of the advent of the messiah—Sabbatai Zevi from Smyrna—found a captive audience, not only in the traumatized victims of the

---

381 Meirav Jones and Yossi Shain, "Modern Sovereignty and the Non-Christian, or Westphalia's Jewish State," *Review of International Studies* 43, no. 5 (2017), 1–17.

382 David Armitage, "The Cromwellian Protectorate and the Languages of Empire," *The Historical Journal* 35, no. 3 (1992), 531–555.

eastern European pogroms of 1648–1649, but also in stable, established Jewish communities all across Europe and North Africa.

This outburst of messianic fervor, known as Sabbateanism, coupled with a widely reported secret repudiation of elements of Jewish law and rabbinic authority, is generally considered to have been a fleeting historical episode, but it was in fact an early herald of modernity and Zionism and the first practical attempt to end the Diaspora mode of existence. Gershom Scholem believed that it drew upon "a new and profound human experience—the experience of liberty" and breached the walls of the late-medieval ghetto. "The Sabbatean heresy made possible the secularization of a traditional society," writes historian Mor Altshuler, "and the modern movements of the Haskalah and Reform Judaism broke through the walls. Secular ideologies like Socialism, Communism and Zionism arose in their wake. They would not have been able to take root in Jewish society if the walls of the spiritual ghetto had not been breached in the days of Sabbatai Zevi."[383]

Sabbatai Zevi's vision of messianic sovereignty gripped the Jewish world and strengthened the bonds between its communities around the globe. It was given a serious boost by a self-proclaimed prophet known as Nathan of Gaza, who served Sabbatai Zevi in a role akin to that of a public relations minister.

Nathan of Gaza was born in Jerusalem in 1643 to parents who had immigrated from Europe. In his twenties, he moved to Gaza where he studied the Kabbalistic writings of Isaac Luria and started having prophetic visions. Nathan spread rumors of the imminent establishment of a Jewish state in Gaza, which he envisioned as "the temporary capital of Israel."

The stories about a "Jewish messiah" who was about to restore

---

383   Mor Altshuler, "Messianic Elements in Early Hasidism: The Controversy between Ben-Zion Dinur and Gershom Scholem," in *Gershom Scholem (1897–1982): In Memoriam: Volume One*, ed. Yosef Dan (Jerusalem: Mandel Institute for Jewish Studies), 6–7 [Hebrew].

his people to their land rippled through Europe's capitals and were latched onto by parties with geopolitical designs to weaken the Ottoman Empire. Prominent European leaders, including the pope and the doges of Venice, sworn enemies of the Turks, took an interest in Sabbateanism and questioned Jews close to them about the rumors from the East.

Historians Mordechai Breuer and Michael Graetz describe the Jews as praying, fasting, putting themselves through purification rituals, and selling their personal property to prepare themselves for the voyage to the Holy Land. They even heeded Zevi's call to celebrate the days of mourning over the destruction of the Temple as days of jubilation—this time, they were truly going home. One eyewitness recalled the indescribable joy in the Hamburg Jewish community whenever letters arrived with news of Sabbatai Zevi. The Portuguese Jewish recipients of the letters would bring them to synagogue and read them out loud. Some Jews even sold their homes, so adamant were they that the Redemption was imminent.[384] This intense anticipation of imminent redemption led Hamburg's Jewish community to dispatch a delegation to Constantinople to pay homage to the messiah. Vienna and Prague rapidly became vibrant centers of Sabbateanism, and 400 Jewish men from Frankfurt began organizing their journey to the Holy Land, in the footsteps of an earlier advance party. In Mainz, rabbis held daily discussions about the latest developments, and Jews in Franconia, and principally around Nuremberg, made urgent preparations for the advent of the messiah.

The saga of Sabbatai Zevi ended in a massive fiasco on September 17, 1666. The Ottoman Sultan offered Zevi the option of converting to Islam or being put to the sword. Zevi chose to abandon

---

384   Mordechai Breuer and Michael Graetz, *German-Jewish History in Modern Times. Volume 1: Tradition and Enlightenment, 1600–1780* (New York: Columbia University Press, 1996).

his Jewish faith. The shock of his conversion created immense cognitive dissonance for his acolytes, who insisted that this must be a cryptic step on the road to salvation. "The conversion of the messiah was shocking to the majority of believers, who felt betrayed and returned to their previous lives with a feeling of profound disappointment and despair," writes Turkish academic Cengiz Sisman. "Once the dust settled…a few of his believers began to reinterpret his conversion as a sort of 'holy apostasy,' a 'secret mission,' deliberately undertaken with a particular mystical purpose in mind."[385]

Many Jews still bore the traumatic legacy of Sabbateanism in the eighteenth century, and mutual recriminations about hidden pockets of false messianism led to intra-communal strife.

The fiasco of Zevi's messianic sovereignty and the chaos that followed his apostasy weakened rabbinical Judaism as a whole. But the episode also harmed the ideal of "ascending" to the Land of Israel and spurred conversions to Protestantism. The Jews' disillusionment, opined Scholem, expedited the advent of the liberal, secular Judaism of the Haskalah, which abandoned the notion of waiting for the messiah to bring redemption. In fact, some of the devotees of Reform Judaism emerged from families who had remained faithful, sometimes covertly, to Sabbatai Zevi and his messianic vision of return.[386]

Spinoza the "Zionist"

Just as the mystical, messianic movement of Sabbatai Zevi to restore Jewish sovereignty was collapsing, a more secular conception was already taking shape in the mind of Benedict Spinoza. In 1670, just a

385 Cengiz Sisman, "Sabbatai Sevi's Conversion to Islam," *Tablet Magazine*, December 22, 2016, https://www.tabletmag.com/jewish-arts-and-culture/220449/sabbatai-sevis-conversion-to-islam.

386 David Klinghoffer, *Why The Jews Rejected Jesus: A Turning Point in Western History* (New York: Three Leaves Press, 2005), 196–197.

few years after the frenzy of Sabbateanism, he published his *Tractatus Logico-Philosophicus*, which had a profound impact on the Sephardic Jewish community of Amsterdam. According to Yirmiyahu Yovel, Spinoza undoubtedly knew about Sabbateanism, and part of his work was an indirect response to Sabbateans themselves. His secular rationalism was the antithesis of the irrational frenzy that gripped Sabbatai Zevi's followers.[387]

Spinoza argued that the Hebrew Bible, like monotheism, was a human creation and had served in the past to mobilize Jewish national identity and lay down the law as the ostensible "words of the living God." The Torah was not a gift from heaven, but the fruit of the national Jewish spirit. Moses was not a prophet to whom God revealed himself, but a statesman and a political leader, full of faith and initiative, who used the language of prophecy to find and consolidate the Israelite nation.

According to Spinoza, the Jews' struggle for sovereignty could similarly draw on Jewish theology. "If the foundations of the [Jewish] religion did not effeminate their hearts," Spinoza wrote, "I would absolutely believe that someday, given the opportunity, they will set up their state again and that God will choose them anew, so changeable are human affairs."[388] In other words, the Jews would one day band together to fight for independence, and their achievement could be spun as God "choosing" his people anew. Securing Jewish sovereignty, Spinoza emphasized, would require the Jews to adopt an activist political stance and sever themselves from religious faith.

Centuries later, Spinoza's thesis would receive great attention from Zionist thinkers, who adopted the modern concept that Jews were members of a nation that should be in command of its

---

387   Yirmiyahu Yovel, "Spinoza and His People—The First Secular Jew?," *Jerusalem Studies in Jewish Thought* (1988), 357–385.

388   Steven B. Smith, *Spinoza's Book of Life* (New Haven: Yale University Press, 2003), 194. See also Yovel, *Spinoza and Other Heretics*.

own destiny. Spinoza sought to secularize history and see events as subject to the mundane laws of nature. He regarded the idea of the Jews as the "chosen people" as a rallying cry for action, not a divinely ordained fact, and rejected the traditional rabbinic belief that redemption would only come as God's reward for ritual devotion. Spinoza's writings inspired the political Zionism of Leon Pinsker and Theodor Herzl, and David Ben-Gurion later embraced him as a Zionist prophet. Philosopher Leo Strauss also deemed him one of the founders of Zionism.[389]

If we compare Spinoza's idea of Jewish sovereignty with Harrington's vision of a Jewish state, there is a certain historical irony—it was the English Christian who envisioned a cultural religious entity, whereas the man born and raised as a Jew saw it in clearly secular terms. Spinoza was indifferent, even hostile, toward what we might now call ethno-nationalism when applied to the Jews, and particularly toward Orthodoxy and its focus on religious observance and passively waiting for the messiah. He was not a tribalist, and he espoused an inclusive Judeo-Christian identity that allowed for pluralism in the public sphere.

In Spinoza's "dogmas of the universal faith," he emphasized that the source of human piety was reason and rejected the elevation of any theology over another. "Holiness of life is not particular to the Roman Church but is common to all. And since we know through this…that we dwell in God and God dwells in us, it follows that whatever it is that distinguishes the Roman Church from the others, it is something superfluous and based merely on superstition."[390]

Until the turn of the nineteenth century, the theories of Jewish sovereignty advocated by Harrington and Spinoza remained on the

---

389   Smith, *Spinoza's Book of Life*, 194.
390   Richard Mason, "Spinoza on Religious Choice," *Philosophy* 69, no. 270 (1994), 453.

intellectual sidelines and failed to allay the misery of Jewish life in western Europe. Even Sabbatai Zevi's initial success and tragic downfall did not lead to a profound break with tradition, because Jewish history was well acquainted with messianic hopes that were dashed.[391] As long as Europe remained a Christian continent, the Jews were unwanted, lacking territorial roots and condemned to eternal wandering. Their communities accepted, to some extent, the mark of Cain they were branded with and tried to rationalize their scattered existence. Their yearning for a renewal of sovereignty remained a matter of theory and theology.

Most Western European Jews in the late Middle Ages and early modern era lived in ghettos, under discriminatory regimes and conditions of persistent uncertainty. This was true of Jews in eastern Europe, who, by the sixteenth century, formed the majority of continental Jewry. Much like those who lived in central and western Europe as well, they almost always inhabited the bottom rung of the social ladder; they lived on the outskirts of cities, were differentiated by their clothing and religion, and lacked legal status. But even there, their situation varied from country to country and region to region, depending on the historical, social, and cultural conditions. Many places in Europe forbade any Jewish presence, and others only let Jews enter during the daytime. Elsewhere, Jews enjoyed extensive economic and religious freedom. This was the case mainly in Calvinist and "multi-religious" Amsterdam, where tolerance reigned, and the Jews flourished.

The founders of the Jewish community of Amsterdam were descendants of conversos from Spain and Portugal. Their ancestors had suffered the forced conversions of the Inquisition, but many of them who were raised as Catholics now returned to openly practicing Judaism. Holland was their preferred refuge after the Treaty of

---

391 Breuer and Graetz, *German-Jewish History in Modern Times*.

Utrecht of 1579, which promised religious tolerance, and the successful rebellion of the Low Countries against the Spanish Empire of Philip II, which led to Dutch independence in 1581.[392] Iberian Jews were joined later by poor Ashkenazi Jewish refugees from the Thirty Years' War and survivors of the depredations of 1648–49, when Jews were massacred by the Cossacks in Lithuania and hundreds of communities were destroyed.

The Spanish-Portuguese community enjoyed a warm welcome in the Dutch Republic "whose prolonged confrontation with Spain aroused considerable identification among citizens with those who were viewed as victims of the Iberian Inquisition and Catholic intolerance."[393] These Iberian Jews turned Amsterdam into "the Jerusalem of the north." Some were involved in international and colonial commerce and often represented the high-power rulers in Europe. Its leaders, among them Menasseh Ben Israel, created the intellectual infrastructure for interfaith dialogue with Protestant philosophers and theologians, including on interpretations of scripture. Ben Israel wrote: "I have held friendship with many great men, and the wisest, and most eminent of all Europe; and also they came to see me, at my house, and I had many friendly discourses with them."[394] However, despite the great differences between Holland and other countries, "the legal status of Dutch Jews, like that of their brethren elsewhere, remained unchanged," according to the historian Jacob Katz. "The Jew had no legal claim to acceptance or toleration."[395]

---

392 The United Netherlands, a union of seven provinces, was officially recognized at the Peace of Westphalia of 1648.

393 Yosef Kaplan, "Genta Politica: The Portuguese Jews of Amsterdam vis-à-vis Dutch Society," in *Dutch Jews as Perceived by Themselves and by Others*, eds. Chaya Brasz and Yosef Kaplan (Leiden: Brill, 2001), 20–21.

394 Menasseh Ben Israel, *Vindiciae Judaeorum, or a Letter in Answer to Certain Questions Propounded by a Noble and Learned Gentleman* (1656), reprinted in *Menasseh ben Israel's Mission To Oliver Cromwell: Being a Reprint of the Pamphlets Published by Menasseh ben Israel to Promote the Re-admission of the Jews to England, 1649–1656*, ed. Lucien Wolf (London: Macmillan, 1901), 137.

395 Katz, *Out Of The Ghetto*, 11–16.

Indeed, the model of religious pluralism that took root in Holland in the seventeenth century did not mean religious *freedom*. On the contrary, the Dutch state enforced a rigid division between religious movements and sects. In 1619, Amsterdam's city elders announced that Jews, as an ethno-religious group, could only be admitted if it were ascertained that they obeyed their own commandments, believed in God and the afterlife, and swore to neither marry nor employ Christians. Jewish community leaders had to provide guarantees that their congregants would all respect this religious separation.[396]

The former conversos, now settled in Holland, had to confront a painful dilemma—having lived for years in Christian society, publicly disavowing their Judaism, and hiding their true identity, Jewish practice was now alien to them. According to scholar Yosef Kaplan, religious identity "could not fully express these Jews' ethnic and social identity."[397] Yosef Hayim Yerushalmi adds: "The remarkable thing is not that they failed, but that so many succeeded [to remain Jewish]."[398]

Given these identity challenges and the Dutch Republic's insistence on religious segregation, Jewish community leaders took an increasingly hardline approach to religion to circumscribe the community and tighten their control over it. They greatly stepped up the use of excommunication as a tool of control; new regulations were also issued to deter community members from straying from strict observance. Offenders were forced to undergo degrading ceremonies

---

396   Dominique Coal, *Civil Society and Fanaticism: Conjoined Histories*, trans. Amy Jacob (Stanford, CA: Stanford University Press, 1997), 183.

397   Yosef Kaplan, *An Alternative Path to Modernity: The Sephardi Diaspora in Western Europe* (Leiden: Brill, 2000), 17.

398   Yosef Hayim Yerushalmi, "Conversos Returning to Judaism in the 17th Century, Their Jewish Knowledge and Psychological Readiness," *Proceedings of the World Congress of Jewish Studies* 9 (1969), 209 [Hebrew].

in synagogues and to pay stiff fines.[399] The late historian Zeev Levy likened the descendants of the conversos who became strictly observant to modern-day, newly religious Jews, some of whom become particularly zealous to protect themselves from their own instincts and surroundings.[400] In his opinion, the reason for Amsterdam Jewry's uncompromising attitude towards Spinoza and others like him was precisely this converso background.[401]

While many are familiar with the story of Spinoza's excommunication, less well-known is the tragic fate of Uriel da Costa, who killed himself in 1640 after the humiliation of being whipped in the synagogue and then trampled on by the congregation.

Da Costa was a Portuguese philosopher, the son of a Catholic father and a mother from a converso family. After learning of his roots, he decided to become a Jew. He moved to Amsterdam, where the fanatical rabbinical Judaism he encountered was far from the biblical faith he had studied in the scriptures. He denounced the rabbis as "Pharisees" who had distorted Mosaic law, and was violently excommunicated until he confessed his sins.

In his *Exemplar Humanae Vitae*, Uriel da Costa described the humiliation that ultimately led to his suicide:

> I made my entrance into the synagogue which was filled with men and women out of curiosity to be spectators. And at the time appointed I went up into the desk which stood in the middle of it and with a distinct voice read over the form of confession

---

399   Yosef Kaplan, "The Struggle against Travelers to Spain and Portugal in the Western Sephardi Diaspora," *Zion* LXIV (1999), 65–100 [Hebrew].

400   Zeev Levy, "On the Sephardic and *Converso* Background to Spinoza's Philosophy," *Pe'amim* 49 (1991), 89 [Hebrew].

401   Ibid.

which they had drawn up for me, viz. that I deserved to die a thousand deaths for the crimes and misdemeanors I had committed.... I stripped myself naked down to the waist, tied a napkin about my head, pulled off my shoes and, holding up my arms above my head, clasped a sort of pillar in my hands to which the door-keeper tied them with a band. Having thus prepared myself for my punishment, the virger came to me and with a scourge of leather tongues gave me nine and thirty stripes according to the custom of the Jews....

This correction being over, I was ordered to sit on the ground and then the Doctor came to me and absolved me from my excommunication. So now the gate of heaven, which was doubly locked and barred against me before, was flung open all on a sudden.... After this I put on my clothes and went to the door of the synagogue, where I prostrated myself, the door-keeper holding up my head whilst all both old and young passed over me, stepping with one foot on the lower part of my legs and behaving with ridiculous and foolish gestures, more like monkeys than human creatures.

Today, ultra-Orthodox Israelis who seek greater freedom and challenge their rabbis' absolute authority might also be ostracized from their communities and families. Those who seek to integrate into Israeli society—serving in the military, finding their own spouses, or accepting the primacy of civil law—are also often met with violence and isolation. Can ultra-Orthodox rabbis use the threat of ostracism to protect their communities from modernity, or will overusing this sanction erode their authority?

In seventeenth century Amsterdam, the Jewish practice of excommunication incensed the Dutch state, which banned its use without explicit permission from civil courts. Its effectiveness later waned because of overuse and the advent of modernity.[402] The growing power of the modern state, and the Jewish bourgeoisie's demands for freedom from the yoke of rabbinical rule, ultimately eroded Jewish communal autonomy and the status of its rabbis and leaders, who had served for generations as "a distant echo of ancient Jewish sovereignty."[403]

Court Jews: Harbingers of Modernity

Outside of Amsterdam, the Jews' segregated ghetto life prevented the formation of a clear doctrine to regulate them as a minority and as an integral part of society and the state. Their integration into the fabric of gentile society by making them equal citizens could have lent them a semblance of normality.

Historian Derek Penslar observes that their exclusion from the trade guilds and agriculture (due to the ban on land ownership) in the Middle Ages compelled wealthier Jews to focus on moneylending, while the poorer majority earned their living from petty commerce. European kings harshly condemned moneylending and money changing, but the industry was an important part of their accumulation of power, as it gave them access to cash without having

---

402   Yosef Kaplan, "The Herem in the Sephardic Community of Amsterdam in the 18th Century," *Proceedings of the Tenth World Congress of Jewish Studies* 2, no. 1 (1990), 195–201 [Hebrew].

403   Mittelman, *The Scepter Shall Not Depart from Judah*, 47.

to overtax their subjects and disrupt government services, both of which would have led to unrest and threatened their regimes.[404] The Catholic Church also condemned usury as a grave sin, and in the thirteenth century, Christian merchants in northern Italy who indulged in the practice were branded as heretics, denied a Christian burial, and sometimes even forcibly banished.

The Christians' perception of Jews as driven by greed was no less a part of their demonization than the blood libels and accusations of ritual murder and black magic. In 1530, a German-Jewish convert to Christianity, Anton Margaritha, wrote a book called *Der gantze Jüdisch Glaub* (*The Whole Jewish Belief*). He argued that it was the Jews' addiction to usury that prevented them from embracing Christ, so they should be forced into physical labor to eradicate their pathology. It was in this spirit that Martin Luther wrote his venomous *On the Jews and Their Lies* a few years later. The father of the Reformation also demanded that they be compelled to perform menial labor and work the land in to erase their criminality on the road to converting them to Christianity.[405]

The economic situation of the Jews was largely determined by the economic situations of the countries they inhabited and local tax collection mechanisms. Ostensibly, the larger a kingdom and its population, the more profitable its tax collection should have been, but there was often a drawback. Azar Gat contends that smaller and socially homogeneous European states such as Holland and England enjoyed effective tax collection, whereas the larger states—notably Spain, France, and the Holy Roman Empire—struggled. For these states, the enormous expenditures involved in waging wars rendered tax collection even more critical. Tax rises induced great poverty and imperiled the countries that ground

---

404   Derek Penslar, *Shylock's Children: Economics and Jewish Identity in Modern Europe* (Berkeley: University of California Press, 2001), 13–18.

405   Ibid.

their populations down, effectively killing the goose that laid the golden egg.[406]

Many kingdoms, notably Spain and France, went bankrupt due to the collapse of banking systems that had extended them credit to wage war and maintain their armies. Their failure to pay their debts not only destabilized and collapsed their financial institutions, but also prejudiced their ability to secure funding because of their poor credit. The result was a diminished fighting capacity and weaker sovereignty.

By 1630, there were almost no Jews in Spain, France, or England. Western Europeans at the time knew the Jews only indirectly, through anti-Jewish books and polemics, or in stereotypes nourished by the fables and folklore of Christian preachers.[407]

The Jews, living as defenseless subjects in the far-flung rural areas to which they had been banished, were dependent on the protection of the local nobility, who needed their money. It was only thanks to the Thirty Years' War and its semi-feudal battles, that their plight marginally improved, because "every feudal household needed the equivalent of the court Jews."[408]

The court Jews formed a small stratum responsible for handling the financial affairs of German princes and other European noblemen. Their influence lasted some 150 years, from the mid-seventeenth century until the French Revolution, and grew against the backdrop of the collapse of centralized governments in the divided societies of German-speaking central Europe. But even when Jews were promoted to the rank of *Hofjude*–court Jew–they remained a convenient target for pillaging by the state, although some rulers grasped that robbing and expelling them jeopardized a source of

---

406   Azar Gat, *War in Human Civilization* (Oxford: Oxford University Press, 2006), 486–488.

407   Kaplan, "Genta Politica," 21.

408   Hannah Arendt, *The Origins of Totalitarianism* (San Diego: Harcourt Brace Jovanovich, 1979), 19.

easy revenue. It was for this reason that the Hamburg city senate rejected the city council's demand to banish the Jews in the wake of the publication of the anti-Semitic pamphlet, *The Wandering Jew.* German princes and their military commanders even protected the Jews from mobs seeking to plunder the ghettos "because they needed the money of the Jews for the conduct of the war."[409]

Penslar explains that by extorting money from Jews in the form of forced loans, European rulers were able to muster resources while honoring the Christian prohibition on usury. Hypocritically, they used this money to finance their activities while calling the Jews robbers. Thus, European rulers demonized the Jews while shielding themselves from censure. They espoused theological arguments, by which the Jews' monopoly over usury allowed Christians to resist the temptation to engage in this despicable practice themselves.

Nevertheless, the decline of religion and the consolidation of the modern state and the free market highlighted the Jews' role in the economy, which became a core issue in their integration into sixteenth-century European society. The court Jews of Germany and Austria stood out in this respect. However, despite their economic and political importance, they remained a despised group, dependent on the favor of the local princes, and "there was no security of tenure, as in bureaucratic organizations, nor could the Court Jew transmit the position to his descendants, as in hereditary service aristocracies."[410]

The German principalities were often burdened by heavy debts, due to the high cost of maintaining their independence. It became enormously difficult for them to obtain loans after the collapse of the European banking system because of the Thirty Years' War, and many principalities could not finance and operate their mercenary forces.

---

409   F. L. Carsten, "The Court Jews: A Prelude to Emancipation," *The Leo Baeck Institute Year Book* 3, no. 1 (1958), 143.

410   Lewis A. Coser, "The Alien as a Servant of Power: Court Jews and Christian Renegades," *American Sociological Review* 37, no. 5 (1972), 577.

The wars between France and the Holy Roman Empire devoured the latter's ability to maintain sovereignty across its territory, foster a stable middle class, collect taxes, and obtain credit from international banks. This situation opened new economic possibilities for Jews with capital and initiative, particularly in German-speaking regions bedeviled by the persistent fear of governmental and institutional collapse.

Sociologist Lewis Coser observes that absolute rulers try to accumulate power that is independent of their subjects and prefer to rely on weak, marginal, downtrodden groups that are not part of the socio-national mainstream. These groups cry out for protection and are grateful for the opportunity to get closer to the centers of power. Therefore, they become the ideal supporters for absolute rulers who find themselves low on resources and power.[411] Such groups are the most dependable and least threatening—like the court Jews in the German principalities and the Habsburg monarchies after the Thirty Years' War. A small minority of the wealthier Jews—including those who traded in jewelry, currencies, precious metals, and tobacco—became attractive to the rulers and were installed as court Jews. They supplied the rulers with loans and tended to the needs of their guards: "Though the Jews were by far the weakest in the triad of forces contending for power and influence, their support was nevertheless central to the victory of absolutist rulers."[412]

Some court Jews were elevated to the nobility, especially in Austria and France. They became landowners and major players in the development of the textile industry, particularly velvets and laces. Their families formed a Jewish aristocracy across Europe through marriages, and they sometimes enjoyed intimate relationships with royal families due to the latter's dependence on them. Some became influential actors in politics, thanks to their close royal ties, and

---

411   Coser, "The Alien as a Servant of Power," 575–576.
412   Ibid., 576.

others were dispatched on international diplomatic assignments. Court Jews enjoyed exemptions from the prohibitions applied to their less fortunate brethren on the fringes of society.

Some became Christians, but as Coser has pointed out, their conversion negated their special status as court Jews. Sometimes princes appointed those who retained their Jewish heritage as representatives to their communities; this was to the chagrin of those communities, who regarded them as a fifth column. Some also became philanthropists, helped to build community institutions and lobbied for improvements to the Jewish condition.

Court Jews and their families remained intensely dependent on individual princes, whose deaths sometimes led to their downfall. They also remained subject to acute hostility from German townsfolk, which often led to sanctions and violence. For example, in 1717, Mannheim decided to bar Jews from wearing clothes adorned with silver or gold. Two years later, the Hamburg senate, the same body that had refused to allow the expulsion of the Jews, forbade them from carrying elaborate walking sticks, swords, and pistols.[413]

Despite the meteoric rise of the court Jews, their well-being was far from assured; they were often scapegoated, as if they bore personal responsibility for the princes' failures. But, as Coser argues, they undoubtedly played a critical role in the growth of the modern German state.[414] Court Jews were the first to be emancipated, paving the way for the general improvement of the Jews' situation in the nineteenth century. According to the French *Encyclopédie*, court Jews also played a supporting role in European politics; it likened them to "cogs and nails needed in a great building in order to join and hold together all its parts."[415]

---

413 Carsten, "The Court Jews," 140–156.
414 Coser, "The Alien as a Servant of Power," 577.
415 Elon, *The Pity of It All*, 28.

The "Economic Jew"

How did it come to pass that, at the turn of the nineteenth century, the image of Jews was transformed from a marginalized, sickly, and impoverished religious sect to that of a powerful cabal that supposedly pulled the strings of global capital and international politics? The rise of capitalism and the Enlightenment inspired them to hope that they would soon expunge the stigma of being an accursed and menacing minority and be accepted as an integral part of European nations. Enlightened Christians hoped the Jews would metamorphose—in their character, habits, occupations, and faith—and become civilized and equal citizens, and even an integral part of the global capitalist economy. No longer was the debate about Jews mainly theological; their status was now discussed predominantly in terms of economics, society, politics, and psychology. This discourse inspired new ideas about the "Jewish Question," which became a core issue of public debate in Europe and international diplomacy.

Jews in Europe remained a scattered minority. Frankfurt, for example, had a Jewish presence since at least the twelfth century, but they suffered regular pogroms, such as the massacre of 1241, when the community was all but wiped out. Frankfurt Jewry was also hit by the Black Death, also known as bubonic plague (1348–1349), which killed tens of millions throughout Europe. The Jewish quarter was devastated not only by the plague but by massacres orchestrated by the Christian flagellation movement; its members accused the Jews of causing the plague by poisoning Frankfurt's wells.

Frankfurt Jewry was gradually revived and even prospered economically until 1462, when Jews were, once again, summarily forced out after Christian competitors complained that they were harming their businesses. They were called "worms" and ordered to move to the ghetto known as the *Judengasse*—a narrow alley abutting a reeking canal outside the city walls, which became their home for the next three centuries.

Even as late as the eighteenth century, the Jews of Frankfurt suffered rioting, looting, and spates of capricious violence. They were compelled to pay a protection tax and barred from owning land, farming, working as craftsmen, and leaving the ghetto after dark. In the daytime, their movement was also restricted. The number of marriages permitted was capped, as were the number of children they could bear.

This was the world into which Mayer Amschel Rothschild was born in 1744. Rothschild established his banking business as a young man in the 1760s and eventually founded the dynasty that would soon own the biggest financial empire in Europe. He and his five sons set up banks in Frankfurt, Vienna, London, Naples, and Paris, drawing on a network of couriers and agents plugged into every source of political and economic information on the continent. They supplied credit to foreign governments and became major players in the bond markets.

The Jews of Frankfurt, like those in many other places in Europe, had always included a small, wealthy minority who rubbed shoulders with powerful and influential individuals and helped to finance the royal families of Europe. Rothschild himself was exceptionally fortunate during the period of the Napoleonic conquests, thanks to his special relationship with Crown Prince Wilhelm I of Hesse (1743–1821), who deposited much of his wealth with the Jewish financier when he fled from Napoleon's armies. Rothschild guarded it zealously and even enlarged it at great risk to himself. When the prince returned after Napoleon's defeat, he rewarded Rothschild generously and spread the word of his honesty and reliability across Europe.

The rise of the Rothschilds in Europe's major capitals in the post-Napoleonic period engendered conspiracy theories about the power of transnational Jewish finance. In the space of a few decades, Jews stopped being stereotyped as the wandering cobblers who betrayed Christ and were now seen as rich, corrupt capitalists. The Rothschilds' financial clout gave them the reputation of "the kings of the epoch," who used their money to direct armies and nations. It also became part of the conversation about "a design to reclaim the Holy Land for the Jewish people" and their alleged plan for "the restoration of Judea to our ancient race."

Historian Niall Ferguson charts the development of these conspiracy theories in his monumental history of the Rothschild dynasty. One article in an American newspaper in 1830 claimed that the Turkish sultan's financial distress might lead him to sell Jerusalem to the Rothschilds. Similar fabrications appeared in France and Russia, where cartoons appeared showing Jews embarking for the Holy Land in first class cabins, financed by Rothschild money. Comparable allegations were made in Germany. In Britain, Scottish philosopher Thomas Carlyle criticized the election to Parliament of Lionel Rothschild—the first Jew to take a seat in the House of Commons—asking, "How can a real Jew...try to be Senator, or even Citizen of any Country, except his own wretched Palestine, whither all his thoughts and steps and efforts tend?"[416]

Emancipation and the "Jewish Problem"

As long as the old monarchical order prevailed, the Jews were not considered a "problem" in need of a solution.[417] The debate about their role in society entered the agenda in the run-up to the French Revolution, as part of the messy transition from the old world to the

---

416   Niall Ferguson, *The House of Rothschild: Money's Prophets 1798–1848 (Vol. 1)* (New York: Penguin Books, 1998).

417   Reinhard Rurup, "Jewish Emancipation and Bourgeois Society," *The Leo Baeck Institute Yearbook* 14, no. 1, (1969), 69.

new. Much was written about integrating the Jews into the changing world, and the debate reflected the dilemmas faced by France, Germany, and other nations in addressing their own political, economic, and social future. In the late-eighteenth century, Europeans become obsessed with the issue—but they almost never let the *Jews* say what *they* thought about it. The calls to better the Jews' situation and integrate them into society were not made from a philo-Semitic position of respect and tolerance, but the simple (and perhaps deplorable) necessity of reordering enlightened life in modern Europe, given the challenges that the Jews posed as the most problematic test case on the continent.

The debate over Jews' place at the intersection of the modern state and the capitalist economy preoccupied many thinkers in Germany, France, and Britain in the seventeenth and eighteenth centuries. The founder of Pietism in Germany,[418] Philipp Jakob Spener, rejected Martin Luther's hatred of Jews and preached Christian love for them as human beings.[419] But, like Luther, he believed that the Jews could be converted to Christianity by consent; the key was not religious, but socio-economic. If the Jews underwent a metamorphosis and abandoned usury and petty trade, their dignity would be restored.

Spener published his treatise on the Jews in 1680—the same year French theologian Claude Fleury's *Mœurs des Israélites* was published. Fleury argued that the Talmud and usury were deviations that arose from life in exile, and he too believed that if the Jews returned to working the land, they could be normalized and converted to Christianity.

In 1714, Irish philosopher John Toland advocated granting the Jews citizenship in Ireland and Great Britain, hoping they could

---

418   Pietism was a religious movement founded after the Thirty Years' War (1618–1648). It placed an emphasis on personal faith, not on the political role of the Church.

419   Alexander L. Ringer, "Handel and the Jews," *Music and Letters* 42, no. 1 (1961), 18.

make a positive contribution to a policy of mercantilism.[420] When they returned under Cromwell, they were not granted British citizenship. Influenced by Hobbes, Locke, and Spinoza, Toland was the first to advocate for their citizenship.

The radical new idea that the "Jewish problem" was socio-economic rather than religious received another push with the publication of German writer Christian Wilhelm von Dohm's highly influential bestseller *On the Civil Improvement of the Jews* in 1781. Von Dohm argued that the Jews of his time were "corrupt", and Judaism encouraged separatism. But he blamed this situation on the Christians for having marginalized and abused the Jews for generations. The Jews, he wrote, were victims of historical circumstances, and any other group that had suffered the same treatment would have been "guilty of identical errors."[421] Von Dohm proposed turning the Jews into manual laborers and farm workers, as well as cutting them off from petty commerce and moneylending.

From the turn of the nineteenth century, Jews gradually became more active and more important players on this stage. Since the dawn of modernity, they had been excluded from the debate about their own condition. Now, they were invited to join, philosophically and organizationally.

The Jews began to intensively debate the nature of Judaism. Were they a communal-religious tribe, a universal culture, or a political nation? This new debate centered around the contours of their identity and community as states and societies evolved around them.

The Jewish Emancipation in western Europe took place in two

---

420   Mercantilism is an economic doctrine that advocates for increasing a nation's capital and assets through protectionism, encouraging exports and limiting imports. Mercantilists operate on the premise that international trade is a zero-sum game. Countries with trade deficits are "losing," while countries with trade surpluses are "winning."

421   Robert Liberles, "Dohm's Treatise on the Jews: A Defense of the Enlightenment," *The Leo Baeck Institute Yearbook* (1988), 34.

stages, according to historian Reinhard Rürup. The first, starting in 1780, was linked to the events around the French Revolution and continued until the Congress of Vienna in 1815. In this phase, the Jews were not yet active in high politics, but attitudes about them were an important indication of whether European nations, in their philosophy and politics, belonged to the old world or the new. Between 1815 and 1840, reactionary forces tried to turn back the wheels of liberty and modernization, but this kindled an emerging nationalism, revolutionary politics and economics, and the rise of socialism.

The second stage of the Emancipation took place between 1840 and 1870 and caused an earthquake in Europe and tectonic shifts in every nation, as it raised unique challenges. Much of the socio-political thought surrounding the "Jewish question" reflected these upheavals. The Jews themselves responded to this new reality with powerful dynamism and creativity, which affected European life and its zeitgeist—and was influenced by them in turn.[422]

In the first half of the nineteenth century, the primary Jewish response to the potential of modernity was to devise their own theories for civil integration, but in the second half of the century, they started thinking in terms of their Jewish nationality—and acted accordingly. This process culminated in the appearance of Zionism, as an organized political movement, by the turn of the twentieth century.

---

422 Rürup, "Jewish Emancipation and Bourgeois Society," 68–70. David Vital, *A People Apart: A Political History of The Jews in Europe: 1789–1939* (Oxford: Oxford University Press, 1999), 99.

Chapter V: The Jews in the Era of the Modern Nation-State: From Passive Pawns to Active Players

The modern constitutional state was founded on the idea that the source of law lies in human reason, not in arbitrary powers or external authorities. The concept of the rule of law—along with the related principles of individual freedoms and equality—was predicated on the belief that human beings alone were the supreme and final arbiters of a nation's values and norms. The rule of human-made "positive" law was conceived as a replacement for the "natural law" that supposedly reflected a cosmological, divine order, as well as the Christian laws that purported to reflect God's will. In a revolutionary turn from the arbitrary regimes of past centuries in Europe, all citizens—and even Jews, in time—would enjoy full equality before the law, without distinction as to ethnicity, faith, or race.

Towards the end of the eighteenth century, the debate over the Jewish question became an integral part of Europe's transition from the old world to the new, which was known as the Enlightenment. Immanuel Kant, the godfather of modern universal ethics, saw Judaism and the Jews as a hindrance to his Enlightenment project and flatly rebuffed attempts to attach any special historical or theological significance to either. Kant saw the Jews as a historical accident, devoid of any divine message or rationale; they had simply survived through sheer happenstance, and it was time to stop treating them as a separate tribe. Their mere existence was a threat to his enlightened model of laws based on practical rationality and human individuality.

In his 1793 work *Religion within the Bounds of Bare Reason*, Kant wrote that the Jews had long ceased to exist as a political entity, as had the Jewish religion, which had never existed at all. Judaism was "merely a union of a number of people who, since they belonged to a particular stock, formed themselves into a commonwealth under purely political laws, and not into a church."[423]

Kant also repudiated the idea that Judaism had made any meaningful contribution to Protestant Christianity and asserted that Jewish law, in both ancient and contemporary times, lacked any moral value. The notion that the Jews might have any effect upon God and his actions through their prayer was a primitive supposition. Nevertheless, Kant thought it was preposterous to convert the Jews to Protestantism—the correct solution was the "final end" of Judaism itself.

Like some of his contemporaries, Kant pondered whether the Jews were at all capable of fully integrating into German society. He believed that they were morally degenerate, and it was uncertain whether political emancipation would terminate their existence. The intensity of the Jewish disease, therefore, demanded the "euthanasia of Judaism [as] a mortal religion," to enable the nascent German state to consolidate into an advanced political entity.[424]

Following in Kant's footsteps, highly influential German political philosopher Georg Wilhelm Friedrich Hegel (1770–1831) also saw the Jews as an obstacle to the founding of the modern constitutional state. His vision was of a strong and effective liberal central government, one that demanded that citizens profoundly internalize the values of the Enlightenment and regard themselves as free from divine commandments, whether Catholic or Jewish.

Like Kant, Hegel also believed that the Jewish world was debased and fated to disappear. To his mind, Judaism had no

---

423 Amy Newman, "The Death of Judaism in German Protestant Thought from Luther to Hegel," *Journal of the American Academy of Religion* 61, no. 3 (1993), 461.

424 Ibid., 455–484.

historical role to play after the Temple in Jerusalem was destroyed and the Jews were scattered into the four winds, especially since its precepts had been universalized by Christianity. For Hegel, Judaism's elimination was the only logical response in the fight against its tribal and introspective encouragement of human alienation.

Hegel contended that Judaism lacked the basic principles of enlightened society, since it rejected the centrality and primacy of the individual. By seeing themselves as the chosen people and their God as the God of the Jewish nation, they represented a backwards primitivism that exposed their flawed consciousness and inability to transcend to universal thought. They were, in short, a threat to the modern state. After Germany freed itself from the domination of Napoleonic France and its attempts to force Jewish emancipation on an unwilling continent, the next stage would be to crush Judaism as a religion and a culture.[425]

The Kantian and Hegelian vision of enlightenment, although a cornerstone of the modern state, remained a matter of pure theory when it came to the emancipation of German Jews. Moses Hess, one of the early progenitors of Zionism in the second half of the nineteenth century, observed in *Rome and Jerusalem: The Last National Question* that it was not a Jewish disease that afflicted Europe but a German one:

> Even baptism does not free him [the German Jew] from the nightmare of German anti-Semitism. The Germans hate less the religion of the Jews than their race, less their peculiar beliefs than their noses. Neither reform nor baptism, neither education [*bildung*] nor

---

425   Newman, "The Death of Judaism in German Protestant Thought," 469–473.

emancipation, completely opens the gates or social life to the German Jews. They therefore desire to deny their racial descent.... [But] Jewish noses cannot be reformed, and the black, frizzy Jewish hair cannot through conversation be turned into blond, nor by means of a comb become smooth. The Jewish race is one of the original races which, despite climatic influences, has reproduced itself with integrity. The Jewish type throughout the centuries has remained the same.[426]

Indeed, in Hess' view, the Germans remained mired in an instinctive, exclusive racism and anti-Semitism, to the extent that even their philosophical universalism was but a rationalization of racist arrogance.

The Jews of the French Republic

The French Revolution was a turning point in the history of the modern age. It thrust the Jewish question to the fore in a dizzying series of different contexts, including nationalism, church and state, race, economics, and society. The model of the French Republic raised, for the first time ever in Europe, the possibility of no longer treating the Jews as an inferior ethno-religious group and transforming them into equal citizens without converting them to Christianity.[427]

---

426 Ken Kotun-Fromm, *Moses Hess and Modern Jewish Identity* (Bloomington: Indiana University Press, 2001), 86.

427 The French revolutionaries started debating the status of the Jews around the same time as the Germans did in the context of the principalities of the Holy Roman Empire. See Shulamit Volkov, *Walther Rathenau: Weimar's Fallen Statesman* (New Haven: Yale University Press, 2012).

Revolutionary France was the first state in Europe to emancipate the Jews. It did so to the displeasure of many members of the National Assembly, who warned of their economic power and disloyalty to the republic and argued that extending their equality would provoke peasant uprisings. Those in favor of emancipation, however, believed that its failure would violate the spirit and precepts of the revolution and that the Jews should be accorded rights as individual citizens, but by no means as a distinct collective. One member of the National Assembly, Count Stanislas-Marie-Adélaide de Clermont-Tonnerre, famously declared: "We must refuse everything to the Jews as a nation and accord everything to Jews as individuals."[428] In 1791, just two years after the outbreak of the French Revolution, France legislated to make the Jews equal citizens, which enabled them to freely practice any profession and even assume elected office.

Newly enfranchised, they were henceforth Frenchmen "of the Mosaic faith." Historian Shmuel Trigano has written that the French establishment demanded that the Jews renounce their attachments to a broader Jewish people and cease to foster any ethno-religious ties among themselves. "The plan which we are developing," wrote revolutionary cleric Abbé Grégoire, "entails the dissolution of Jewish communities."

Nonetheless, after the revolution, France established a centralized state institution, the Israelite Central Consistory of France, which protected the Jews' rights to religious observance as individual citizens. In 1808, Napoleon surprised them by decreeing that they must submit to this agency's authority. The emperor appears to have been influenced by Catholics who warned him of the supposedly treacherous nature of the Jews as "dishonest peddlers and usurious lenders."

---

428   Lynn Hunt, *Inventing Human Rights: A History* (New York: W.W. Norton, 2007), 158.

The Consistory was to standardize and oversee all aspects of Jewish life, including taxation, legislation, worship, education, and rabbinical powers. This new model, dubbed *franco-judaïsme*, allowed them to be Jewish at home and French outside *("Juif l'internaute, citoyen au dehors")*. Its motto–*patrie et religion*–proudly emphasized loyalty to the French nation as its supreme purpose. Nevertheless, contrary to the vision of the Emancipation, by creating separate institutions for the Jews, France emphasized their being an ethnic faith community at the expense of absolute Frenchness.[429]

The emancipation did not dissolve French Jewry as a community but redefined it via a centralized state institution. Moreover, French Jews managed to sustain their intra-Jewish ethnic loyalty under various pretexts, including raising money for philanthropic projects to assist oppressed Jews overseas.

A gulf had emerged between the declared aims of the emancipation and the institutions entrusted with regulating Jewish life in accordance with those aims. This gap was particularly clear from the establishment of the Alliance Israélite Universelle in 1860, the first transnational Jewish organization devoted to fighting anti-Semitic persecution around the world. It acted in the spirit of the emancipation, concurring that no distinct Jewish community existed in France–although its basic premise was that a worldwide Jewish people certainly *did* exist.

The French Republic's insistence on making the Jews an exception to its model of undifferentiated, secular Frenchness proved that the Jewish question was not about the ability of Jews to integrate as citizens, but France's inability to eradicate the plague of anti-Semitism, as would become evident during the Dreyfus affair in 1894. Yet

---

429   Shmuel Trigano, "Is There a Future for French Jewry?," *Azure* 20 (2005). See also Jonathan Judaken, *Jean-Paul Sartre and the Jewish Question: Anti-Semitism and the Politics of the French Intellectual* (Lincoln: University of Nebraska Press, 2009), 10.

even when anti-Semitism in France peaked on the eve of World War II, the Jews tried to deny it.

Although the drive for assimilation had left French Jews politically vulnerable, the leaders of the Consistory battled against the odds to embrace "ultra-patriotism…as the best antidote to anti-Semitism." They even naively tried to cooperate with the Vichy regime. The tragedy of French Jewry, notes historian Michael Marrus, was their almost blind adherence to the emancipation, even as most Frenchmen cast it aside. The state failed to protect the Jews after the war broke out, and the model of *franco-judaïsme* fell by the wayside. Out of the 300,000 Jews living in France when the Nazis invaded in 1940, some 80,000 of them were deported to Auschwitz by the Vichy regime.[430]

French Jewry, however, rose from the dead after the defeat of the Nazis. Jews who had fought in the resistance established the CRIF (the Representative Council of French Jewish Institutions), a non-religious umbrella organization that rivaled the Consistory. In the 1950s and 1960s, the community flourished and its numbers doubled due to the mass influx of Jews from North Africa. While the Consistory's leadership remained Ashkenazi, incoming Jews from Morocco, Tunisia, and Algeria transformed the face of French Jewry.

In recent decades, French Jewry has been undergoing a deep process of convergence with Israel—the process that I call the "Israelization" of Judaism. In 2015, amid a spate of terror attacks and a violent resurgence of Muslim anti-Semitism, Israeli Prime Minister Benjamin Netanyahu called on the Jews of France to emigrate to Israel. In response, French Prime Minister Manuel Valls made an emotional speech urging them to stay in their French homeland, saying: "I regret Netanyahu's statements…. The place for French Jews is in France."[431]

---

430   Michael Marrus, "European Jewry and the Politics of Assimilation: Assessment and Reassessment," *The Journal of Modern Jewish History* 49, no. 1 (1977), 105–106.

431   "French PM Manuel Valls Tells Jews to Stay in France," *Jerusalem Post*, February 16, 2015, https://www.jpost.com/Diaspora/French-PM-Manuel-Valls-tells-Jews-to-stay-in-France-391167.

In a speech to the National Assembly memorializing the victims of recent terror attacks in Paris, Prime Minister Valls said:

> History has shown us that a reawakening of anti-Semitism is the symptom of a crisis of democracy, a crisis of the Republic…. How can we accept that in France—the Jews' land of emancipation two centuries ago but also, 70 years ago, one of the lands of their agony—how can we accept that shouts of "Death to the Jews!" can be heard in our streets? How can we accept the acts I've just recalled? How can we accept that French people can be murdered because they are Jewish?
>
> There's an anti-Semitism people call historical, going back many centuries, but above all there's this new anti-Semitism born in our neighborhoods against the backdrop of the Internet, satellite dishes, abject poverty and hatred of the State of Israel, advocating hatred of the Jew and of all Jews. We must say this! We must utter the words to combat this unacceptable anti-Semitism…. Yes, let's say it directly to the world: without France's Jews, France would no longer be France![432]

---

432 "Tribute to the Victims of the Attacks: Speech by M. Manuel Valls, Prime Minister, in the National Assembly," January 13, 2015, authorized translation on the website of the French government, https://www.gouvernement.fr/en/tribute-to-the-victims-of-the-attacks.

The Jews in International Relations and the Congress of Vienna

The French defeat at Waterloo brought Napoleon's military empire to an end, liberating the states of Europe from French occupation. In September 1814, delegations of all the major European states convened in Vienna to draw up the terms of a new peace settlement that would lay the foundations for what became "one hundred years of peace" on the continent, which lasted almost without interruption until World War I in 1914. The spirit of the Congress of Vienna held firm in a tempestuous Europe during what became known as the "Spring of Nations"—the Revolutions of 1848—and later the respective unifications of Italy and Germany. The consequences for the Jews were immense.

The dominant nations at the 1814–1815 Congress of Vienna were the "Big Four"—Russia, Prussia, Austria, and Great Britain, all of which had defeated Napoleonic France and now sought to reach a new European equilibrium and block each other's imperial ambitions. The debates were also marked by titanic struggles over borders and legitimacy, principles by which peace should be established, and the desired political order of the emerging European states.

One struggle between rival visions at the Congress of Vienna centered around the question of the unification of Germany, which was splintered into multiple political entities. The conflict between the rival German principalities over the nature of unification aroused nationalist sentiments and a concomitant hostility toward national minorities.[433] The issue of the emancipation of Germany's Jews loomed in the background; scattered among dozens of German states, large and small, they had briefly enjoyed full political equality

---

433   Louis Greenberg, *The Jews in Russia: The Struggle for Emancipation* (New Haven: Yale University Press, 1965), 138.

under French occupation. Now, liberated from French rule, the envoys of the German states at Vienna demanded the full restoration of their sovereignty and the abrogation of the civil status accorded to the Jews by the French occupiers.

Opposing these demands were Austrian foreign minister (and later chancellor) Klemens von Metternich and the Prussian delegate, philosopher Wilhelm von Humboldt. In the spirit of Hegelian liberalism, and with the backing of Austria's Jewish financial elite, they demanded that Germany become a constitutional state governed by the rule of law, granting equality to all Jews in the new German confederation.

The status of German Jewry was debated for three weeks at the Congress of Vienna, and three main solutions were proposed. The first was gradual liberalization, predicated on the argument that they would have to change their social mores as a precondition for legal equality. One version of this approach was based on Christian Wilhelm Dohm's axiom that "the Jew...was a human being even more than he was a Jew." It called for full legal equality for Jews and envisaged a state-run process lasting some fifty years to encourage their "civil betterment" and prepare the Christians to accept them.

Another version of the gradual liberalization approach was proposed by Prussian official Friedrich von Schuckmann, who, in his 1785 work *On Jewish Colonies,* had warned *against* granting the Jews equality for fear of provoking friction between them and their Christian neighbors. He wrote:

> So long then, as the [German] nation as a
> whole looks upon the Jews as an inferior kind
> of people and takes offence at being treated
> on a par with them; so long as the prejudice
> against them rules the hearts of the greater
> part of the constituted Christian authorities

and of the clergy who guide the people; for
so long it will be impossible to protect them
entirely from oppression by promulgating
laws.[434]

The second approach to the Jewish question debated at the
Congress of Vienna was the "interventionist" answer, which called
for immediate legislation to make the Jews equal citizens. This revolutionary demand was presented by yet another Prussian official,
who argued that the transformation of the Jews need not take long;
they had waited long enough and could be enfranchised quickly
without causing undue social damage. Humboldt backed this approach, arguing that "a gradual process of emancipation has the
effect of confirming the separation which it is designed to remove."
He pushed for a giant leap forward to give the Jews full equality
in one bold stroke, since "it is impossible to conceive of any legal
reason why the Jew who is willing to fulfil all the duties of Christians
should not also enjoy the same rights."[435]

The third—and ultimately triumphant—approach to the Jewish
question was the "particularist" answer, which opposed legal equality
for Jews as a universal principle. It did so by means of an indirect argument that emphasized the right of the German principalities and
city-states to make sovereign decisions and annul the laws imposed
by the Napoleonic occupiers. This was how the fractured territories
of Germany foiled the Prussian-Austrian attempt to coerce them into
a united Germanic federation and perpetuated the inferior status of
the Jews—all as a symbol of their sovereign independence.

---

434 Werner E. Mosse, "From '*Schutzjuden*' to '*Deutsche Staatsbürger Jüdischen Glaubens*': The Long
and Bumpy Road of Jewish Emancipation in Germany," in *Paths of Emancipation: Jews, States,
and Citizenship*, eds. Pierre Birnbaum and Ira Katznelson (Princeton: Princeton University Press,
2016), 65–68.

435 Edward Timms, "The Pernicious Rift: Metternich and the Debate about Jewish Emancipation
at the Congress of Vienna," *Leo Baeck Institute Year Book* 46, no. 1 (January 2001), 3–18.

Humbolt and Metternich, the liberals, failed in their bid to secure Jewish emancipation across Germany. They were outmaneuvered by anti-Semitic German nationalists, who cunningly introduced tortuous formulations into the treaty that effectively forced the continued exclusion of the Jews and, in the words of the historian Edward Timms, created "state-sanctioned or officially approved antisemitism...[whereby] an educated German Christian could despise the Jews with a good conscience, knowing that he had the law on his side, quite apart from the blessing of the churches."[436]

Germany would not adopt the Jewish emancipation policy born in the French Revolution until 1870, when the dozens of independent German entities formed a unified Reich. But even after unification, Germany never instituted any national policy that recognized the Jews as a distinct community—until the Nazis' rise to power and the Nuremberg Laws.

The Jews Become a "Question"

Karl Marx's 1843 work *On the Jewish Question* is still regarded as one of most venomous anti-Semitic screeds of all time. The essay was Marx's answer to the German philosopher Bruno Bauer, who had contended that the Jews would achieve civil equality only after shedding their religion and joining in the secular state. Marx argued that the Jewish question was not a matter of religion—it was a matter of the Jews' pathological connection to money and capitalism. Marx did not object to Jewish political emancipation—that is, to formal equality—but maintained that Jews could not be emancipated as human beings if their very essence was defined by a bourgeois mentality and the practice of selling and buying.

---

436 Ibid., 17.

Hence, "the social emancipation of the Jews is the emancipation of society from Judaism."[437]

The questions that were raised about the Jews were part of a broader European conversation on other "questions," such as the "Eastern question" or the "woman question." Historian Holly Case demonstrates that the popular urge in nineteenth century Europe to settle or "solve" questions was expressive of a widespread European desire to devise analytical means to structure society and politics. Dealing with Jews as a "question" also became part of Zionist discourse. The "Jewish question" was a core component of Moses Hess's 1862 work *Rome and Jerusalem: The Clash of Ancient Civilizations*, and Theodor Herzl's 1896 Zionist manifesto *The Jewish State*. Case writes that the nature of any given question determined the range of solutions that were considered possible or desirable. The Jewish question was the question that most vexed the Europeans. Eventually, it invited a "Final Solution."[438]

The realization of full emancipation, however, demanded compliance from the Jews themselves—and it was not clear that they wished to accept the model of assimilation purportedly on offer from modern European states. The new reality obliged them to prepare for major changes in their identity, organization, community, and sense of nationality. It forced them to actively confront the question of whether they were ready to surrender their relative isolation as an ethno-religious community and broaden the contact—and concomitant friction—between them and their Gentile neighbors.

It was time for the Jews to work out who their true allies were in the non-Jewish world and what cultural outlook they would pursue.

---

437   Shlomo Avineri, "Marx and Jewish Emancipation," *Journal of the History of Ideas* 25, no. 3 (July–September, 1964), 445–46.

438   Holly Case, "The 19th Century as the Century of Questions and the Diplomatic Revolution from Below," paper presented at the International History Seminar at Georgetown University, April 4, 2013. Citation by permission.

On the organizational level, they had to choose their tactics: Would they keep a low profile or make their presence felt?[439] Furthermore, they had to decide how far they were willing to transfer responsibility for their fate from communal institutions to national governments, and in particular, to what extent, if at all, they were prepared to accept those governments' decisions on questions connected to halakha and tradition. One burning question was how far to cooperate with Gentile authorities on policing and law enforcement in situations where a member of the community transgressed. Such questions remain acute, and arguably even more so, in the sovereign State of Israel, where ultra-Orthodox politicians play a role in the national leadership but many of their voters still shun the state's authority an institutions in principle.

The Enlightenment (and its Jewish analogue, the Haskalah) had revolutionary implications inside communities. Enjoyed at first mainly by the Jews of western Europe, it spread eastward into the Russian Empire. In a seething and splintered Germany, the Jewish question was a remarkably important indication of the country's transformation from the old world to the new. While the Jewish populations of France and Britain were relatively small and practically marginal, in Germany they saw themselves as "another 'tribe' among many; to be absorbed, like others, into the great German nation-in-the-making."[440] They came to play a central role in Germany's dilemmas about progress, politics, and society. As Reinhold Rurup put it: "Germany was thus the country where the fate of European Jewry in general would largely be determined."[441]

Germany's Jews wrestled with the question of whether, and how, they could preserve their religious-cultural heritage and communal

---

439   Ezra Mendelson, *On Modern Jewish Politics* (Oxford: Oxford University Press, 1993), 5.

440   Volkov, *Walter Rathenau*, 5.

441   Rurup, "Jewish Emancipation and Bourgeois Society," 67–69.

life as the ghetto walls came tumbling down, tempting and compelling them to integrate into Germany's modern, open society. Until the second half of the century, most Jews lived in Orthodox religious communities in rural areas. In the cities, however, young intellectuals banded together to advocate enlightenment and integration into Germany's open society. They devised a radical new theology or philosophy that ascribed common ideological roots and a common national fate to Jews and Germans.[442] Yet it was far from clear that Germans would ever accept such a common bond, so long as the Jews maintained their own separate tribal-communal identity.[443]

In France and Britain, unified countries with effective central governments, the dilemmas provoked by the Emancipation about Jewish religious observance and communal identity were partially solved, or at least eased, by the fact that the authorities continued to relate to the Jews as a separate community. Unlike in Germany, the Jews had their own communal institutions to represent them on a national level. The Board of Deputies of British Jews was founded in 1760 as an informal body after the death of King George II to write a loyal address to the new ruler. It is still considered the formal body to represent the interests of British Jewry at the national level today.

The post of chief rabbi in Britain was created in 1704, when all Jews were Orthodox, yet the increase in the liberal and non-Orthodox streams raised questions about whether he could speak on behalf of all Jews. Nevertheless, the chief rabbi still enjoys a semi-official status and is commonly seen as a spokesman for Britain's Jews. This became evident ahead of the 2019 general election, when the chief rabbi issued an unprecedented warning about Labour's anti-Semitism.

---

442   Michael A. Meyer, "Jewish Religious Reform and Wissenschaft des Judentums: The Positions of Zuns, Geiger and Frankel," *Leo Baeck Institute Year Book* 16, no. 1 (1971), 20.

443   Volkov, *Walter Rathenau*, 4–5.

From Jewish Questions to Jewish Questioners

At the turn of the nineteenth century, the question of the nature of Jewishness, and whether it could exist outside of a religious framework, arose with full force. German Jews wished to integrate into their Christian surroundings while avoiding conversion to Christianity. To achieve their goals, they had to devise alternatives to Orthodox Judaism, which was seen as a fossilized relic and hostile toward the German model of enlightenment. Thus emerged Reform Judaism as an attempt to reconcile a Jewish communal faith with a German national identity, which was a compound of Protestantism, liberalism, rationalism, and nationalism.

It was Moses Mendelssohn (1729–1786), the "German Socrates," who created an impossible synthesis between past and present, reason and emotion, Christianity and Judaism, and between two national cultures that sought not only to define themselves in tribal terms, but in the language of universal morality.

Mendelssohn, in his life and in his writings, reflected the painful drama of the Jewish transition from the old world to the new. His intellectual efforts to forge a new Judaism, one that could combine the Jewish tradition with German Enlightenment's values and nationalism, formed a momentous philosophical and literary enterprise. His personal contribution was so great that, as one scholar wrote, "At that time in Europe, there were no other Jews who played such a substantial role in Europe's literature and its culture."[444]

Mendelssohn breathed life into ancient Hebrew texts. His work resonated enormously, and he won the admiration of the great thinkers of his generation, among them Immanuel Kant. He was a source of inspiration and influence for Christian von Dohm, who advocated emancipation for the Jews "as human beings." Amos Elon

---

444   Simon Rawidowicz, "Moses Mendelssohn," *Hatekufah* 26–27 (1929), 477 [Hebrew].

wrote that many Jews would celebrate Mendelssohn as their own "patron saint," who would lead them "beyond the stagnant confines of religious identity."[445]

But criticism was quick to come. Because of the inevitable internal contradictions in his heroic efforts to bridge deep philosophical chasms, and uncertainty about the future and role of the Jews in modern Germany, Mendelssohn became the object of censure among Orthodox and liberal Jews alike. Naturally, he was also suspected by Gentiles and a target for anti-Semites. Even though elite German thinkers admired the breadth of his intellect, they did not spare him criticism over his determination to advance the Jews and their cultural heritage. They derided his efforts to preserve Jewish particularity together with integration into German society as inconsistent. Johann Gottfried Herder, the father of German nationalism, asked Mendelssohn contemptuously, "Why are you a Jew?" Worst of all was Protestant theologian Johann Kaspar Lavater, who saw Mendelssohn as the greatest of all Jews—and therefore tried to convert him in a historic bid to precipitate the "conversion of the entire Jewish nation to Christianity."[446]

Indeed, Mendelssohn's personal adherence to his identity as an observant Jew did not stop his children from embracing Christianity in the name of reason, and his story became a tragic symbol for German Jewry, many of whose members opted for German rationalist idealism over Judaism—a path that soon became a one-way road to catastrophe.

Mendelssohn, an Orthodox Jew himself, was the man who paved the way for Reform Judaism, since he saw the Jews as a religious and cultural community and not a national one. In fact, he opened the door for a new theology, which undermined tribalism

---

445   Elon, *The Pity of It All*, 63.
446   Ibid., 46.

and reduced the sanctity of the principle of mutual responsibility based on kinship ties. The validity of the Jewish faith, he believed, stemmed not only from Judaism's unique ancient culture, but mainly by virtue of its humanistic, moral mission.

Mendelssohn's philosophical and theological revolution, intended to undermine Orthodoxy, was adopted by Reform Jews who wanted to reconstitute Judaism as a Western culture and tradition, free from halakhic constraints and tribal loyalties. The failure of Orthodox Judaism to embrace the institutional and theological changes necessary to retain Jews who hoped to integrate into German society created an unbridgeable gap between Orthodoxy and the values of the Enlightenment. This provoked the modern reaction represented by Reform Judaism—a new configuration that combined religious tradition with a secular order.

Reform Judaism changed the face of the Jewish world. Its goal was integration, not sovereignty. As sociologist Stephen Steinberg explains, it sought to transform Judaism from being a despised "sect" on the margins of society, living by outdated halakhic codes, into a legitimate "church" centered around a rational, constitutional state. In this sense, Reform Judaism was similar to the advanced stages of the Protestant Reformation, which revolutionized Christianity. It was the only religious current in western Europe that aimed to reestablish Jewish life based on modern philosophy, seeing the Jews as a "church movement."[447] It aspired to adapt traditional Jewish life to the philosophical, theological, and civil values of modernity, to integrate Jews into the German nation-state—and eventually the United States—as loyal citizens. The Reform "church movement" sought to diminish, as far as possible, the differences between the Jews and their Gentile surroundings.

---

447   Stephen Steinberg, "Reform Judaism: The Origin and Evaluation of a 'Church' Movement," *Journal for the Scientific Study of Religion* 5, no. 1 (Autumn 1965), 117–129.

Reform Jews opposed the idea that they were a people who aspired to have a sovereign state; their religiosity was drawn along the same lines as the civil religion of Protestant states. Just as Hegelian Protestantism had been designed as a Germanic civil religion, Reform Judaism was presented as the civil religion of German Jews.

Like Protestantism, Reform Judaism was a means to forging a moral and universal "practical rationality" that promoted German values and civil culture. It was to do so by realizing the concept of *Bildung*—a German term for a sweeping process of personal and cultural maturation and self-betterment. For German Jews, Bildung meant embracing a broad, scientific education, fluency in German as a substitute for the Yiddish of the shtetls, Protestant ethics, a refined manner, and rules of conduct that reflected their enlightenment, judiciousness, and membership of a flourishing and modern bourgeoisie.[448] For Germany as a whole, the realization of Bildung was considered a harbinger of the Hegelian "end of history"—the pinnacle of human cultural development and the secular reincarnation of the Christian "End of Days." Reason, argued Hegel, would reveal God's work. For the Jews of the Haskalah (the Jewish Enlightenment) the cult of Bildung became an all-encompassing philosophy to replace halakhic Judaism.

Thus, Reform Judaism was a marriage of Judaism and enlightened German Protestantism. To achieve this metamorphosis, Reform Jews launched a long-term process of transitioning away from Torah scholarship toward a universal education in the German tongue.

Rabbi Abraham Geiger (1810–1874) is considered the founding father and intellectual architect of Reform Judaism in Germany. He asserted that the Jews who transitioned from being a "compact nationality" into "a diaspora in which Jews lived among the nations

---

448   David Sorkin, "Religious Reform and Secular Trends in German-Jewish Life: An Agenda for Research," *Leo Baeck Institute Year Book* 4, no. 1 (1995), 169–184.

whom they were destined to instruct" were endowed with a "religious genius" that gave them "a unique insight into God and His teachings."[449] This genius lay in the fact that it was a constantly evolving religious culture. In Germany, this meant establishing Bildung as an overarching worldview and part of the religious communal experience—a kind of Germanization of Judaism, if you will.

For centuries, Geiger argued, the Jews had been enslaved by a code of religious law that had become an untamed growth of contradictory pagan commandments, preventing Orthodox Jews from participating in the Enlightenment. He called for intellectual elites to uproot these weeds and acquire their education at leading universities rather than in religious seminaries. To Geiger's mind, only Jewish theologians fully endowed with Bildung and deeply aware of the historical structure of their faith would be able to lead the Jewish people to the realization of their destiny. Their role would be to liberate Jewish civilization by releasing it from the chains of the anachronistic halakha. The new Jew, he argued, would evolve from being a pedantic student of halakha into an enlightened scholar of the "Science of Judaism" (*Wissenschaft des Judentums*)—no longer a "vessel of divine law" but rather a "living bearer...of the moral, religious and scientific spirit at its historical stage."[450]

Moses Hess, Herald of Jewish Sovereignty

Reform Judaism represented, for the first time in modern Jewish history, a theology based on universal ethical teachings, not ritual law. It stressed the common values that bourgeois Jews shared with

---

449   Arnold Eisen, *The Chosen People in America: A Study in Jewish Religious Ideology* (Bloomington, IN: Indiana University Press, 1983), 20.

450   Meyer, "Jewish Religious Reform and Wissenschaft des Judentums," 31.

their non-Jewish neighbors.[451] This was a model of Diaspora life that was not based on the paradigm of sovereignty, exile, and return. On the contrary, Reform Jews shifted their focus away from Jewish nationalism and its quest for sovereignty towards a model of integration as part of other nations. They rejected the notion that the essence of Judaism was national survival and the reclamation of the Jews' long-lost independence. Their aim was to replace the story of destruction and restoration as Judaism's core ethos with a broad system of ethics to instead become a "light unto the nations," nourished by the universal morality of the ancient prophets. Reform Judaism emphasized the moral and spiritual aspects over sovereignty and worship, inspired by the ancient prophets' eternal rebukes of the corrupting nature of power and ritual. In the new Reform doctrine, Prophetic Judaism was depicted as hostile to the idea of sovereignty—a dichotomy later criticized by Zionist thinker Ahad Ha'am:

> Certain modern historians are quite wrong when they assert that the Prophets hated the State as such, and desired its destruction, because they regarded its very existence as essentially inconsistent with that spiritual life which was their aim. This political asceticism, this desire for the annihilation of the flesh of the national organism as a means to the strengthening of its spirit, was in reality quite repugnant to the view of the Prophets.[452]

---

451 Lawrence Englander, "History of Reform Judaism and a Look Ahead: In Search of Belonging," ReformJudaism.org, https://reformjudaism.org/history-reform-judaism-and-look-ahead-search-belonging.

452 Ahad Ha'am, "Flesh and Spirit," in *Selected Essays by Ahad Ha'am*, ed. and trans. Leon Simon (Philadelphia: Jewish Publication Society of America, 1912), 152–153.

As the Reform Jews devised a doctrine based on denying that the Jews were an ethno-national tribe and framing their Jewish revival as a "universal church" that would promote social justice, an intensely nationalistic tribalism erupted across Europe. In Germany, a romanticized nationalist idealism challenged the dominant vision of the liberal state and placed kinship and blood ties over civil values and institutions of the modern state. Indeed, some Reform rabbis concluded that their cosmopolitan vision was alien to the prevailing spirit of Germany and fled to the United States.

America, a nation of immigrants, proved to be fertile soil for the spread of their progressive religious ideology. The Reform Jewish mission was uniquely suited to life in America, which rabbis called "the new Zion." At the turn of the twentieth century, America would become "the ideal stage on which the mission to humanity could convincingly be proclaimed and publicly enacted."[453]

After German rabbis landed on America's shores, Reform Judaism emerged as the dominant stream of American Jewry. It declared the biblical commandments non-binding, focusing instead on the universal calling of the chosen people. But over time, this rhetoric emptied the Reform movement of its particularist content. American Reform Judaism became a progressive ethical doctrine centered around social justice, human rights, and the universalistic imperative of *tikkun olam*—"repairing the world."

Samuel Adler, who moved his family from Germany to New York City in 1857, presided over Temple Emanu-El, which became "the flagship of Judaism's new reform movement." His son, Felix Adler, who went to study in Germany, returned to New York City in 1874 and incorporated the Society of Ethical Culture with the blessing of the Reform community, which opened the first school based on the Ethical Culture tradition. "Ethical culture struck a chord with

---

453   Eisen, *The Chosen People in America*, 20.

some of the nation's new Jewish immigrants," writes Judith Colp Rubin, "many of them Germans who had fled the reactionary aftermath of Napoleon's defeat and failed democratic revolutions."[454]

The humanistic optimism of German Reform Jewry was swiftly subjected to serious stress, including during the infamous Damascus affair of 1840. Since the 1820s, tensions between Jews and Christians in Damascus had been rising as a result of commercial rivalries and competition for the support of the Ottoman authorities. The Ottomans had generally favored the loyal Jews over the larger Christian minority, who they perceived as a threat to Syria's Islamic character.

To win over the Muslims, Christian leaders accused the Jews of ritually murdering a monk and his Muslim servant. Historian Moshe Maoz wrote that the scheme was "to delegitimize and dehumanize the Jews, and to represent them as a satanic enemy of the entire population…and to put them outside the law." The leaders of the Jewish community were tortured; some of them were killed and others "confessed." One leader even converted to Islam to save his life.

Maoz writes that the Damascus blood libel "planted the seed of antisemitism in the souls of many Muslims…and Muslims in Syria and the Land of Israel have since then occasionally taken up the weapon of the blood libel in order to settle scores with Jewish adversaries or to extort money from them."[455]

Although they took place in Muslim lands, the events in Damascus were, for European Jews, a painful reminder and warning sign of the destructive forces of tribal nationalism and anti-Semitism lurking in Christianity, despite the spirit of the Emancipation. Many were alarmed by the magnitude of the dissonance between the

---

454 Judith Colp Rubin, "My Alma Mater's Jewish Problem: Ethical Culture? Maybe Not So Much," *Commentary*, February 2020.

455 Moshe Maoz, "The Background to the Damascus Blood Libel," *Pa'amim* 20 (1984), 3–29 [Hebrew].

rhetoric of progress and enlightenment and the primeval, poisonous Jew-hatred in Damascus. Even Moses Hess (1812–1875), one of the most important socialists of his generation and a contemporary of Marx and Engels, experienced agonizing emotional and intellectual turmoil as he witnessed the blood libel unfolding. He would soon turn his back on the cosmopolitan vision of proletarian revolution to become the most ardent advocate of Jewish sovereignty in the Land of Israel as the only logical answer to the Jewish question. In so doing, Hess became an early harbinger of the necessity of sovereignty and perhaps the earliest prophet of the Israelization of the Jewish people.

Hess's treatise *Rome and Jerusalem* was the first modern Jewish nationalist text and a severe indictment of Reform Judaism's vision for the Diaspora. He opined that any Jew who denied his Jewishness was a traitor to his faith, and even more gravely, to his people. The Jews were, above all, a nation, not just a religion and a ritualistic tradition, and those who converted were betraying the wider family.

At several points in *Rome and Jerusalem*, Hess mentioned the personal grief that the 1840 Damascus blood libel caused him. At the time, he had already felt an acute dissonance between his love for his people and its heritage and his own determination to advance the international proletariat:

> Twenty years ago, when an absurd and false accusation against the Jews was imported into Europe from Damascus it evoked in the hearts of the Jews a bitter feeling of agony. Then it dawned upon me for the first time, in the midst of my socialistic activities, that I belong to my unfortunate, slandered, despised and dispersed people. And already, then, though I was greatly estranged from

Judaism, I wanted to express my Jewish patriotic sentiment in a cry of anguish, but it
was unfortunately immediately stifled in my
heart by a greater pain which the suffering
of the European Proletariat evoked in me.[456]

Hess gradually moved away from his advocacy of socialist humanism toward Jewish nationalism, and as early as 1841, he called
for Jewish settlement in Palestine as a fitting solution to the Jewish
question in Europe. Seven years before the revolutions of 1848, Hess
was already wondering how "the political rebirth of a people [could]
be realized without its own free and powerful will—and that will is
here totally absent."[457] Indeed, as historian Jacob Talmon wrote, it is
astonishing that even during the upheavals of 1848:

The Jews, of all the peoples and tribes of
Europe, were the only ethnic group not to
be affected by nationalist sentiment. On the
contrary, they greeted that year as the fulfilment of the promise of full equality and
general fraternity. They believed it would see
the last barriers between nations and religions
falling. Some of them went so far as to call
upon their coreligionists to show an example
by shedding all separatist distinctness.[458]

Hess saw the European Jews' indifference as a nation to the

---

456   Moses Hess *Rome and Jerusalem: A Study in Jewish Nationalism*, trans. Meyer Waxman (New
York: Bloch Publishing Company, 1918), 86–87.

457   Ken Koltun-Fromm, *Moses Hess and Modern Jewish Identity* (Indiana: Indiana University
Press, 2001), 46.

458   Jacob Talmon, *The Myth of the Nation and the Vision of Revolution: The Origins of Ideological
Polarisation in the Twentieth Century* (New Brunswick, NJ: Transaction, 1991), 189.

events of 1848 as a missed opportunity for the national rebirth of the Jewish people. He argued that "no modern people, struggling for its own fatherland, can deny the right of the Jewish people to its former land, without at the same time undermining the justice of its own strivings."[459] He scathingly decried the blindness of the German Jewish advocates of assimilation, especially those who cloaked themselves in an aura of enlightenment and German culture in a bid to belittle or deny the Jews' existence as a nation:

> Among the nations believed to be dead and which, when they become conscious of their historic mission, will struggle for their national rights, is also Israel—the nation which for two thousand years has defied the storms of time, and in spite of having been tossed by the currents of history to every part of the globe, has always cast yearning glances toward Jerusalem and is still directing its gaze thither....

> But while the unprejudiced stranger considers the problem of Jewish Nationalism a timely one, it appears to cultured German Jews unreasonable. For it is in Germany that the difference between the Jewish and German races is emphasized and used both by the reactionary as well as by the liberal Anti-Semite as a cloak for their Judeophobia. It is there that the existence of Jewish nationality is still employed as an argument against

---

459 Hess, *Rome and Jerusalem*, 87.

the granting of practical and civil rights to
the Jews. And this in Germany, where the
Jews, from the time of Mendelssohn, in
spite of their participation in all cultural and
moral movements and their notable contribution to these fields, and notwithstanding
their continual disavowal of Jewish national
culture and their painstaking exertions to
Germanize themselves, have striven in vain
to obtain equal rights.[460]

Today, Theodor Herzl, is widely celebrated as the founder of
Zionism, yet he acknowledged that Hess had gotten there first.[461]
Herzl first read *Rome and Jerusalem* in 1901, after writing *The Jewish
State*. He responded enthusiastically: "What an exalted, noble spirit!
Everything we have tried is already in his book.... Since Spinoza,
Jewry has brought forth no greater spirit than this forgotten, faded
Moses Hess!"[462]

Rome and Jerusalem was indeed a prophetic work; it was written
in the spirit of the German nationalism of Johann Gottfried Herder,
who tried to combine romantic nationalism with a vision of a
modern humanistic state. Herder believed that the most important,
binding factor in any liberal social order was the existence of an
organic national community—the *Volk*. Moses Hess, for his part, saw
the Jews as a Volk and Judaism as an amalgamation of the Jewish
Volksgeist (national spirit), heritage, temperament, education, ethics,
and psychology. For Herder, and later Hess, the sovereign state was

---

460   Ibid., 86–87.
461   Shlomo Avineri, *Varieties of Zionist Thought* (Tel Aviv: Am Oved, 1999), 51 [Hebrew].
462   Shlomo Avineri, *Herzl: Theodor Herzl and the Foundation of the Jewish State* (London: Weidenfeld and Nicolson, 2013), 248.

the territorial expression of the national community and the primary means for its preservation and prosperity.

The other critical dimension of the nation as a Volk was its language. Every nation's language weaves together its ways of thinking, traditions, history, religion, and other essential traits. It was not possible, according to Herder and Hess, to express a nation's culture in a foreign language. Since language was the heart of any nation, the existence of multiple languages inside a nation-state and the corruption of the national tongue constituted grave threats to the unity and purity of the Volk. Indeed, the revival of the Hebrew language is perceived by many as the most critical element of the Jewish national awakening in our time. The Israelization of Judaism has grown dramatically by the very fact that Hebrew is increasingly becoming the *lingua franca* of the Jewish world.

Herder saw the Jewish people, from their earliest days, as an organic whole and not a conglomeration of individuals. The "Jewish question" was therefore not a religious matter but a political one. Its resolution would not be attained by interfaith debate and certainly not by conversion to Christianity. Herder believed that the people's national character had degenerated throughout history because of their failure to reach national maturity in their own land. If they wished to survive, their critical task was to renew their sovereignty in their historical homeland, Palestine.[463]

Herder, like Hess, was skeptical about whether the Jews really wanted to live a sovereign independent life and whether they were even ready to leave Europe and return to the Land of Israel. But both men were certain that they retained their Volksgeist, which could yet be resuscitated. Hess, therefore, assailed the diasporic vision of Reform Judaism:

---

463 Ibid., 535.

Their reforms have only a negative purpose—
if they have any aim at all—to firmly establish unbelief in the national foundation of
the Jewish religion.... The Jewish reform-
ers...know so little of the value of national
Judaism, that they are at great pains to erase
carefully from their creed and worship all
traces of Jewish nationalism.

They fancy that a recently manufactured
prayer or hymn book, wherein a philosophical theism is put into rhyme and
accompanied by music, is more elevating
and soul-stirring than the fervent Hebrew
prayers which express the pain and sorrow
of a nation at the loss of its fatherland. They
forget that these prayers, which not only
created, but preserved for millenniums, the
unity of Jewish worship, are even today the
tie which binds into one people all the Jews
scattered around the globe.[464]

Over 150 years later, his rebuke remains the most trenchant criticism of Reform Judaism ever made in the name of Jewish nationalism.

Germany as a "Jewish Homeland"

For Reform Jews, Germany was a Jewish homeland in the making,
and they were busy fusing their culture mainly with Protestant
German culture. Their status as an equal and integral part of German

---

464   Hess, *Rome and Jerusalem*, 95–101.

society was ratified with the approval of a new emancipation law in 1871. Between 1871 and 1878, thirty-six Jews were elected to the *Reichstag.*[465]

But the subterranean currents of anti-Semitism still flowed unabated. German-Jewish philosopher Gershom Scholem explained their desire to assimilate and blend into their surroundings in *From Berlin to Jerusalem* saying that "most Jews lacked discrimination in all matters affecting themselves, yet in all other matters they mustered that faculty for reasoning, criticism, and vision," and adding that this was a gripping and tragic story of "self-deception." It pushed prominent Jewish intellectuals, including Ludwig Geiger (son of Abraham, the founder of Reform Judaism) into denial and "self-censorship… as a method."[466]

Until the end of the nineteenth century, German Jews were strengthened in their resolve to pursue a diasporic, non-Zionist vision of the future; the radical ideas of Moses Hess remained peripheral. Most German Jews rejected Herzl's Zionist movement as a threat to their national status and as a naïve, narrow-minded agenda at the dawn of the twentieth century.

Until his dying day, leading German-Jewish intellectual Hermann Cohen (1842–1918) clung to his belief that the Jews would eventually be welcomed with open arms in Europe, change their mores, and assimilate into the German nation. He believed that despite Jews' profound theological link to the Land of Israel, the Jewish character and Judaism as a religion and a culture were essentially non-territorial. For him, Diaspora life was the embodiment of the Jewish purpose. He talks about the "duality of Israel's political fate" and the fact that "the [ancient Jewish] state declined, while the people were preserved…. No state, but yet a people. But

---

465   Elon, *The Pity of It All*, 205–206.

466   Gershom Scholem, *From Berlin to Jerusalem: Memories of My Youth* (New York: Schocken Books, 1980), 26–27.

this people is less for the sake of its own nation than a symbol of mankind. Israel, as a nation, is nothing less than the mere symbol for the desired unity of mankind."[467]

For Hermann Cohen, Zionism was an expression of Judaism's inferiority and weakness. It condensed it to the proportions of a mere national tribe, whereas its ultimate form lay in its merger with modern German nationhood. Judaism's contribution to German culture, Cohen believed, was the universal ethical foundation that Moses Mendelssohn had discerned. Over the generations, it had fused with Protestantism, and the Jews' diasporic existence was now their universal, religious, and moral calling–a substitute for their ancient nationalist consciousness.

Hermann Cohen dismissed Zionism as a mendacious, magical formula for the dim and impulsive and as a vision that was liable to erode Judaism's historical contribution. The humanistic heritage of Kant, Schiller, and Beethoven that had flourished in Germany could not have existed without the Judaism of the prophets, who had bequeathed the idea of the rule of a benevolent God over the whole of humanity. Cohen, in effect, took the Reform thesis one step further–Germany was nothing less than a Jewish nation and homeland.

This idea, which German Jews clung to until the Nazis' rise to power, was later imported to the United States by those who came to America and laid the foundations of the most powerful and prosperous Diaspora community in Jewish history.

How ironic, then, that most of the Jews who eventually made America their home came not from Germany, but from the Russian Empire and eastern Europe, where, in the words of Yuri Slezkine in *The Jewish Century*, "Everyone (and most particularly the Jews)

---

467 Hermann Cohen, *Religion of Reason out of the Sources of Judaism*, trans. Simon Kaplan (New York: F. Ungar, 1972), 253.

assumed that the Jews were nonnative, temporary exiles; that they depended on their customers for survival; and that the country—however conceived—belonged to the local[s]."[468]

---

468   Slezkine, *The Jewish Century*, 106.

Chapter VI: The View from Eastern Europe

While the Jews' separate communal existence raised theological and practical difficulties in western Europe, those in eastern Europe remained mired in poverty. Most of them knew little or nothing about what was happening to Jews in the West.[469] They dutifully obeyed their rabbis and entertained no thoughts of integrating into Gentile society. The Jewish Emancipation played no part in the socio-political life of the Russian Empire; this reality reinforced the separateness of Russian Jewry from the rest of Russian society.

In nineteenth century Germany, the major question was how a nation divided into multiple political entities could find a path to unification, and if the Jews could be part of this process. In Russia, the tsars' greatest challenge was maintaining effective government over their vast realms and the many ethno-national minorities they contained. Their solution for the Jews was to confine them to their old places of domicile, which Russia annexed from Poland on the western reaches of the empire, extending from Black Sea port cities such as Odessa, and taking in what are today Lithuania, Belarus, eastern Poland, Moldova, and western Ukraine.

As a rule, the Jews were segregated outside the major areas of ethnic Russians and were prohibited from migrating to other parts

---

469   Jacob Talmon, *Myth of the Nation and Vision of Revolution: Ideological Polarization in the Twentieth Century* (New Brunswick, N.J.: Transaction, 1991).

of the empire.[470] In the later part of the century, the success of this policy was confirmed by the fact that over 90 percent of the Jews resided in twenty-five provinces of the Pale of Settlement, legally barred from residing permanently in other parts of the empire.[471] At the time, this population constituted the largest segment of Jews in the world.[472]

The differences between modern, industrialized Germany and the backward, pre-industrial Russian Empire led the Jews in each country to think and act differently regarding the viability of sovereign independence versus Diaspora-based solutions to their plight. First, the huge disparity in the size of the two communities—Germany's was relatively small, Russia's was enormous—affected how they thought about and acted upon their situations. Secondly, the fact that German Jews spoke German eroded their sense of belonging to a distinct tribe; within a short period, modernity had almost demolished the ghettos and the halakhic way of life. Many scholars believe that without the racial anti-Semitism that flourished in post World War I Germany, the Jews there might have assimilated and disappeared altogether.

This phenomenon had no significant parallel in imperial Russia, apart from Odessa, where there was no exclusively Jewish quarter and a modern Jewish community flourished. Only when the Nazis occupied Odessa during World War II was a ghetto first established there.

The Jews of the Pale of Settlement never faced a substantial

---

470   As of 1804, a small minority of Jews was permitted to reside temporarily outside the Pale for the purpose of acquiring higher education. In 1835, a similar privilege was extended to Jewish merchants who conducted business in the cities of inner Russia. See Salo W. Baron, *The Russian Jew Under Tsars and Soviets* (London: Macmillan, 1964), 78–79.

471   Yvonne Kleinmann, "Jewish Society Beyond the Pale of Settlement" in *The History of the Jews of Russia: 1772–1917*, ed. Ilia Lurie (Jerusalem: Zalman Shazar Center, 2010), 141 [Hebrew].

472   Richard H. Rowland, "Geographical Patterns of the Jewish Population in the Pale of Settlement of Late Nineteenth Century Russia," *Jewish Social Studies* 48, no. 3–4 (Summer–Autumn 1986), 207–234.

threat to their identity or communal lifestyle. Life on the periphery of an anti-modernist, multinational empire that forcibly segregated and excluded them only reinforced their communal, ethno-national cohesion.

In the second half of the century, buds of "selective integration"—to use a term coined by historian Benjamin Nathans—began to appear, but they declined after the assassination of Tsar Alexander II in 1881, an event that turned the lives of Russian Jews upside down. Pogroms in the southwest of the empire, with the backing of Tsar Alexander III, extinguished any thoughts of possible integration. By the turn of the twentieth century, the attacks had accelerated the process of mass Jewish migration (principally to the United States), stirred up internal Russian revolutionary angst, and prompted the emergence of a pro-sovereignty Zionist movement. These events and the rise of Zionism were the context in which new, diasporic survival strategies emerged, joining the revolutionary vision of overthrowing the tsarist *ancien regime*. The debate among Russian Jews over the Diaspora versus sovereignty was a historic turning point on the question of who spoke for the Jews and with what authority.

The Jews of the Russian Empire

Until 1772, Jews had been forbidden to reside within the borders of the Russian Empire. Only after the partition of Poland, when the Jewish communities of Byelorussia came under Russian rule, did the Russian authorities begin to consider their legal status. They adopted the institution of the *kahal*, which had existed under the Polish-Lithuanian Commonwealth for centuries. The Polish crown had used the Jews for economic gain and granted them substantial rights to live as an autonomous people and maintain their traditional society. The authorities served as their protectors as long as they met the financial demands of the kingdom. This was the origin of the kahal as a self-administered community with a legal personality. "It was with this legal status," writes historian John D. Klier, "that Jews entered the Russian Empire."[473] The kahal system was ultimately abolished by Tsar Nicholas I in 1844.

The story of the Jews under the Russian tsars is primarily a story of remarkable demographic growth.[474] Between 1795 and 1880, the Russian Jewish population more than quadrupled; by the end of the nineteenth century, they numbered over five million, despite mass emigration to America in the last two decades of the 1800s. In fact, between 1882 and 1914, their population in the Russian Empire increased by 50 percent. This enormous natural growth (an annual birth rate of forty per 1,000 people) was due to the custom of early marriages and large families, a decrease in infant mortality, communal institutions that provided effective health care, and isolation from the famines and epidemics that blighted the Russian peasantry.

Unlike in the West, and particularly in Germany, mixed marriages and conversions were rare in Russia. In Lutheran Germany, the power of religion had diminished considerably; baptism had become a perfunctory act to acquire an "entrance ticket to European culture," in the words of convert Heinrich Heine. Conversion to Christianity, as Israeli writer Amos Elon put it, was "facile, almost casual…a brief ceremony without, apparently, any prior instruction or preparation," which entailed no sanctions from one's family, because "family ties were more powerful than religious solidarity."[475]

---

473 John D. Klier, "The Ambiguous Legal Status of Russian Jewry in the Reign of Catherine II," *Slavic Review* 35, no. 3 (1976), 506.

474 Benjamin Pinkus has written that this nineteenth-century demographic miracle made Russia home to the world's biggest Jewish population, although the Jews never saw Russia as their own country and certainly never saw it as their homeland. See Benjamin Pinkus, *Jews of the Soviet Union* (Cambridge: Cambridge University Press, 2009).

475 Elon, *The Pity of It All*, 82.

By contrast, in Russia, which remained tribal and devout, conversions to Christianity were almost always the result of coercion, often undertaken by Jews brutally conscripted into the tsarist military. Even when echoes of the Enlightenment had begun to penetrate the Pale of Settlement, conversions were rare and solidly opposed by a traditional Jewish society that took firm action against what it saw as "the plague of apostasy that was spreading amongst the intellectual followers of Mendelssohn, a society that saw in any manifestation of enlightenment the start of the path to abandonment of Judaism."[476]

Since the foundation of the Duchy of Muscovy in the fourteenth century, the Russian Empire, which saw itself as heir to the Byzantine Empire and defender of the Orthodox Church, had expanded through a five-century-long series of conquests. By the mid-nineteenth century, it stretched from Finland in the north to the Caucasus in the south and from Poland in the west to the Pacific Ocean in the Far East. This vast expanse was ruled by the Romanov dynasty, which headed a small elite group that held all the political and military power.

The Russians were only one of the many nationalities inhabiting the empire, and they weren't even the most highly developed. Other nations had much more economic and cultural clout. Nevertheless, the autocratic efforts of the tsarist regime were relatively successful, as long as the feudal aristocracy, with the backing of the church, retained the fealty of the oppressed peasantry. The empire used local elites to impose the tsar's will on the non-Russian peoples, with a combination of oppression, assimilation, and Orthodox Christianity; sometimes it maintained equilibrium by establishing more liberal autonomous institutions.

---

476 Yehuda Slutsky, *The Jewish Enlightenment Movement in Russia* (Jerusalem: Zalman Shazar Center, 1977), 12 [Hebrew].

With time, however, the Romanovs' ability to govern the empire waned. They had built it up not by arranged marriages with other dynasties, like other imperial powers, but through war and conquest. Most of the empire's subjects were not Russians, and there was no federative arrangement between the semi-independent constituent states. The tsarist regime became the object of criticism and attacks by enlightened, would-be modernizers and national minority groups and ultimately also the target of the socialist and anarchist revolutionaries who brought it down in 1917.[477]

In the absence of ethnic cohesion, and in order to sustain the tsarist regime's stability and survival, the Romanovs tried to inculcate their subjects, including non-Russians, with patriotic sentiments to forge a multinational kingdom based on cultural Russification. This included aggressive military conscription, the forced spread of the Russian language, and above all, the use of Orthodox Christianity to create a melting pot of uniformity. Despite or perhaps because of this conscious attempt to Russify the empire's minorities, traditional Jew-hatred remained intense. The Jews were perceived as a threat to—and the antithesis of—Russianness; for their part, they regarded the Russification drive as forced apostasy.

There were around one million Jews in the lands that the Tsarist Empire occupied after the partition of Poland between 1772 and 1795. The Jewish Question occupied the imperial government and bureaucracy from the very beginning. Along with the traditional Christian attitude that saw Jews as a superstitious, greedy, and morally degenerate race, the tsar's officials held semi-modernizing positions that aimed to improve them and turn them into "useful members of society."[478]

The vision of "improving" the Jews, incorporated in many

477   Aviel Roshwald, *Ethnic Nationalism and the Fall of Empires: Central Europe Russia & The Middle East, 1914–1923* (London: Routledge, 2001), 19–27.

478   Pinkus, *Jews of the Soviet Union*, 15.

legislative enactments from the early nineteenth century, was similar to the western European demand for the Jews to change. However, there was no socioeconomic basis or political and ideological hunger to further these reforms in eastern Europe. Unlike in the Germany of Kant, Hegel, and Humboldt, in the rural, devoutly Christian Russian Empire, illiteracy and resistance to progress blocked the drive to Russify and "improve" the Jews. Historical Jew-hatred ran so deep that officialdom deemed thoughts of advancing their status within society as dangerous.

This deep-seated hatred was shared by Tsar Nicholas I. As a young officer, he wrote in his diary that the Jews were "veritable leeches who attach themselves to the populace and suck its blood."[479] As monarch, he issued an 1844 edict barring Jews from serving in state institutions unless they converted to Christianity.[480]

Tsar Nicholas's Russification program obligated Jews to perform military service. His 1827 conscription order, which abolished the policy of allowing subjects to purchase exemptions from the draft, heralded a vicious, aggressive campaign in which boys as young as eight or nine years old were press-ganged into serving for twenty-five years, and many of them were forced to convert to Christianity. The formal age of enlistment in the imperial army was eighteen, but they were forcibly drafted in special training facilities called "Cantonist Battalions." Between 1827 and 1854, approximately 50,000 children of poor families were literally abducted by Jewish collaborators known as *khappers*. They were appointed by kahal leaders and handed over to the Russian army.[481] In a letter to a friend, a contemporary Jewish scholar, Y. B. Levinson, described the

---

479   Gerard Israel, *The Jews in Russia* (New York: St Martin's Press, 1975), 23–24.

480   Benjamin Nathans, *Beyond the Pale: The Jewish Encounter with Late Imperial Russia* (Berkeley, CA: University of California Press, 2006).

481   Adina Ofek, "Jewish Children as Soldiers in Tsar Nicholas's Army," *Modern Judaism* 13, no. 3 (1993), 277–308.

brutal "dragging away of children from their mothers, just as if they were piglets."[482]

Jewish communities were forced to supply a quota of boys to the military. Alexander Herzen, a prominent radical Russian thinker, painted his meetings with conscripts aged eight to fourteen in the harshest colors. They had been handed over to the authorities by Jewish communities as cannon fodder and were often abused and humiliated by sadistic officers. Herzen recalled the horrifying sight:

> Pale, exhausted, with frightened faces, they stood in thick, clumsy, soldiers' overcoats... fixing helpless, pitiful eyes on the garrison, soldiers who were roughly getting them into ranks. The white lips, the blue rings under their eyes bore witness to fever or chill. And these sick children, without care or kindness, exposed to the raw wind that blows unobstructed from the Arctic Ocean, were going to their graves.[483]

Indeed, for almost the entire nineteenth century, the tsarist regime implemented a paradoxical policy toward the Jews; their integration was seen as both an essential condition for the stability and cohesion of the empire and a threat. This contradiction led to ersatz swings between legislation to promote integration and manifestations of violence and segregation. For their part, the Jews wanted equality with their fellow subjects but also did everything they could to preserve their ethno-religious particularity.

---

482   Slutsky, *The Jewish Enlightenment Movement in Russia*, 75 [Hebrew].

483   Cited in Zvi Gitelman, *A Century of Ambivalence: The Jews of Russia and the Soviet Union: 1881 to the Present* (Bloomington: Indiana University Press, 2001), 5.

Before the assassination of Alexander II in 1881 and the almost immediate outburst of anti-Semitism that followed, there were hopes that Russia might undergo a liberal metamorphosis. The empire's defeat in the Crimean War of 1853–1856 and the succession of Alexander II in 1855 led to a brief respite in tsarist tyranny and became known as the epoch of the Great Reforms. Herzen, who reacted enthusiastically to the policy of emancipating the peasantry from their serfdom, likened the move to the Christian revolution in the Roman Empire, which sounded the death knell for paganism.[484]

The succession of Tsar Alexander II after Nicholas I's death provided a great gust of liberalization, giving a boost to Jewish optimism and to the rise of the Russian-Jewish enlightenment movement. Jewish intellectuals expressed their faith in progress and confidence that Jew-hatred would vanish sooner or later, and Russian Jews would achieve the emancipation enjoyed by their brethren in western Europe.[485] According to historian John Klier, unlike Tsar Nicholas's tendency of punishing "bad Jews," Tsar Alexander's government aimed to reward "good Jews."[486] This policy of selective integration cut military service down to five years and allowed more Jews to live outside the Pale of Settlement; merchants and craftsmen were also given more freedom of movement. Medical professionals who completed twenty-five years' military service and other educated persons, including Jews, were encouraged to enter public service.

Alexander II introduced his liberalizing reforms mainly out of economic considerations, not values or ideological motives. He wanted to enlist only a small minority of Jews, who would contribute capital, professional expertise, and military and cultural prestige

---

484   Alexander Herzen *My Past and Thoughts: The Memories of Alexander Herzen*, trans. Constance Garnett (Berkley: University of California Press, 1982), xxxii.

485   Slutsky, *The Jewish Enlightenment Movement in Russia*, 17 [Hebrew].

486   John Doyle Klier, *Russia Gathers Her Jews: The Origins of the "Jewish Question" in Russia, 1772–1825* (De Kalb: Northern Illinois University Press, 1986).

to his empire. During Alexander's reign, the legal status of Jews also improved, and they served as officials in local governments (the *zemstvos*), and as lawyers, doctors, statisticians, and other professions. The new military conscription system that went into effect in 1874 gave a wholesale exemption to Russian high school graduates; as a result, even Orthodox Jews preferred to enroll their sons into Russian schools rather than yeshivas.[487] The Jews arguably became "the most loyal [group] to the government of Alexander II." They were grateful to the new tsar for removing the harsh restrictions imposed by his predecessor, although their economic situation and social status barely improved.[488]

From Cultural Autonomy to Embryonic Zionism, 1860-1881

For many generations, Jewish communities in the Russian Empire and the Polish-Lithuanian Commonwealth enjoyed a large degree of administrative and cultural autonomy, whether through the Council of Four Lands in Poland or the elected local kahal Jewish community committees in tsarist Russia. In many senses, Jewish autonomy under autocracies formed the basis of Simon Dubnow's later thinking about Jewish autonomism—the cause of Jewish autonomy in the Diaspora, including within a future democratic, multicultural Russia.

Between 1580 and 1764, the Council of Four Lands was principally in charge of collecting taxes from the Jews on behalf of the royal treasury. Sometimes regarded as heir to the Sanhedrin of antiquity, the council functioned in what is known as Greater Poland,

---

487 Kleinmann, "Jewish Society Beyond the Pale of Settlement."
488 Greenberg, *The Jews in Russia*, 146.

Little Poland, Galicia (with Podolia), and Volhynia, and its members were acknowledged as the leaders of Polish Jewry in secular affairs.

The council met twice a year to discuss and arrange interactions with the authorities on both religious and secular matters. For the first hundred years of the its existence, leading rabbis were the dominant force, but in time, the difference between the secular council and the rabbinical leadership became more and more pronounced. In 1688, the council forbade rabbis from interfering in matters of taxation. Five decades later, in 1739, it reiterated this demand and insisted that the rabbis confine themselves to matters of religion.[489]

The shift in the council's leadership away from the rabbis and toward lay leaders was influenced by the budding Enlightenment movement in western Europe and the growing desire of Polish Jews to strengthen their oversight of their communal representatives.

The Jews of the Polish-Lithuanian Commonwealth would experience profound change in the coming decades after the tsarist empire annexed the Polish provinces and introduced a new policy of coercive governance, combined with limited integration for the minorities under its rule. In 1791, imperial authorities created the institution of the kahal as a decentralized successor to the council. Kahal committees were formed in the roughly 1,000 separate Jewish communities in the Pale of Settlement. Each committee numbered five to nine members and functioned as an administrative and enforcement body under the auspices of the imperial regime, and executed its will. It soon became the central element in Jewish life. According to historian Benjamin Pinkus, even before the kahal system, Jewish autonomy "was fuller than that conceded to other national and religious minorities within Belorussia."[490] The kahal was governed according to Jewish law and was responsible for collecting taxes from

---

489   S. Zeitilin, "The Council of Four Lands," *The Jewish Quarterly Review* 39, no. 2 (1948), 212.

490   Pinkus, *Jews of the Soviet Union*, 12.

Jews, representing and policing members of the community, and issuing identity documents.

During the reign of Alexander I, some called for the integration of the Jews as "good and useful citizens." But this budding liberalism and the opening it offered for western-style enlightenment lacked the administrative foundation for any meaningful reform. The tsarist regime preferred a policy of segregation based on the kahal structure as an effective means of control. At times, Tsar Alexander I tried to form a Jewish advisory body and even tried to help to combat blood libels.

Under the tyrannical rule of his successor, Nicholas I, this dialogue-oriented attitude gave way to a harsh dynamic of arbitrary coercion. In 1827, Nicholas abolished the practice of purchasing exemptions from military service and ordered Jewish community leaders to supply conscripts as a collective responsibility; with this, the kahal system's moral authority quickly waned in the eyes of many Jews, as did solidarity and confidence in their own representatives, whom they now perceived as lackeys of the tsarist regime. Jews accused these community leaders of corruptly exploiting their power to decide who was, and who was not, doomed to conscription. Any contacts with the authorities that were perceived as excessively close evoked suspicion, and any cooperation with the government's proposed reforms were feared as the prelude to forced Christianization. Nonetheless, the kahal system remained the only structure that enabled the Jews to enjoy a high level of communal cohesion under their own elected leadership.[491]

In 1844, the Russian government changed its policy toward the Jews overnight. Their autonomy was deemed too broad and threatening, and Tsar Nicholas abolished the kahal system. A year later, it was decreed that within five years, the wearing of traditional Jewish garb would be totally forbidden. According to Benjamin Pinkus, the

---

491   Baron, *The Russian Jew Under Tsars and Soviets,* 112.

abolition of the kahal system meant that elected Jewish leaders were stripped of their powers and "synagogue authorities were forbidden to exercise any pressure, except reprimand and warning."[492]

Even without the kahal committees, "Jewish communities continued to deliver taxes and conscripts, as the state required of them."[493] Over time, however, their internal leadership lost their status and powers. Rebellious youngsters and intellectuals, as well as entrepreneurs and rich merchants, challenged the old guard and its traditional system of control. The community was divided over the key question that keeps recurring: Who speaks for the Jews, and on what authority?

The tsarist regime's erratic flip-flopping between wanting to rule the Jews as a collective and fearing that their cohesion would constitute a threat reflected its growing apprehension about national minorities in general. The Poles, Ukrainians, Byelorussians, and Caucasian peoples all awaited the opportunity to assert their independence. Tsar Nicholas's ferocity and frequent, unanticipated policy swings compelled the Jews to reconsider their future. Increasingly concerned that he would take devastating steps against them, they came up with innovative initiatives to ensure the continued existence of their collective life outside (or after) an imperial Russia.

However, most residents of the Pale of Settlement were unaffected by the romantic ideas of the Enlightenment in Germany and could conceive of no solutions beyond their traditional way of life. Hasidic Judaism remained the dominant force among Russian Jewry until the second half of the nineteenth century. Under the rule of Alexander II, more and more educated Jews began trying to fit into the empire along the lines of the western European model—as fully equal citizens.

---

492 Pinkus, *Jews of the Soviet Union*, 16.
493 Nathans, *Beyond the Pale*, 34.

The reforms during his reign, the upheavals in western Europe, and the revolutions of 1848 laid the foundation for the emergence of anti-establishment Jewish nationalist movements. They fed upon the socialist and liberal revolutionary trends in the West while also drawing inspiration from the Bible and ancient Jewish sovereignty. After Russia's defeat in the Crimean War, Alexander II became increasingly dependent on the taxes paid and services rendered by affluent and educated Jews. They became indispensable to the rehabilitation of Russia's infrastructure, and since the regime was so dependent on private capital, a small cadre of merchants became significant financial players for the Russian government.

The new Jewish elites also became the principal mediators between the imperial regime and their own communities. In the 1870s, wealthy Jews, notably the Günzburg family, were known for their philanthropy and efforts to sway the government on Jewish affairs. They succeeded in getting some of the restrictions on settlement abolished, as well as expanding the Jews' freedom of occupation outside the Pale. Their role was similar to that of the court Jews of central Europe after the Thirty Years' War, and they secured an elevated legal status for themselves.[494] These developments and Tsar Alexander's reforms spurred an internal debate about the opportunities and dangers inherent in Russification versus the preservation of a distinct Jewish existence. Some of the wealthy and educated Jews in cities such as Odessa and St. Petersburg were active in reshaping community life with the emphasis on liberal Jewish-Russian integration.

The story of Odessa is a fascinating example of Jewish flourishing in eastern Europe. In 1790, according to an unofficial census, there were a few hundred Jews living in the city, mostly petty traders. By 1860, their ranks had swelled to 17,000, about one-quarter of the

---

494 Ibid.

city's population. By the turn of the century, Odessa was spoken of as a "Jewish city" and the Jews had become its economic engine, and in the early twentieth century, two-thirds of the craftsmen and industrialists in Odessa were Jews. Odessa, in the words of historian Charles King, "was New Russia's answer to the shtetl"–a place where Jews were not isolated. Instead, they fit into society, were nourished by the prevailing enlightenment, and were optimistic that they could convince the Russian authorities of their value.

Imperial authorities cooperated with the modernizers by banning the wearing of the *kapotah*, the knee-length jacket donned by Orthodox Jewish men, who were now battling for the survival of their traditional way of life. They sometimes used underhanded methods to do this, such as levelling false accusations of subversion against poet Judah Leib Gordon, one of their harshest critics. They reported him and his wife to the Russian authorities, who banished them on the pretext of anti-tsarist subversion.

Hasidic Jews saw Odessa as a den of Jewish thieves and heretics. In *Fishke the Lame (The Book of Beggars)*, by S. Y. Abramovitsch, the father of Yiddish literature known by his pen name Mendele Mocher Sforim, the main character, Fishkeh, sums it up by saying: "Your Odessa is not for me."[495]

Among the Jewish intellectuals in Russia were early Zionists who preached progress but condemned the Western tendencies toward assimilation. They produced flourishing Hebrew literature that drew upon biblical sources and extolled the glory of Jewish sovereignty of ancient times. Avraham Mapu (1808–1867) became one of the most important heralds of modern Hebrew literature, arousing the national consciousness of young Jews with his 1853 book *Love of Zion*, the first modern Hebrew novel.

---

495   Charles King, *Odessa: Genius and Death in a City of Dreams* (New York: W. W. Norton & Co., 2011), 97–106.

Mapu blazed a path for the celebrated writer Peretz Smolenskin (1842–1885), who called for the revival of Hebrew nationalism and denounced Jewish integration in Russia as a shameful surrender on the part of an ancient nation. Smolenskin, influenced by the Polish national uprising in 1863, condemned both the rabbinic establishment and the forces of assimilation. Having grown up in a small village in Byelorussia and having been a fervent rebel against the yeshiva world he was raised in, Smolenskin was also the harshest and most prominent critic of Reform Judaism and the Enlightenment ideas of Moses Mendelssohn, which he was exposed to after moving to Odessa. He continued his relentless struggle against them from Vienna, where he founded the Hebrew monthly *Hashachar* ("The Dawn"), devoted to the revival of the Hebrew language, in 1869.

In advocating Hebrew nationalism as a substitute for assimilation, Smolenskin was advancing a similar ideology to Moses Hess, but his was based on and couched in the Hebrew language. Like Hess, and unlike other Russian Jewish intellectuals who admired what modernity and enlightenment had achieved for their brethren in the West, Smolenskin condemned the Reform model for making Judaism an empty, lifeless, universal religion. He despised it for erasing the yearning for Zion from the liturgy, for abandoning Hebrew and replacing it with German, and for giving up the solidarity of the People of Israel and their symbiosis of nation and religion. He argued that religion and nationalism went hand-in-hand in Judaism, and the Hebrew language was the essential foundation of both. Those who renounced the use of Hebrew in their prayers were betraying their people and their religion; to his mind, without the Hebrew language, there was no Torah, and without the Torah there was no Jewish nation.[496]

On the spectrum between Orthodoxy, which wanted to remain

---

496   Greenberg, *The Jews in Russia*, 141.

aloof from the rest of the Russian Empire, and the forces of innovation and modernity, which sought integration and progress within the empire, there were also the voices of some educated rabbis who, decades before Pinsker and Herzl, emphasized that a commitment to Jewish nationhood was no less important than a commitment to religion—and perhaps even took precedence. They believed the preservation of the Jews' tribal nature mandated them to maintain strong ties to their historical homeland and to Hebrew as an everyday language, not only as a sacred tongue. These pre-Zionist rabbis spoke in messianic terms of the "Restoration of Israel." They were inspired by rabbis from outside the Russian Empire, most prominently Nachman Krochmal, Zvi Hirsch Kalischer, and Judah Alkalai, all of whom were early harbingers of Religious Zionism in the Land of Israel. The ability of Orthodox rabbis to adopt these messianic and revolutionary calls for settlement in what was then a neglected corner of the Ottoman Empire is a testament to the latent potential within the Jewish religion to adapt itself to the world of modernity.

Zionism, Autonomism, the Bund, and Migration to America

By 1880, Russian Jews could still not integrate along the western European model, but they did enjoy a reasonable level of personal and public security, like other imperial minorities, both in the Pale of Settlement and the cities. The tsarist regime did not degenerate into mass murder, notwithstanding some violent, arbitrary outbursts on the government's watch, as well as substantial oppression and discrimination. But the assassination of Alexander II in 1881 and the succession of Alexander III led to an abrupt change in the lives of Russia's Jews.

The waves of pogroms in 1881–1882 became known as the "Whirlwinds in the South," in an allusion to the Book of Isaiah.

They continued at differing levels of intensity and capriciousness over the next two decades with the backing of the regime. The tsars directly encouraged harsh legal measures and indirectly approved "spontaneous" attacks on Jews. Every day brought fresh peril, and their fear of this arbitrary violence disrupted their vision of progress and integration under the Romanov monarchy.

Even the flourishing community of Odessa—about whom the Yiddish phrase "You can live like a king in Odessa" was coined—was abruptly transformed from being a place of great hope for tolerant cosmopolitanism into a place of anti-Semitic chaos. Like the Golden Age in Spain, the promise and calamity of Odessa were a repetition of what could happen to the Jews without Jewish sovereignty.

This insecurity and chaos gave a boost to Zionism and the forces of liberalism. It also strengthened the spirit of socialist revolution—although in the early years of the twentieth century, up to the October Revolution, Jews "broadly rejected socialism in any guise...as the solution to the problem of the Jews in Russia."[497] Despite this, many who were motivated by the winds of secularization and political instability wanted to be part of the overthrow of autocracy.[498] In the end, however, the irresistible allure of the American Dream and the drive to migrate westward proved supreme. Between 1881 and 1914, two million Jews left the Russian Empire for the United States, accounting for some 80 percent of the their emigration from eastern Europe. Some brought revolutionary, left-wing ideas to the US and featured among the leaders of its socialist and communist movements. Only a handful of Russian Jews went to Palestine, many of them influenced by the Lovers of Zion (*Hibat Zion*) movement, which had become the exemplar and catalyst of organized Zionism in Eastern Europe.

---

497 Michael Stanislawski, "Why Did Russian Jews Support the Bolshevik Revolution?," *Tablet*, October 25, 2017.

498 Jonathan Frankel, "The Jewish Socialism and the Bund in Russia," in *The History of the Jews of Russia: 1772–1917*, 255 [Hebrew].

The American Jewish community was transformed by this mass migration. With time, the United States would become the most important Jewish community in the world. However, toward the end of World War I, there were still more Jews in the teetering and soon-toppled Russian Empire than anywhere else in the world because of tremendous natural growth rates, despite the trauma of the pogroms. At the turn of the twentieth century, the number of Jews in Russia was estimated at between five and seven million.[499]

The constant fear of pogroms and revolutionary ferment drove many Jews to political activism. Disgusted at the passivity and fatalism of their parents' generation, young Jews refused to accept further affronts to their dignity or to wait to be slaughtered. They mobilized to fight the violence and depredations against their people at all levels of society and the state. The Jews of imperial Russia reached their breaking point with the infamous Kishinev pogrom of 1903, immortalized in Hayim Nahman Bialik's chilling poem "On the City of Slaughter":

> Arise and go now to the city of slaughter;
>
> Into its courtyard wind thy way;
>
> There with thine own hand touch, and with the eyes of thine head,
>
> Behold on tree, on stone, on fence, on mural clay,
>
> The spattered blood and dried brains of the dead.[500]

Many Jews realized that eastern Europe had become a death-trap. But those who were so versed in commemorating calamities

---

499   Anna Geifman has noted that in 1903 there were 136 million people in the empire, including seven million Jews. See Anna Geifman, *Thou Shalt Kill, Revolutionary Terrorism in Russia, 1894–1917* (Princeton: Princeton University Press, 1995), 32.

500   Hayim Nahman Bialik, "In the City of Slaughter," in *Complete Poetic Works of Hayyim Nahman Bialik*, ed. Israel Efros (New York: Histadruth Ivrith of America, 1948), http://faculty.history.umd.edu/BCooperman/NewCity/Slaughter.html.

were also adept at denying reality and snapping back to old routines. A debate emerged: What should the future hold for the Jews of the Russian Empire? They grappled with many different ideas, both before and after the overthrow of the Romanovs in 1917, including Jewish sovereignty and new ways of living in the Diaspora. At one end, Zionism called for the "negation of the diaspora" and the creation of a Jewish state. At the other, there were demands for full integration in the Diaspora based on civil, economic, and political equality. Yet others called for Jewish autonomy *in* the Diaspora. Jews also debated two models of cultural autonomy after the fall of the tsars; one model envisaged the Jews as a minority like any other recognized national group in a proletarian Russian state while the other saw them enjoying self-rule as part of a federative arrangement in a liberal state in which national groups would have cultural (but non-territorial) autonomy. The latter was the vision of Simon Dubnow, who declared:

> It is our duty to fight against the demand that the Jews give up their national rights in exchange for rights as citizens.... Such a theory of national suicide that demands that the Jews make sacrifices for the sake of equal rights, the like of which are not demanded of any other nationality or language group, contradicts the very concept of equal rights and of the equal value of all men.[501]

One element cropped up in every discussion of the Jewish future—the definition, status, and location of the Jewish homeland.

---

501 Simon Rabinovitch, "The Dawn of a New Diaspora: Simon Dubnov's Autonomism, from St. Petersburg to Berlin," *Leo Baeck Institute Year Book* 50, no. 1 (January 2005), 270.

In the dispute between advocates of sovereignty and those who favored a diaspora-based solution, the appearance of the Hibat Zion movement gave a significant boost to the Zionist idea. However, Zion argued that Jews would forever be foreigners in Russia, and the way out of their distress was emigration to their historic homeland. Diasporists and proponents of autonomy emphasized the concept of "hereness" (*doykeit* in Yiddish), which meant that Jews belonged to the places where they lived, just like any other nation.

Prominent among the diaspora advocates was the Bund (Yiddish for "union"), a movement founded in 1897 as a "General Union of Jewish Workers" in Russia, Poland, and later, Lithuania. It was the first social-democratic organization in the Russian Empire and became a mass movement. As such, it was the most modern and popular diasporic model in eastern Europe and a key component in the formation of the socialist movement in Russia and the pan-European left.

There were two contradictory streams within the Bund—one universalist and the other specifically Jewish. The first advocated unity with all socialist movements, Jewish and non-Jewish, for the sake of the proletarian class struggle; the second called for joining with other Jewish movements to preserve and bolster Jewish particularity and national solidarity. The Bund's attempt to maintain an independent Jewish entity within the Russian Social Democratic Labor Party created internal contradictions and provoked clashes with both Jewish and non-Jewish bodies. In Jewish circles, its universalism aroused opposition due to the fear of assimilation and erosion of tradition.[502] But among Russian socialists, the majority—including Lenin in his early role as the socialists' leader-in-exile—saw

---

502   Charles E. Woodhouse and Henry J. Tobias, "Primordial Ties and Political Process in Pre-Revolutionary Russia: The Case of the Jewish Bund," *Comparative Studies in Society and History* 8, no. 3 (April 1966), 331–360.

the Bund's goal of becoming an independent ethno-national party as a threat to the unity of the working class.

In 1903, Lenin contended that the Jews had long ceased to be a nation, "for a nation without territory is unthinkable." He dismissed the notion of diaspora nations in general and of a Jewish diaspora nation in particular, claiming: "The idea of a Jewish nationality runs counter to the interests of the Jewish proletariat, for it fosters among them, directly or indirectly, a spirit hostile to assimilation, a spirit of the 'ghetto.'" Historian Zvi Gitelman writes that "for Lenin, there was no Jewish nation, only a 'Jewish Problem'"—and this problem would only be solved if the Jews assimilated and abandoned their distinct cultural identity.[503]

Dubnow's "Diaspora Nation"

The Bund never succeeded in finding the right formula to ensure the survival of the Jewish tribe in alliance with other socialists. At the same time, Jewish thinkers proposed two other agendas that were not as politically influential as the Bund's but still had an impact. The more important of these was Jewish autonomism, Simon Dubnow's vision of Jewish autonomy as diaspora nation. The other was Yiddishism, socialist intellectual Chaim Zhitlovsky's idea for a "Yiddish language community" to replace the Jews' religion-based identity, which he thought was going to disappear. Zhitlovsky's form of autonomy would first be established in the multicultural Russia that would emerge from the embers of the revolution. He suggested that Yiddish would be the language of instruction in schools and the working language of other institutions. Yiddishists held a conference

---

503 Zvi Gitelman, "The Jews: A Diaspora within a Diaspora," in *Nations Abroad: Diaspora Politics and International Relations in the Former Soviet Union*, eds. Charles King and Neil Melvin (Boulder, Colorado: Westview Press, 1998), 61.

in Bukovina in 1908 and declared Yiddish "a national language of the Jewish people."[504]

Zhitlovsky was something of a Zionist before taking a sharp turn and backing the Bolsheviks. Realizing his mistake, he later fled to the United States and promoted the idea of turning the Land of Israel into a Yiddish–not Hebrew–national cultural center. He predicted that masses of Jews would stream to a Yiddish-speaking national home. Historian Zvi Gitelman sardonically said: "Whether Zhitlovsky seriously thought that Sephardic Jews would adopt Yiddish, or whether he simply ignored their existence, is not clear, but telling."[505] Zhitlovsky died in Canada, together with his eccentric proposal.

Simon Dubnow showed some sympathy for Yiddishism but did not see it as the heart of the national culture of eastern European Jewry. For him, the Jews were a multilingual people and speakers of Russian, Yiddish, and Hebrew. Dubnow, a gifted historian, considered himself a missionary for Jewish history. He made a great contribution to the study of eastern European Jewry and called upon them to proudly brandish their past as the key to ensuring their national future. He advocated the study of history and the documentation of Jewish life as a modern alternative to Torah study. He also earned the widespread recognition of social scientists as the leading expert in the field of diaspora studies, a branch of the study of nationhood.

Dubnow was a member of the intellectual elite and emerged in the Byelorussian part of the Pale of Settlement; he later moved to St. Petersburg, Odessa, Kaunas, Berlin, and Riga. The Kishinev pogrom of 1903 shocked him deeply and led him to cooperate with Ahad Ha'am and Hayim Nahman Bialik in investigating the massacre. "Stunned by the thunder of Kishinev," he later wrote, "we each

---

504 Joshua M. Karlip, *The Tragedy of a Generation: The Rise and Fall of Jewish Nationalism in Eastern Europe* (Cambridge, MA: Harvard University Press, 2013), 10.

505 Gitelman, "The Jews: A Diaspora within a Diaspora," 61.

sat in our own homes in Odessa with broken hearts and seething with impotent anger. When the horrendous news reached our town, so close to the martyrs, the pen dropped from my hand and I could not return to my historical work for many days."[506]

Dubnow, Ahad Ha'am, Bialik, and fellow intellectuals Yehoshua Rawnitzki and Mordechai Ben Ami, who were all neighbors in Odessa, published an anonymous manifesto in Hebrew, penned by Ahad Ha'am, which became a clarion call for Jewish self-defense:

> Brothers.... It is a disgrace for five and a half million souls to place themselves in others' hands, to stretch out their necks and cry out for help, without trying to defend themselves, their property, and the dignity of their lives. And who knows if it was not this disgrace of ours that did not cause the start of our degradation in the eyes of all the people and to turn us into dirt in their eyes?... It is only he who knows how to defend himself who is respected by others. If the citizens of this land had seen that there is a limit, that we too, although we will not be able nor willing to compete with them in robbery, violence and cruelty, are nonetheless ready and able to protect what is precious and sacred to us, until our last drop of blood. If they had actually seen it—there is no doubt—they would not have fallen upon us

---

506   Simon Dubnow, "Ahad Ha'am's Scroll of Mysteries (25 Years Since the Kishinev Massacre)," *Hatekufah* 24 (1934), 416 [Hebrew].

with such nonchalance; because then a few hundred drunkards would not have dared to come with clubs and pickaxes in their hands to a large community of Jews of some forty thousand souls to kill and to violently rob to their hearts' content. Brothers! The blood of our brethren in Kishinev cries out to us: Shake off the dust and be men! Stop whining and begging, stop reaching out to those who hate you and ostracize you, that they should come and save you. Let your own hand defend yourself![507]

Even after the Kishinev pogrom, Dubnow retained his faith that the Jews could achieve a life of dignity and meaning as a nation within the framework of social and cultural autonomy in the Diaspora, in nation-states where they were a minority. He considered the Jews the prototype for diaspora nations and formulated his own radical doctrine for Jewish nationhood, writing:

When a people loses not only its political independence but also its land, when the storm of history uproots it and removes it far from its natural homeland and it becomes dispersed and scattered in alien lands, and in addition loses its unifying language; if, despite the fact that the external national bonds have been destroyed, such a nation maintains itself for many years, creates an independent existence, reveals a stubborn

---

507   Ibid., 416–420 [Hebrew].

determination to carry on its autonomous development—such a people has reached the highest stage of cultural-historical individuality and may be said to be indestructible, if only it cling forcefully to its national will.[508]

In the Israeli Century, the idea that the Jewish people's mobility strengthens and deepens its culture, and that non-territorial nationhood is the pinnacle of moral achievement because it is unencumbered by borders and the monopoly over the use of force has become a pet thesis for liberals and internationalists.

While the Hibat Zion movement was sending pioneers to the Land of Israel, Dubnow opposed the Zionist program of securing territorial sovereignty, deeming it impractical. Amid the pogroms sparked by the assassination of Tsar Alexander II in 1881, he argued that isolating the Jews in the backwater of Ottoman Palestine would degrade them culturally and ethically, and they would "sink into Asiatic culture." He wrote to Moshe Leib Lilienblum, who had decided to join the Lovers of Zion, that sovereignty was a "straw to clutch at, and those who grasp at it will surely drown…in ignorance and barbarism."[509] He also disagreed with his friend Ahad Ha'am's idea that the Jews could establish a center of modern life in Palestine. Dubnow maintained that from a moral perspective, a diaspora national existence was preferable to an exclusivist, territorial-sovereign nationhood, which would inevitably cling to chauvinistic tribal nativism and state violence.

Dubnow's adherence to the idea of diasporic autonomism was rooted in his faith that Russia would one day become a liberal,

---

508   Rabinovitch, "The Dawn of a New Diaspora," 281.
509   Miriam Frenkel, "The Medieval History of the Jews in Islamic Lands: Landmarks and Prospects," *Peamim* 92 (2002), 32.

multinational state. This remained his opinion up until the Russian democrats surrendered to the Bolsheviks during the 1917 Revolution.

In 1922, he took refuge in Berlin. Despite the failure of the Jews to integrate in Soviet Russia and the early success of Zionism in Palestine and the Balfour Declaration, Dubnow continued to believe that the national future of the Jews lay in Europe. He rejected assimilation as unnatural both psychologically and morally, and as a threat to the Jewish people. Only a vibrant diaspora nation, united and organized, without territorial sovereignty, could serve as the inspiration for a progressive, pluralist, and multicultural society. Dubnow's vision was to build on the Jews' proven success in keeping their ethnic particularity, via their language, culture, and education, and their ability to maintain national institutions. He wanted to revive the kahal system, but not based on religious principles or hierarchy as it had been in the Middle Ages and in the Russian Empire. The kahal he wanted to recreate would be of a democratic-republican nature with a clearly secular national orientation. The Jewish diaspora nation would serve as the model for multiethnic life in modern states whose populations were not ethnically homogeneous and did not demand assimilation into the predominant group.[510]

Even after the pogroms of 1903 and other upheavals, Dubnow believed Russia would become a multiethnic, liberal, democratic country in which the Jews could flourish with national/non-territorial autonomy. After the 1905 Revolution, when elections for parliaments (*Dumas*) were first allowed, he played a key role in the formation of the League for the Attainment of Full Rights for the Jewish People of Russia. The goal of the league was "the realization in full measure of civil, political, and national rights for the Jewish

---

510   After Dubnow wrote the "Diaspora" entry in the *Encyclopedia of Social Sciences* in the 1930s, the term "diaspora" became almost exclusively linked to the history of and political sociology of the Jews. Recent decades have seen a revival of diaspora studies as a subfield of international relations, and Dubnow remains a primary source and a model for the study of this phenomenon.

people." It organized as a pressure group, not as a party, and mobilized Jewish voters to ensure "the elections of candidates, preferably Jewish, who would strive for full rights for the Jews and a democratic regime of Russia."[511]

Indeed, many Russian Jews voted in the 1906 elections for the liberal party, the Kadet, because of its commitment to constitutional order and universal suffrage. Thousands of Jews "who had previously no contact with political life were now drawn into it by the exercise of their franchise. Russian Jews could feel as they had never felt before that they had a stake in the future of Russia."[512] By the time the Bolsheviks' seized power, almost all Russian Jews, who were officially emancipated in the democratic 1917 February Revolution, were anti-Bolsheviks. But when the Russian Civil War broke out and anti-Bolshevik forces of the White Army committed anti-Jewish atrocities, many Jews adopted the Bolsheviks as allies.[513]

As he saw fascism rising in Europe and the Jewish national home in Palestine becoming a reality, Dubnow still clung to his faith that the diaspora nation would be the dominant mode of Jewish life, even if a Jewish state were to be established. He did not agree that people must constantly strive for sovereignty to be a nation.

Dubnow was murdered by a Latvian collaborator during the Nazi occupation of Riga in 1941. For many, his cruel death became the symbol of the disaster inherent in the naïve faith of living a secure Jewish life as a scattered diaspora nation.

---

511   Sidney Harcave, "Jews and the First Russian National Election," *The American Slavic and European Review* 9, no. 1 (February 1950), 33–41.

512   Ibid., 41.

513   Michael Stanislawski, "Why Did Russian Jews Support the Russian Revolution?," *Tablet*, October 25, 2017.

Chapter VII: "Die Goldene Medina"

Until the late 1860s, the United States was virtually unknown to the majority of Jews residing in the Pale of Settlement. For the rabbis and leaders of most of Russian Jewry, "anyone who moved to America was traveling to a godless place with no Torah."[514]

However, for the small number of eastern European Jewish intellectuals who had migrated to western Europe, America was developing a reputation as the land of the free. Indeed, after the American Civil War, it became increasingly attractive to Russian Jews, who briefly tasted the air of liberation after the accession of Tsar Alexander II, who had put an end to years of bondage and brutality under Tsar Nicholas I. He opened Russia to the West, and America was no longer just a *"Treife Medina"*—an unkosher land—but a utopian *"Goldene Medina."* Only after the catastrophe of the pogroms following the assassination of Alexander II, however, did it become an irresistible magnet for massive Jewish migration.

It was exactly at this juncture when the European Jewish press began asking whether Jewish migrants should go to America or to Palestine. In the 1880s, the Holy Land was known as a far-away place for a small spiritual elite studying the Torah and living off charitable donations from the Diaspora. But the Whirlwinds in the South pogroms ignited Russian Zionism, and the idea that the Land of Israel could become a refuge gained momentum. Soon after

---

514   Israel Bartal, *To Redeem a People: Jewish Nationalism and Enlightenment in Eastern Europe* (Jerusalem: Carmel, 2013) 245 [Hebrew].

Leo Pinsker published *Auto-Emancipation* (1882), which called for the creation of a national territorial homeland for the Jews,[515] more than 5,000 Russian Jews arrived in the Holy Land. Encouraged by Hovevei Zion, they joined the 26,000 Jews who already lived in the holy cities of Jerusalem, Hebron, Tiberias, and Safed.

Most of the new immigrants were poor and could hardly face the harsh reality in Palestine. The existing Jewish population there (the "old *Yishuv*") was ill-equipped to absorb the large numbers of newcomers, and its leaders worried that the new arrivals would compromise their own standing with Ottoman authorities, who quickly decreed a ban on immigration.[516] At that point, the choice between the Land of Israel and the Goldene Medina had never been so clear.

Only after the appearance of Theodor Herzl on the world stage did Palestine become a central focus of Jewish national sentiment. He laid the ideological and organizational foundations for the Zionist movement. His pamphlet *Der Judenstaat* (*The Jewish State*, 1896) called for the massive evacuation of Jews from Europe and the restoration of a Jewish state in the Holy Land. *The Jewish State* was a prophetic document, preaching the ingathering of exiles as the solution to the Jewish Question in Europe, and granting the Jews equal status among the nations.[517]

Herzl provided concrete answers on how to transplant Jews from Europe to Palestine, and how build political and financial institutions, schools, and settlements. A charismatic and relentless figure, he traveled the capitals of Europe and beyond, building international backing of imperial powers and alliances with other actors on the world stage. In many ways, Herzl is the first modern Jewish

515 Dimitry Shumsky, "Leon Pinsker and 'Autoemancipation!': A Reevaluation," *Jewish Social* Studies 18, no. 1 (Fall 2011), 33–62.

516 Margalit Shilo, "The Immigration Policy of the Zionist Institutions 1882–1914," *Middle Eastern Studies* 30, no. 3 (July 1994), 601.

517 Aharon Klieman, "Returning to the World Stage: Herzl's Zionist Statecraft," *Israel Journal of Foreign affairs* 4, no. 2 (2010), 76.

statesman, who paved the way for diplomacy in Israel both before and after statehood, and also for Diaspora Jewry.

In August 1897 Herzl presided over the First Zionist Congress in Basel, Switzerland. After three days of remarkable deliberations, with hundreds of enthusiastic Jewish delegates from seventeen countries in attendance, as well as many non-Jews and European journalists, Herzl confided to his diary: "If I were to sum up the Basel Congress in a single phrase—which I would not dare to make public—I would say: in Basel I created the Jewish State."

From 1904 to 1914, the yishuv in Palestine absorbed a significant wave of new migrants from Eastern Europe, known as Second Aliyah. These newcomers emerged as the new social and political elite that replaced the old, religious one with a modern revolutionary vanguard. Zionist thought (and later historiography) glorified these *olim*, stressing their mission and superior stature over the "simple" eastern European Jews who migrated to the United States only to improve their lot. Historian Gur Alroey wrote that Zionist historiography deliberately downplayed the story of Jewish migration from Russia to the United States to distinguish between the "uniqueness" of Jews who chose Palestine and the banal masses who rushed to America with "no national purpose and its moral level was undoubtedly lower than that of Aliya to Palestine."[518]

Even after the Holocaust and the establishment of Israel, America long remained the preferred destination of most Jews. Israelis stigmatized them as pining for the fleshpots of Egypt, but Jews who arrived in the United States rarely saw their move as a waystation on the road to their ancient homeland. America was their new Promised Land, the "true Zion."

Today, over seventy years after the establishment of the State

---

518   Gur Alroey, *An Unpromising Land: Jewish Migration to Palestine in the Early Twentieth Century* (Stanford: Stanford University Press, 2014), 2017.

of Israel, there is no longer a real debate over which is the true Jewish homeland. Even the most patriotic American Jews, who would never think of uprooting themselves for a home overseas, understand that Israel is increasingly the dominant force in the Jewish world and the only country that can claim to be a homeland of the Jews.

America's unique relationship with both the Jews and the Hebraic heritage dates to before the nation's founding. New England's Puritans of the seventeenth and eighteenth centuries took great interest in the Old Testament and Jewish history. They saw themselves as "the new Israelites," and Boston was often called "New Jerusalem." They also hailed the Hebrew language as "the mother of all languages," and the earliest Harvard presidents were Hebraists.

But the Puritans were not philo-Semites. In fact, they rarely met Jews in their lives, and like other Christians, suspected them for rejecting Christ. While Puritans prayed for mass conversion of the Jews, they mistrusted the motives of individual converts who might be under spell of the Devil and, therefore, ready to backslide to "the prejudices of their education."[519]

The first Jews to set foot in America were Sephardic, immigrating from Spanish and Portuguese domains in South America, the Caribbean, and the Iberian Peninsula. The settlers who came from the Dutch colony in Brazil to New Amsterdam in the 1650s were Sephardic as well; in 1654, they founded Shearith Israel, the first Jewish congregation in America, and the only synagogue in New York City until the arrival of German Jews in the 1820s.

Jews also arrived in Rhode Island after the colony declared in 1652 that "all men of whatever nation soever they may be...will have the same privileges as Englishmen." Though the purpose of the colony was "the spread of Christianity," and a 1663 Rhode Island

---

519   Milton M. Klein, "A Jew at Harvard in the 18th Century," *Proceedings of the Massachusetts Historical Society* 97 (1985), 135–145.

law stated that "only Christians can be admitted to the Colony," in 1684, the Rhode Island legislature decided that "Jews might expect as good protection as any stranger being not of our nation."

In 1762, when the Rhode Island Superior Court denied naturalization to new Jewish arrivals, claiming that the colony was full, Ezra Stiles, an eminent American theologian remarked: "Providence seems to make everything work, for mortification of the Jews, and to prevent their incorporation into any nation; that thus they continue as distinct people.... [It] forebodes that the Jews will never become incorporated with the people of America, any more than in Europe, Asia, or Africa."[520] Stiles, who became the seventh president of Yale (1778–1795), studied Hebrew regularly and was infatuated by Jewish traditions. By 1768, Rhode Island's Jews included twenty-five families, and of the 2.5 million colonists in 1776, Jews were a negligible minority, numbering around 2,000.

Throughout the nation's first decades, Jews in the United States made every effort to make their adopted country their new homeland. In fact, those who called for Jewish salvation in Palestine in the early years of the republic were invariably Christians.

On the morning of October 31, 1819, a large crowd crammed into the Old South Church in Boston to hear a young priest named Levi Parsons. He told his congregation that the Jews had "taught us the way to salvation," and it was the Christians' mission to restore them to their ancient homeland. He urged his flock to become missionaries in the Holy Land and prepare the ground for the return of the Jews, who in turn would welcome the second coming of Christ. Thus, the Jews would inaugurate the "millennial age of peace and spiritual solidarity," and all would recognize the sovereignty of Christ.[521]

---

520   Oscar Reiss, *The Jews in Colonia America* (Jefferson, NC: McFarland & Company, 2000), 49.

521   Michael Oren, *Power, Faith, and Fantasy: America in the Middle East, 1776 to the Present* (New York: W. W. Norton, 2007), 80–81.

It is often little understood in Jewish circles the extent to which Christian Zionists in the United States consider the existence and fate of the Jewish state a critical component of their own identity. Everyone knows that Israel depends on the United States as a superpower patron; less well known is that Israel has a profound impact on the character and identity of America itself. How did it happen that the internal debate about American values, culture, heritage, and international mission is shaped by what goes on in faraway Israel?

How the Jews Shaped American Identity

From its inception, American Jewry developed and defined itself in light of changes in American identity and the United States' place in the world. In the early nineteenth century, the country was still an ethnic nation-state, based mainly on an Anglo-American Protestant culture, with more than a dash of race and religion. It conceived of itself as a Christian country that was fulfilling the ancient Israelites' dream of life in the Promised Land, with the Hebrew Bible as its guide.

The small number of Jews who lived in the United States tried to fit into this Protestant paradigm. They were relatively invisible until the arrival of a large group of German Jews in the 1840s, who "got along very well with their non-Jewish neighbors, although American conception of Jews in the abstract at no time lacked the unfavorable elements embedded in European tradition."[522] German-Jewish immigrants spread rapidly throughout the United States, creating the communal and religious structures that would form the backbone of American Jewry and making every effort to

---

522 John Higham, "Social Discrimination Against Jews in America, 1830–1930," *American Jewish Historical Society* 47 (September 1957), 3.

be part of the American "chosen people." Inspired by the Jewish Reform Movement they had imported from Germany, these immigrants worked to replace Orthodox Judaism—which they saw as too tribal and trapped in ritual and theology—with a universal code of morality.

The immigration of German Jews came against a backdrop of a larger mass immigration. The population of the United States ballooned between 1815 and 1860, when some five million immigrants arrived from Europe, particularly from Ireland, Britain, and Germany. According to the 1860 census, there were over 31 million people in the United States. This period witnessed increasing hostility from Protestant Americans against Catholics, many of whom were refugees from the Irish Potato Famine. The Jews were, at this juncture, a drop in the ocean, but they started to organize. As early as 1840, when the United States was already home to 15,000 Jews, the community rallied to pressure President Martin Van Buren to intervene in the Damascus blood libel affair.[523]

By the eve of the 1860 presidential election, after an influx of thousands of immigrants from Germany, the number of Jewish US citizens had risen to 50,000. Their leaders started to organize as a nationwide lobby group to protest the abduction of Edgardo Mortara, a Jewish-Italian boy kidnapped by the Vatican in 1858 after a family servant claimed that she had secretly baptized him. The incident profoundly shocked liberal society across Europe and caused shockwaves in the American Jewish community. Anti-Catholic sentiment in the United States no doubt helped the Jews to find sympathy for their protests against Catholic abuses of Jews in Europe and the Middle East, and they rode this wave.[524]

---

523   Alexander DeConde, *Ethnicity, Race, and American Foreign Policy* (Boston: Northeastern University Press, 1992), 52.

524   David I. Kertzer, *The Kidnapping of Edgardo Mortara* (New York: Vintage Books, 1998), 125–127.

It was around then that Abraham Jonas, a close Jewish friend to future president Abraham Lincoln, started recruiting Jews to the Republican Party, having despaired of receiving help in the Mortara case from President James Buchanan, a Democrat, and Secretary of State Lewis Cass. Despite the antebellum Republican Party's nativist trends, which targeted Jews and other foreigners, Illinois Representative Abraham Lincoln swam against the tide and passionately decried not only slavery but also anti-Semitism. In a speech in New York in 1859, he declared:

> I know of no distinction among men, except those of the heart and head. I now repeat that, though I am native born, my country is the World, and my love for man is as broad as the race, and as deep as its humanity. As a matter of course I include native and foreign people, Protestant and Catholic, Jew and Gentile.[525]

Nevertheless, during the Civil War, some states forbade Jews from holding public office and anti-Semitism was in the air. General Ulysses S. Grant accused the Jews of being "unprincipled." He refused them permits to come South, forbade his officers from allowing them to move with the army, and even expelled all the Jews from his military district in 1862. "They come in with their carpet-sacks in spite of all that can be done to prevent it," he complained.[526] When he was elected president after the war, Grant publicly apologized to

---

525 Jonathan D. Sarna and Benjamin Shapell, *Lincoln and the Jews: A History* (New York: St. Martin's Press, 2015), 46.

526 Joseph Lebowich, "General Ulysses S. Grant And The Jews," *Publications of the American Jewish Historical Society* 17 (1909), 71–79.

the Jews, but some would argue that his anti-Semitic legacy had still not entirely disappeared from the ranks of the US Army.[527]

Two decades after the American Civil War and Lincoln's assassination, the United States was home to some 250,000 Jews. As the country expanded westward, it was flooded with some 30 million immigrants from southern and eastern Europe: Italians, Poles, Hungarians, Czechs, Slovaks, Russians, and of course, Jews. They changed the face of the United States, which by the late nineteenth century became a multiethnic, pluralistic country.

The anti-Semitic violence that erupted in the Russian Empire after the assassination of Tsar Alexander II in 1881 prompted a mass exodus of Russian Jews. From 1880–1914, some 2.5 million abandoned the Pale of Settlement. In 1880, New York City was home to roughly 80,000 Jews; by 1910, there were 1.1 million; and by 1920, their numbers had risen to 1.5 million, or more than 30 percent of New York's population. In 1927, the number of Jews in the United States hit 4.2 million.

Zionism and the New American Jewish Community

The young Zionist leader Haim Arlosoroff visited the United States from Palestine several times between 1926 and 1928 and recorded his impressions of American Jewry's meteoric development in a series of fascinating letters. He saw it as a unique historical experiment, which had no parallel with any model of Jewish existence throughout history and could not be explained in terms borrowed from western and eastern European experiences. He wrote that American Jewry was the most important phase in Jewish history since the Second Temple era and could even be seen as a messianic miracle.

---

527   Joseph W Bendersky, *The "Jewish Threat": Anti-Semitic Politics of the U.S. Army* (New York: Basic Books, 2000).

He described the "overnight" emergence of American Jewry as "a finger of God in our national life" and a "beacon for all Jews."[528]

Initially, this mass influx of eastern European Jews caused a split within American Jewry. Jewish politics were also revolutionized, reorganizing around hundreds of *landsmannschaften*–mutual aid societies set up to help Jewish immigrants from specific eastern European towns to integrate into American society.[529] The wealthy German Jews were anxious lest an influx of poor, traditional eastern European Jews–the alien hordes–impinge their status as veteran members of society.[530] They also feared the arrival of the Zionist national spirit imported by Russian Jewish supporters of Hovevei Zion, which would surely sully their reputations as patriotic Americans. The descendants of German Jewish immigrants, who affiliated with the Reform Movement, wanted to put an end once and for all to the incessant questions about their national loyalty. In 1885, they adopted the Pittsburgh Platform, which declared that the Jews were "no longer a nation, but a religious community."[531]

Meanwhile, millions of Jewish immigrants from eastern Europe sidelined their "aristocratic" German-born brethren. They built a vibrant Yiddish subculture, established Jewish schools and kosher restaurants, opened Jewish summer camps, choirs, and theater troupes, and developed a vast literature and press, which dwarfed the Jewish institutions from western Europe. This was all accompanied

---

528   Haim Arlosoroff, "New York and Jerusalem" (letter 5 in "Letters on American Jewry), *Hatekufah* 26–27 (1930), 466–467 [Hebrew].

529   Daniel Soyer, *Jewish Immigrant Associations and American Identity in New York: 1880–1939*, (Detroit: Wayne State University Press, 2001), 49–81.

530   In his bestselling book about eastern European Jews' impact on American Jewry, Irving Howe recalls how in 1908, New York Police Department Commissioner Theodore Bingham claimed that 50 percent of criminals in New York City were eastern European Jews, calling them "burglars, firebugs [arsonists], pickpockets and highway robbers–when they have courage." See Irving Howe, *World of Our Fathers: The Journey of the East European Jews to America and the Life They Found and Made* (New York: New York University Press, 2005), 127.

531   "The Pittsburgh Platform (1885)," Central Conference of American Rabbis, https://www.ccarnet.org/rabbinic-voice/platforms/article-declaration-principles/.

by radical working-class politics. Left-wing Jews, who arrived as part of the massive wave of immigration in the 1880s, bolstered the more radical forces and became a powerful branch of the global Left and arguably influenced the Jewish revolutionaries in the Russian Empire. Nevertheless, as Arlosoroff wrote, eastern European Jews "were washed in a stream of forceful Americanization, which could neither be stopped nor glossed over."[532]

While liberal Jews in America were still recoiling from the rumblings of early Zionism, the country also witnessed the emergence of an early Christian Zionism. In the late nineteenth century, evangelical leader William E. Blackstone secured the signatures of more than 400 members of the American elite–including Supreme Court justices, senators, businessmen, and journalists–to pressure President Benjamin Harrison to promise the return of the Jews to their historic homeland. In his 1878 book *Jesus is Coming*, Blackstone wrote that the second coming of Christ depended on the ingathering of the Jews in the Land of Israel. That is, the Jewish people's homecoming and the restoration of their sovereignty were critical stages in the Christian messianic vision of the End of Days. Blackstone visited Zionist pioneering communities in the Land of Israel in the 1880s and raised funds for the settlers. In many senses, he laid the foundations for the enduring bonds between evangelical Christianity and Zionism. Many liberal Jews today would be surprised to learn that Louis Brandeis, the father of liberal Jewry, hailed Blackstone as "a Father of Zionism."[533] Perhaps counterintuitively, liberal American Jewry was tied at its inception to evangelical Zionism.

Born in 1856 in Louisville, Kentucky, to an assimilated family, Brandeis had little connection to Jewish heritage. Over the years, he became increasingly vocal about his identity and ultimately

---

532   Arlosoroff, "New York and Jerusalem," 476 [Hebrew].

533   Timothy P. Weber, *On the Road to Armageddon: How Evangelicals Became Israel's Best Friends* (Grand Rapids, MI: Baker Academic, 2004) 106.

articulated a vision of symbiosis between American Jews' commit-ment to Zionism and their commitment to America. "Loyalty to America demands that each American Jew become a Zionist," he said. "To be good Americans, we must be better Jews, and to be better Jews, we must become Zionists."[534] This mantra eventually became the moral basis of the bond between liberal American Jewry and the State of Israel, which resonates even today.

As a young lawyer of repute, Brandeis was initially quiet about his Jewish identity and happy to go along with the Puritanical vision of America as the Holy Land and white evangelicals as the new chosen people. Historian Jonathan Sarna writes that Brandeis "grew up to share his mother's distaste for formal religion; and...fulfilled her hopes for a character formed by a 'pure spirit and the highest ideals.'"[535]

As a young man, Brandeis established a special bond with his brother-in-law, Felix Adler (1851–1933), who had come to America from Germany as a boy. His father, Samuel Adler, moved his family to New York City to become the rabbi of the Reform Temple Emanu-El, and Felix later went back to Germany to take doctoral studies. After his return to the United States, he championed a doctrine he called "The Judaism of the Future" and launched the "ethical culture movement," which had little trace of God-centered religion. This doctrine won over many followers, but among even progressive Jews, many felt that Adler has emptied their Jewish identity, and he came to be seen, according to one historian, "as a dangerous threat to the seemingly stable nature of the American Jewish community."[536]

Brandeis himself was also a humanist. He saw a deep connection

---

534 Louis Brandeis, *On Zionism* (Washington, DC: Zionist Organization of America, 1942), 11, 49–50.

535 Jonathan D. Sarna, "The Greatest Jew in the World Since Jesus Christ: The Jewish Legacy of Louis D. Brandeis," *American Jewish History* 81, no. 3/4 (Spring/Summer 1994), 347.

536 Benny Kraut, *From Reform Judaism to Ethical Culture: The Religious Evolution of Felix Adler* (Cincinnati: Hebrew Union College Press, 1979), 107.

between Protestant ethics and the heritage of the Hebrew prophets. Yet for him, the employment of Jewish heritage as universal democratic creed should not come at the expense of cultivating Jewish uniqueness. As he came to appreciate the life of eastern European immigrants, he concluded that American Jews should not assimilate, but thrive as an ethnic community by strengthening their own kinship ties and connecting tribal tradition to the cultural and intellectual heritage of the United States. They could do so by devoting themselves to the cause of Zionism.

Indeed, the idea that Herzl's Zionism should be an integral element in Jewish American identity appeared after the first Zionist Congress in 1897. It was Richard James Horatio Gottheil, a professor of Semitic languages at Columbia University and the president of the American Zionist Federation from 1898 to 1904, who formulated the thesis that Herzl's Basel Plan spoke only about a *national home* and not a *state*, and thus could fit harmoniously with the aspiration of American Jews without exposing them to charges of dual loyalty.[537]

In 1905, Brandeis, already a well-known lawyer, experienced a profound identity shift and publicly professed his Judaism for the first time. Although he implored his Jewish brethren to refrain from defining themselves as "hyphenated Americans," he encouraged them to remold their communities and religious-cultural heritage in the spirit of American democracy. In so doing, writes Allon Gal, Brandeis gave a stamp of approval to "clear ethnic politics."[538]

Jewish artists and intellectuals played a central role in shaping the discourse over American identity and the place of ethnic groups

---

537 Zohar Segev, "European Zionism in the United States: The Americanization of Herzl's Doctrine by American Zionist Leaders-Case Studies," *Modern Judaism* 26, no. 3 (October 2006), 279.

538 Allon Gal, "Louis Brandeis and American Zionism," in *The Legal and Zionist Tradition of Louis D. Brandeis*, ed. Allon Gal (Jerusalem: Academy of Arts and Sciences, 2005), 62 [Hebrew].

in the new American patchwork. Consider the play *The Melting Pot* by the Russian-born Jewish playwright Israel Zangwill, which opened on Broadway in 1908. It tells the story of a young composer, David, who arrives in New York from Russia and composes a symphony celebrating the city's ethnic harmony. He dreams of marrying a beautiful Christian girl, unencumbered by his Jewish identity:

> America is God's crucible, the great Melting-Pot where all the races of Europe are melting and reforming!... Here you stand with your fifty groups, with your fifty languages...and your fifty blood hatreds...into the Crucible with you all! God is making the great American.

In the climactic scene, the young composer stands with his beloved Vera on a Lower Manhattan rooftop, with the Statue of Liberty gleaming in the distance, and excitedly points to the metropolis below. "There she lies, the great Melting-Pot—listen! Can't you hear the roaring and the bubbling?... Celt and Latin, Slav and Teuton, Greek and Syrian, black and yellow—" Vera cuts him off and whispers back: "Jew and Gentile."[539]

Zangwill's play won critical acclaim across America. When it was staged in Washington, DC, President Theodore Roosevelt called out from his box: "That's a great play, Mr. Zangwill, that's a great play."

Zangwill himself was married to a Christian woman. Although he backed the idea of a Jewish state after meeting Herzl in 1895, he did not think that it had to be in Palestine. He imagined a safe haven

---

539 Arthur M. Schlesinger, *The Disuniting of America: Reflections on a Multicultural Society* (New York: W. W. Norton & Co., 1992), 32–33.

for the Jews along the lines of New Zealand or Australia, namely as "a large Jewish colony under the protection of the British Crown."[540] His play was panned by Jewish critics for giving a green light to assimilation, and indeed, the philosophy of the melting pot became the intellectual basis for an aggressive policy of Americanization, which erased immigrants' connections to their original countries and native cultures.[541]

It did not take long, however, before the idea of the melting pot became the ethos of American Jewry. The Jews embraced the patriotic vision of America as the new chosen people perhaps more enthusiastically than any other European immigrants, despite being the only non-Christian group. They felt that, perhaps for the first time ever, their religion and ethnic identity were tolerated, notwithstanding minor bursts of anti-Semitism. Jewish artists and intellectuals, who became the leading theoreticians and drivers of the emerging American identity, combined their ethno-religious identity with an ethos of American patriotism. At the outset, major organizations—including the American Jewish Committee, B'nai B'rith, and the American Jewish Congress—modelled themselves as all-American, cosmopolitan institutions that stressed their loyalty to America in conjunction with their promotion of universal human rights.

One Russian-Jewish immigrant, Mary Antin, described George Washington and other founding fathers as "our forefathers" and said of the United States: "The country was for all citizens, and *I was a citizen*, and when we stood up to sing 'America!' I shouted the words

---

540 Mira Yungmann, "Zangwill versus Herzl and Pinsker: Three Approaches to the Jewish Problem," in *Proceedings of The Eleventh World Congress of Jewish Studies part 2, vol. 2* (Jerusalem: World Congress of Jewish Studies, 1993/1994), 171–177 [Hebrew].

541 President Roosevelt himself used the metaphor of the "crucible" when he said: "We can have no 'fifty-fifty' allegiance in this country. Either a man is an American and nothing else, or he is not an American at all." See Schlesinger, *The Disuniting of America*, 32–35.

with all my might."[542] Her choice of the words "our forefathers" incensed some American Protestants, who stubbornly saw the Jews
as foreign implants. When Jewish anarchist Jacob Abrams was tried
for sedition in 1914 and invoked in his defense "our forefathers of
the American Revolution," the judge incredulously interjected to
ask whether he meant to refer to "the founders of this nation as
your forefathers" and asked him bluntly: "Why don't you go back
to Russia?"[543]

During World War I, suspicions arouse about American Jews'
dual loyalties because of their ties to Germany. Americans also questioned the Jews' loyalties because of their communal institutions
and transnational attachments to European Jewry and Zionism, a
separatist national movement.

Most spokesmen for American Jewry eagerly lauded American
nationalism as their civic identity, but in 1915, Horace Kallen, a
German rabbi's son, assailed Zangwill's vision of the melting pot in
an influential essay titled "Democracy Versus the Melting Pot." He
argued that Zangwill's representation of American life was inaccu-
rate, and the melting pot was a poor vision for it. In its place, Kallen
proposed cultural pluralism. Instead of erasing ethno-cultural differences between groups in American society, this diversity—including
Jewish identity—should be cherished as an asset in the cultivation of
a vibrant democratic society. In his vision, the United States would
be a diverse federation of minorities inspiring each other and coexisting under the banner of civic loyalty to the institutions of American
democracy. Only cultural pluralism, Kallen argued, would guarantee
the country's national resilience.

World War I aggravated the debate about loyalty and identity
in America. To begin with, wars always demand unwavering loyalty

---

542 Lawrence H. Fuchs, *The American Kaleidoscope: Race, Ethnicity, and the Civic Culture* (Hanover
NH: Wesleyan University Press, 1990), 67–68.

543 Ibid.

and bind citizens to their country through the ultimate sacrifice. The war also raised uncomfortable questions about immigrants' loyalties to their countries of origin, especially if those countries were at war with the United States. Some 250,000 Jews enlisted in the US Army; some 3,500 of them were killed in battle. However, once Americans started suspecting dual loyalties on the part of German immigrants, including Jews, many started seeing Kallen's vision of cultural pluralism as a threat to the American nation.

Kallen was not alone in his beliefs. In 1916, a radical young journalist named Randolph Bourne published an article in which he feted America as a transnational nation of cultural affinities to diverse home countries. He slammed the vision of America as an isolationist Anglo-Protestant nation, and his essay "Trans-National America" would also enter the canon of texts about American identity.[544]

That same year, American philosopher John Dewey denounced those who spread fear about immigrants' ties and loyalties to their home countries. He argued that "such terms as Irish-American or Hebrew-American or German-American are false terms," because they presupposed that America was a static entity "to which other factors may be hitched on." However, "the typical American is himself a hyphenated character...he is international and interracial in his make-up."[545]

This internationalist pluralism cut against the winds of nationalism that swept through America in the early twentieth century. Americans were already deeply suspicious of and hostile towards second- and third-generation "aliens," and their suspicions were only heightened during the war. President Woodrow Wilson said:

---

544   Ralph Bourne, "Trans-National America," *The Atlantic*, July 1916, https://www.theatlantic.com/magazine/archive/1916/07/trans-national-america/304838/.

545   Nathan Glazer, *We Are All Multiculturalists Now* (Cambridge, MA: Harvard University Press, 1997), 86.

"You cannot become thorough Americans if you think of yourselves in groups. America does not consist of groups." He added that those who regarded themselves as "belonging to a particular national group in America" were not worthy "to live under the Stars and Stripes."[546]

American Jews during World War I watched the unfolding disaster wrought on their kin in eastern Europe with horror, as the Jews fell hostage and victim to the warring sides. The Russians treated the Jews of eastern Europe as a fifth column; in spring 1915, they cruelly expelled more than half a million Jews from the area of the front against Germany and Austria-Hungary. When the Russian army retreated, it slaughtered masses of Jews in Poland and eastern Galicia, torching dozens of villages with their inhabitants inside. Eastern Europe became "a physical and spiritual graveyard for Jews," in the words of historian Aviel Roshwald, who has documented how they fell prey to the Russians and Germans alike. The Germans conquered vast swathes of Russian territory at the start of the war and operated a slick propaganda campaign that promised the Jews liberation from tsarist oppression but still treated them as treasonous dirt. Many Jews suffered under the yoke of anti-Semitism and were dispatched for hard labor in what were effectively concentration camps.[547]

Many American Jews had families trapped in the carnage in eastern Europe, and news of the devastation spurred them into establishing aid organizations that sent money, personnel, and supplies to Russia and Poland. This mission gave birth to the modern network of American-Jewish international aid organizations, including the American Jewish Joint Distribution Committee, which still provides humanitarian aid to distressed populations around the world.[548]

---

546   DeConde, *Ethnicity, Race, and American Foreign Policy*, 83.

547   Aviel Roshwald, "Jewish Cultural Identity in Eastern and Central Europe during the Great War," in *European Culture in the Great War: The Arts, Entertainment and Propaganda 1914-1918*, eds. Aviel Roshwald and Richard Stites (New York: Cambridge University Press, 1999), 89–126.

548   Sarna, *American Judaism*, 210–211.

Thus, while the Jews of eastern Europe suffered acute persecution, their brothers and sisters who had sailed to safety in America grew stronger as a community.

Indeed, America gave the Jews of eastern Europe a safe haven and fertile soil on which to express their Judaism. They, in turn, cherished the United States as a national home with an open democratic society and free market ethos. America allowed them to be patriots while enjoying a Jewish religious and cultural renaissance. With the "Jewish Question" no longer a serious worry, the Jews were able to focus on securing their place in American society and politics. The United States' role as the undisputed new Jewish homeland made American Zionists a marginal factor within both American Jewry and the Zionist movement, as few of them intended to personally fulfil Herzl's vision and move to the Land of Israel. There was no need for Zionism in the United States; the Jews believed that they had cracked Herzl's dilemma of how they could live in peace. In the words of historian Robert Wiebe: "What could Zionism, a wandering minstrel of a movement, offer them?"[549]

Louis Brandeis, Woodrow Wilson, and the Balfour Declaration

World War I precipitated the collapse of mighty empires and thrust the question of national self-determination to the fore. In so doing, it compelled American Zionists to reconsider their attitude toward Jewish nationalism. In June 1914, Louis Brandeis assumed the leadership of the Provisional Executive Committee for Zionist Affairs. He backed Zionism out of an understanding that the evolving American identity had to be made amenable to Jewish ethnic identity, and

---

549 Robert H. Wiebe, *Who We Are: A History of Popular Nationalism*, (Princeton: Princeton University Press, 2002), 35–36.

he saw Zionism as a means with which to strengthen American-Jewish identity. He believed that American Jews needed to connect to their national roots to form a coherent group based on more than liberal religion and guarantee that Judaism did not dissipate into the broader American population, but rather constituted a meaningful part of it.

According to historian Jonathan Sarna, Brandeis's personal charm and public reputation gave Zionism tremendous momentum in the United States. Many American Jews joined the ranks of the Zionist movement, and its coffers grew fuller than ever. The fact that a man of Brandeis's stature backed it gave more public legitimacy after he was appointed the first Jewish associate justice of the US Supreme Court in 1916. His support induced other famous Jews to declare their support for Zionism as the framework through which they could reconcile their universalist, progressive ideals with their latent Jewish identity. Thanks to Brandeis, Zionism became something of a civic religion for secular American Jews, a religion that aspired, in Sarna's words, to create "a model state in the Holy Land—freed from the economic wrongs, the social injustices and the greed of modern-day industrialism."[550]

By cultivating a synthesis between loyalty to America, loyalty to the Jewish people, and a commitment to the notion that the Jews deserved an independent polity, Brandeis encouraged Reform Jews, who considered Judaism to be just a religion, to mellow their opposition to Zionism.[551] His earnest desire to assist the Zionist movement, even from afar, made him a central player in promoting the

---

550 Sarna, *American Judaism*, 204–205.

551 Brandeis's Zionism must be understood in the context not just of the plight of Jews in eastern Europe but also the struggle over American-Jewish identity. Brandeis and his American Zionist colleagues were only distantly involved in the Jewish state-building project in Palestine and to a large extent were "armchair Zionists." See Gal, "Louis Brandeis and American Zionism," 70–71 [Hebrew].

Jewish nation-building project in Palestine under President Wilson's administration.

At the outbreak of World War I in 1914, Wilson took a defensive line and kept the United States out of the fighting. In time, however, he set his sights on replacing the imperial world order with one based on the "universal principles of liberty and justice through institutionalized international cooperation."[552] The US entry into the war on April 6, 1917, the collapse of the Ottoman empire, and the impending British takeover of Palestine energized the Zionist diplomatic campaign for British support for a Jewish national home. On April 21, 1917, Zionist philanthropist James de Rothschild, together with the Zionist leader Chaim Weizmann, asked Justice Brandeis to secure President Wilson's approval for Britain's plans for Palestine in a telegram:

> Unanimous opinion [is that the] only satisfactory solution [is a] Jewish Palestine under British protectorate. Russian Zionists fully approve. Public opinion and competent authorities here [are] favorable.... It would greatly help if American Jews would suggest this scheme before their Government.[553]

Upon receiving this appeal, Brandeis and his American Zionist colleagues started lobbying the president. Brandeis met President Wilson on May 6, 1917, and argued that a Jewish state would fulfill the conditions of the type of peace settlement he envisaged, as well as replace Ottoman tyranny with a democratic state in which the

---

552   Erez Manela, "The Wilsonian Moment and the Rise of Anticolonial Nationalism: The Case of Egypt," *Diplomacy and Statecraft* 12, no. 4 (December 2001), 102.

553   Richard Ned Lebow, "Wilson and the Balfour Declaration," *The Journal of Modern History* 40, no. 4 (December 1968), 502.

Jews, an oppressed minority, would be able to freely pursue their cultural and economic development. Brandeis also met British Foreign Secretary Arthur Balfour.

Wilson endorsed the idea of a Jewish national home in Palestine not just because it matched his commitment to self-determination (as listed in his famous Fourteen Points of January 1918), but also for internal political reasons, namely the Jewish vote. Zionism spoke to Wilson's heart, and his religious faith propelled him to accept the Balfour Declaration—the first formal recognition by the British government of Jewish national rights in Palestine.

Although President Wilson saw himself as a historic partner in the restoration of the Jews to their homeland, he still wavered about alienating Ottoman Turkey as a potential ally.[554] Only after the defeat of the Ottoman Empire did he publicly declare his support for the establishment of a Jewish national home in Palestine, and in January 1918, Congress adopted its own resolution supporting a Jewish Commonwealth in Palestine.

An intensive campaign of Jewish diplomacy insured that the historic declaration was enshrined in the Paris Peace Conference. The Balfour Declaration also became part of the preamble of the League of Nations mandate, acquiring full legal standing in international law. The Allied powers, the league announced, made Britain "responsible for putting into effect the declaration originally made on November 2, 1917 by the Government of his Britannic majesty, and adopted by the said Powers."[555]

Martin Kramer has written that the Balfour Declaration is justly considered the beginning of the Jewish nation-state's legitimation by other nations, and therefore a subject of attack by Israel's enemies. However, while in the collective memory of American Jewry the

---

554 Lebow, "Wilson and the Balfour Declaration," 501–523.

555 Martin Kramer, "The Forgotten Truth about the Balfour Declaration," *Mosaic*, June 5, 2017.

declaration was secured by Louis Brandeis and President Wilson, Zionist historiography and Israel's collective memory remember Chaim Weizmann as the genius behind it. After the declaration was issued, the leader of Revisionist Zionism, Ze'ev Jabotinsky, said: "The declaration is the personal achievement of one man alone: Dr. Chaim Weizmann.... In our history, the declaration will remain linked to the name of Weizmann."[556]

Weizmann, who became Israel's first president in 1949, grew up in the Russian shtetl with deep roots in Jewish tradition, but outgrew his East European mentality to become "an Englishman." After moving to Britain in 1904, he earned great reputation as a biochemist who developed the acetone-butanol-ethanol fermentation process, yet his true passion lay in Zionism. He used his professional success and prestige to climb the ladder of the Zionist movement, which had been thrust into turmoil by the sudden death of Herzl in 1904. He gained prominence as a British Zionist activist and used his celebrity status among Britain's elite to raise money and support to build a university in Palestine. In 1921, Weizmann conquered American Zionism as well, effectively staging an organizational coup with Brandeis's American rivals, who removed Brandeis from his leading position of the American Zionist Organization. According to historian Ben Halpern, Weizmann defined Zionism as "Palestine first" and believed that Brandeis and his allies "were not Jewish nationalists at all."[557]

As a man who could bridge eastern and western Europe, he understood that he needed American Jewish support more than anything else. "They can give up on us, but we cannot give up on them," was his mantra regarding American Jewry.

Only 60,000 Jews lived in Palestine in 1918, while the population in America was growing by leaps and bounds. Prominent

---

556   Ibid.

557   Ben Halpern, "The Americanization of Zionism, 1880–1930," *American Jewish History* 69, no. 1 (September 1979), 15–33.

non-Zionist American Jewish leaders, including Louis Marshall and Cyrus Adler, had feared that supporting Zionism would raise allegations of dual loyalties, but Wilson's statement enabled them to retroactively endorse the Balfour Declaration.[558] Soon after it was signed, Marshall conceded that "to combat Zionism at this time is to combat the Government of England, France and Italy, and to some extent our Government in so far as its political interests are united with those of the nations with which it has joined in fighting the curse of autocracy."[559]

Marshall became a critical partner of Chaim Weizmann in raising funds among American Jews for the Zionist project in Palestine. However, he and his colleagues at the American Jewish Committee refused to endorse Palestine as a national home for the Jewish people at the same time, making do with supporting a "center for Judaism." They insisted that "the Jews of the United States have established a permanent home…and recognize their unqualified allegiance to this country." For them, this was axiomatic. They also insisted that Jewish citizens of other democratic countries would continue "to live…where they enjoy full civil and religious liberty." Although they acknowledged that many Jews were moved by a traditional yearning for the Holy Land, they limited their support to a "center for Judaism…for the stimulation of our faith…and for the rehabilitation of the land," and decidedly *not* for an independent national polity. This remained the official position of the American Jewish Committee until the eve of World War II.[560]

---

558   In a letter sent in 1910 to Jacob Schiff, one of the most prominent leaders of early twentieth century American Jewry, Marshall wrote: "As you know, I am a non-Zionist but not an anti-Zionist. I object fully as much as you do to being publicly connected with a Zionistic undertaking. Yet I can see no objection to the acceptance of financial aid from a Zionist or Zionistic organization." See Jerome C. Rosenthal, "A Fresh Look at Louis Marshall and Zionism 1900–1912," *American Jewish Archives* (November 1980), 115.

559   David Vital, *A People Apart* (Oxford: Oxford University Press, 1999), 699.

560   Stuart E. Knee, "Jewish Non-Zionism in America and Palestine Commitment: 1917–1941," *Jewish Social Studies* 39, no. 3 (Summer 1977), 210–211.

Indeed, Weizmann invented the remarkable formula that allowed the alliance between Palestinian Zionists and American Jews to advance the cause of Jewish nationalism in the twentieth century by collaborating with Louis Marshall. That formula, which he labelled "shared duty and mutual responsibility," meant the following division of labor: we in Palestine will give our sweat and blood, and you, our brothers and sisters in America, will give your financial resources and political support. After the establishment of the State of Israel, the AJC gradually became the most important diplomatic organization among Diaspora Jewry, working to safeguard the security and international standing of Jews worldwide and in the State of Israel.[561]

America, the New Promised Land

The stronger the Zionist movement grew, the more strongly American Jews also identified with the United States. American Zionists did their utmost to avoid accusations of dual loyalties or a lack of patriotism. Even during the Holocaust, when the Jews of Europe desperately needed their help, American Jews took little public action, out of fear of undermining their standing as loyal Americans. In his book *The Abandonment of the Jews*, David Wyman documented how American Jews chose to champion American interests during the war at the expense of saving European Jewry.[562] This raises the disturbing question: Did this excessive loyalty to President Franklin D. Roosevelt allow him to ignore the genocide of the Jews as a factor in weighing US interests?

---

561   On Weizmann's complex relations with American Jews see Motti Golani and Jehuda Reinharz, *The Founding Father: Chaim Weizmann, Biography 1922-1952* (Tel Aviv: Am Oved, 2020), 119-148 [Hebrew].

562   David S. Wyman, *The Abandonment of the Jews: America and the Holocaust 1941-1945* (New York: Pantheon Books, 1984).

However, the battle to defeat fascism in Europe also opened the door for American Jews to at long last harmonize Jewish values with universal American values. In her research on American-Jewish soldiers during and after World War II, historian Deborah Dash Moore showed how the war provided Jews an entry ticket to American society. White Anglo-Saxon America, which the Jews had never been a part of, now had one supreme mission: to fight for freedom and crush fascism. Ironically perhaps, while the Jews of Europe were being incinerated in the name of the Nazis' vision of racial purity, the Jews of America were offered a golden opportunity to prove their allegiance to the American spirit, to make anti-Semitism and anti-Jewish discrimination unacceptable, and to secure complete social integration. This process effectively transformed them into members of white society and faithful adherents of the American creed that embraced Catholics and Protestants, emphasizing their liberal common ground over religious differences.

During the 1950s, this creed would evolve into a conception of "Judeo-Christian" culture.[563] The Judeo-Christian idea, which appeared before World War II, was used as a philosophical affirmation of anti-fascism after the sinking of the USAT *Dorchester* in 1943, when Protestant, Catholic, and Jewish chaplains drowned together at prayer.[564]

Over the years, the idea of Judeo-Christian culture came to refer to shared values and principles between Christianity and Judaism and was said to form the basis of Western civilization. The concept gave legitimacy to Jews and Judaism as a pillar of the American ethos.[565]

---

563 Deborah Dash Moore, "Jewish GIs and the Creation of the Judeo-Christian Tradition," *Religion and American Culture: A Journal of Interpretation* 8, no. 1 (Winter, 1998), 31–53.

564 Anna Grzymala-Busse, "Once, the 'Judeo-Christian Tradition' United Americans. Now It Divides Them," *Washington Post*, April 17, 2019, https://www.washingtonpost.com/politics/2019/04/17/once-judeo-christian-tradition-united-americans-now-it-divides-them/.

565 Will Herberg, *Protestant-Catholic-Jew: An Essay in American Religious Sociology* (New York: Anchor, 1960).

It was also used to embellish the "natural" alliance between Israel and the United States. In fact, President Barack Obama invoked the phrase to eulogize Shimon Peres, and President Donald Trump used it to underline the historical alliance of Israel and the United States against radical Islam.

American Jews began enlisting American ideas and Jewish institutions in the service of the Zionist project soon after Pearl Harbor. At the 1942 Biltmore Conference in New York, when the enormity of the catastrophe in Europe began to dawn on them, they gave Ben-Gurion their go-ahead to pursue Jewish sovereignty. They mobilized to support Zionism more actively after the Holocaust and during Israel's War of Independence. However, in the 1950s, during the Eisenhower administration, they weighed their actions cautiously when American and Israeli interests clashed. During the 1956 Suez Campaign, in which Israel colluded with British and French forces to invade the Sinai Peninsula over the objections of Eisenhower, they distanced themselves from the Israeli actions. Political scientist Michael Barnett observes that, while Israel considered itself responsible for the historic mission of saving the Jews and expected Diaspora Jews to immigrate to their ancient homeland, American Jews believed even after Israel's establishment that *they* represented the safest and most prosperous Jewish future. Nevertheless, Diaspora Jews accepted their role as political advocates and fundraisers for Israel without protesting too loudly that Israel often treated them as less authentically Jewish. Thus, Israel and the Diaspora established balanced and consensual kinship and working ties.[566]

The nascent State of Israel developed into a critical component of American Jews' identity and supporting Zionism from afar became a substitute for nourishing ethnic and religious communal ties in the United States. Support for Israel allowed many American

---

566   Barnett, *The Star and the Stripes*, 257.

Jews to preserve their *Jewishness* without observing their *Judaism*, and Israel became a means for renewal and community mobilization. By donating to Israel, American Jews felt a sense of mission and partnership in the greatest Jewish adventure of our time. It was only in the late 1960s, after the Eichmann trial and Israel's victory in the 1967 Six-Day War, that American Jews' tribal-national attachment to Israel took a huge turn, and commitment to the tribe began trumping the ethos of Jewish cosmopolitanism. This development occurred amid the countercultural revolution, when many American Jews were looking for a tangible identity that would reconcile American interests and values with broader Jewish and Israeli national interests.

After Israel won the Six-Day War and improved its international standing in Washington, American Jews discovered new directions for their communal identity and Jewish faith. From the 1970s, Israel became one of their core projects and an integral part of their identity. The focus on Israel also spurred a religious and spiritual renewal, which allowed them to slow the process of Americanization, which stressed the humanistic and universal motifs of the Jewish tradition at the expense of its tribal and rabbinical sides.

The American Jewish renewal was part of the growing spirit of multiculturalism in American society, based on a rejection of white supremacy in favor of a liberal vision of civil rights and affirmative action. This spirit gave minorities the green light to emphasize their ethnic heritage as integral parts of the American mosaic and thus gave a certain legitimacy for "ethnic" Americans to reaffirm their ties with their home countries *without* being suspected of dual loyalties.

Yet for American Jews, unlike other minorities, their European points of origin were no longer relevant—*Israel* became their symbolic "country of origin," and they started building institutions around the Jewish state while trying to influence its identity in a manner that would reflect their own liberal worldview. Political support for the modern and democratic State of Israel became their new civic religion; donating to the Zionist project became a religious rite.[567] By speaking up for an Israel under attack from the Communist bloc and Third World states, American Jews were speaking up for the values of America itself.

Their growing identification with Israel after the Six-Day War bolstered their sense of global Jewish mutual responsibility. It also spurred an intense focus on Holocaust commemoration as part of a collective American identity and animated their public struggle to force the Soviet Union to let the Jews leave, under the battle cry of "Let My People Go!" The intensity of American Jews' commitment to their brethren in the Soviet Union can be partially explained by their sense of guilt at having "abandoned" the Jews of Europe during the Holocaust. Second- and third-generation Jewish immigrants, feeling secure in the United States, took it upon themselves to correct their parents' traumatic failure to honor mutual Jewish responsibility. Their extensive activism in defense of the Jews' right to emigrate from the Soviet Union made them players in the Cold War and influenced the course of the superpower conflict. The US Congress passed the Jackson-Vanik amendment to the Trade Act of 1974, which prevented states that restricted their citizens' freedom of emigration from receiving preferential trading relationships with the United States.

The amendment was adopted despite opposition from the White House; Israeli officials also feared that it would backfire and obstruct the emigration of Jews from the Soviet Union, thousands of whom had started leaving in recent years. President Richard Nixon and Secretary of State Henry Kissinger were committed to a policy of détente between Washington and Moscow and argued that it would be better to keep quiet on the matter of Soviet Jewry than enter a full-on confrontation with the Kremlin. The Watergate scandal

---

567   David Biale, *Power and Powerlessness in Jewish History* (New York: Schocken Books, 1986), 197.

forced Nixon out of the White House in August 1974, and his successor, President Gerald Ford, signed the Jackson-Vanik amendment into law in January 1975. Israeli Prime Minister Yitzhak Rabin sent President Ford and the resolution's congressional sponsors a letter to thank them on behalf of the Israeli people and Jewish communities worldwide.

In their campaign to free Soviet Jewry, American Jews became the most high-profile advocates of freedom against the "evil empire." They worked to ensure that Soviet Jews be recognized as refugees under US law, granting them residency rights in the United States. The large majority of *refuseniks*–Jews denied the right to emigrate from the Soviet Union to Israel and persecuted for alleged treason– wanted to reach the United States as a second choice. In general, however, the Israeli government asked American Jews to intensify the campaign for the refuseniks' right to reach the Promised Land. This demand often caused friction between Israeli authorities and American-Jewish leadership, but the latter ultimately deferred to the official Israeli position because Russian Jews "were wanted and needed and stood a better chance of remaining Jews" in Israel.[568]

In his book, *Chutzpah*, Alan Dershowitz describes how the complicated relationship between the State of Israel and American Jewry impacted on the struggle for the refuseniks and the Prisoners of Zion (Jews imprisoned by the Communist regime for Zionist activities). Dershowitz and future Canadian justice minister Irwin Cotler defended famous refusenik Anatoly (Natan) Sharansky, who was charged with espionage by the Soviet Union. Soviet authorities accused him of subversion for joining dissident physicist Andrei Sakharov in the Helsinki Watch group, who demanded to oversee the implementation of the Helsinki Accords. The Soviet Union had

568   Fred Lazin, *The Struggle for Soviet Jewry in American Politics: Israel versus the American Jewish Establishment* (New York: Lexington Books, 2005), 3.

signed the 1976 landmark treaty to respect fundamental liberties and human rights in exchange for détente with the United States. Sharansky was convicted of treason, spying for the United States, and spreading anti-Soviet propaganda; he was sentenced to thirteen years in jail. His struggle not only elicited an international outcry and spurred an unprecedented mobilization of American Jews, but it also created friction between the State of Israel and American Jewry. For although he had become a symbol of the human rights struggle in the Soviet Union and the Jewish campaign for freedom behind the Iron Curtain, Israel decided not to focus on the release of a man now seen as a "dissident," preferring instead to focus specifically on Prisoners of Zion and refuseniks sentenced for the "crimes" of Zionism and attempting to emigrate.

Dershowitz writes that Israel rebuffed his request to inspect documents connected to Sharansky's trial and imprisonment because it deemed his case too "universal" and argued that focusing on him might prejudice the wider struggle to open the gates of the Soviet Union to Jewish emigration. According to Dershowitz, Israel declined to officially assist Sharansky because it wanted to avoid a head-on collision with the Soviets, while American Jews were fighting for their brethren out of a broader concern for human rights. Israel, he added, took a realist approach based on its own national interests and the good of its citizens (and citizens-to-be), and it effectively abandoned Sharansky.

Only under massive pressure from the Diaspora did the State of Israel ultimately adopt Sharansky's cause. He was handed over to American authorities on February 11, 1986, as part of a Cold War prisoner exchange and landed at Ben Gurion Airport to a hero's welcome.

The gulf between Israel's official position and American Jews' campaign for Natan Sharansky and other refuseniks shows just how intense the disagreement could be over who could speak on behalf of the Jewish people and with what authority. Dershowitz writes that Israel, as a democratic sovereign state, wished to limit its involvement to its particular national interests; but American Jews, who were not Israeli citizens, adopted a universalist agenda that emphasized that they were neither legally nor morally answerable to Israel and had their own set of priorities: "We, of course, understood our limitations.... Private citizens do not carry anywhere near the influence that states do; but neither do they have some of the constraints."[569]

Dershowitz's analysis of the division of labor between Israel and the Diaspora in the campaign to free Soviet Jewry, however, overlooks one critical point. Starting in 1952, the Israeli prime minister's office operated Nativ (the "Liaison Bureau")—a clandestine organization for maintaining contact with Jews in the Eastern Bloc. Nativ was Israel's invisible hand, steering the struggle of Soviet Jewry; it spurred Diaspora Jews and other actors into action, raising awareness and pressure in defense of the Prisoners of Zion and the Jews' right to emigrate. Nativ swayed international thinking by winning the favor of Western journalists and intellectuals, organizing international conferences, and "handling" Jewish and non-Jewish politicians, who had no idea who was steering them. It was also responsible for indirectly influencing American public opinion and institutions, creating vast transnational support for the cause of Soviet Jewry.[570] While Dershowitz and other American Jews focused on universal rights and political freedoms, one former director of Nativ told this author that "the Jews and others could say what they wanted—the most important thing was that the overwhelming majority of Soviet Jews ultimately reach Israel."[571]

---

569   Ibid., 255.

570   Peter Hagel and Pauline Peretz, "States and Transnational Actors: Who's Influencing Whom? A Case Study in Jewish Diaspora Politics during the Cold War," *European Journal of International Relations* 11, no. 4 (December 2005), 467–493.

571   Ibid.

For years, it was an integral part of Israel's foreign policy to act in manifold ways and on multiple fronts to rescue Jews—not only in the Soviet Union—and bring them to Israel. Oftentimes, Israel agreed to shady arms deals with autocratic regimes in return for "buying" their Jews. This was true of its relations with the dictatorships in Ethiopia, Argentina, Iran, and Romania.[572] Questions of morality were a running sore in the ties between Israel's sovereign interests and Diaspora activists' commitments to universal, prophetic justice. The tension between morality and state interests became clear, for example, in the argument over Israel's relations with the apartheid regime in South Africa, which left American Jews angry and exposed to bitter criticism at home, especially from African American quarters.

There were also vibrant moral dilemmas over internal Jewish matters. After the collapse of the Soviet Union, high-profile American Jewish leaders rallied to rehabilitate Jewish communities in eastern Europe and lobby for restitution of property stolen during and after the Holocaust. They discovered, to their dismay, that Israel refused to join their struggle. In the 1990s, Stuart Eizenstat, a senior Clinton administration official, led the campaign to seek justice for the "double victims": Jews victimized by both the Nazis and the Communists.

Israel had absolutely no interest in helping to rehabilitate the Jewish communities of eastern Europe, however. Repeated entreaties to Prime Minister Benjamin Netanyahu and his successor Ehud Barak fell on deaf ears. "I told them that Israel should be embarrassed by its disengagement," recalled Eizenstat, but the Israeli government stuck to its belief that strengthening Jewish communities in eastern Europe would undermine efforts to encourage Jews to come to Israel instead.

Israel also had other interests vis-à-vis eastern European countries, which did not overlap with those of American Jewish leaders.

---

572   Aaron S. Klieman, *Israel's Global Reach: Arms Sales as Diplomacy* (Washington and London: Pergamon-Brassey's 1985).

"It was ironic," added Eizenstat, "that the government that purports to represent the interests of world Jewry would have left the field [of property restitution] to the U.S. government."[573]

American Jews' great advantage in promoting Israel's cause and speaking for oppressed Jews around the world has always been due to their strength in the media and politics and their self-image as spokespeople for universal morality. The late neoconservative intellectual Irving Kristol wrote that American Jews "located themselves on the cutting edge of American acculturation to secular humanism as an integral part of their own Americanization...because it has assured them of an unparalleled degree of comfort and security."[574] The sovereign State of Israel, meanwhile, acts out of a realist assessment of its *raison d'état*, exposing itself to international censure on questions of might and morality. Yet increasingly, American Jews are called on to adapt themselves to what this sovereign state sees as the implications of Jewish tribal loyalty. Challenges related to identity and loyalty, including the definition of who is a Jew and the debate over Israel's borders, have intensified over time and liberal American Jews are trapped between a desire for Israel to validate their own Jewishness and their universalist ideology and other imperatives of survival in American society.

"The Israeli as Witness"

American Jews, who always promoted cosmopolitan values, also became the leading proponents of the separation between church and state. Progressive Jews became opponents of expressions or symbols of Christianity in public spaces. The gradual erasure of

---

573   Stuart E. Eizenstat, "Imperfect Justice," *New York Times*, February 23, 2003), https://www.nytimes.com/2003/02/23/books/chapters/imperfect-justice.html.

574   Irving Kristol, *Neoconservatism: The Autobiography of an Idea* (New York: The Free Press, 1995), 448–449.

doctrinal and traditional differences between liberal Jews and Christians, whose faith was also being Americanized, gave them a sense that anti-Semitism was in retreat. Yet their cultural integration in American society exacerbated trends of full-blown assimilation among younger American Jews. "Even if these young Jews approve of Jewish survival...," wrote Irving Kristol, "there are an awful lot of Jews, young and not-so-young, who are less interested in Jewish survival than in the universal sovereignty of secular humanism.... American Jews, living in their suburban cocoons, are likely to be the last to know what is happening to them."[575]

The erosion of Jewish identity among liberal American Jews provoked Orthodox hostility in Israel and the United States to the Reform and Conservative movements, which, in turn, sought secular allies in Israel, alarmed by growing religiosity in society and politics. Data shows that while a very high proportion of Orthodox American Jews had visited Israel, only a small minority of Reform Jews thought that visiting Israel was important to maintaining Jewish identity in the United States. Scholar Charles Liebman wrote that Israel was just a "symbol" for Reform Jews, while Orthodox Jews were more invested in the Jewish state out of concern about secular Zionism's influence on Judaism, including their own Judaism in America.[576]

For decades, progressive Jewish movements in the United States refrained from intervening in domestic Israeli affairs, but this changed dramatically at the end of the twentieth century. The more that American Jewish identity seemed to be weakening, and Israel seemed to be steaming towards greater Orthodoxy and na- tionalism (with the encouragement of politically conservative and religiously orthodox actors in the US), the Reform and Conservative movements upped their involvement in the hope of averting a rift

---

575 Kristol, *Neoconservatism*, 449–450.

576 See Yossi Shain, *Kinship and Diasporas in International Affairs* (Ann Arbor, MI: University of Michigan Press, 2007), 71.

between the State of Israel, where the Orthodox held a monopoly on religious institutions including both the chief rabbinate and the religious public school system, and a largely liberal Diaspora.

Reform and Conservative Jews in the United States understood that a titanic battle was underway in Israel between liberal secularism and religious nationalism, which reached a violent climax with the assassination of Prime Minister Yitzhak Rabin in 1995. They also understood that they had to enter the battlefield between Tel Aviv and Jerusalem, so to speak, and realized that the culture wars and political sparring in Israel could determine the future of Judaism itself and their own status as Jews. They could no longer stand aside and claim that what happened in Israel was none of their business.

It was in this context that the Reform Movement adopted the new Pittsburgh Platform in 1999, which embraced Zionism and affirmed the "unique qualities of living in...the land of Israel," but also called for cultural and religious pluralism in the country. The progressive movement hoped to reinforce its legitimacy and institutional standing in the United States by deepening its involvement in Israel. Ismar Schorsch, the chancellor of the Jewish Theological Seminary, said explicitly that building a strong presence for Conservative Judaism in Israel was essential for "revitalizing the Conservative movement in North America." Rabbi Richard Hirsch, the executive director of the World Union of Progressive Judaism, expressed similar sentiments at a Reform convention in Jerusalem in 1999. It was out of this understanding that both denominations built institutions in Israel and upped their involvement in legal battles in Jerusalem over religion and state, especially surrounding formal recognition of non-Orthodox movements, funding for their institutions, egalitarian worship at the Western Wall, and more.

When Israel and the Palestine Liberation Organization signed the Oslo Accords in 1993, liberal American Jews believed that Israeli and American Jewry were at the dawn of a new liberal age. It seemed that Israel, now secure, would soon shake off the burden of its constant preoccupation with national security and embrace cosmopolitanism. In 1996, when Benjamin Netanyahu rose to power in the wake of the Rabin assassination and tried to reverse the liberal trends, and also embraced the pro-Israel evangelical right in the United States, liberal Jews fought him with all their might and lent their support, as did the Clinton administration, to the election of his rival Ehud Barak as Israeli prime minister in 1999. The outbreak of the Second Intifada in September 2000, however, was a breaking point for hopes of a new Jewish world after Oslo, and the cosmopolitan dream definitively collapsed a year later, after the 9/11 terror attacks.[577]

The forces of religion and nationalism in twenty-first Israel represent an open challenge to the cosmopolitan spirit of liberal American Jewry. This was the context, back in the 1970s, for the emergence of the unapologetically pro-Israel and heavily Jewish neoconservative movement. While left-wing American Jews complained that their Orthodox brethren were becoming more fervent Zionists and neglecting their obligations to weaker nations (including Palestine), Jews on the American cultural and political right believe that progressives have forgotten what it means to be loyal Jews. The change sweeping the American Jewish community can be seen, in part, from the demographic and political rise of Orthodox and even ultra-Orthodox forces at the expense of the more liberal streams.

An even more significant change is the alliance between Orthodox Jews and the pro-Israel evangelical right, which progressive Jews still perceive as not only anti-Semitic, but the biggest threat to the progressive, secular order in America that Jews have spent a century fighting to build. Centrist and neoconservative American

---

577   Yossi Shain, "The Transnational Struggle for Jewish Pluralism," in *Democracy and The New Religious Pluralism*, ed. Thomas Banchoff (New York: Oxford University Press, 2007), 85–112.

Jews, who emphasize the importance of Israel and the US-Israel alliance, have taken a view that sees evangelicals as more powerful and trustworthy allies than the increasingly anti-Israel American progressive left—including the Jews in its ranks.[578]

The US-Israel special relationship, which deepened after the 1973 Yom Kippur War, has enabled many American Jews to identify with two homelands—the United States and Israel—at once. Major US Jewish organizations promoted Israel's cause, arguing that they were thereby promoting the values and interests of the United States. But over time, sections of liberal Jewry started seeing this convergence as a burden, and they regarded "blind loyalty" to a "religious and nationalistic Israel" as too great a deviation from the cosmopolitan values underpinning their loyalty to America.

This was the context for the establishment of J-Street as a liberal alternative to AIPAC, the biggest pro-Israel lobby group, in 2007. For its part, the Jewish far-left sees support for Israel, the "occupying power," as an abject betrayal of its values. While both Israel and other mainstream sections of American Jewry treat this fringe as beyond the pale, they are disturbed when major US figures, like Senator Bernie Sanders, snub liberal Zionists. In 2020, Sanders boycotted AIPAC's annual Policy Conference, calling the organization "a platform for leaders who express bigotry…and [opposition to] basic Palestinian Rights."

Despite their criticism of Israel, however, liberal American Jews struggle to reconcile with the United States as their permanent home. Life is good, they have no plans to move to Israel, and they foresee their children and grandchildren as Americans. International relations scholar Michael Barnett, himself a liberal American Jew, admits that, despite their achievements and prosperity, "American

---

578 Murray Friedman, *The Neoconservative Revolution: Jewish Intellectuals and the Shaping of Public Policy* (New York: Cambridge University Press, 2005), 245.

Jews can still feel as if they are outsiders, in danger of overstaying their welcome...[and] privately, many American Jews worry that their amazing run of luck will end."[579]

Non-Orthodox American Jewish conservatives draw surprising inspiration from the liberal Christian theologian Reinhold Niebuhr, who understood that a desire for community in a cosmopolitan world would lead Jews to embrace religion as a moral framework, not just as a matter of tribal belonging. It was Niebuhr who persuaded Will Herberg, the American-Jewish intellectual who embraced Americanization, to remain Jewish.

While many American Jews refused to accept the notion that their religion set them apart from their neighbors—even secularizing the Bar Mitzvah ceremony into a general rite of adolescence and entry into American society—Niebuhr vigorously defended the preservation of a particular Jewish identity and became one of the most vocal Christian supporters of the Jews' right to political self-determination in their historical homeland. He did so in defiance of liberal Jewish theologians and many of his Christian peers, who rejected sovereignty and power in favor of universalist ethics. Niebuhr fiercely attacked the pacifistic Christian worldview adopted by many Jews, which aspired for an amorphous liberal, Christian, universalistic utopia.

At the outbreak of World War II, Christian pacifists believed that no dictatorship was so dangerous as to justify the United States entering the war. Niebuhr, however, argued that it was not only absurd but also *criminal* to think that Hitler might be defeated through passive resistance.[580] He became an avowed Zionist and argued that only an independent Jewish state would do justice to Jewish religion and culture. He cheered Israel's victory in the Six-Day War.

---

579   Barnett, *The Star and the Stripes*, 245.

580   Reinhold Niebuhr, *The Children of Light and Darkness* (New York: Charles Scribner's Sons, 1944; University of Chicago Press, 2011), 142–143.

After his death in 1971, when liberal Christians criticized Israel's control of Jerusalem in the journal he founded, *Christianity and Crisis*, his widow demanded that his name be removed from the masthead.[581]

The Six-Day War, which mobilized many American Jews in defense of the Jewish national cause, also turned many evangelical Christians into supporters of Israel. In the Netanyahu era, senior Israeli officials are often much closer to the evangelicals' messianic religious worldview than to the outlook of liberal Jewry in terms of values and foreign policy. But liberal Jews' long-term emphasis on universal values and recoil from the evangelicals' religious fervor were mainly rooted in centuries of experience, which showed that anti-Semitism was inherent in Christianity and nationalist movements. The commitment to liberal activism was an important component in American Jews' efforts to forge alliances with other minorities in the United States, including the African American civil rights movement, out of an understanding that strengthening American cosmopolitanism would also help Jews around the world.

Recent years, however, have seen a sea change. Until recently, some liberal American Jews threatened that if Israel's behavior were to bring Zionism and liberalism into tension, they would have to opt for the latter. But Israel seems to have taken little notice of this threat and has entrenched its alliance with *non*-liberal sections of America.

For some quarters of evangelical Christian society, loyalty to Israel has become a critical, defining element of American patriotism. The Zionist Organization of America was fiercely criticized for hosting Steve Bannon, Donald Trump's controversial advisor, at a gala dinner in 2018. Many American Jews saw Bannon as a far right,

---

581   Seymour Siegel, "Reinhold Niebuhr: In Memoriam," *American Jewish Year Book* 73 (1972), 605–610.

anti-Semitic ideologue. Bret Stephens, a conservative columnist opposed to Trump, slammed the alliance between the American-Jewish right and Steve Bannon as a "disgrace" in a *New York Times* op-ed.[582] Mort Klein, the president of the ZOA, insisted nonetheless that Bannon was "a great friend of Israel and Jews."[583]

The increasingly intimate relationship between the evangelical American right and the Israeli right is rooted in their common faith in God's promise to restore the Jews to the whole Land of Israel. Evangelicals are ardent devotees of Hebrew scripture–their children read the Hebrew Bible and pore over the map of the Land of Israel, which they increasingly see as their second home. The Land of Israel is the place where their savior, Jesus Christ, was born; it is where he preached his Gospels and was crucified and rose from the dead. Many evangelicals frequently fly to Israel on pilgrimage missions to retrace Jesus's steps. To a large extent, they believe that the Promised Land belongs to them no less than to Israelis.

In the Middle Ages, the wretched Jews of Europe bore witness to the supremacy of Christianity and victory of Jesus Christ, but in the Israeli Century, the sovereign Jewish state is the most compelling testament of the impending realization of prophecy and the second coming of Christ at the End of Days. Like Augustine's conception of "the Jew as witness," today, the paradigm has shifted to "the Israeli as witness."

In this brave new world, we must ask: Have we reached a point where the Israeli-Evangelical alliance might eclipse mutual Jewish responsibility, and does Israelis' religious commitment to sovereignty over the territories conquered in the 1967 Six-Day War mean that

---

582   Bret Stephens, "Steve Bannon Is Bad for the Jews," *New York Times*, November 16, 2017), https://www.nytimes.com/2017/11/16/opinion/steve-bannon-israel-anti-semitism.html.

583   Amir Tibon, "Israeli Ambassador to U.S. Hosted Bannon for Dinner, Thanked Him for Support," *Haaretz*, November 18, 2017), https://www.haaretz.com/us-news/israeli-ambassador-to-u-s-hosted-bannon-for-dinner-thanked-him-for-support-1.5466470.

it will prefer a partnership with evangelical Christianity over a covenant of fate with progressive Jewry?

Chapter VIII: The Israeli Century

Israel was born as a Jewish state. The new state sought to liberate the Jewish people from enslavement to foreign powers and the rule of Gentiles. This was its purpose, its mission, and its goal. It was born as a safe haven for Jews and has indeed given refuge to millions of immigrants and always remains open for more. But from Zionism's early days, it was also understood that Israeli independence would have a moral mission beyond the mere establishment of a safe haven. Ever since the rebirth of Jewish sovereignty, Jews in Israel and across the Diaspora have been asking how the new Jewish national home should be built and what its cultural and philosophical foundations should be.

To what extent should Israel be a modern, "normal" nation-state ("a nation like any other")? Should Israel and its society express a distinctly "Hebrew" character? How is this identity different from a Jewish character? To what extent should the sovereign State of Israel promote a "just society," and what are the proper values of social justice? How appropriate is it for Israeli sovereignty to be built based on "Jewish ethics," and what are the foundations of Jewish ethical principles? To what extent should the Jewish state serve as a "light unto the nations"? How committed should Israel be to engaging with and protecting Diaspora Jews, including from the specter of assimilation (out of a conviction that Jews are members of one big family and all "responsible for one another")? Is Israel's only purpose the good of the Jews or must it promote and protect the humanistic values of human rights? In what sense should Israel be the state of its minority, non-Jewish citizens? To what extent must the state nurture society's attachment to the Jewish religious tradition? Is it appropriate for Israel to encourage its citizens to live a religious life, and can it establish a "Zionist halakha"? Must Israel be democratic?

Jews have been asking different variations of these questions throughout history, from the days of sovereignty under the Hasmoneans in antiquity and through long centuries of statelessness. But only in the Israeli Century have almost all the big questions that Jews ask themselves, and that others ask about them, boiled down to the experience of Jewish sovereignty.

In antiquity, brief periods of sovereignty collapsed because of military or political weakness in the face of greater external forces. Yet the Jews generally blamed infighting or sins against God for these disasters. In the Israeli Century, Israelis believe that external forces have less and less power to destroy their country, but their talk of existential threats still drifts into rhetoric about endemic internal strife and divine intervention.

This happened in 2018, during the fierce debate over the Nation-State Law and the questions it raised about identity, citizenship, and equality in modern Israel. This argument intensified the profound polarization in Israel, widened the rift between the Israeli government and non-Orthodox movements in the Diaspora, and even made waves in the West, where people wonder where an independent Israel is taking its Judaism and democracy.[584]

This dramatic trend, whereby Israel sets the agenda for Jews around the world, will only intensify in the coming years. As a sovereign state, it is the main driver of a Jewish history that was decentralized for two millennia. It is also concentrating that history in a

---

584   "Israel: Jewish or Democratic," *The Economist*, July 26, 2018, https://www.economist.com/middle-east-and-africa/2018/07/26/israels-jewish-nationalist-identity-is-outweighing-its-democratic-one.

single geographic spot, as the nation redefines itself and its wishes. Although Israel continues to battle hostile forces in the Middle East, and peace with the Palestinians remains a far-off prospect, the most glaring feature of the Israeli Century is the growing confidence in Israel's power, stability, and vitality as it ingathers the Jewish people back into the Land of Israel.

Some will dispute this conclusion, maintaining that the persistence of the Israeli-Palestinian conflict and Israel's pariah status in parts of the world prove that the Jewish state has not yet broken the pre-sovereign paradigm of exilic existence and its assorted dilemmas. Its instability arguably points to *continuity* with the Diaspora condition, the argument goes, not a break from it.[585]

Others warn that deepening domestic divisions and disputes could lead to civil strife, chaos, and the end of Israeli independence. It is important to listen to these voices of alarm. However, I still believe the Israeli experience is fundamentally different from any other the Jews have known. For there is no longer any serious question about Israel's existence—or its necessity for the continued existence of Jews and Judaism.

Israel's continued existence is obviously a genuine challenge given the situation in the Middle East, but its preoccupation with security is also a consequence of the Jewish paradigm—the cyclical story of exile and return, which continues to shape the collective Jewish consciousness. This paradigm is profoundly influenced by memories of persecution and trauma, but in the Israeli Century, these unpleasant historical experiences are cautionary tales that serve to justify Israel's power. The Jews and Israel face serious threats, but their sovereign power now means that any attempt to destabilize or

---

585   Major-General (ret.) Shlomo Gazit, who served as the head of Israeli military intelligence, claimed in the summer of 2018 that seventy-one years after the UN decision to partition the land and create two states, "Israel's War of Independence has not yet been won…[even if many] live in a fantasy that the war for our existence is already behind us," Shlomo Gazit's weekly newsletter, August 11, 2018 [Hebrew].

annihilate them is a threat to world peace. If Israel's existence were ever truly in doubt, world leaders know it would not hesitate to use its doomsday weapons. This is the essence of the Jewish people's historic shift, from the condition of "the surprise of chaos" as a stateless minority to a reality of sovereign stability.

A century ago, decades before the creation of the Jewish state and the Nazis' rise to power, Jewish national poet Hayim Nahman Bialik argued that attaining independence had the potential to break the paradigmatic cycle of exile and sovereignty. In his 1925 speech at the inauguration of the Hebrew University of Jerusalem on Mount Scopus, he said:

> Ladies and Gentlemen! You all know what has become of our old Spiritual strongholds in the Diaspora in recent times and I need not dwell upon this theme now. For all their inner strength, and for all the energy the nation had expended upon creating and preserving these centers, they stood not firm on the day of wrath; by the decree of history they are crumbled and razed to the foundations and our people is left standing empty-handed upon their ruins....
>
> Through cruel and bitter trials and tribulations, through blasted hopes and despair of the soul, through innumerable humiliations, we have slowly arrived at the realization that without a tangible homeland, without private national premises that are entirely ours, we can have no sort of a life, either material or spiritual. Without Eretz

> Israel—Eretz means land, literally land—
> there is no hope for the rehabilitation of
> Israel anywhere, ever.[586]

The Israeli Century has fundamentally transformed the Jewish condition, even if it has not cured the mood swings that Jews suffer (in Israel and the Diaspora), between apocalyptic visions and messianic reveries. The Israeli reality of grave external threats, interspersed with great achievements, victories, and periods of normality, causes misconceptions about Israel's power and, thus, a sense of vulnerability. Historically, the Jewish national psychology was nourished by an awareness and discourse of existential doubt—a belief that normality is a short-lived condition and disaster is always around the corner.

Despite its resilience, Israel has not yet broken free of this mindset. On the eve of the Six-Day War, Israelis joked darkly that the last person to leave the country should switch off the lights. During the Yom Kippur War, they spoke of the "destruction of the Third Temple," meaning the state. Even today, attempts to discuss long-term planning for the country are often greeted with an instinctive Israeli response of "if we still *have* a country then." Why should anyone believe that the cycle can be broken?[587]

But the State of Israel is more prosperous, dynamic, and strategically strong than the "*gevalt* syndrome" mentality typical of periods of chaos since time immemorial. There are ups and downs in Israel's security situation and in the mood of Israelis and Diaspora Jews, but other nations and minorities experience similar volatility. Sometimes Israelis and Diaspora Jews go through painful times, but the Israeli Century is defined by its continuity and stability, not

---

586   Chaim Nahman Bialik, "At the Inauguration of the Hebrew University Jerusalem, January 4, 1925," in *The Zionist Idea*, ed. Arthur Hertzberg, 283–284.

587   Amotz Asa-El, *The Jewish March of Folly* (Rishon LeZion: Yediot, 2019) [Hebrew].

its precariousness. This reality is what is driving the Israelization of Judaism, essentially making the State of Israel into an insurance policy for every Jew around the world—admirers and detractors alike.[588]

So why are so many Jews not content with just having a nation-state and the security it provides? Why does it often seem that the daily grind of statehood is "beneath" some Jewish intellectuals? The answer is that while the Jews supposedly negated the exile by returning to their homeland, many in Israel and the Diaspora are unwilling to forgo the freedom and flexibility of global, cosmopolitan life, unbound by the travails of sovereignty, confined to a single homeland. Many Jews still believe that a diasporic life is the key to their survival and sovereignty in a single geographic location exposes them to the risk of total annihilation. Can the Jewish people strike the right balance between sovereignty as the guarantor of national survival and the diverse traits they acquired as a transnational people, which made them unique among the nations but also vulnerable to unspeakable crimes? To answer this, we need to look at how Jews understand their own past—and how the Israeli Century has dramatically recast the idea of Jewish history itself.

Writing History, Making History

The Jews were the first people to bequeath the writing of history to the Western world. They believed it was a basic theological imperative to transmit truth from father to son. They were the first to break with the assumption that time is cyclical, and that events and people recur throughout history. In antiquity, the present was always thought to be a reiteration of the past—but the Jews invented

---

588   Yossi Shain, *The Language of Corruption and Israel's Moral Culture* (Or Yehuda: Kinneret-Zmora-Dvir, 2010), 187–192 [Hebrew].

linear history. For them, the past mattered not only as a means of understanding the present but as part of the ancestral journey that had brought them where they were, and through which they could discover their historic mission. This was why they meticulously recorded family genealogies. Historian Thomas Cahill writes that the Jews were the first to broach the idea that something new might occasionally appear on the stage of history and even welcomed this element of surprise. In so doing, they "radically subverted all other ancient worldviews." He believes the Jews, during their ancient independence, were "the first people to live—psychologically—in real time."[589]

But when the ancient Jewish kingdom crumbled, they stopped recording their own history. After Josephus wrote his history of the destruction of the Second Temple, the Jews started treating the Torah as if it contained all the history worth knowing. "History had nothing to explain and little to reveal to the man who meditated the Law day and night," wrote the historian Arnaldo Momigliano. "The whole development of Judaism led to something unhistorical, eternal, the Law, the Torah."[590] The Jews started placing greater emphasis on the Torah and the Talmud, eclipsing their earlier fascination with history. Without sovereignty, time lost all meaning, because as the Talmud says, "there is no earlier and later in the Torah."[591] The Talmud went as far as to say that God himself, no longer playing an active role in history, "sits and engages in Torah study" all day long.[592] In a life without politics, a life that meditated solely on the eternal and timeless, the Jews no longer had a reason to appeal to history.

---

589   Thomas Cahill, *The Gifts of the Jews: How a Tribe of Desert Nomads Changed the Way Everyone Thinks and Feels* (New York: Doubleday, 1998), 128–129.

590   Momigliano, *The Classical Foundations of Modern Historiography*, 23.

591   Babylonian Talmud, Pesachim 6b trans. William Davidson, available from the Sefaria Library at Sefaria.org.

592   Babylonian Talmud, Avodah Zarah 3b, trans. William Davidson.

But although the Jews no longer recorded history, they did obsessively record something else. Legal scholar Arye Edrei stresses that "the Jews were very committed to recording their spiritual creativity," meaning their new insights into the Torah. For example, there are no Jewish historical writings about the atrocities inflicted on the Jews of the Rhineland during the Crusades. Instead, the eleventh century is remembered as the time when Rashi, the famous French rabbi, wrote his commentary on the Hebrew Bible and Talmud. So, too, the expulsion from Spain in 1492 was not recorded in Jewish annals. The key milestone of that period was the composition of the *Shulkhan Arukh*, which Rabbi Joseph Caro wrote a whole generation after the Inquisition. The rabbis, thereby, emphasized that Torah study and the promotion of religious interests were superior to the politics of a sovereign national life, and that "the intellectual enterprise associated with Torah learning constituted the most important event, and one might say the only event, worthy of preservation."[593]

Only at the dawn of the nineteenth century, when modern Jews started imagining a future for themselves in their countries of domicile (and later, in their own independent state), the writing of Jewish history began again in earnest. A power struggle immediately broke out between historians and rabbis, and Jews and Gentiles, over how to read and interpret the past, and over who possessed authoritative knowledge. In Berlin in 1819, a group of young intellectuals formed the Society for the Scientific Study of Judaism. The writing of Jewish history became *Wissenschaft des Judentums*–the science of Judaism. The society's manifesto stated that it would not focus narrowly on Judaism as a religion. Rather, it would span "religion, philosophy, history, law, literature in general, civil life and all the

---

593   Arye Edrei, "Holocaust Memorial: A Paradigm of Religious Memories in the Religious and Secular Society in Israel," in *On Memory: An Interdisciplinary Approach*, ed. Doron Mendels (Oxford: Peter Lang, 2007), 80–81.

affairs of man." The organization defined this science as an objective enterprise, which "begins without any preconceived opinion and is not concerned with the final result." Leopold Zunz and Mordechai Jost, who is considered the first person to have chronicled Jewish history as an academic endeavor, were members of this association. They argued that the resumption of Jewish history writing was not just a pure science, but also a psychological need for Jewish self-determination. They also argued that studying Judaism using conventional scientific methods would give it a special status and dignity, which would unify major forces in the Jewish people. This scientific approach secularized Jewish history, because modern science categorically rejected the notion of divine providence as the driver of it. In modern Jewish historiography, human and institutional actors are the driving forces.[594]

Scholar Asaf Yedidya notes that Orthodox Judaism suffered an unprecedented shock when secular Jews—so-called *apikorsim*, or apostates—started writing Jewish history, snatching Judaism out of the rabbis' hands and diminishing their stature. The most prominent "apostate" was historian Heinrich Graetz, who achieved global fame with his monumental series *History of the Jews*. He was widely seen as disparaging the Orthodox Judaism of eastern Europe, which he believed was failing to keep up with the modern world.

The modernist revolution in the writing of Jewish history provoked a counterreaction. Orthodox Jews feared the growing influence of modernity and the secular study of Judaism and were pushed to create a more traditional, religious alternative to the "rational" writing of history. Some rabbis established the Orthodox Science of the Jews, centered on the transmission of knowledge and respect for Jewish texts and the commentators and thinkers of the rabbinical

---

594 Yosef Hayim Yerushalmi's lecture in memory of Shelomo Dov Goitein, cited in *Shelomo Dov Goitein 1900–1985* (Princeteon, NJ: The Institute for Advanced Study, 1985), 25–26.

tradition. The Orthodox Science of the Jews had many different schools and champions, including Ze'ev Yavetz, one of the founders of Mizrachi, the Religious Zionist movement, who wrote his history as a challenge to Graetz.[595]

At the dawn of the twentieth century, Jewish-Russian doctor and historian Yehuda Leib Katzenelson observed that modern Jewish historians divided Jewish history into two great eras: "The first [was] from the birth of the Hebrew nation till the Babylonian Exile, and the second era from the Babylonian Exile till the present day. They called the first era *Geschichte der Israel*—the History of Israel, and the second *Geschichte der Juden*—the History of the Jews." Katzenelson was the successor of Simon Dubnow, the father of the Jewish Autonomism movement and chief editor of the *Iibrskyh Encyclopaedia*, the first Russian-language Jewish encyclopedia. But after visiting the Land of Israel and falling in love with the Jewish settlement movement, he changed his mind and dropped his support for Jewish autonomy in the Diaspora. On the eve of World War I, Katzenelson predicted that the Jewish people were at the threshold of a new lease of life on their historic, national soil.[596]

The writing of Jewish history has undergone a major shift in the Israeli Century. Suddenly, the historical, cultural, and political has centered on sovereignty. In the Israeli Century, scholars of Jewish history from antiquity to modernity, including the period of the Holocaust and the creation of the State of Israel, are profoundly divided. They continue to debate facts, the credibility of archaeological findings, and above all, the writing and interpretation of the narrative of Jewish nationhood and sovereignty. During the pre-state Yishuv and Israel's early independence, historians and archaeologists

---

595   Asaf Yedidya, *Criticized Criticism: Orthodox Alternatives to Wissenschaft des Judentums 1873–1956* (Jerusalem: Bialik Institute, 2013), 199 [Hebrew].

596   Y. L. Katzenelson, "Religion and Politics in the Chronicles of the Ancient Hebrews," *Hatekufah* 25 (1931), 358 [Hebrew].

focused on strengthening the rationale for Israeli sovereignty and proving the connection of the diverse and scattered Jewish people to their homeland. (Some might say they were even recruited for this role.)

"Zionist" historians divided Jewish history into three periods. First came antiquity, when nationalism was the engine of the Jewish people's identity; this period ended with defeat to the Romans in the first and second centuries CE. The second period, between the second and twentieth centuries, was a long life of exile, a history of suffering and destructive, messianic passivity. They depicted the third period, starting with the emergence of Zionism, as an active national history, climaxing with Israeli independence after the Holocaust, and Israel's victory in the Six-Day War.

In the 1980s, the "New Historians" and post-Zionist scholars emerged with a wave of revisionist interpretations that challenged the Zionist interpretation of history. Some of these historians and "critical sociologists" framed Jewish national historiography as a malevolent, colonialist conspiracy to dispossess the Palestinian people. Some even cast doubt on the Jews' basic right to be called a nation; others argued that the depiction of Israel as a success that contrasts with the failure of the Diaspora is a historical fiction. The Jewish nation itself was described as an "invented people."[597]

Debates over Jewish identity and sovereignty in the Israeli Century have included fierce arguments about the historical truth of the biblical account of the ancient Israelite kingdoms, the credibility of Josephus's *The Jewish Wars* and his account of the destruction of the Second Temple, the New Historians' interpretation of Israel's twentieth-century rebirth, the events of the War of Independence and the creation of the Palestinian refugee problem, and how Israel

---

597   Eric Mecholuan, "What is the Meaning of Jewish History?," *Mosaic*, August 12, 2018. See also Shlomo Sand, *The Invention of the Jewish People* (New York: Verso, 2009).

should interpret Jewish texts in making moral decisions. The arguments over the political and theological drivers of the Israeli and Jewish story often veer from factual to ideological questions about the Jewish people's right to their ancient land, the Israeli occupation of the West Bank, and the nature of Israeli society and democracy. In modern Israel, every archaeological finding can spark a political flare-up over religion, nationality, and the state's desire to prove its connection with the past. Israel has sought to make the biblical story the historical foundation of Jewish and Israeli identity, and archaeological discoveries are a powerful tool for creating a national consciousness and social solidarity. However, new findings can also challenge the integrity of this biblical story and provoke intense controversy.[598]

Many scholars of Jewish and Israeli history operate in the grey area between writing objective history and shaping collective memories; the boundaries between research and politics are frequently transgressed by demagogic rhetoric and obscured by disputes about historical forgetfulness, denial, conspiracies, or exaggerations.

These fierce debates have played a key role in the consolidation of Jewish identity in the Israeli Century. They also affect Israel's relations with the Diaspora, as seen from controversies over Israel's place among the nations and internal Israeli arguments over who should rightfully lead the whole Zionist project.

The Israeli education system provides the clearest illustration of this interplay between history and politics. In 2016, The Biton Commission, headed by the Israel Prize-winning Mizrahi poet Erez Biton, was tasked by the education ministry with recommending how to empower Sephardic and Mizrahi Jewish heritage in the Israeli

---

598   Yehoshua Dorfman, *Tension Before the Surface: The Interrelationship of Archaeology and Politics in Israel* (Or Yehuda: Kinneret, Zemora-Bitan, Dvir, 2015) [Hebrew].

education system. Its report found that the history studied by Israeli children "paints a rather bleak picture":

> "The general narrative that seems to pervade the curriculum was written from a European perspective, which superficializes the history of Sephardic and Mizrahi Jewry and its place in the annals of the Jewish people...a situation...that creates painful dilemmas and identity crises for Sephardic and Mizrahi Jews, who are oblivious to Jewish heritage in their countries of origin, to the cultural treasures created there, and to the contribution of these populations to Jewish society through the generations."

Is it really possible to generalize about the Jewish people and their history? Is Jewish history a meaningful concept or simply the sum of the experiences of discrete religious and ethnic communities? Is there a logical consistency to it or a linearity leading to the rebirth of a sovereign Israel? Zionist historians, such as Ben-Zion Dinur, have written that "Jewish history is the history of the Jewish Nation.... Jewish history is unified by a homogeneous unity that includes all periods and places, each of which illuminates the others."[599] Other historians believe this approach "politicizes" history with a view to creating a "usable past" for the Israeli public.[600]

But in the Israeli Century, reality is much more powerful than any debate over how history should be written. Most Israelis are untroubled by questions about historical justifications for their

---

599 Ivan G. Marcus, "Israeli Medieval Jewish Historiography: From Nationalist Positivism to New Cultural and Social Histories," *Jewish Studies Quarterly* 17, no. 3 (2009), 247.

600 Moshe Rosman, "Zion: A Story of Tension," *Zion* 75, no. 4 (2010), 485–496 [Hebrew].

connection to their homeland. They are busy building a flourishing country in their own image as Israelis and writing its history with their blood and actions in an accelerated push to consolidate their national home. And this is the key point—since the early days of Zionism, the Jews have been less concerned with *writing* history than *returning* to it. They've cared less about the *theory* of history than what making history means in *practice*.

Secular and religious Zionists alike conceived of the settlement of the Land of Israel and sovereignty there as the Jewish return to history. For secular Zionists, this meant taking their fate into their hands and acting as an independent nation on the international stage. This was how the Jews would reassert ownership over their own people's spiritual and creative assets, which had been expropriated by other nations over history. None of the Jews' unique contributions to humanity were conceived as uniquely *Jewish* contributions. For religious Zionism, the return to history was an expression of God working in mysterious ways because the renewal of Jewish life in the Land of Israel was a fulfillment of the ancient biblical prophecies.[601]

The Zionist return to history is also the Jews' return to their original home. From the birth of Zionism, immigration to the Land of Israel and the resettlement of biblical cities were considered ways in which the Jews could return to their own history.

Hiking around the country has always been a key element of Israel's national education and its efforts to make patriots out of schoolchildren and youth movement members. By exploring the great outdoors, the "new Jews" were able to reclaim heritage sites lost to their people thousands of years ago. One scholar who studied the purpose of these hikes during the British Mandate era wrote that they combined the Bible with Zionism to make the youth feel

---

601   For the return to history, see Eliezer Schweid, "The Return to History in Twentieth-Century Jewish Thought," *Daat*, http://www.daat.ac.il/daat/history/hevra/hashiva-2.htm [Hebrew].

that they lived in a "land of ideals" and were taking an active part in the redemption of the Land of Israel.[602] In his letters, legendary officer Yoni Netanyahu (the brother of Israeli Prime Minister Benjamin Netanyahu), who lost his life during the heroic hostage rescue mission at Entebbe in 1976, passionately described how he walked the length of the land to familiarize himself with "every tree and rock," waxing romantically about the ancient homeland.[603]

Masada, the desert fortress where the Jews committed mass suicide in antiquity to avoid falling to the Romans, became an international symbol of their return to history, under the slogan "Masada shall not fall again." Of this, Nitsa Ben-Ari has written:

> Many years later, hikers still remembered ascending in the dark, part of the way with a rope, and their guides' infectious excitement. They remembered the difficult path up the mountain, the vegetation, the natural scenery, and the rain that poured without warning. What had they to do with the Masada suicides, with Eleazar Ben Jair or the traitor Josephus Flavius? Like all who came before and after them, they had endured a powerful sensory experience and panic; and they had invested strength, power, and endurance in this strenuous and difficult test. In so doing, they had achieved an Israeli

602   Yuval Drori, *National Education through Mutually Supportive Devices: The Zionist Story* (Jerusalem: Magnes, 2008), 71 [Hebrew].

603   Yonatan Netanyahu, *Self-Portrait of a Hero: The Letters of Jonathan Netanyahu (1963–1976)* (New York, NY: Random House), 82.

identity, a sense of homeland, group cohesion—together, us, everyone.[604]

As the Israeli Century takes shape, the notion of returning to
history remains the profound creed of Zionism. Almost on a daily
basis, right-wing Israeli leaders speak in sweeping historic terms about
their commitment to the integrity of the Land of Israel and its historic sites. This stands in stark contrast to the traditional Orthodox
conception of Judaism, which has sought to downplay sovereignty
as the reason for and guarantor of Jewish existence since the destruction of the Second Temple. Instead, halakha provided the Jews a
closed circuit of rigid concepts, which replaced national sovereignty
as what defined them in exile. This religious framework was vital for
Diaspora Jews in exercising their self-rule without possessing the coercive powers of the state. To this day, ultra-Orthodox Jews employ
harsh measures, including excommunication, to enforce communal
compliance with religious law and thereby guarantee conformity
and collective continuity.[605]

The concept of the return to history is also an affront to the
ultra-Orthodox view of the world. The ultra-Orthodox are disinter-
ested in writing or studying history and prefer to focus on halakha,
permanent and unchanging, which requires no further additions.
Thus, they deny that the establishment of the State of Israel marks
a historic shift in the Jewish condition and do not regard Israeli independence as marking the end of the paradigm of exile and return,
but rather as one more stage in a long chain of generations, and one
more stop in a longer sequence of wanderings. What makes the existence of an independent Israel important was not sovereignty but

---

604 Nitsa Ben Ari, *S. Yizhar: Story of Life, Part B* (Tel Aviv: Tel Aviv University, 2017), 87
[Hebrew].

605 Gershon Scholem, "Who is a Jew," 71 [Hebrew].

the reconstruction of the world of Torah scholarship and yeshivot destroyed in the Holocaust.

In the 1940s and 1950s, Chazon Ish (Rabbi Avrohom Yeshaya Karelitz), the great spiritual leader of ultra-Orthodoxy, opposed giving the Holocaust a special status in the timeline of Jewish history. He feared that the theological difficulty of explaining why God stood by while the Jews were being slaughtered, and why the great rabbis failed to save their communities, would encourage Torah scholars to start having heretical thoughts. He and other ultra-Orthodox rabbis wanted to focus not on the genocide of European Jewry but on rebuilding the vibrant world of Torah scholarship that existed before it. Post-Shoah yeshivas are named after places destroyed in the fires of the Holocaust.[606]

Even today, many ultra-Orthodox communities do not regard the State of Israel as the Jews' return to history; they completely reject the national-religious notion that Israel has a sacred status and marks "the beginning of the redemption." Some ultra-Orthodox Jews see Israel as a convenient political framework for the existence and cultivation of rabbinical Judaism, a world which, as Yeshayahu Leibowitz stresses, "was not designed for a reality of Jewish political independence."[607] When ultra-Orthodox groups demand to "restore the crown to its former glory," they often mean a return to the Torah and the Diaspora tradition—not the sovereignty that predated the fall of Jerusalem in antiquity.

Until the nineteenth century, in the absence of national independence, the Jewish tribe was held together in part by its hostile environment. As Jean-Paul Sartre argued, "It is the anti-Semite who *makes* the Jew."[608] But with the advent of modernity, the defensive

---

606   Edrei, "Holocaust Memorial," 52.

607   Eliezer Goldman, *Judaism Without Illusion* (Jerusalem: Shalom Hartman Institute, 2009), 319 [Hebrew].

608   Jean-Paul Sartre, *Anti-Semite and Jew* (New York: Schocken Books, 1948), 69.

walls of rabbinical Judaism were breached by the Emancipation. The attractiveness of the new world and threatening nature of the old world pushed the Jews, willingly or unwillingly, to become citizens of their countries of residence and shape the history of other nations. The Jewish people conceived of manifold ways to sustain a national existence far away from their historic homeland, whether through socialism, progressivism, integration in other people's nationalism, or modernized adaptations of religion. These models had a profound influence on the rest of Western civilization and sometimes even shaped identities of countries. But with the possible exception of American Jewry, these innovations failed to save the Jews from the "surprise of chaos." Their host countries often spat them out, and this chaos climaxed with the Holocaust. By contrast, the American Jewish community has been warmly embraced—but this embrace encourages many to assimilate and lose their distinctly Jewish identity.

The fact is that only in the State of Israel, thanks to the stability of sovereignty, can the Jewish return to history safeguard the development of a pluralistic Judaism, without fear that leaving the bunker of religious tradition will endanger its very existence. Nevertheless, in recent decades, the principle of the Jewish return to history has become a volatile threat to Israel's national cohesion, because rival interpretations about the *meaning* of return are fueling ideological and political strife. For most secular Zionists, Israel's establishment and consolidation represent the fulfilment of the return to history. But others, especially religious Zionists, have a broader concept of sovereignty, which includes the future annexation of Judea and Samaria or the West Bank, as part of an unfolding messianic process. For core sections of the religious Zionist movement, the Jews have not yet fully returned to history because returning to the homeland means not just building settlements in Judea and Samaria but rebuilding the Temple in Jerusalem.

In effect, ever since Israel was created out of a commitment to a complete Jewish return to history, rival concepts of loyalty and tribal belonging have become more deeply entrenched. The debate is over *how far back* to return in time, and *where to* in space.

"Home Away from Home"

Gershom Scholem was a German-born scholar who became one of Israel's leading philosophers and historians. As early as 1909, he wrote that the great promise of Zionism was to liberate Jews who had "fossilized in the Diaspora...and become disconnected from reality," by forging a new life in an independent state where they could "strike roots and feel at home."[609]

But is Israel really a home? On the eve of Israel's seventieth Independence Day, celebrated Israeli author David Grossman argued that a "strong Israel may be a fortress, but it is not yet a home," because "home is a place whose walls–borders–are clear and accepted; whose existence is stable, solid, and relaxed; whose inhabitants know its intimate codes; whose relations with its neighbors have been settled. It projects a sense of the future."[610]

Israel may be far from perfect as a home, but Israelis have a stronger sense of home than citizens of other "settled" countries. Every Israeli knows the motto of El Al, the national airline: "Home Away From Home." The prevailing feeling is not only that the State of Israel is a home, but that the Jewish people are a family–no matter how conflicted.

Some members of the Israeli family are deeply dissatisfied by

---

609   Gershom Scholem, *Explications and Implications*, 367 [Hebrew].

610   David Grossman, "'Israel Is a Fortress, but Not Yet a Home': David Grossman's Memorial Day Speech to Bereaved Israelis and Palestinians," *Haaretz*, April 18, 2018, https://www.haaretz.com/israel-news/full-text-speech-by-david-grossman-at-alternative-memorial-day-event-1.6011820.

what goes on in this home. While newcomers quickly maintain that Israel is *their* home and complain that they have not been fully welcomed or represented, many descendants of the original Zionist pioneers feel that their home has been "stolen" from them. Yet others maintain that the country does not meet their lofty expectations, disapprove of how Israel behaves regionally and internationally, or feel that the Israeli home is small and claustrophobic.

These feelings attest to a protracted power struggle over the "interior design" of the Israeli home—but a home it remains. Israel's leaders must therefore exercise extreme caution when wading into the question of home ownership. By exacerbating arguments about national loyalty within the home, they risk eroding its foundations.

By international standards, Israelis have an impressively high sense of patriotism.[611] They are constantly debating and complaining, but this debate is based on the common understanding that the Jews belong to and rightfully own this home.

Jews in other countries, including the United States, cannot have the same conversation. Although they fervently insist that they are at home in the countries where they are citizens, they do not feel entitlement to these countries *as a collective* and certainly do not claim ownership in the name of Judaism.

Israelis, in contrast, regard Israel as their home and see themselves as constant "home improvers." If, in the 1950s and 1960s, emigration was seen as a reasonable option for a better life, in recent decades fewer Israelis have seen other countries as viable alternatives, despite traveling abroad more than ever.

Many Israelis do, however, occasionally discuss emigrating and living abroad. During the massive protests of 2011 over the cost of living and economic inequality, Israeli emigration to Berlin made

---

611   "10 Most Patriotic Countries in the World," Borgen Magazine, https://www.borgenmagazine.com/10-patriotic-countries-world/.

headlines as if it were a threat rather than a nuisance. "Forgive me if I'm a bit impatient with people who are willing to throw the only state the Jews have into the garbage because it's easier to live in Berlin," said Yesh Atid party leader Yair Lapid.[612] In reality, Israelis are always keen to fly abroad and breathe some fresh air, but they quickly realize that there's no place like home. Even when trekking in faraway places, they fully expect that Israel will always come to their aid if needed—because *home* entails a strong sense of collective responsibility.

The real argument among Israeli Jews, therefore, is over who controls this shared home, not over who belongs in it. Alexander Yakobson, a prominent scholar and voice on Israeli identity, argues that it is an almost fantastical achievement for Israel, as a multicultural and multiethnic state, to have achieved such cohesion.[613]

Shmuel Rosner and Camil Fuchs highlight Israel's great success in creating a revolutionary new cultural identity, which they call "Jewsraeli." Multiple studies reveal that an absolute majority of Israeli Jews regard themselves as Jews first but think that "that being a good Jew means living in Israel: i.e., to be Israeli. In order to be *Jewish* first, one must first be *Israeli*.... These are the buds of a new culture—of Israeli Judaism. A culture that bears both fresh thinking and fresh features."[614]

Of course, questions of belonging and attachment are fundamentally different for Israeli Arabs. They also consider Israel their

---

612   "Don't Scrap Home Because It's 'Easier to Live in Berlin,' Lapid Tells Israelis," *Haaretz*, October 1, 2013, https://www.haaretz.com/.premium-finance-minister-slams-israeli-financial-expats-1.5342789.

613   Alexander Yakobson, "Zionism and Multiculturalism," *Law & Business: IDC Law Review* 14 (2012), 682 [Hebrew]. See also this English-language adaptation: Alexander Yakobson, "A Jewish State, Multiculturalism, the Law of Return, and Non-Jewish Immigration," in *The Nation State and Immigration, The Age of Population Movements* Anita Shapira, eds. Yedidia Z. Stern, Alexander Yakobson, and Liav Orgad (Brighton: Sussex Academic Press, 2014).

614   Shmuel Rosner and Camil Fuchs, *#IsraeliJudaism*, trans. Eylon Levy (Jerusalem: Jewish People Policy Institute, 2019), 79.

home; they see themselves as natives and the Jews as invaders. They have a different claim to a national home, a Palestinian state, and are neither willing nor able to become part of the Jewish-Israeli national vision. But many Israeli Arabs do see the State of Israel as a state to which they can belong and even contribute to as citizens.

As a reaction to demands from Israeli Arabs and activists of the Israeli Left for Israel to become a "state of all its citizens," recent decades have seen growing calls to enhance the state's Jewishness. A large majority of its Jewish citizens believe that the Land of Israel is a core component of the Jewish religion, and the Jewish religion a core component of Jewish nationality.

The Nation-State Law, a quasi-constitutional "basic law," is an expression of these tendencies. The law stipulates that Israel is the nation-state of the Jewish people and the "historical homeland" where they alone "realize its natural, cultural, religious and historical right to self-determination." It also states that Hebrew is the "state language," while Arabic has only a "special status."[615] It does not explicitly undermine Israeli Arabs' status as citizens, but neither does it specify that their citizenship is of equal value to that of Jews.

After the Nation-State Law was passed, Yakobson warned that it might erode the impressive fabric of Israeli society and aggravate Israeli Arabs' sense of being second-class citizens. He believes that a state that fulfils the Jewish people's right to self-determination should aspire for no citizen to feel that the state does not also belong to them.[616]

Today, it is clear to Jews and others around the world that Israel is the Jewish national home, and the Jews always have somewhere to

---

615   "Basic Law: Israel–The Nation State of the Jewish People," unofficial translation by Dr. Susan Hattis Rolef, https://knesset.gov.il/laws/special/eng/BasicLawNationState.pdf.

616   Author's interview with Alexander Yakobson, July 19, 2018.

go.[617] In summer 2018, against the backdrop of rising anti-Semitism in Jeremy Corbyn's Labour Party, one British Jew who decided to leave Britain for Israel said:

> At a point you think, enough is enough.... The biggest irony is, it's the likes of Jeremy Corbyn and...all the anti-Israel people who make you want to live in Israel. They are trying to suggest that Israel caused anti-Semitism but historically it's the other way round. Anti-Semitism is what caused people to become Zionists and say, 'We just want to get out of here and find a safe homeland.'[618]

Indeed, the Israeli Century is witnessing a non-stop homecoming—every year new immigrants arrive in Israel, not just from countries in crisis but also increasingly from developed states that Jews have considered home.

Israel has experienced tremendous upheavals since the early days of Zionism. During the pre-state Yishuv and its early independence, the founders' generation sought to create a Hebrew national identity as different as possible from the passivity of the Diaspora and its fatalistic rabbis. The *sabra*—the native-born Israeli—was a Jew who was starting afresh, untainted by persecution, death, passivity, weakness, or the physical effects of spending all day crouched

---

617   In the controversial 2015 novel *Submission*, the French novelist Michel Houellebecq describes a dystopia in which Islamist political parties compete against Marine Le Pen's National Front over the future of France. The protagonist, a non-Jewish scholar, learns that his Jewish girlfriend Myriam is leaving with her parents for Israel "till things calm down in France." As he kisses her goodbye, he says, "For me there is no Israel." Michel Houellebecq, *Submission: A Novel*, trans. Lorin Stein (New York: Farrar, Straus and Giroux, 2015), 89.

618   Laura Smith-Spark, "Anti-Semitism Is So Bad in Britain That Some Jews Are Planning to Leave," CNN, August 17, 2018, https://edition.cnn.com/2018/08/17/uk/uk-anti-semitism-intl/index.html.

over books. He was a tanned warrior-hero who worked the land and had no interest in the Talmud, the Siddur, or Diaspora heritage. In fact, he repressed and even reviled them. Sabras also wished to disconnect from "naive" Jewish cosmopolitanism. These native-born Israelis were different in their language, mores, and identity from Diaspora Jews and observant immigrants. The sabra was a symbol of the native-born Hebrew youth, charged with leading the revolutionary switch as a nation from Judaism to "Hebraism." For them, the establishment of the State of Israel was a fundamentally secular event. In the early 1950s, the German-Jewish religious philosopher Akiva Ernst Simon even asked, "Are we still Jews?"[619]

Writer Aharon Appelfeld bemoaned the sabras' hostility to the Diaspora and especially the Zionists' disgust at the Jews' helplessness during the Holocaust, going "like lambs to slaughter." This attitude led the state's founding generation to adopt a narrative that was disconnected from the Jewish story in Europe. Appelfeld argued that:

> In the final analysis, we are paying a terrible price for it. We are paying for it in the form of the diminishment of the Jewish soul.... I feel close to Yiddishkeit and to Zionism as well; to the communists and to the assimilators, too. Because I saw them there. I saw them all being killed in the same pit. Therefore, I feel sympathy for them. And I have this basic understanding that both [ultra-Orthodox] Agudat Israel and [socialist] Hashomer Hatza'ir are part of the Jewish fate. Both Kafka and Rosa Luxemburg and Ariel Sharon, too, are different modern responses

---

619   Ehud Ben-Ezer, *Unease in Zion* (New York: Quadrangle Books, 1974), 15.

to the Jewish fate. All are part of the same
Jewish story....

There was an attempt here to amputate internal organs of the soul. That caused incapacity, a serious cultural incapacity. Therefore, I
think that today the Jewish people [in Israel]
is waging two existential wars simultaneously. One for the body, against the Arabs, and
a second war for the soul, against itself. The
identification of Judaism with a religion from
which people are trying to dissociate themselves is creating a very serious vacuum here.
The result is a black hole of identity. That is
why there is a deep recoil from everything
Jewish. But without some sort of Jewish identity, we will not be able to exist. There will be
nothing by which to exist in Israel. A society
without true roots is a society without a
future.[620]

Until the early 1960s, the term "Hebraism"—*ivriyut*—was the
banner of Jewish nationalism, which was secular and indigenous
in character. The Hebrews, who revered Hebrew as their national
tongue and suppressed their parents' exilic languages, were mostly
not religious but always saw themselves as part of the Jewish nation,
stretching back through history and across the seas. They were loyal

---

620 Interview with Ari Shavit, "A Jewish Soul," *Haaretz*. February 11, 2004, https://www.
haaretz.com/1.4714221.

to the notion of a common Jewish national destiny and staunchly committed to the Land of Israel as the national homeland.[621]

In this respect, Hebraism differed fundamentally from the cultural movement of the 1940s known as Canaanism, which hoped to build a home for the Hebrew nation but integrate it into the wider Middle East. Canaanism defined itself in opposition to rabbinical religion, the exilic history of the Jewish people, and the Diaspora condition. Its vision was to forge a Hebrew nation and state, calling on Jews to disconnect from their exilic religion and tradition and create a new Jew, proud and connected to the soil. But as the late Israeli journalist and left-wing leader Uri Avnery wrote, after the Holocaust "the Canaanites were forgotten and everybody became remorseful super-Jews."[622]

The vision of a "Hebrew" state was undercut by the great waves of immigration in the 1950s. The new arrivals include religious and traditionalist Jews from Europe and the Arab world, who neither wanted nor needed to disconnect from their Jewish past, nor did they wish to join the sabras' scorn for religion and faith. They believed they could build a Zionist state and live strong, independent lives there, at ease with the Jewish past and its traditions.[623]

Post-Zionist scholars have focused on the experience of these Mizrahi immigrants as the basis for calling into question the legitimacy of Zionism itself. According to the historian Amnon Raz-Krakotzkin, the Zionist notion of Hebrew sovereignty, based on the negation of the exile, tried to forcibly impose the traumas suffered

---

621 The late Amos Oz wrote: "Bialik, Kaznelson and Gordon never believed that we should 'raze the old world to the ground.' Even Brenner never said to the Jews of Halakhah, 'you can keep your holy scriptures and other antiquated baggage.' They said, 'we too are heirs to Jewish culture—not sole heirs, but legitimate heirs.'" From Amos Oz's essay "A Full Cart or an Empty One," republished in "Between Zionism and Hellenism: Amos Oz on the Meaning of Secular Judaism," *Haaretz*, January 28, 2019, https://www.haaretz.com/israel-news/culture/.premium.MAGAZINE-amos-oz-there-is-no-judaism-without-debate-over-the-meaning-of-judasim-1.6875342.

622 Uri Avnery, "Jews, Arabs: It's Time We Decided Who We Are," *Haaretz*, August 7, 2018, https://www.haaretz.com/opinion/.premium-jews-arabs-it-s-time-we-decided-who-we-are-1.6406242.

623 Ben-Ezer, *Unease in Zion*.

by Ashkenazi Jews onto the worldwide Jewish experience. He argues that the Jewish experience in eastern Europe did not represent Jewish life in Islamic lands, which was relatively peaceful but chillingly depicted by the early Zionists as a never-ending tale of persecutions to make it fit into the Zionist ethos of the negation of the exile.

In his view, Ashkenazi Zionists tried to forcibly "rehabilitate" Mizrahi Jews to cure them from the supposed traumas of exile.[624] Post-Zionist sociologist Yehouda Shenhav goes much further, contending that Jewish life in Muslim lands was good, respectable, and safe until Zionism—an Ashkenazi invention—came along to wreak havoc. Jews were attacked, expelled, and forced to flee, all because of Zionism. Shenhav also rejects the notion of a shared Jewish fate, arguing that there is no such thing as a collective national identity. Instead, he believes, there was always a distinct "Arab Jewish" ethno-national identity, which was different from the identity of the Ashkenazi Jews who defined Israeli culture.[625]

But many post-Zionist scholars are in denial about the complicated predicament of the Jews of Muslim lands, which changed dramatically between the medieval Golden Age and the modern era. Many Middle Eastern Jews lived in small, traditional communities until the twentieth century, and were the completely dependent subjects of Muslim patrons, accepting subordination in exchange for protection. The Jews of the Atlas Mountains, for example, were effectively hostages to the whims of their patrons, who occasionally authorized attacks on them to satisfy their Muslim loyalists.[626]

---

624   Amnon Raz-Krakotzkin, "Exile Within Sovereignty: Critique of 'The Negation of Exile' in Israeli Culture," *Teoria U'Vikoret* 4 (Fall 1993), 23–54, and 5 (Spring 1994), 113–132 [Hebrew]. See also abridged English adaptation in *The Scaffolding of Sovereignty*, eds. Zvi Ben-Dor Benite, Stefanos Geroulanos, and Nicole Jerr (New York, NY: Columbia University Press, 2017).

625   Yehouda Shenhav, *The Arab Jews: A Postcolonial Reading of Nationalism, Religion, and Ethnicity* (Stanford, CA: Stanford University Press, 2006).

626   Moshe Shokeid and Shlomo Deshen, *The Generation of Transition: Continuity and Change among North African Immigrants in Israel* (Jerusalem: Ben-Zvi Institute, 1999), 24–26 [Hebrew].

Of course, North Africa was also home to descendants of Jews expelled from Spain, who were more cosmopolitan and rose to prominence in their countries' economic and diplomatic life, but these bourgeois families formed a limited upper-class, which collapsed after the French conquest. They distanced themselves from the Jewish masses residing in ghettos known as the *Malach*. Historian David Korkos has written that, as he opted to settle in Israel in order to safeguard his heritage, more than two-thirds of his vast upper-class family, who held the rank of "merchants of the sultan," moved to Europe or North America, and many converted to Christianity.[627]

Shenhav and likeminded scholars also ignore the attachment and longing that so many Middle Eastern Jews felt for the Holy Land, as well as their awareness of a common Jewish historical destiny in the Mediterranean Basin and beyond. Gideon Kressel argues that the post-Zionist attacks on the idea of the negation of the exile are politically motivated, falsify Jewish history in the Arab world, and only sow division in Israeli society.[628]

One fascinating feature of the Israeli Century is how third- and fourth-generation Mizrahi immigrants are stubbornly preserving their ancestral heritage and revitalizing old customs, making them part of Israel's broader national culture. The Moroccan-Jewish festival Mimouna, celebrated at the end of Passover, has become a national festival, for all intents and purposes.

By contrast, if the young descendants of the original eastern European Jewish immigrants wished to revive the culture of eastern Europe, they would probably not know how—they have no reference points to cling to. As historian Aviad Kleinberg observes, the original Zionist elites did not want to recreate eastern European culture in

627   Michel Abitbol, *The Korkos Family and the History of Modern Morocco* (Jerusalem: Ben Zvi Institute, 1977), 5 [Hebrew].

628   Gideon Kressel, "Yehouda Shenhav, *The Arab Jews:* Nationality, Religion and Ethnicity," *Megamot* 43, no. 4 (2005) [Hebrew].

Israel. They wanted to forge "a new Israeli, out of nothing," returning to their biblical roots and putting the misery of the Diaspora behind them. As such, "the culture that Jews from Islamic lands were expected to adopt was not that of eastern European Jews, but the culture the latter had voluntarily adopted while systematically demolishing their own historical roots." In reality, the Western culture associated with Ashkenazim in Israel today is the culture of the Enlightenment, not the shtetl culture they reviled and discarded.[629]

The popular discourse over the so-called ethnic divide in Israel, between Mizrahim and Ashkenazim, is mostly vulgar, shallow, and politically manipulative. But at the core of this divide is a serious concept—that of *traditionalism*. By looking at Israelis' dynamic relationship with Jewish traditions, we can work out one of the most important inner tensions in Israeli society, one that will ultimately come to have a powerful effect on discussions of Jewish identity around the world.

The modern West, including the American Jewish community, accepts the existence of a dichotomy between secularism and religious traditionalism, and this dichotomy was accepted by the dominant factions of the early Zionist movement. Secular Zionism objected to piety and religion in principle, regarding them as restraints on the same personal freedom that so many in the West had fought for in the name of the Enlightenment and the Haskalah. But today, only a small section of Israel's population is actively hostile to tradition and religion for ideological reasons. Many Israeli Jews who identify as "secular" define themselves as such in opposition to the Orthodox religious establishment and religious coercion, and as a statement of their own personal autonomy. Researcher Hizky Shoham writes that there is no real theological debate in Israel

---

629   Aviad Kleinberg, "The Invention of Ashkenazi and Mizrahi Identity," Aviad Kleinberg's Blog, July 11, 2016, [Hebrew].

between religious and secular factions, and many secular Jews actually conduct "lives that are partially religious but unaffiliated with
a community and at an arm's length from the rabbinical establishment." He explains:

> Jewish Israeli society is fairly religious in its
> actions and beliefs but treats its religion as
> a non-binding tradition.... In other words,
> modern secularism does not necessarily
> mean a diminution in the importance of
> the religious tradition and practice, some-
> times the opposite. It means that religion is
> becoming a non-binding cultural reservoir,
> without coercive powers, a remnant of the
> past—but a meaningful remnant, that mustn't
> be forgone. In a modern lexicon, that's what
> you might call tradition.[630]

However, in contrast to the Western dichotomy, Middle
Eastern Jews imagine a graded spectrum of levels of religiosity and
tradition, where pure secularism is not even a possibility. In a 2018
survey conducted ahead of Rosh Hashanah, 54 percent of Israeli
Jews said they believe in God, and a further 21 percent said they
believe in a "higher power." According to the poll, most Mizrahi
Jews believe in God; moreover, they believe in his providence and
active involvement in the world.[631]

In the Israeli Century, traditionalism has become the hallmark

---

630 Hizky Shoham, "'Religion,' 'Secularity,' and 'Tradition' in the public thought of Israel,"
Iyunim Bitkumat Israel 24 (2014), 35 [Hebrew].

631 Chemi Shalev, "Haaretz Poll For Rosh Hashanah, a Picture of Israel's Muddled Jewish
Soul," *Haaretz*, September 9, 2018, https://www.haaretz.com/israel-news/.premium-for-rosh-ha-
shanah-a-picture-of-israel-s-muddled-jewish-soul-1.6462847.

of Mizrahi Jews, for whom "ethnic identity and traditionalist-Jewish identity are complementary organs in a complex system of self-definition, which also includes familial, national, gender, and class identities."[632] In contrast, Ashkenazi identity has become synonymous with European culture, distant and detached from the Jewish tradition. Uriel Abulof argues that many Israelis have developed a "sentimentalism" towards Mizrahi culture, viewing it as a more "authentic" expression of Jewish tradition—the same sentimentalism that characterized the "Orientalist" approach of the early secular Zionists towards their brethren in the East.[633]

An important synthesis is offered by philosopher Meir Buzaglo, who argues that the Zionists' conflation of secularism with Israeliness and Jewishness with the Diaspora, is driving a wedge inside the Jewish people. He regards traditionalism as a potential bridge between secular and religious Israelis because traditionalist Jews share many values with both their secular and religious peers. "It is neither secularism nor ultra-Orthodox religiosity; it is neither fanatical about the concepts of progress and the Enlightenment, nor is it Haredization. It should also be distinguished from folklore or popular culture, although Judaism in Israel has transferred the 'crown of popularity' to the Mizrahim."[634] Traditionalism, he argues, is the glue that binds a rich and pluralistic Jewish culture. Israeli Jewish identity, he says, must step back from rootless, universalistic ideologies, confrontational secular and religious absolutes, and also from an ethnic tribalism that glorifies immigrants' native cultures and seeks to replicate an imagined golden age. Traditionalist Jews inhabit the modern world but retain a familiarity with Judaism and

---

632 Yaacov Yadgar, *Beyond Secularism: Traditionism and the Critique of Israeli Secularism* (Jerusalem: Van Leer Institute, Hakibbutz Hameuchad, 2012) [Hebrew], 108.

633 Abulof, *Living on the Edge*, 228 [Hebrew].

634 Meir Buzaglo, "Mizrahiness, Tradition, Melting Pot: A Philosophical-Political Study," in *Inequality in Education*, ed. Dafna Golan-Agnon (Tel Aviv: Bavel, 2004), 209–235 [Hebrew].

their heritage, and they exercise judgment in choosing what to take from that tradition–and what they will never accept. For Buzaglo, "Israel is the only place where Jews are compelled to fight for a common purpose, and the only place where Zionism facilitated the existence of secular Jewish life." Israeli sovereignty liberates Jews to be completely Jewish, completely modern, and completely Zionist at the same time, and successfully resolve contradictions whenever they arise.[635]

The bond between Judaism and Israeli identity evolved from the early days of the state. It was further tightened with the Likud Party's rise to power in 1977. Menachem Begin, the first Likud prime minister, is known for opening up the national home, and giving a place and a voice to traditionalist Jews of Middle Eastern origin, who had felt like second-class citizens for years. Begin gave greater weight to rabbinical history–not just biblical history–than his socialist predecessors. He spoke of the different ethnic groups in Israel as his "brothers" and sought to strengthen the mutual responsibility between Jews and Israel's common destiny with the Diaspora. Begin also famously sponsored legislation to bar the extradition of Israeli citizens accused of crimes abroad, out of a commitment not to abandon even criminal Jews to "Gentile" authorities–they would serve their sentences in Israel's Jewish-run prisons instead.[636]

The question of home has always included the Jews of the Diaspora. Israel hoped to make Jews around the world feel that it is their national home. Most Diaspora Jews see it as such and identify with it–even if they criticize it. In this respect, they are compelled to engage with the Jewish state because it necessarily impinges on their own identity and condition as Jews. In the past, if Diaspora Jews

---

635   See also Arie Kizel, "Buzaglo's Traditional Alternative: Not Fit to Fight over a Mizrahi'ism Dissociated from Judaism (Book Review)," *Studies in Education* 4 (2011), 218 [Hebrew].

636   David Weiner, "All of Israel Are Responsible for One Another," in *David Weiner Volume on Criminal Law and Ethics* (Tel Aviv: Israel Bar Association, 2009), 226 [Hebrew].

mobilized to support a "fragile" Israel from the outside, its fiercest Jewish critics are now actively involved *inside* Israel in the hope of shaping it. All in all, they seek to influence Israel from the inside because the Israeli Century affects their own identity and status as Jews, both in their own eyes and in those of their neighbors. Every important Jewish movement or organization in the Diaspora, therefore, has a branch in Israel.

Today, Diaspora engagement with Israel is seen as critical for the preservation and cultivation of Jewish identity worldwide. It has led to the creation of Birthright Israel, among other initiatives, which has brought more than half a million young Diaspora Jews to visit Israel. Birthright's backers hope these trips will make Diaspora youth feel a profound sense of tribal belonging and understand their historic role in safeguarding the Jewish people; this hope appears to be substantiated by recent long-term studies comparing the Jewish engagement of former participants versus non-participants.[637]

But alongside recent initiatives to bring Israel and the Diaspora closer, another trend is emerging–the Israeli right wing, governing in coalition with ultra-Orthodox parties, is actually leading Israel *away* from the liberal Judaism of the Diaspora. Ronald Lauder, the president of the World Jewish Congress and a politically conservative figure, complained about this in the *New York Times*. He wrote that Israel's religious-nationalist tendencies, which are being anchored into law, imperil a sense of common destiny between Israel and the Diaspora, partly because of the tension between Orthodox hegemony and democratic values:

> These events are creating the impression that
> the democratic and egalitarian dimensions

---

637   Graham Wright, Shahar Hecht, and Leonard Saxe, "Jewish Futures Project: Birthright Israel's First Decade of Applicants: A Look at the Long-Term Program Impact, October 2020" (Waltham, MA: Brandeis University, 2020).

of the Jewish democratic state are being tested.... Passing the torch to this younger generation is already a difficult undertaking—as many leaders, educators, rabbis and parents will attest. But when Israel's own government proposes damaging legislation, this task may well become nearly impossible.[638]

The argument with American Jewry has escalated in recent years. Many feel that Israelis are damaging what they define as Judaism and sabotaging their reputation in the United States. But Israelis believe that they are busy defending the national home and Judaism, while spoiled Americans have the luxury of constantly criticizing and preaching universal morality from a safe distance. For many right-wing Israelis, liberal American Jews are a lost cause, if not a hostile crowd. Haggai Segal, editor of the national-religious *Makor Rishon* newspaper, wrote that Israel's attempts to encourage them to immigrate are "good for the soul and one's conscience, but hopeless.... Our brothers in the Diaspora will continue assimilating en masse even if we break into a heavy sweat trying to strengthen their ties to Judaism and to us. It's a waste of money, a waste of emotional energy, and most of all a waste of time."[639] Segal, who was convicted of membership in the radical Jewish Underground and violent attacks on Palestinians in the 1980s, speaks for a growing segment of nationalist Israeli society that does not regard liberal American Jews as an asset for the Jewish people. This approach is growing more prevalent among the younger generation of religious-nationalist Israelis, even if the older generation remains wary. Rabbi Chaim Druckman, an

---

638 Ron Lauder, "Israel, This Is Not Who We Are," *New York Times*, August 13, 2018), https://www.nytimes.com/2018/08/13/opinion/israel-ronald-lauder-nation-state-law.html.

639 Haggai Segal, "The New Jewish Agency Chairman Should Offer Diaspora Jews One Solution: Move to Israel," *Makor Rishon*, June 29, 2018 [Hebrew].

elder of the Religious Zionist world, reacted with dismay to Segal's remarks, saying, "I am shocked! There are Jews who are out at sea, and some people are telling them—Drown!"[640]

The disagreement over the future of the territories has also caused divisions within the Diaspora itself. After 1967, some Diaspora Jews supported expanding the country's borders to include its newly acquired territories; many even leapt at the opportunity to be pioneers, make history, and personally settle in Judea and Samaria, which are now home to around 60,000 American Jews. As strange as it might seem, many Jews who moved from the United States to West Bank settlements saw the settlement enterprise as a continuation of the American Jewish liberalism of the late 1960s. They associated the values of the civil rights movement in the United States with the right of Jews to settle their ancient homeland.[641] But today, the question of Israeli settlements is making it increasingly difficult for liberal American Jews to reconcile their support for Israel with their progressive values.

Under Prime Minister Benjamin Netanyahu, the "national camp" came to embrace the ultra-Orthodox parties as an inseparable part of the Israeli right wing. Shas and United Torah Judaism used to be thought of as non-Zionist parties, but their followers hold increasingly extreme nationalist positions—calling for a full Israeli annexation of the occupied territories—and exhibit extreme hostility towards Arabs.[642]

They also dispute the basic entitlement of liberal Diaspora Jews to a share in the Israeli national home. In 2015, the late religious affairs minister David Azoulay said that Reform Jews were not

---

640   Guy Ezra, "Rabbi Druckman on the Column in *Makor Rishon*: 'I Am Shocked!,'" July 5, 2018 [Hebrew].

641   Sara Yael Hirschhorn, *City on a Hilltop: American Jews and the Israeli Settler Movement* (Cambridge: Harvard University Press, 2017) .

642   Sagi Elbaz, "The Ultra-Orthodox Are the New Israeli Right," *Haaretz*, August 8, 2019, https://www.haaretz.com/opinion/.premium-the-ultra-orthodox-are-the-new-right-1.7649293.

really Jewish, but trying to "fake" it and did not observe religious law properly. He even called Reform Jews "a disaster to the people of Israel."[643] And yet the Nation State Law enshrines Israel's obligation to "act, in the Diaspora, to preserve the ties between the State and members of the Jewish people," and "to preserve the cultural, historical and religious heritage of the Jewish People among Jews in the Diaspora."

In recent years, new ground is emerging in the effort to strengthen the bond between Israel and the Diaspora in the global economy. This includes collaborative initiatives between Israeli and Diaspora Jews to promote investment in Israeli start-ups. Israel is also known as a hothouse of groundbreaking innovation and life-saving medical research. Thus, efforts are made to combine its technological prowess with the tremendous abilities of Diaspora Jews in a process that also reshapes old patterns of Jewish philanthropy.

A wealthy country in its own right, Israel will no longer go hat in hand to its wealthy American uncle. For years, many American Jews who were willing to donate to Israel did not see the country as a good place to do business. But now, at the core of this vision for the future of global Jewish cooperation are commercial and scientific ventures, underpinned by their partners' sense of a common identity. Israeli Jews will find a force-multiplier for their innovation, and American Jews will receive a boost to their national-tribal identity. This interaction between the Diaspora and the Start-Up Nation will provide both with commercial opportunities, reinforce their Jewish identity, and strengthen their sense of mutual responsibility.

If, in the twentieth century, Zionists sought to negate the Diaspora, and Diaspora Jews saw a fragile homeland that needed their support and protection, in the Israeli Century, the balance of

---

643   Isabel Kershner, "Israeli Minister Says Reform Jews Are Not Really Jewish," *New York Times*, July 7, 2015, https://www.nytimes.com/2015/07/08/world/middleeast/israeli-minister-says-reform-jews-are-not-really-jewish.html.

global Jewish responsibility has shifted. Today, Israel has become a strong and confident home, in the eyes of both Israelis and Jews around the world, including many of its critics. While the vision of the negation of the exile, which was so central to early Zionism, has not entirely disappeared, it looks completely different in the Israeli Century.

The Israeli Century and the Entry Pass to the Jewish People

But whose home is it? By gaining an independent state, the Jews also gained a special power to define the boundaries of their nation, just like other sovereign states can decide who may enter their territory or become citizens. The shift the Jewish people underwent, from being a stateless nation to having nation-state, also reformulated the historic question of identity—"who is a Jew?"—which had pre-occupied them since the Babylonian Exile. In the Israeli Century, the answer to this question is chiefly expressed through the Law of Return, which sets the criteria for who is considered Jewish and auto-matically entitled to citizenship. Initially passed in 1950, the Law of Return allows one to belong to Israel's Jewish majority community on the basis of one's extended kinship ties. In 1970, the law was amended to include anyone with at least one Jewish grandparent—a definition deliberately meant to echo the Nazi-era Nuremburg Laws. If you are Jewish enough to be persecuted for it, the reasoning went, you are welcome in our home. Yet the definition of who is a Jew for the purpose of Israel's official religious authorities—who control marriage, divorce, and burial—requires one to be born to a Jewish mother or formally undergo Orthodox conversion.

The burning question, therefore, is whether the Law of Return is just an entry pass to the State of Israel or also to the Jewish people. Hundreds of thousands of Israeli immigrants who received citizenship as Jews, on the basis of the Law of Return, are considered not Jewish under a strict halakhic definition even though they regard themselves as Jewish people. For Jews in the Diaspora, and many in Israel, this raises a legitimate question as to why converts through non-Orthodox denominations should not be included as well. But for Orthodox Jews, of course, "a subjective sense of belonging is completely irrelevant to the definition of who is a Jew."[644]

Despite the Orthodox monopoly on defining conversions, the reality of the Israeli Century proves that in a sovereign Jewish state, one can effectively join the Jewish people even without a formal conversion at all. In fact, many immigrants from the former Soviet Union, who are not Jewish according to religious law, were accepted based on the 1970 amendment and have been deeply integrated into Israeli Jewish society. They speak Hebrew, serve in the Israel Defense Forces, are patriotic, raise their children in the national education system, and adopt Israeli customs, including traditional Jewish rituals. They are not Jewish according to halakha, but they *feel* Jewish and identify with the majority in Israel. They have effectively undergone a "sociological conversion,"[645] and the Israeli Jews they marry care nothing for their family trees.

Moreover, the fact that the Israeli Central Bureau of Statistics distinguishes between "Jews and others" and "Arabs" shows that Israel *de facto* considers citizens who are neither Jewish nor Arab as part of the broader Jewish population.[646] This hints that it might be possible to join the Jewish people by the same principles that permit membership of other modern nations. According to Alexander Yakobson, these "sociological conversions" do not weaken Israel's

---

644   Yisrael Rosen, "Who Is a Jew in 2000?," in *Who Is a Jew Today: Symposium on Jewish Identity*, eds. Maya Leibowitz et al. (Tel Aviv: Yediot Aharonot/Hemed, 2006), 41–47 [Hebrew].

645   Asher Cohen, *Non-Jewish Jews in Israel* (Jerusalem: Hartman Institute, 2006) [Hebrew].

646   Yaacov Yadgar, *Beyond Secularism: Traditionism and the Critique of Israeli Secularism* (Jerusalem: Van Leer Institute, Hakibbutz Hameuchad, 2012), 81, footnote 10 [Hebrew].

Jewish character but only change it, and the nature of Jewish nationalism, in a way that makes it more multicultural and multi-ethnic.[647] Notwithstanding the historical debate over who is a Jew and the dominance of the Orthodox rabbinate, it seems that only in Israel can one become *de facto* Jewish over time even without formally converting.

There are also people who have no Jewish family ties whatsoever, but were born in Israel to foreign workers and refugees. Many of them speak Hebrew as their first language, have no sense of commitment to their parents' home countries, become Israeli patriots over time, and effectively join the Jewish people. Israelis who object to the expulsion of foreign workers with Israeli-born children as "anti-Jewish" believe that they should be embraced. One commentator went as far as to say that Israel should transfer its budgets for activities for Diaspora Jews, "who do not speak Hebrew [and] have no interest in living in Israel," to absorbing foreign workers who speak Hebrew, live in Israel, and are committed to raising families within Israeli Jewish society.[648]

Israel's Orthodox establishment is fighting these trends, annulling conversions that were not performed according to their own strict interpretation of religious law—even those performed by some modern Orthodox rabbis in the Diaspora—and subjecting those whose Jewish status is in doubt to stringent restrictions. But they are struggling to hold back the tide; in trying to draw the narrowest possible boundaries for Jewish belonging, they are making themselves increasingly irrelevant to whole sections of the Israeli population, and many Jews in Israel take no account of their pronouncements.

In the early twentieth century, decades before Israeli

---

647   Alexander Yakobson, "Zionism and Multiculturalism," 717 [Hebrew].

648   David Chinitz, "Israel Should Keep Its Filipinos and Drop Birthright," *Haaretz*, August 21, 2019, https://www.haaretz.com/opinion/.premium-israel-should-keep-its-filipinos-and-drop-birthright-1.7725550.

independence, Gershom Scholem foresaw that Jewish sovereignty would completely transform Jewish identity.[649] The Jewish people in Israel are multicultural and multi-ethnic, and the state also treats Diaspora Jews and "non-Jewish Jews" as belonging to the same nation. Israel is a country of immigrants, which integrated newcomers from Europe and the Arab world and elsewhere, in an attempt to create a melting pot in which the *state* would define its Jewish citizens' national and tribal attachments.

It has also managed to welcome "honorary Jews" into the family.[650] The Druze, an Arabic-speaking ethnic community, are intensely patriotic Israelis and have distinguished themselves in the ranks of the Israeli army. They have forged what Israelis call a "covenant of blood" with the state's Jewish citizens and are "brothers in arms." Thus, when the Knesset passed the Nation-State Law in 2018, which stated that Jews have an exclusive right to national self-determination in Israel, the Druze community took to the streets in protest at being marginalized. Veteran broadcaster Yaron London warned that if the Druze concluded that their status as "quasi-Jews" became seen as precarious, the survival of the Jewish-Druze national alliance would be thrust into serious doubt.

Over 20 percent of Israelis are Arabs, and either Muslims or Christians. Among them, a minority serve in the country's security forces and feel proud to be Israeli, even if they do not feel they share a common destiny with the Jewish Diaspora. Yet the large majority of Israeli Arabs see themselves as a distinct national minority, separate from the Jewish people; the Israeli state, in turn, treats them with suspicion. Nevertheless, the picture of Israeli Arabs in the Israeli Century is a complex one. They live side-by-side with Israeli Jews in a state of perpetual conflict and profound hostility, but there

---

649   Scholem, "Who Is a Jew," 76 [Hebrew].

650   Yaron London, "The Fracturing of the 'Covenant of Blood'—This in Just a Preview," *Yediot Aharonot*, August 1, 2018.

is also surprising harmony, and many Arabs see themselves as part of a "civil" Israeli nation.

Scholars have taken different views of the prospects of full integration of Israeli Arabs into the fabric of the Jewish State. Some, like Dan Schueftan, take a pessimistic approach. He argues that Israeli Arabs have become increasingly radicalized since Israel's establishment and have turned from a defeated party into a large and assertive national minority, which poses a danger to the Jews. In his view, the Arab minority is led by radical forces who identify with Israel's enemies and deny its legitimacy as a Jewish state. This anti-Israel and anti-Jewish hostility characterizes the elites of the Palestinians in Israel and trickles down to the general Arab Israeli public, resulting in expressions of support for Israel's sworn enemies.[651] When on May 11, 2021, fierce violence of Arab youth erupted in mixed Jewish-Arab towns, amid growing clashes in Jerusalem's Temple Mount, Jewish Israelis were once again shocked to witness the powerful sense of kinship of Arab-Israeli citizens with their fellow Palestinians in the West Bank and Gaza. The fact that Arab-Israeli rioting took place just when millions of Israelis where rushing to bomb shelters from Palestinian Hamas's rocket barrage on Tel Aviv and other major cities, immediately awakened the demons of the Second Intifada of two decades earlier, with its deadly wave of suicide bombings. Israel declared a state of emergency in the city of Lod, and Israel's police chief commented: "We have not seen this kind of violence since October 2000."

Such dramatic events present a challenge to the more optimistic approach championed by scholars like sociologist Sammy Smooha. He speaks about Israeli Arabs undergoing increasing "Israelization." The Arabs are not part of the Jewish people but feel that they belong

---

651   Dan Schueftan, *Palestinians in Israel: The Arab Minority and the Jewish State* (Or Yehuda: Kinneret, Zemora-Bitan, Dvir, 2011) [Hebrew].

to a civil Israeli nation. Indeed, research consistently shows that large numbers of Israeli Arabs are proud of Israel's achievements and see it as their home.

The Israelization of Israeli Arabs is also clear from their categorical rejection of the notion of emigrating to other Arab countries, including a potential Palestinian state. They consider life in Israel, and especially its economy, as an enormous advantage and consider the country their own. When studying abroad, they tend to connect socially with Israeli Jews far more than with Arabs of other countries.

The Israelization of Israeli Arabs is also clear from the younger generation's declining use of the Arabic language. Even amongst themselves, they increasingly speak a Hebraized form of Arabic. In the Israeli Century, there has been a huge growth in the number of Arab students at Israeli higher learning institutions where the main language is Hebrew.[652]

The tension between the polar approaches about the future of Arabs in the Israeli state, radicalization versus integration, came to the fore in a dramatic fashion in March 2020, a time of both political upheaval and the beginning of the Covid-19 pandemic. On March 2, Israel held national elections, and the Arab Israeli Party "The Joint List" won a record fifteen Knesset seats, thereby gaining a potentially pivotal role in the efforts to replace Netanyahu's coalition. The prime minister and his allies immediately denounced the opposition effort to include the Arab Party in "the Israeli equation" as illegitimate and even treasonous. Although they insisted that this was targeted at Arab parties, which are expressly non-Zionist, rather than citizens, many commentators saw it as indicative that Arabs were second-class citizens when it came to political representation, calling Israeli democracy itself into question.

---

652   Lior Datal, "80 Percent Jump in Arab Students in Academia," *The Marker*, January 24, 2018 [Hebrew].

The same month, however, the pandemic exploded nation-wide. Suddenly, many Israelis "discovered" that 20 percent of Israel's medical personnel, including those at its leading hospitals, are Arab doctors and nurses, many of whom voted for the same Arab list that the prime minister denounced as "terrorist."

On the other hand, in the face of a global pandemic, many in the Arab communities were also "awakened to the fact" that they were indeed Israelis, protected by the same public health system that protected everyone else. Images of IDF troops distributing boxes of meals and other necessities to Arab communities to reduce potential exposure and prevent the spread of the virus, all during the holy month of Ramadan, were widely seen. The Covid-19 crisis demonstrated how the power of Jewish sovereignty and the mobilization of the state apparatus worked in times of peril for all Israelis, Jews, and non-Jews alike.

The crisis also brought to the surface the glaring fact that, in times of emergency, Israel prioritized its own citizens over Jews in the Diaspora, who were forbidden from visiting the country, just like all other foreign visitors.

Halakha and the State

Israel has managed to bring different cultures together, both Jewish and non-Jewish, but there remains an antagonistic divide between the ultra-Orthodox and the rest of Israeli society. The opposition of many ultra-Orthodox Israelis to the modern values of Israeli society is a ticking time bomb—a problem that has become even more acute during the Covid-19 epidemic. Is a violent confrontation inevitable?

In the late twentieth century, amid the euphoria of globalization and the signing of the Oslo Accords between Israel and the Palestinians, some argued that secular fears of a resurgence of old, reactionary forms of religious Judaism were overblown. Yigal Elam wrote that the threat posed by the national-religious and ultra-Orthodox streams was illusory, and "historical Judaism" would soon be overpowered by the unstoppable forces of modernity. Rabbinic Judaism, Elam added, had always been on the defensive when facing progress and modernity, acknowledging its inferiority to its advanced secular surroundings. This was true before the establishment of Israel, and it remained the case in modern Israel, where "historical Judaism" had been fighting a hopeless rearguard battle since 1948 and had "reached the end of the road."[653]

Two decades after Elam's book was published, is this still the state of affairs? Israel is flourishing, but the forces of ultra-Orthodoxy and religious nationalism are growing stronger politically and demographically, raising fears that the fragile balance between religion and modernity will be upset. Identity polls in Israel show that "religious outlooks, or a lack thereof...mark the deep fissures within Israeli Jewish society. They differentiate of course between ultra-Orthodox, religious-Zionist and traditionalist Jews, but also mark secular Jews."[654] Many Israelis fear that a growing religious extremism and coercion could deteriorate a culture war into a civil war.

The struggle between modernity and Orthodoxy in Israel is playing out in multiple arenas—in the military, in the economy, in education, in culture, in welfare policy, and even on questions of the environment. One of the most acute issues is the role of women in Israeli society, especially in the context of military service, political representation, workforce participation, and personal status issues. The status of women is always a key indicator of any country's embrace of modernity and democracy. So, when religious Zionist rabbis actively oppose women's combat service and urge religious

---

653   Yigal Elam, *The End of Judaism: The Religion-Nation and the Realm* (Tel Aviv: Yedioth Aharonot, 2000), 278–279 [Hebrew].

654   Shalev, "Haaretz Poll For Rosh Hashanah, a Picture of Israel's Muddled Jewish Soul," *Haaretz*.

youth not to serve in mixed-gender units, many Israelis fear that their modern democracy is in jeopardy.

Is Israel's sovereignty threatened by this extreme religious and nationalist assault on its secular, democratic institutions? When the head of the extremist Jerusalem Faction, Rabbi Tzvi Friedman, tells his disciples that "it would have been better if this state had never been established" and "the army is impure, not sacred,"[655] can we infer that the Israeli Century is steamrolling toward becoming a theocracy? Or is the opposite happening, and do these rabbis' extreme statements prove that religious leaders are panicking, fearing that their communities are edging closer to the Israeli mainstream?

While most of the secular public believes there is religious coercion, the ultra-Orthodox public believes there is secular coercion.[656] Indeed, the political sociologist Guy Ben-Porat argues that, despite the trends of increasing religiosity in Israel, there is also a profound movement toward greater secularism. These trends have intensified since the 1990s, thanks to the mass immigration of largely secular Jews from the former Soviet Union and the liberalization of the Israeli economy, opening it up to the world. He also argues that the Israeli public sphere is becoming more universalist and secular, and many religious and ultra-Orthodox Israelis are now exposed to the winds of globalization and uncensored media. This influences their family values, participation in the labor market, and consumer behavior.

But he believes this secularization does not attest to a secular political order because the public status, symbols, and leadership of the religious world have all grown stronger, especially in the Netanyahu era, when ultra-Orthodox parties were a permanent fixture in Israel's governing coalitions. Ben-Porat argues that secularism is the natural consequence of life in Israel and is both a political and apolitical

---

655   Yaki Adamker, "Rabbi Auerbach's Successor: Secular Jews Are Goyim, Better if Israel Had Never Been Born," *Walla!*, June 19, 2018 [Hebrew], https://news.walla.co.il/item/3166932.

656   Rosner and Fuchs, *#IsraeliJudaism*, 143.

force. It is political because it has caused institutional changes, and apolitical, as it allows individuals, especially those in and above the middle classes, to live a free, unencumbered.

For other observers, however, this is a misleadingly rosy picture that downplays the recent shift in the balance between religion and state in Israel in favor of religious forces.[657]

Philosopher Michael Walzer argues that many twentieth-century national liberation movements were rooted in revulsion for religious life and the messianic ethos of passively waiting for God. This was true of India's struggle for independence from the British Empire under the leadership of Mahatma Gandhi and Jawaharlal Nehru and the Algerian struggle against French colonialism. Walzer argues that the Zionists who raised the banner of activism, progress, innovation, and new beginnings developed as the antithesis of the religious pathology of submitting to the decrees of fate. Yet years later, these liberation movements are under assault from a religious revivalism that challenges their founding cultures.

Religion is therefore back with a vengeance in India, Algeria, and Israel, because these countries' founders were elitists, who failed to properly understand the people they led and failed to develop democratic alternatives to tradition, family life, and community befitting daily life after independence. The "paradox of liberation" is that religion, repressed at the moment of the national awakening, later reemerges in the guise of a religious fanaticism that imperils the free institutions and secular character of these countries.[658]

However, Walzer's thesis is somewhat limited, and his comparison between Zionism and other postcolonial movements is artificial. It ignores the fact that Zionism, despite supposedly being

---

657   Guy Ben-Porat, *Between State and Synagogue: The Secularization of Contemporary Israel* (Cambridge: Cambridge University Press, 2013).

658   Michael Walzer, *The Paradox of Liberation: Secular Revolutions and Religious Counterrevolutions* (New Haven: Yale University Press, 2015).

secular, never completely avoided messianic motifs, even if it moderated them. Moreover, religious movements played a key role in the Zionist revolution, and their utopian theories were not so different from the secular Zionists' vision of redemption. This utopian messianism helped to make *mamlakhtiyut*–Ben-Gurion's statist ideology of prioritizing national over sectoral interests–into a kind of civic religion in Israel's early days.

Furthermore, the process of national liberation did not end with independence in 1948–it continued with other major events, above all the conquest of Judea, Samaria, and the Old City of Jerusalem in 1967. These and other milestones naturally provoked changes in Jewish national liberation theories. They also awakened Religious Zionism, turning religion from a passive to an active force.

In Israel's early years, the socialist spirit of Labor Zionism reigned supreme, and its role models were the workers, not the urban bourgeoisie. Israeli values were thought to be inconsistent with liberal democracy, which prioritized individual liberty, rights, and economic prosperity. One indication of the early zeitgeist was how Israelis spoke contemptuously of American Jews as indulgent hedonists, despite their dependence on the generosity of American Jewry as the "wealthy uncle" and their awe of America. Indeed, America threatened Israel in its early years as a magnet for emigration; many Israelis left the moment they could for the *Goldene Medina*. But ironically, today, it is the Religious Zionists who can lay the strongest claim to being the heirs of the founders' ethos, while the kibbutzniks, who were thought of as the physical incarnation of the founders' vision, have neglected it.

In 1952, Jewish-American anthropologist Samuel Koenig, who researched Israeli society in the first years after independence, wrote that "the *kibbutz* is engaged in a life-and-death struggle," and that "the spirit of capitalism and bourgeois living standards are on the rise, while socialism is on the downward road."[659] Nevertheless, the lead figures and voices in the formation of Israel's early collective values were the pioneers and their successors in the labor movement. They were the IDF's combat soldiers and commanders, and their fighting spirit shaped the ethos of the Hebrew state. In Israel's early days, religious Jews played a marginal role in the secular Zionist image of heroism. True to Koenig's observations, after the Six-Day War, and especially after the Yom Kippur War, Israelis gradually transitioned from statism to liberalism and increasingly prioritized the individual and the free market.

Accordingly, Israel's collective national morality was undermined; the founding generation's role models and institutions fell from grace. They were replaced by new forces, whose representatives achieved positions of influence in politics, the economy, society, the legal system, the army, and other national institutions. New elites started to take hold in the name of rising sections of Israel's diverse, multicultural society.

After the Six-Day War, Israel's democracy and economy were opened up, but this did not stop the quest for a vision of cooperation across society. In the 1970s, a battle between the new pretenders to moral ownership of the Land of Israel, the Gush Emunim settler movement, and the dovish Peace Now began. While Gush Emunim pushed with a messianic fervor to continue the founding generation's mission and settle the territories "liberated" in the Six-Day War, Peace Now lobbied no less fervently for Israel to return the territories in exchange for an immediate and comprehensive peace. The grandchildren and heirs of the original Gush Emunim activists settled in Judea and Samaria, won the hearts and minds of the Israeli right wing, and are now among the leading forces in the shaping of

---

659 Samuel Koenig, "Immigration and Culture Conflict in Israel," *Social Forces*, 31, no. 2 (December 1952), 144–148.

the Israeli Century. In contrast, Peace Now has been marginalized, trying without success to hold back the advance of the settlement movement.[660]

One of the major forces holding the Israeli collective together is Israel's security situation, which demands the ongoing mobilization of civilians, especially during times of war (which are becoming smaller and less frequent). Such was the case in late 2001, when the Kinneret Covenant was signed by dozens of public figures and intellectuals who represented the full spectrum of Israeli Jewish society, amid fears that profound divisions it would jeopardize the national effort to fight the horrific suicide bombings of the Second Intifada. The covenant represented an attempt to reach a broad political and social consensus during an acute emergency:

> We are members of one people. Our past and our fate are linked. Despite the differences of opinion and the divergent outlooks between us, we are all committed to the continuation of Jewish life, to the continued existence of the Jewish people, and to ensuring the future of the State of Israel.[661]

The security situation does not affect everyone equally, but it has profound implications for Israeli society. Not all Israelis are directly affected by security threats in the West Bank, in communities adjacent to the Gaza Strip, and along the Lebanese border; some are even completely disengaged. Yet the security situation affects everyone, as terrorism and missiles threaten to reach the center of Israel, and even those not directly affected on a daily basis send their

---

660 I owe this insight to a conversation with Prof. Ruth Gavison on December 24, 2018.

661 "The Kinneret Covenant (2001)," unofficial translation in "Supporting the Covenant," *Haaretz*, January 2, 2002, https://www.haaretz.com/1.5472827.

children to the IDF and remain committed to the ethos of collective national defense.

The responsibility for national defense and reverence for soldiers' sacrifices used to be the preserve of the secular, socialist founding generation, but these have since migrated to other sections of Israeli society. In particular, the religious Zionists are positioning themselves as the nation's new fighting heroes and consider themselves the heirs of the original pioneers and the most devoted Zionists.

After the Six-Day War and the occupation of the territories, religious Zionists started increasing their engagement with the army by performing shortened service through the *yeshivat hesder* program, which enabled them to focus on their yeshiva studies while making a meaningful contribution to national security. From the late 1980s onward, with the advent of pre-army religious preparatory academies (*mechinot*), national-religious youth started enlisting for full combat duty, becoming the backbone of the IDF ground forces and a key part of its officers' corps, including in elite units. According to Yagil Levy, an expert in Israel's civil-military relations, "As the religious presence in the IDF strengthened, the organized religious community sought not only to establish arrangements to protect its conscripts' [religious] culture, but also to influence the army's character and even its deployments."[662] Levy speaks of a "takeover" of the IDF's collective military ethos and fighting forces by religious Zionist soldiers and their rabbis. He believes this has led the IDF to adopt religious values, even during times of combat, and give precedence to religious soldiers, whose connection to Jewish tradition it considers an advantage.[663]

Rabbi Eliezer Shenvald, who heads a yeshivat hesder and

---

662   Yagil Levy, "The Theocratization of the Israeli Military and Its Drivers," *The Public Sphere* 13 (2018), 176–177 [Hebrew].

663   Ibid., 188–192.

attained the rank of colonel in the IDF, rejects Levy's claims of rabbinic influence in the IDF and religious coercion, dismissing them as "political." He argues that it has always conducted a dialogue with the full breadth of Israeli society and can debate questions of values unimpeded. IDF Chief Education Officer Brigadier-General Zvika Faireisen also rejects claims of religious coercion as "mendacious," describing them as "rooted in fear and intolerance and bound to sow ignorance and discord," and maintaining that "the IDF has no desire or goal to change the identity of any soldier."[664] He stressed that it was Ben-Gurion who emphasized the importance of bringing the Hebrew Bible and the vision of the prophets into the IDF. In his view, its Jewish education schemes have nothing to do with religion, just familiarity with Jewish culture.

When Israel was still a young country, its Jewish society was essentially a "nation in uniform." The IDF's job was not just to defend the country, but to settle the land, educate the people, and teach new immigrants Hebrew. In the last five decades the reverence for the IDF has waned somewhat, and sections of society are proudly anti-militaristic. Yet military service still plays an enormous role in the Israeli experience, not just for religious Zionists. Many Israeli teenagers take a strong interest in military service while still at high school; while American teenagers are busy writing college applications, Israeli teenagers are trying out for different IDF units. Moreover, the Israeli education system still sees itself as responsible for preparing children for "meaningful" military service, and the media regularly publish tables of enlistment rates from different schools and towns.[665] Although the military ethos has lost its sheen for some of the secular public, "meaningful military service" (as it

---

664   "Q&A with Brig.-Gen. Zvika Faireisen," *Shvii*, April 20, 2018 [Hebrew], 26, https://www.dmag.co.il/pub/shvii/302/26/.

665   Yoav Zeitun, "Enlistment Statistics: Index of Contribution to IDF by Population Center," *YNet*, December 5, 2017 [Hebrew], https://www.ynet.co.il/articles/0,7340,L-5051837,00.html.

is called) remains a badge of honor that influences one's status in Israeli society.

Despite the debate over the influence of religious Zionists on the IDF, it also plays an increasingly crucial role in building Israel's status as a technological superpower, largely on the strength of secular Israeli recruits. After 1948, Israel made a limited effort to develop its security forces' scientific and technological expertise. It set up the IDF Science Corps, which later became Rafael Advanced Defense Systems, and built its first nuclear reactor at Nahal Soreq in the 1950s. The IDF opened its first computer unit in 1960, but only in the 1970s did the state undertake to revolutionize its scientific and technological capacities. Israel's military industries and universities started taking a great interest in research and development after French President Charles de Gaulle slapped an arms embargo on Israel after the Six-Day War.[666]

In recent decades, as the threats to Israel's security have shifted, the IDF has worked to channel the finest young minds into its technological units, most famously Unit 8200, developing several tracks to help it find, filter, and train a scientific and technological elite, with cooperation with Israel's leading universities, in everything from cyberwarfare to drones, battlefield communications, and counterterrorism. During the COVID-19 pandemic, many Israelis learned about Unit 81 of the intelligence corps, a kind of R&D unit tasked with rapidly developing ventilators to distribute across the country for the first time.[667]

Such elite programs include not only young men and women from wealthy towns, but also thousands of underprivileged prodigies, who are brought into advanced training schemes at various

---

666   Dan Breznitz, *Innovation and the State: Political Choice and Strategies for Growth in Israel, Taiwan and Ireland* (New Haven: Yale University Press, 2007), 41–47.

667   Uri Berkovits, "Hush-Hush IDF Intel Unit Takes on Covid-19," *Globes*, April 20, 2000, https://en.globes.co.il/en/article-hush-hush-idf-intel-unit-takes-on-covid-19-1001325867.

institutions of higher learning. Gifted youngsters are scouted while they are still at high school and directed to the IDF's technological units. Service has long been widely admired by Israeli society and is a great résumé builder in Israel's hi-tech industry.[668] Eviatar Matania, one of the founders of Israel's national cyber-defense systems, told me, "If it weren't for mandatory conscription, it would have been very difficult to recruit the finest youth for these jobs, because the universities and technology-rich industries would have snapped most of them up, like in many Western countries."[669]

Former IDF Chief of Staff and Air Force Commander Lt.-Gen. Dan Halutz also believes that catching the finest minds young and enrolling them in technological units gives Israel an extraordinary edge, putting the country at the forefront of global technology.[670] Matania also says that "Israeli culture, which cherishes meaningful mandatory service as a national value, allows talented youngsters to have a completely free higher education, and in turn they make the IDF one of the best militaries in the world."

Given the manifold types of military service, therefore, is there really a threat of "theocratization" in the IDF, as Levy claims? Or does its technological momentum advance the cause of modernity and signal that Jewish Israeli identity will become less religious in future?

The role of Religious Zionists in the IDF came under significant public scrutiny in the wake of the assassination of Prime Minister Yitzhak Rabin in 1995. At the time of the murder, Israel was in the grips of a culture war. One side belonged to a secular, globalized culture, which found expression politically through the

---

668 Tali Heruti-Sover, "The Army Is Making the Deal of Its Life: It Receives Manpower from Talpiot, Who Wouldn't Stay a Day in the Professional Army," *The Marker*, Sepember 9, 2010 [Hebrew], https://www.themarker.com/career/1.590639.

669 Author's interview with Eviatar Matania.

670 Author's interview with Dan Halutz.

Oslo Accords and Shimon Peres's vision of the "New Middle East." Prime Minister Rabin also believed that the basic condition of the Jewish people was changing in the new globalized world, and it was time for Israel to shake free of feelings of isolation and integrate among the nations.

Opposing the Rabin government were Religious Zionists, who considered the Land of Israel sacred and feared that the Oslo Accords spelled its moral and political doom. They led a hostile and often violent resistance to the peace process. Rabin was attacked in the streets and called names drawn from rabbinic literature—*rodef*, meaning one who pursues another with an intent to kill, and *moser*, meaning one who hands a fellow Jew over to Gentile authorities.[671]

Although the Rabin assassination and the terror attacks of the late 1990s undermined public support for the Oslo Accords, it was the Second Intifada, launched in 2000, that changed the face of Israel by dealing the Oslo vision a deathblow. Religious nationalists were delighted to have won over disillusioned leftists, crowning Ariel Sharon, the lion of the settlement movement, their leader. But this bubble soon burst as well. Sharon "betrayed" them when he ordered the 2005 disengagement from the Gush Katif settlement bloc in the Gaza Strip, which amounted to "the ideological destruction of faith in the vision of Greater Israel and settlement in all parts of the land that is in our hands."[672] Religious Zionists were traumatized by the images of settlements in rubble and evacuees in tears and the shattering of the messianic vision that these implied. Once again, the threat of insurrection hung in the air. Yair Sheleg describes how the young generation of religious Zionists wrestled with themselves, having lost the "naive romanticism of [their] faith in the state and its

---

671   Ofer Aderet, "Rabin in 1976 Interview: Settlements Are a Cancer," *Haaretz*, September 26, 2015, https://www.haaretz.com/.premium-rabin-in-1976-settlements-are-a-cancer-1.5402552.

672   Yair Sheleg, *The Loss of Naïveté: The Impact of the Withdrawal from Gaza on Religious Zionism* (Jerusalem: Israel Democracy Institute, 2015), 6 [Hebrew].

intentions" after the disengagement; some even sought an alliance with the ultra-Orthodox to forget about the Zionist national enterprise altogether.

In reaction to the disengagement, the rabbis at the national-religious hesder yeshivas and pre-military academies, including leaders of the settlement movement, tightened their grip on the IDF's combat forces, in order to thwart any future evacuations. Yagil Levy points to this process as one cause of the growing theocratization of the IDF. But while some fear that rabbis are eroding the authority of its commanders, many others point to the evacuation of Gush Katif as proof that religious soldiers have profoundly internalized the importance of the national interest, which is why few religious soldiers disobeyed orders.

The theocratization of the IDF might not be a linear process and could trigger a counterreaction. "Pushing the boundaries of religious influence has spurred secularists to fight back…over female service, the exclusion of women, and the Yizkor [memorial] prayer," concludes Levy. "This battle led religious Israelis to hold back…. But the less interested the secular middle class is in what goes on in the army, the greater the space will be for theocratization to develop."[673]

The IDF and the Ultra-Orthodox

When Napoleon drove the Prussians out of Warsaw and awarded the duchy to King Frederick Augustus I of Saxony, he forced Poland to adopt a French-style constitution, giving all men equal rights. In theory, this abolished all laws that differentiated between Christians and Jews. However, Poland's new overlords, who did not think Christians and Jews were vaguely equal, did not have to make too

---

673   Yagil Levy, *The Divine Commander: The Theocratization of the Israeli Military* (Tel Aviv: Am Oved and Sapir Academic College, 2015), 375–377 [Hebrew]. See also Yagil Levy, "This Is How Eisenkot Institutionalized Religionization in the IDF," *Haaretz*, January 17, 2018 [Hebrew].

much of an effort—the Jews themselves saw this newfangled equality as bad news. "They knew that if they enjoyed the same rights as everyone else, they would also have to bear the same obligations to the kingdom," wrote Polish-Jewish historian Ezriel Nathan Frenk, "and then they would be unable to avoid military service, which would force them to violate the Sabbath, eat non-kosher food, shave their beards and sidelocks, and commit other crimes against God." Jewish community leaders in Warsaw lobbied King Frederick and Napoleon to make them unequal again, but since the new constitution could not simply be amended, they requested and duly received a temporary reprieve. On October 17, 1808, the king signed an edict depriving Jewish residents of the Duchy of Warsaw and of political rights for ten years, in the hope that they would use this time to discard all the peculiarities that differentiated them from everyone else.

When the Duchy of Warsaw annexed western Galicia in 1809 and brought it under its new French-style constitution, the Jews asked to be exempt from military service, which was mandatory for all males between the ages of twenty-one and twenty-eight. This time, the Jews lobbied Prince Józef Poniatowski, the minister of war, who agreed to grant them an exemption from the draft, in exchange for a special tax of 700,000 złoty a year. Poniatowski wrote to the king of Saxony and said the Jews were not suited for the honor of military service—experience had proven that they could not be trusted with national defense without great caution. The king agreed to exempt the Jews from the draft, and they honored Poniatowski with the nickname "the righteous duke."[674]

Fast forward to the Israeli Century. While religious Zionists hope to shape the religious implications of Israeli sovereignty through military service, many ultra-Orthodox Israelis prefer to

---

674   Ezriel Nathan Frenk, "On the History of Jews in the Duchy of Warsaw: Archive Materials," *Hatekufah* 4 (1929), 451–498 [Hebrew].

dodge the questions of sovereignty and military service altogether. They wish to signal that a truly religious Judaism is hostile to the prioritization of the national interest or at least wants no part in it. In November 2016, at an ultra-Orthodox conference, Prime Minister Benjamin Netanyahu was welcomed with all the honors afforded to a Hasidic rebbe. He embraced his (once and future) coalition partners and praised them for being "loyal [and] devoted, with a warm Jewish heart," and sharp-witted. Yaakov Litzman, the health minister from the United Torah Judaism Party, lavished Netanyahu with praise and said: "Mr. Prime Minister, we trust you and vote with you on every issue, *even matters we have no interest in like...foreign affairs and defense* [my emphasis]. We demand and receive the prime minister's support [on matters of] Shabbat, the needs of yeshivas, and the scrapping of the Conscription Bill."[675]

One of the most salient questions facing modern Israel is: What does the future hold for the coalition between the Israeli right and the ultra-Orthodox, and can it last? Whereas the Israeli right defines national loyalty in terms of commitment to Jewish sovereignty and territorial control of the whole Greater Israel, the ultra-Orthodox seem to care less for these issues and some are even actively hostile.

The rise of a new governing coalition in June 2021 that opposed the ultra-Orthodox demands and put Netanyahu in opposition showed the limits of what such a marriage of convenience can deliver for them.

Ultra-Orthodox natural growth rates have increased dramatically in the last forty years. In 1979–1995, their number doubled from around 140,000 to some 290,000. Over the next twenty years, as of late 2017, their population grew almost four-fold again, rising to 1,033,000, or 12 percent of Israel's population, according to

---

675 Yaki Adamker, "Among His Natural Partners: The Evening Netanyahu Spoke 'Haredi,'" *Walla*, November 21, 2016 [Hebrew].

THE ISRAELI CENTURY   399

the Central Bureau of Statistics. The growth rates of the ultra-Orthodox population are the fastest in the developed world, at 4.4
percent a year, compared to 1.4 percent for the rest of the Israeli
Jewish population. If these trends continue, it will take them sixteen
years to double in size, compared to fifty years for everyone else.
Demographers forecast that the ultra-Orthodox will constitute one-
third of Israel's Jewish population by 2050.

This demographic bomb will have tremendous economic
implications. The average income of an ultra-Orthodox man is 43
percent lower than that of a non-ultra-Orthodox Jewish man. The
monthly income of non-ultra-Orthodox households is 65 percent
higher than that of ultra-Orthodox homes. Since the average ultra-Orthodox home has twice as many members as other Jewish
households, and since fewer ultra-Orthodox men earn a living
(and those who do have lower wages), there is a gulf of 171 percent
between the income of an ultra-Orthodox home and everyone else.
Economists warn that without a dramatic change in ultra-Orthodox growth rates and patterns of education and employment, the
existing arrangement will cause the Israeli economy to slow down
dramatically and possibly even collapse.[676]

How did Israel reach a situation where the ultra-Orthodox
might imperil the future of the Israeli Century? How could the state
have facilitated and encouraged these trends? Can they still be re-
versed? World War II made Zionism the leading movement in the
Jewish world. Before that, the ultra-Orthodox world had been hostile
to the Jewish national movement. Yet after the Holocaust, on the
eve of Israel's independence, new, pro-Zionist voices could be heard
even among ultra-Orthodox Jews who had survived the destruction

---

676 Shahar Ilan, "Against the Forecasts: Haredim Will Reach 26% of the Israeli Population
in Only 40 Years," *Calcalist*, May 17, 2018 [Hebrew], https://www.calcalist.co.il/local/arti-
cles/0,7340,L-3738304,00.html; Shahar Ilan, "Haredi Employment: The Right-Wing Government
Pushes back and Pushes in," *Calcalist*, December 31, 2017 [Hebrew], https://www.calcalist.co.il/
local/articles/0,7340,L-3728480,00.html.

of their communities in Europe and reached Israel. Although the ultra-Orthodox regarded Zionism as a fundamentally secular, anti-religious project, the power struggles over the nascent state led many of them, if only fleetingly, to see Israel as a political framework in which "ultra-Orthodox Judaism could also find its place and fight for its values."[677] Yet as time passed and ultra-Orthodox communities found their bearings, the Hasidic rebbes who openly identified as Zionists disappeared, and ultra-Orthodox hostility to the state became the rule and intensified.[678]

For the ultra-Orthodox, this ideological split from religious Zionism was critical for the preservation of their distinct identity. Over time, their hardline, uncompromising positions on questions of religion and state have aggravated their rivalry with Zionists, both secular and religious.

Brown writes that, on the one hand, this ultra-Orthodox zealotry was moderated by the trauma of the Holocaust and the birth of the State of Israel, "which absorbed refugees from violence and enabled the resurrection of the Torah world." However, as they settled into their new lives in Israel, and as Judaism became a hot potato in fights over religion and state, their initial sense of awe waned in favor of an internal ultra-Orthodox solidarity and a desire to build a "society of yeshiva scholars."[679] For religious Zionists, Independence Day celebrates the prophesied "beginning of the growth of our Redemption," but for many ultra-Orthodox Jews, it is a day of mourning.

Historian Kimmy Caplan describes the growing "Haredization" in Israel since the 1970s. [680] The ultra-Orthodox have become more

---

677 Benjamin Brown, "Ultra-Orthodox Judaism and the State," in *When Judaism Meets a State* Yedidia, eds. Z. Stern et al. (Tel Aviv: Yedioth Ahronoth & Israel Democracy Institute, 2015), 108 [Hebrew].

678 Ibid., 109 [Hebrew].

679 Ibid., 112.

680 Kimmy Caplan, *The Internal Popular Discourse in Israeli Haredi Society* (Jerusalem: Zalman Shazar Center, 2007), 46 [Hebrew].

geographically and culturally isolated and committed to the "society of scholars"—the notion that men's primary occupation should be Torah study, not paid employment. Haredization happened due to an extraordinary rate of demographic growth and on the instructions of senior rabbis, who argued that ultra-Orthodox society must defend itself from the infiltration of "foreign" influences that threaten Judaism's integrity.

Indeed, in many ways the Haredi community of Israel is acting as a "state within a state." Yet the Covid-19 pandemic also exposed a deep sociological paradox: Haredim in Israel continue to think like tenants, but they have long since become landlords. In stark contrast to ultra-Orthodox communities in the Diaspora, who can still regard themselves as strangers in a strange land, Haredi Israelis now manage an ideologically fraught relationship with a government of which they form a key part. Haredi parties have key ministers in the Israeli government who carry cabinet responsibility for all the decisions of the Israeli government. At one level, the reality that the Haredi Israelis are critical partners of the Israeli Right and are deeply embedded within state institutions has created a de facto acceptance of governmental sovereignty and legitimacy within the Haredi world. Yet when the pandemic hit, the depth of that acceptance became less clear, as Haredi ministers were torn between the state rulings to shut down religious institutions and the order by rabbis to keep them open.

Ultra-Orthodox communities have expanded greatly in the United States and Britain in recent decades, but authorities in both countries are becoming increasingly suspicious of and hostile toward these communities' self-segregation and use of public funds at their own separate schools.[681] This concern has grown especially in New

---

681 "Majority of British Jews Will Be Ultra-Orthodox by End of Century, Study Finds," *The Guardian*, October 16, 2015, https://www.theguardian.com/uk-news/2015/oct/16/majority-of-british-jews-will-be-ultra-orthodox-by-end-of-century-study-finds.

York City, where parts of the community have defied state and municipal authorities during the Covid-19 crisis, opening schools, holding mass events, and exhibiting significant patterns of transmission above that of the general population along a similar pattern to what happened in Israel.

The growth of these communities outside of Israel depends on their ability to remain closed, since their natural growth rates are so high, and their anti-modern culture is so restrictive. However, many are poor and struggle to subsist on state welfare and Jewish philanthropy.

Will the ultra-Orthodox despair of a life of poverty in Israel, where they receive such generous support and assistance from state institutions? Or will they take over the state's institutions and levers of power, tightening their grip and overpowering its sovereignty and modernity? And in the Diaspora, will they continue to cut themselves off from the rest of the Jewish community, drawing strength from the example of their cousins in Israel? These are crucial questions for the future of the Israeli Century.

Jewish Ethics, State Ethics

The question of who gets to define the Jewish mission and Jewish ethics has become a major bone of contention between the State of Israel and Diaspora Jewry. In the Israeli Century, this question is also at the heart of quarrels and powerplays inside Israel over the nation's character (i.e, Where does it land on the spectrum from Jewish to democratic?) and the nature of its control of the territories. Diaspora Jews have an important role to play in the debate over Jewish morality, but the moral parameters of Judaism will be defined mostly by the power struggles inside Israel and the battles over the country's future, borders, identity, and institutions. A. B. Yehoshua argues that today, Jewish values are being tested primarily "by what happens here [Israel]." They "are tested by our actions, not just our words.... This often reveals the ugly face of Judaism, but this is the truth—for better or worse."[682]

Jewish morality and ethics took shape over many generations, first as a tribal-sovereign code of morality, then as religious-communal ethics, and in the modern era, as two competing visions: universal morality versus Zionist state ethics. Before the modern era, the Jewish people were "not a people, except in their Torah," as medieval philosopher Rabbi Saadia Gaon averred. Their identity and values were based mainly on ethnic kinship and a commitment to halakha and the Torah.

But this situation changed with modernity. Yeshayahu Leibowitz observed that since the Emancipation, it has been impossible to agree on a "specifically Jewish ethical content" that all who are conscious of their Jewishness can recognize as Judaism.[683] Besides traditional religious ethics, two new types of Jewish ethics emerged. One universalist version of Judaism was built on the principles of the Emancipation and the ethics of citizens demanding equal rights in their countries of residence. The Zionist version of Judaism, by contrast, was built on the idea that only national independence could guarantee Jewish survival.

Throughout the Israeli Century, Jews have been arguing about whether the universal ethics cultivated by those who lacked the power of a state and territorial control can be reconciled with the Zionist ethics of a sovereign Israel. Is it even possible to reconcile the ethics of a particularist, realist state with the ethics of an idealist, universalist people?

Universalists in the Diaspora sometimes feel that Israel's state morality demands that they stretch their own morality to legitimize the illegitimate. But in Israel, many also argue that Jews who speak

---

682 A. B. Yehoshua and Nicole Krauss discussing Jewish Affairs, Mishkenot Sha'ananim, Jerusalem, August 10, 2014, https://www.youtube.com/watch?v=1FrCYC5kGNQ.

683 Yeshayahu Leibowitz, *People, Land, State* (Jerusalem: Keter, 1992), 75 [Hebrew].

in the name of "universal morality" and criticize Israel's alleged "immorality" are disconnected from the necessities of preserving sovereign life and are even sabotaging Israel's international standing.

In antiquity, the Jews treated the protection of their sovereignty and national community as the highest moral imperative. This included adhering to the Jewish laws of war, which some still wish to follow in the Israeli Century. Hence, in Israel's early years, IDF Chief Rabbi Shlomo Goren set out to aggregate the war-related commandments and laws in Judaism, including ancient Jewish military practices, with a view to imbuing the IDF's fighting techniques and sense of mission with an "ancient glory." He believed that these "eternal laws of justice" could guide Israel's various security services.[684]

He also strove to make the IDF a place "where religious Jews could feel at home."[685] Goren pushed for synagogues and kosher kitchens to be built in all military bases. He also strongly advocated a state-centric interpretation of Jewish law whereby Judaism's supreme value, higher even than Sabbath observance, is the defense of the Jewish people in the Land of Israel.

The photographs from the Six-Day War of Rabbi Goren running alongside IDF paratroopers through the Lions' Gate, into the Temple Mount, and down to the Western Wall, carried on the shoulders of Israeli troops and blowing the shofar, are some of the most powerful images of the Israeli Century. Among religious Zionists, he became a mythical figure, and his words to the IDF soldiers who liberated the Western Wall in 1967 were nothing less than a messianic injunction:

> I am speaking to you from the plaza of the
> Western Wall, the remnant of our Holy

---

684   Rabbi Shlomo Goren, "Army and War in Light of Halakha," *Mahanayim* 97 (1965) [Hebrew].

685   Yossi Klein Halevi, *Like Dreamers: The Story of the Israeli Paratroopers Who United Jerusalem and Divided the Nation* (New York: HarperCollins, 2013), 80–81.

Temple. 'Comfort my people, comfort them, says the Lord your God.' This is the day we have hoped for, let us rejoice and be glad in His salvation. The vision of all generations is being realized before our eyes: The city of God, the site of the Temple, the Temple Mount and the Western Wall, the symbol of the nation's redemption, have been redeemed today by you, heroes of the Israel Defense Forces. By doing so you have fulfilled the oath of generations, 'If I forget thee, O Jerusalem, may my right hand forget its cunning.'[686]

Since 1967, religious Zionists have increasingly accepted the priority of Jewish laws of war and commandments to settle the Land of Israel. In 1992, when Yitzhak Rabin was elected Israel's prime minister and pursued a peace policy with the Palestinians based on the formula of "land for peace," religious Zionists and settlers launched an aggressive campaign to discredit him as a "traitor." It was at that point that extreme anti-state attitudes laid the groundwork for his assassination three years later. Religious zealots even called for mutiny in the IDF.

Decades later, such attitudes continued to persist among the more extreme rabbis of the settlement movement. In 2012, Attorney General Yehuda Weinstein decided to close the case against two religious nationalist rabbis, Yitzhak Shapira and Yosef Elitzur, who had been accused of encouraging "price tag" attacks in their book *The King's Torah*, legitimizing attacks on Arabs and their property.

---

686   Alan Balfour, *The Walls of Jerusalem: Preserving the Past, Controlling the Future* (Hoboken, NJ: Wiley Blackwell, 2019), 171–172.

The rabbis and their supporters argued that the decision to ban the book, arrest them, and question rabbis who had allegedly endorsed the killing of Arabs was a grievous violation of their freedom of expression. Supreme Court Justice Elyakim Rubinstein, himself Orthodox, rejected a petition against Weinstein's decision to close the case, yet stressed that religious writings were not automatically exempt from laws about incitement. "We're dealing with a book," he added, "that wears Jewish garb but is truly anti-Jewish because it defames Judaism."[687]

The ancient ethics of the Jews were determined in accordance with the political strength of their God. Sociologist Max Weber wrote that after the Babylonian exile, the biblical prophets developed a new "ethics of the subjugated" as a substitute for the state morality of the fallen Jewish kingdom. Their morality was based on a new and "realistic recognition of the external political situation," according to which conquest by foreign empires was "a fate apparently desired by God." The Jews' devotion to religious law developed during the Babylonian exile and under foreign rule in Palestine and encouraged them to accept their subjugation to foreign empires as a divine decree. This mindset endured even after the Maccabees' stunning victories against the Seleucid Empire. In the second century BCE, bands of Jewish zealots tried to subvert the political authority of the ruling Hasmonean dynasty, believing that Hasmonean rule was undermining religious devotion by placing the kingdom above God.[688]

After the destruction of the Second Temple, the priesthood collapsed as the institutional mediator between the Jewish people and God. The Talmud and halakha gradually became the comprehensive corpus of Jewish law and ethics in the Diaspora. They acted

---

687   Sharon Pulwer, "High Court Blocks Petition Calling to Indict Authors of 'King's Torah,'" *Haaretz*, December 10, 2015, https://www.haaretz.com/israel-news/.premium-court-blocks-rabbi-incitement-case-1.5436193.

688   Weber, *Economy and Society: Volume 1*, 591–593.

as a barrier against Christian and Muslim kingdoms, which claimed to exercise exclusive moral authority over their subjects. Halakha dictated the daily life and practices of individual Jews and their communities, and rabbinical courts followed it within the boundaries of communal autonomy. Unlike the rest of Christendom, of course, the Jews refused to accept the divinity of Jesus as the basis of universal ethics and charted their own moral code.

Starting in the eighth century, most of the Jewish world came under the centralized rule of the Abbasid Caliphate in Baghdad, which spanned from Iberia to Persia and united the Jews of the Land of Israel and Mesopotamia with many others around the world. The Abbasid Caliphate granted the Jews legal and cultural autonomy, and the Talmud and halakha flourished, shaping the lives of Jewish communities worldwide under the rule of the Jewish Exilarch (*reish galuta*). In fact, it was the Muslim conquest that enabled the Geonim, the leaders of the Babylonian Talmudic academies, to impose the Babylonian Talmud on the vast majority of the world's Jews, and "the Talmud's ongoing dominance, at least in official Jewish medieval culture and living, was a *result* of the Muslim revolution, not an independent *cause* of a 'Jewish' Middle Ages."[689]

When the Jewish autonomous center in Babylon collapsed, and Jews migrated to western Europe and North Africa, they entered a period of chaos, without a central authority to govern them. It was against this backdrop that halakhic civil law, or *mishpat ivri* ("Halakhic law"), developed as a doctrine of social morality. Unlike ritual laws, which focused on Jews' obligations to God, civil law was about their obligations to their fellow Jews. Also, unlike other forms of law, Hebrew law developed without a unified government to enforce it through coercive powers. Instead, Israeli

---

689   Ivan G. Marcus, "Israeli Medieval Jewish Historiography: From Nationalist Positivism to New Cultural and Social Histories," *Jewish Studies Quarterly* 17, no. 3 (2010), 248.

Supreme Court Justice Moshe Zilberg argues it was an outgrowth of the "moral consciousness" and free will of Jewish communities, living in isolation from their Gentile surroundings. Scattered across the world, the Jews devised a legal system that was "religious in its essence, national in its purpose, and secular in its manner of enforcement." Hebrew Law was devised as a code of law to govern interactions between Jews in the absence of sovereignty, on foreign soil. Its legal validity was rooted in the collective Jewish consent and commitment to preserving its integrity as a tribe and resisting assimilation until the Jews could return to their ancestral homeland in the messianic age. According to Zilberg, "Every legal provision, commandment, law, and regulation was examined first and foremost in terms of its efficacy for protecting the Jewish people as a people."[690]

This strict and detailed system of law drew no distinction between the ethical and the legal because Hebrew law, like ritual aspects of halakha, was essentially *religious* law, and in Jewish religious law, crimes against one's fellows are considered *religious* offences. Hebrew law incorporated the Talmud, biblical verses, and the great codifications of Jewish law: the twelfth century Mishneh Torah, the fourteenth century Tur, and the sixteenth century Shulkhan Arukh. The Jews adopted and followed these codes of law even though their communities lacked any legal or political means to enforce compliance with them. Rather, the rabbis' powers of enforcement rested on their own scholarly reputations and expertise in halakha, which had tremendous social force even without the coercive powers of the state. Social sanctions—including divine curses, excommunication, and ostracism—proved effective threats, because Jews did not really have anywhere else to go if they left their communities.

---

690 Moshe Zilberg, *Law and Morality in Hebrew Jurisprudence* (Jerusalem: Magnes, Hebrew University, 1951), 20 [Hebrew]. Emphasis is mine.

Even in the sovereign State of Israel today, many ultra-Orthodox Jews fear being excommunicated if they transgress. They have their own institutions, parallel to those of the state; sometimes they use social sanctions to enforce compliance with rabbinic decrees more effectively than the State of Israel can enforce compliance with its own laws. In modern Israel, one "transgression" that puts young ultra-Orthodox Jews at risk of excommunication is service in the IDF. Naama Idan, an ultra-Orthodox woman who has written about the violent harassment of ultra-Orthodox soldiers by extremists in their own communities, notes that the groups campaigning against the military draft have turned the IDF uniform into "a symbol of a transgression against the ultra-Orthodox world…and transgressors are ostracized." This threat of violence forces many ultra-Orthodox soldiers to change out of uniform before returning home, fearing for their personal safety.[691]

In the seventeenth century, the Sephardic Jewish community of Amsterdam excommunicated Benedict Spinoza for breaking this religious fear barrier. Spinoza argued that there was no reason for Jews to continue obeying Jewish law and ethics in the absence of sovereignty. The Jews were fundamentally a *political* tribe, and there was no moral significance or gain to religious observance and Torah study, because they would not survive without national independence.

Spinoza was the first to reduce the Jews and rabbinical Judaism back to national and political terms. But in the modern era, when Jewish communities in the West started to fray, people started asking what remained of "Jewish" ethics and how they differed from Protestant state morality. Under challenge from modernity, Jews in western Europe and later in the United States redefined morality as

---

691 Naama Idan, "Attacks on Ultra-Orthodox Soldiers: An Organized Campaign?," *Ice*, June 4, 2017 [Hebrew], http://www.ice.co.il/opinions/news/article/538306.

the set of values that would allow them to integrate as equal citizens in their countries of residence.

When the Haskalah movement started taking root and extolling human reason, Moses Mendelssohn still insisted that the halakhic tradition remained morally relevant in the relationship between man and his Creator. Unlike Spinoza, Mendelssohn believed that religious Judaism still had an important role to play in shaping a modern, rational religion—the biblical commandments did not *reveal* the divine truth but pointed the way to discover it. He also believed that the Jewish ethical tradition was valuable not only for polities, like the ancient Israelite kingdoms, but also as a philosophical doctrine.[692] But the difficulty of practicing halakhic Judaism during the Emancipation led thinkers and rabbis in the West to chart new Jewish doctrines. They created new Jewish creeds, in which cosmopolitan, liberal, or socialist values could go hand-in-hand with traditional principles—allowing the Jews to remain Jewish but simultaneously be like everyone else. However, these Herculean efforts soon got entangled in a web of theoretical and practical tensions. Loyalty to a separate clan, it turned out, was inconsistent with universal morality and ethics. Philosopher Hermann Cohen, for example, who rejected Zionism but still wished to be a loyal German Jew, said that if Judaism got bogged down in politics, it would lose its essence and role as the beacon of universal ethics. A "normal" Jewish state would erase what made Judaism unique. Paradoxically, however, when World War I erupted, he still called on Jews to fight and sacrifice themselves for the German nation. The embrace of universalism, therefore, did not stop the Jews from assimilating into particular non-Jewish national movements.

Indeed, it is the nature of universal norms to clash with realist

---

692   David Biale, *Not in the Heavens: The Tradition of the Jewish Secular Thought* (Princeton: Princeton University Press, 2011), 102–103.

raison d'état. Today, "Jewish morality" in Israel is defined above all by Israel's dominance and needs as an independent nation-state. It prides itself on having "the most moral army in the world" and providing humanitarian assistance during emergencies around the world. Israel wants to appear, for its own sake and in the eyes of others, as a particular nation that never abandoned its universal calling. Yet this does not change the fact that its foremost imperative is its own *raison d'état,* and it does not wish to sacrifice its soldiers in the name of a universal morality. Indeed, Christian theologian Reinhold Niebuhr said this about Israel's "national morality":

> The dishonesty of nations is a necessity of political policy if the nation is to gain the full benefit of its double claim upon the loyalty and devotion of the individual, as his own special and unique community and as a community which embodies universal values and ideals. The two claims, the one touching the individual's emotions and the other appealing to his mind, are incompatible with each other, and can be resolved only through dishonesty. This is particularly evident in war-time. Nations do not really arrive at full self-consciousness until they stand in vivid, usually bellicose, juxtaposition to other nations.[693]

Israel's national morality is obviously different from the Jewish liberalism that informs large segments of the Diaspora. After the

---

693   Reinhold Niebuhr, *Moral Man and Immoral Society: A Study in Ethics and Politics* (New York: Charles Scriber's Sons, 1932), 194–195.

Six-Day War, liberal Jews in the United States were inspired by Israel's achievements and saw Zionism as an opportunity to reengage with their national tribe, hoping to connect their own identity with their historic homeland in a manner that would protect them from cultural assimilation. They also boasted of Israel's morality and depicted the Jewish state as a model country. Prominent Zionist thinkers in the West wanted to believe that the historic project of Jewish independence after the Holocaust would transcend the "morality of nations." They felt that it was possible to establish a sovereign, national Jewish life nourished by universal ethics, creating a form of nationalism in which responsibility for the other would become a supreme moral imperative. The hope was that the Jewish "model state" would fulfil the utopian ambition and that being Jewish meant aspiring to justice and humanity, so wrote and believed the French-Jewish philosopher Emmanuel Levinas, as did the American modern-Orthodox philosopher Eliezer Berkovits.

But the hope that a state, which must always operate under *raison d'état*, might successfully operate by universal and non-territorial principles was doomed to failure–especially in the jungle that is the Middle East. The Israeli Century, therefore, threatens to terminate the idea of "Jewish morality" as a liberal, universal code of ethics.

Universal Jewish ethics flourished in the United States–"the country God created for the Jews, so they could have somewhere to flee to in times of crisis," in the words of one of the heroes of Sholom Aleichem's stories. In the early twentieth century, Reform Jews based their identity and institutions on the mass recruitment of immigrants from eastern Europe, who wanted to get away from Orthodox Judaism. They extolled American individualism and argued that it fit neatly into the Jewish tradition that sanctified the life and liberty of the individual. Liberal Jews conceived of America as a home for the fulfilment of the ideal of human liberty and hoped to express their allegiance to the American civic religion by subordinating and adapting Jewish practice to the Constitutional wisdom of the United States. Human reason, especially in its American expression of "liberty and justice for all," now took precedence over religious tradition.[694]

In the early and mid-twentieth century, the liberal Jewish commitment to justice drove the American-Jewish campaigns against anti-Semitism and for minority rights. The legacy and organization of "Jewish liberalism" played an important part in the struggle of African Americans for civil rights.[695] In fact, the cooperation of these two groups in the early 1960s constituted the core of the great coalition that became the civil rights movement.

Decades earlier, during President Franklin D. Roosevelt's New Deal reforms, American-Jewish identity was associated with the struggle for "social justice," later reinvented as *tikkun olam* (literally, "repairing the world")—itself a byword for liberal Jewish universal morality in the United States. Researcher Erin McClanahan writes that Reform leaders adopted the term in the 1950s in an effort to cope with the trauma of the Holocaust and danger of assimilation in America.[696]

Over time, tikkun olam became the slogan of progressive Judaism. Reform Jews, for example, concluded that adopting it, although it came from the same Kabbalistic doctrine they reviled, would let them express their moral universalism in a "Jewish" fashion. They believed that almost anything could be solved *through* it, and almost any American or Jewish social obligation could be defined as tikkun olam. Thus, they could preserve both their Jewish particularism and their commitment to global humanity.

---

694   Yitzhak Englard, *Introduction to the Theory of Law* (Jerusalem: Yahalom, 1990), 28 [Hebrew].

695   Jonathan Kaufman, *Broken Alliance: The Turbulent Times between Blacks and Jews in America* (New York: Simon & Schuster, 1994).

696   David Mamet, *The Secret Knowledge: On the Dismantling of American Culture* (London: Sentinel, 2011), 150.

The Reform Movement officially adopted tikkun olam in its doctrine in 1997, and it quickly became synonymous with progressive politics. Even President Barack Obama used the term to describe his own American moral doctrine. Ruth Messinger, the former Manhattan borough president and head of the American Jewish World Service, an international development and emergency relief organization, argued that tikkun olam would "deter anti-Semitism by demonstrating that Jews work to provide social justice and dignity for all people regardless of race, religion, and ethnicity."[697]

Michael Barnett argues that the cosmopolitan orientation of Jewish American foreign policy came to juxtapose Jewish ethics against Israel's own allegedly problematic morality: "Tikkun olam might be crowding out Israel," he writes, inasmuch as "there could only be one banner at the temple, and Israel had made way for Darfur." The Israeli anthropologist and peace activist David Shulman, born and raised in the United States, discusses whether the universalistic Jewish morality that has flourished in the Diaspora can be reconciled with the reality in Israel. He writes that, at his parents' home in Iowa, it was axiomatic that an "intimate link" existed between Judaism and universal human rights. "My parents and grandparents were Roosevelt Democrats, to the point of fanaticism," he said. "They thought that the Jews had invented the very idea, and also the practice, of social justice; that having started our history as slaves in Egypt, we were always on the side of the underdog and the oppressed." His parents believed that "the core of Judaism as a religious culture was precisely this commitment to human rights, and that all the rest—the 613 commandments, the rituals, the theological assertions—was no more than a superstructure built upon a strong ethical foundation." This "comfortable illusion"

---

697 Barnett, *The Stars and the Stripes*, 3.

was "shattered" when Shulman moved to Israel at the age of eighteen and met a very different world.[698]

Shulman believes that the struggle over the nature and future of Jewish morality today is being waged almost exclusively in Israel; its primary test is Israel's control of the Palestinian people and occupation of the West Bank, and whether Israelis are open to Western, universal ethics. The battles over Jewish morality, he writes, manifest themselves at the Israeli Supreme Court where questions of migrant expulsions, torture, land confiscations, and other occupation-related injustices are being determined. Shulman, who sees Israeli society and politics as becoming increasingly radicalized and hostile to human rights, argues that the Supreme Court is the last bastion where the state's power and brutality can still be curtailed in the name of morality and law. But from the perspective of moral Jewish responsibility, Israel's courts are a confusing place. On the one hand, he writes, the Supreme Court grants the Israeli state a stamp of legitimacy for its occupation of the Palestinians. On the other, it is the only body capable of blocking arbitrary attempts to harm non-Jews. Shulman has not given up hope. He still believes that Israel is committed to Jewish universal morality, even if a bellicose, security-oriented "state morality" is the dominant force.

Israel's democracy confronts many complicated situations that raise questions about war, ethics, and terrorism, including incidents in which hostile actors use civilian populations as human shields. While Israel insists that it invests more effort in avoiding civilian casualties on the battlefield than any other military on earth, critics contend that its conduct in confronting these challenges is immoral.

Such hostility often finds expression through the growing political use of international law to paint Israel as a criminal state.

---

698   David Shulman, "The Last of the Tzaddiks," *New York Review of Books*, June 28, 2018, https://www.nybooks.com/articles/2018/06/28/jews-human-rights-last-tzaddiks/.

This was the case with the UN Human Rights Council's Goldstone Report, which accused it of grave violations of international humanitarian law and war crimes during Operation Cast Lead in the Gaza Strip, in the winter of 2008–2009. The fact that Israel is obsessively denounced as a criminal state at international forums leads some observers, often justly, to conclude that old anti-Semitism has morphed into a new kind of hatred directed at the Jewish state.

Since its early days, the State of Israel has claimed responsibility for "Jewish interests." Seven decades later, it routinely claims to speak on behalf of Jews throughout the world, and hatred of Jews is increasingly expressed as a hatred of the State of Israel. Indeed, criticism of Israel is often motivated by, or expressed through, old-style anti-Semitism—but it is crucial for Israel to understand that these are two radically different creatures in the Israeli Century.

First, the fact that Israel is considered—and considers itself—a power has naturally flipped the moral equation. From the perspective of universal morals, Israel is now Goliath to the Palestinians' David.

Second, even when fallacious statements are made about its conduct, or the facts are deliberately twisted, Israel and its allies around the world have the means to refute these lies and fight for the truth to come to light. In April 2011, in a rare move following years of intense public backlash, judge Richard Goldstone backtracked on the scathing report he had written two years earlier:

> If I had known then what I know now, the Goldstone Report would have been a different document…. While the investigations published by the Israeli military and recognized in the UN committee's report have established the validity of some incidents that we investigated in cases involving individual

soldiers, they also indicate that civilians were not intentionally targeted as a matter of policy.[699]

Third, faced with the might of the Israeli state, there is no strategic reason for its enemies to use classically anti-Semitic rhetoric. Such remarks only bolster solidarity inside Israel, engender empathy from Diaspora Jews, and mobilize support for Israel in the West, which is appalled by old-style anti-Semitism. In May 2018, Palestinian Authority Chairman Mahmoud Abbas provoked fierce criticism for anti-Semitic remarks he had made in a speech in Ramallah. Even the *New York Times*, hardly a supporter of Israeli policies, called on him to resign, and he was forced to apologize in order to mitigate the damage.[700]

Fourth, Israel's national leaders do not consider old-style anti-Semitism a major threat, even if its politicians tend to overuse the term "anti-Semitism" to censure enemies and political rivals. In its foreign relations, Israel meets with, talks with, and strikes deals with its rivals, pursuing a realist approach that tolerates a certain degree of anti-Israel hostility, so long as it can still maximize its national interests and defend itself. Israel and Israelis are less sensitive than Diaspora Jews to old-style anti-Semitism and respond to it with a contempt and hostility of their own.

Elyakim Ha'etzni, a key figure in the settler movement, argues that Israelis are fed up with moral dilemmas and the label "the chosen people," which is understood in so many different ways along social, religious, and political lines that "the Jewish people has

699   Richard Goldstone, "Reconsidering the Goldstone Report on Israel and War Crimes," *Washington Post*, April 1, 2011, https://www.washingtonpost.com/opinions/reconsidering-the-goldstone-report-on-israel-and-war-crimes/2011/04/01/AFg111JC_story.html?noredirect=on.

700   "President Abbas Says He Did Not Intend to Offend Jews," Wafa News Agency, http://english.wafa.ps/page.aspx?id=5eEbb9a97537550946a5eEbb9.

no idea what is expected of it." In contrast to the more messianic elements of the settler movement, he believes that the notion of a national "mission" threatens Israel's ability to function, arguing that it is time for the Jewish state to stop feeling "obliged to sit at the head of the class like the Jewish child in exile who had to work harder than the native schoolchildren in order to reach the same place." According to Ha'etzni, Israelis should not stop aspiring to be moral, "as long as no such mission [of 'chosenness'] is registered in the state's official record." He argues: "The State of Israel is a living organism. As such, it needs no justification for its existence. Its existence is its justification."[701]

The tension between the ethics of the state and the ethics of the prophets is a cornerstone of the Jewish tradition dating back to the Bible itself. The real heroes of ancient Judaism were the prophets, who had a troubled relationship with power and government authority. The prophets were men of God, visionaries, preachers, and seers who demanded justice, without fear, favor, or concern for the personal consequences of their words. They earned their reputations by pummeling the nation's kings and priests with non-stop criticism and calling for the Jewish people and their leaders to abide by the ethical standards set in the Torah. The prophet Nathan's rebuke of King David in the story of the Poor Man's Ewe in II Samuel, for example, is perhaps the best-known moral parable in the Judeo-Christian tradition.

There are no more prophets in the Israeli Century, of course, but there are still recognized moral preachers in the form of religious leaders and intellectuals. In Israel's early years, philosopher and scientist Yeshayahu Leibowitz was one of the boldest voices criticizing the priority given to state interests. He reminded Ben-Gurion that the Israelite hero King Jeroboam expanded Israel's borders "from

---

701   Elyakim Ha'etzni, "The Jewish State: The Next Fifty Years," *Azure* 6 (1999).

the entrance of Hamath unto the sea of the Arabah...and...recovered Damascus, and Hamath, for Judah in Israel"[702]—yet the prophet Amos furiously prophesied against him: "Jeroboam shall die by the sword, and Israel shall surely be led away captive out of his land."[703] Leibowitz was a Zionist and saw the State of Israel as an important means for securing Jewish continuity, which was worth fighting and making sacrifices for. But he refused to see it as a constitutive factor in Jewish nationality and fiercely criticized the belief that the state had sanctity in itself.

After the Six-Day War, Leibowitz became a prophet of doom and railed against what he called "a corrupting occupation." He vociferously attacked the religious establishment as "fascists." Nevertheless, he adamantly refused to repudiate sovereignty and stressed that he was a Zionist "and that's that."

In recent years, Israel's rowdy political debate has been fierce enough to drown out these nagging moral voices. In its culture wars, few prophets have not yet been assailed as a "spokesman" carrying water for a particular cause, and few figures are able to make their words resonate beyond the short-term national conversation.

Who Controls Morality—Judges or Legislators?

In Israel, democratic but deeply divided over identity and ideology, efforts to grapple with the question of Jewish morality have increasingly turned to legal battles, often making the courts the supreme arbiters of it. Legal scholar Menachem Mautner argues that in Israel's early years, when its society was characterized by strong collective norms and solidarity, the Supreme Court mostly kept a low profile, and its rulings had little international resonance. The Supreme Court

---

702   2 Kings 14:25–28 (JPS Version).
703   Amos 7:11 (JPS Version).

suppressed, and perhaps even concealed, its true liberal impulses. But as Israel's internal solidarity began to wane and its society began to open up and embrace liberalism over collectivism, the Supreme Court became more actively involved in promoting liberal values.

Supreme Court President Aharon Barak, perhaps more than anyone else, steered this judicial revolution in the late 1990s and early 2000s, promoting a conception of law as the shield of enlightened democracy and beacon of Israeli moral values against the forces of political corruption. As attorney general in the 1970s, he had written:

> As jurists, we are not restricted to interpreting and implementing existing law. We are at the forefront of the hope for a more desirable law, a better law. Law that takes into consideration not only the needs of the collective, law that looks not only at the individual, but law that balances the two. We are the architects of social change, we have the skills to build a better, more just legal method. We do not perceive our role as being limited to legal technicalities; we perceive our role as including legal statesmanship.[704]

In recent decades, judicial activism witnessed a vigorous pushback when many Israeli jurists and politicians protested, insisting that the demands to restrict the power of elected politicians and grant the judicial branch a veto over decisions with ethical dimensions were anti-democratic. Celebrated scholar Ruth Gavison wrote

---

704   Aharon Barak, "The Rule of Law," in *Innovations and Developments in Legislation and Law*, ed. Shimon Shitreet (Jerusalem: Hebrew University Legal Faculty, 1977), 25 [Hebrew].

that "there is nothing in [judges'] training that gives them the right, the authority, or the ability to be makers of law and morality."[705]

This titanic battle between the Knesset and the Supreme Court has been raging for several decades. It is a battle for hierarchy—for the status of supreme moral and sovereign authority in the Jewish nation. Like other modern democracies, Israel was founded on the principle that democracy is based on law making *by* human beings and *in the name of* human beings. But this left the question of which state authority would reign supreme in matters of law and values open. This is the essence of the separation of powers and the democratic concept of checks and balances.

One answer is to look to the social contract or constitution as the product of a broad ethical consensus. But not every question has an answer lurking in the constitution, because life is dynamic. Needs change, and societies routinely run into problems for which there are no known solutions, not even in rigid constitutions. Israel, which has no written constitution, instead relying on a series of "Basic Laws" whose constitutional status is itself a matter of dispute, is an excellent example of the difficulties in reaching a constitutional consensus in a reality constantly rocked by upheaval and change.

In the absence of a consensus on the irrefutable source of supreme authority, there is perpetual tension between the Supreme Court, which largely purports to represent the liberal, rational values inherent in the law, and the Knesset, which fervently claims the authority to both pass and amend laws, for better or worse. This situation has led to tension between those who believe that only the Supreme Court can defend core values, moral integrity, ethics, and individual rights, and those who argue that, as flawed as the political process may be, it is the core premise of democracy that elected officials alone hold the keys to enshrining a nation's values in law.

---

705 Ruth Gavison in an interview with Ari Shavit, *Haaretz*, November 12, 1999 [Hebrew].

The influence of the court reached its apex with the passage of Basic Law: Human Dignity and Liberty (1992) and Basic Law: Freedom of Occupation (1994), which Barak interpreted as granting the court the right to strike down laws, with his declaration of a "constitutional revolution" in 1992.[706] In 2002, Robert Bork, the American critic of judicial activism and former federal judge whose 1987 nomination for the US Supreme Court was famously rejected by a Democratic-controlled Senate wrote: "The Israeli Supreme Court is making itself the dominant institution in the nation, an authority no other court in the world has achieved."[707]

However, since the late 1990s, the balance has shifted drastically as the Supreme Court's public standing and legitimacy have been eroded through constant clashes with the political echelon and under growing criticism from legal scholars. Indeed, defenders of the 2018 Basic Law: The Nation State, argued that it was necessary, as a corrective to the basic laws of the 1990s, to put the idea of the Jewish State on equal footing with its democratic values.

The argument over the scope of judicial oversight goes further than a straightforward question of judicial review of Knesset legislation. The court's critics accuse of it "judicialization," or stepping on the toes of lawmakers and the government by wading into decisions about security, identity, ethics, and public administration. They argue that, by following the Barak-era policy of treating everything as open to a test of "reasonableness" and dramatically expanding the judicial concepts of standing and justiciability, the court has been undermining the sovereign authority of the legislature, including on major issues that underpin the existence of Israel's Jewish society.

One can reasonably argue that pressing needs left the Supreme

---

706 Aharon Barak, "The Constitutional Revolution: Protected Human Rights," *Mishpat U'mimshal* 1 (1992–1993). Cf. Hillel Neuer, "Aharon Barak's Revolution," *Azure* 3 (Winter 1998).

707 Robert H. Bork, *Coercing Virtue: The Worldwide Rule of Judges* (Washington, DC: AEI Press, 2002), 111.

Court no choice but to fill a moral vacuum. When lawmakers fail to do their jobs properly, it is compelled to step in and lay down the law on matters of ethics, justice, morality, and even defense, and that is exactly what it does, even without explicit constitutional authority. It finds its own "legal sources," practically out of thin air, like the state's unwritten "founding values." In Israel, the debate over judicial activism has become the main partisan boxing ring in the argument over values and authority.

In the coming years, the State of Israel will likely continue to grow prosperous and powerful in ways the Jewish people have never known. Assuming that the paradigm of sovereignty and exile has been broken, and statelessness is no longer an option for the Jewish people, Israelis must decide more clearly how to define Jewish values in using power to counter internal and external threats. Part of the answer will come from the political, social, religious, cultural, and institutional power plays in Israel and the Jewish world. Another part will come from how Israel confronts challenges beyond its borders. It will need to give the Jewish people and other nations answers about how it will use its might in a moral manner. This is Israel's soft underbelly, because it always wants to have things both ways—to be both mighty *and* moral. Sometimes, it will face pressure to use force in a way that will gnaw at the Jewish people's moral and international standing. It will also face counterdemands to forgo resources of power—namely, territory—that might imperil the gains of the Israeli Century. Even Israel's most bitter enemies recognize this vulnerability and use contorted moral reasoning to try to stigmatize the Israeli Century. They argue that the Jews managed to reach extraordinary heights as a stateless people, while the State of Israel has reduced them to a moral nadir. "What has the Occupation achieved?" asked Hamas leader Yehiya Sinwar, who spent decades in Israeli prison for murder and who is designated as a terrorist by the United States government. What is Israel's purpose, he asked, "To raise murderers? ... Once the Jews were like Freud, Kafka, Einstein. They were famous for mathematics, for philosophy. Now it's for drones. For extrajudicial executions."[708]

The internal Jewish debate over the right balance between might and morality, the essence of the historical clash between kings and prophets, all but completely disappeared after the destruction of the Second Temple. But it is back with a vengeance in the Israeli Century, resonating not just in Israel and the Jewish Diaspora but across the whole world. This debate now requires Israel to have exemplary spiritual and religious leadership, with the foresight to understand the challenges facing the Jewish people as well as their remarkable strengths. This is the historic mission facing Jewish leaders in the Israeli Century–to work out their friends and foes and chart a course for the Jewish people in a nation-state that cherishes its history and embraces its open future.

Jewish Universal Morals in the Israeli Century

On September 19, 2020, on the eve of the Jewish New Year, US Supreme Court Justice Ruth Bader Ginsburg died. Ginsburg, an American icon, was renowned for leading the court's liberal wing and for her fierce struggle in promoting progressive jurisprudence and gender equality. Her passing generated national grief, with tens of thousands gathering online and on the Supreme Court steps to mourn her death. She was both the first Jew and the first woman to lie in state at the US Capitol. For the first time in American Jewish history, a traditional Jewish funeral was held in the Great Hall of the Supreme Court, presided over by a female Conservative rabbi

---

708   Francesca Bori, "A ceasefire as far as I'm concerned is complete calm. And the end of the blockade–Interview with Hamas leader in Gaza, Yehiya Sinwar," *Yediot Aharonot*, October 5, 2018 [Hebrew].

alongside Chief Justice John Roberts. Ginsburg was laid to rest at Arlington National Cemetery.[709]

The passing of Ginsburg made headlines all over the world. In Israel it received special attention and was covered in conjunction with its own internal debate about the Supreme Court as an instrument of Jewish morality. Ginsburg was eulogized by Prime Minister Netanyahu, who called her "one of the great judicial leaders of our time," and said, "She was proud of her Jewish heritage and the Jewish people will always be proud of her." Ester Hayut, Israel's Supreme Court president, said that Ginsburg's "legacy will affect many generations throughout the world."

In 2018, Ginsburg visited Israel to accept the Genesis Lifetime Achievement award—a prize informally known as the Jewish Nobel. The award was presented by none other than Aharon Barak. "Without a doubt," he said of Ginsburg, "she is one of the great legal minds of our time; an outstanding Jewish jurist whose fearless pursuit of human rights, equality and justice for all stems from her Jewish values." In her acceptance speech, Ginsburg referred to Barak as "one of the world's most brilliant, humanitarian jurists."[710]

For American Jews, the passing of Ginsburg was a moment that invited self-reflection. Liberal Jews, have crowned her as a role model in balancing between their American and Jewish identities. Some religious progressive Jews compared her to a Torah sage, or *gadol*. "More than just a mere expert, a gadol's very persona is revered," wrote Ben Greenfield, a young rabbi in Brooklyn, in a column called "Hasidic Jews Have Rebbes, Secular Jews Have Ruth

709 Jonathan D. Sarna, "In Death, as in Life, Ruth Bader Ginsburg Balanced Being American and Jewish," *The Conversation*, September 25, 2020.

710 "Ruth Bader Ginsburg Receives Genesis Lifetime Achievement Award in Israel," i24News, July 6, 2018, https://www.i24news.tv/en/news/israel/178670-180704-ruth-bader-ginsburg-in-israel-to-receive-genesis-lifetime-achievement-award.

Bader Ginsburg." "They symbolize not just a canon of knowledge," he wrote, "but an entire community's aspirations for itself."[711]

The editors of *Jewish Currents*, a magazine "committed to the rich tradition of thought, activism, and culture of the Jewish left," announced that the religious tenor of Jewish grief that swept many synagogues in the United States "reflects the particular role Justice Ginsburg has played in the liberal American Jewish psyche—and the way the constituent parts of this identity have fused with American liberalism nearly subsuming Jewishness."[712]

Thus, when the *Guardian* wrote an obituary that questioned Ginsburg's Jewishness, stressing she "abandoned her faith" at seventeen because she was not allowed to join a *minyan* to mourn her mother's death, many Jews felt insulted and pushed back. Liberal American Jews—who were upset by the *Guardian's* omission of Ginsburg's Jewishness (which was later corrected)—were less concerned with alleged antipathy towards Israel, but anxious about the spreading of the notion that Judaism is "only a religion, when it's obviously so much more."[713] They wanted to emphasize the multiple meanings of Jewishness and pointed to the danger of belittling Ginsburg's Jewish attachment, which undercuts the very essence of Liberal Judaism in the modern era. Indeed, Ginsburg herself declared that "I am a judge, born, raised, and proud of being a Jew. The demand for justice, for peace, and for enlightenment runs through the entirety of Jewish history and Jewish tradition."

Ginsburg's iconic stature among American liberals imparted progressive Judaism with added legitimacy at a time when American Jewish liberals were facing an uphill battle to retain their ethnic

---

711   Rabbi Ben Greenfield, "Hasidic Jews Have Rebbes, Secular Jews Have Ruth Bader Ginsburg," *Jerusalem Post*, September 27, 2020, https://www.jpost.com/judaism/hasidic-jews-have-rebbes-secular-jews-have-ruth-bader-ginsburg-643586.

712   "Responsa: Justice You Shall Pursue," *Jewish Currents*, October 9, 2020.

713   PJ Grisar, "Why did the Guardian Say Ruth Bader Ginsburg 'Abandoned' Her Faith?," *Forward*, September 22, 2020.

communities, protect their institutions, and keep young Jews within the tribe. Novelist and filmmaker Jennifer Weiner wrote in the *New York Times* that Ginsburg was, for her, the most exemplary American Jew, because she pursued justice:

> A Jewish identity has little to do with whether you keep Kosher or attend services every Friday, and everything to do with your culture, your ethnicity; with the way you see the world and the way the world sees you. It's an identity we can't slip, even if we want to…. If you've been excluded, you fight for inclusion. If you've been made to feel less-than, because of your gender or your sexual orientation or your race or your religion, you stand up for others who've been denied a seat at the table. The notion of tikkun olam, that the world is broken and that each of us has a role in its repair, is a value that would lead someone to a life like hers. It is a value that overlaps with the highest American ideals.[714]

Ginsburg always spoke of her life story in a mode of "mainstream" American Jewish Liberalism. Her story encompasses the climactic events of the last century; these experiences informed both her Jewish-American identity and her jurisprudence, as if they were seamlessly integrated. Whenever she recounted her life story, it was through the prism of blending American ideals and Jewish morality, which for her was the essence of Judaism.

---

714 Jennifer Weiner, "The Very Jewish R.B.G.," *New York Times*, September 29, 2020, https://www.nytimes.com/2020/09/29/opinion/ruth-bader-ginsburg-jewish.html.

In her speeches, she often mentioned how she was raised as a daughter of migrant families that escaped the horrors of eastern Europe: "It took just one generation, my mother's life and mine" to enjoy "the good fortune to be a Jew born and raised in the U.S.A." She stressed how she was impacted by the nightmare of Nazism and "how fortunate I was to be a child safely in America during the Holocaust." Her personal narrative also included early Zionist inspirations, especially American heroines like poet and essayist Emma Lazarus (1849–1887), and Zionist activist Henrietta Szold (1860–1945). Lazarus was a pioneer in her calls for a Jewish home in Palestine as the solution of "the Jewish problem of Eastern Europe." Many years before Herzl and Louis Brandeis, she wrote that allegiance to the spirit of Judaism does not conflict "in any way with the Jew's duties or sentiments as a citizen of a non-Jewish state,…on the contrary, an intensifying of the noblest Hebrew spirit would tend to make better [American] citizens."[715] By invoking Emma Lazarus and American Jewish Zionist leader and Hadassah founder Henrietta Szold, Ginsburg signaled that American Zionism and support of Israel do not conflict, but are natural extension of American patriotism.

Ginsburg was never a Jewish nationalist, however. Her life embodied the spirit of post-war America and the coming of age of liberal Jews who benefited from the decline of anti-Semitism, growing acceptance of minorities as members of the American nation, and the openness of society to pursue the American dream of higher education in universities and colleges. During this period, the US Supreme Court, led by Chief Justice Earl Warren, greatly expanded the concept of rights and was celebrated by American liberals, many of them Jews, as a vehicle to remedy injustices.

---

715   Bette Roth Young, "Emma Lazarus and Her Jewish Problem," *American Jewish History* 84, no. 4 (December 1996), 305.

After Ginsburg's passing, the editors of *Jewish Currents* wrote, "The fact that the Supreme Court's vaunted period as a force of social progress coincided with the era of large-scale Jewish upward mobility...[led] many American Jews [to] look back on this experience as proof of America's exceptional goodness. Ginsburg certainly did."

In 2003, Ginsburg contributed a short piece to a volume in memory of Jewish American Journalist Daniel Pearl, who was kidnapped by Islamist terrorists in 2002 and brutally murdered in Pakistan. Like other contributors to the volume, she was asked to address Pearl's last chilling words before he was beheaded: "I am Jewish." Ginsburg wrote that "[we] are fortunate to...live at a time when Jews residing here face few closed doors and do not fear letting the world know who they are."

Yet her passage also brought some of the deepest tensions that Jews of the Diaspora will face in the Israeli Century to the surface. Following Ginsburg's death, Judea Pearl, Daniel's father, adopted a confrontational tone:

> I can't help but imagine RBG's disappointment upon finding out her grandchildren are becoming increasingly hesitant to let the world know who they are. Had they applied to UCLA or USC, for example, they might well be deemed unfit to serve in student government by virtue of being Jewish, highly suspect of Zionist affiliation, beliefs or aspirations. And Zionism, so university administrators tell us, is not a word their lawyers

would permit them to spell, let alone respect
or protect in public.[716]

Judea Pearl is a former Israeli, and like most Israelis in America,
he is an ardent Zionist. However, many of the grandchildren of older
liberal Jews, who for decades drew moral sustenance from their bond
with the small, egalitarian, and romantic Israel, are no longer in love
with the Jewish state. Conservative scholar Ruth Wisse pointed out
that Israel today does not fit the "liberal paradigm," while American
liberal Jews, who adopted Israeli heroism for a short period of time
after the Six-Day War, have long since returned to their early twentieth century non-Zionist roots.[717] Indeed, a growing number of
young Jews have become part of the West's anti-Israel camp. At a
time when Israel is wealthier and less vulnerable than ever before,
often as a direct result of its acting through sovereign *raison d'état*,
young liberals in America often have a hard time reconciling it with
universal Jewish morality.

Undoubtedly, the majority of Israeli Jews are turning more to
the right and to religion, but American Jews are undergoing their
own changes that may, in fact, mitigate the rift with Israel. American
Jewish journalist Ethan Bronner, who spent several years in Jerusalem
as the *New York Times* bureau chief and is married to an Israeli-born
psychologist, reminds us that it's not so simple for American Jews to
disconnect from Israel if they wish to remain Jewish:

> Many liberal secular American Jews who do
> not send their children to religious or Zionist
> schools and camps, teach them Hebrew, or

---

716 Judea Pearl, "Ginsburg on 'Being Jewish,'" *Jewish Journal*, September 23, 2020, https://
jewishjournal.com/culture/321992/ginsburg-on-being-jewish/.

717 "The Liberal Betrayal of the Jews," the Tikvah Fund, March 31, 2020, tikvahfund/videos/
tikvah-live-with-ruth-wisse-can-liberals-confront-anti-semitism/201467144489450.

have them spend time in Israel are watch-
ing them abandon not only Israel but organized Jewish life…. While it remains true,
then, that the more left-leaning and secular
members of the American Jewish community are less devoted to Israel than they once
were, the shift is probably more drift than
rift. Their children are simply turning their
attention elsewhere.

In fact, while older American Jews kept Israelis in their hearts
in the 1960s and 1970s while having little interaction with them,
"today, the traffic in both directions is heavy and steady…more than
40 percent of Israeli Jews have been here and 40 percent of US Jews
have been there," Bronner adds. "Those numbers keep going up.
The organization Birthright Israel has taken hundreds of thousands
of young American Jews for a free visit…. Israelis seem increasingly
unbothered when their friends and cousins spend time in the US,
and some end up staying. Nor do Israelis talk about expecting all Jews
to join them…. In addition, an estimated 400,000 Israelis now live
in the US and are integrated into Jewish communities. Israelis are on
college faculties, in Silicon Valley, and on synagogue boards. They
own real estate and businesses. Their children remain devoted to
Israel, adding another dimension to the relationship. In Israel today,
nearly everyone speaks English and absorbs American culture. Over
here, Israeli films and TV series such as *Shtisel*, *Our Boys*, and *Fauda*
are popular on Netflix and HBO."[718]

With these developments in mind, what will constitute the
content of "American Jewish morality" in the future? Is the liberal
legacy of Brandeis and Ginsburg enough to sustain it? This question

---

718   Ethan Bronner, "Stuck," *New York Review of Books*, April 9, 2020.

becomes especially acute in light of the rise of the new radical Left, who attack not only conservatives but also the foundations of lib- eralism as well.[719] While religious and politically conservative Jews have always claimed that Jewish American liberalism was an empty vessel destined to disappear because of its failure to encourage tradi- tion and Jewish kinship, today, even the most progressive Jews seem to agree. Thus, the editors of *Jewish Currents* recently questioned whether drifting American Jews should continue to subscribe to the morality of Ginsburg's jurisprudence or even to the story of her journey as Jew in America. "These narratives—one about the Jewishly inflected righteousness of the Court, and one about the reality of the American dream—have run their course." They also maintain that progressive Jews cannot see how Ginsburg's DNA as a justice could remain the guideline for future Jews in America:

> In conflating Jewishness with American lib-
> eralism, we risk condemning it to go down
> with the ship—and foreclosing possibilities
> to reckon with and remake our tradition.
> Ginsburg, who left behind the strictures of
> traditional Jewish observance, was of gen-
> eration whose relationship of Jewishness
> was strong enough to be characterized by
> rebellion rather than reinvention or redis-
> covery. That won't work for us today; at this
> point, even pervasive Jewish assimilation has
> ceased to be a source of generative angst and
> becomes instead a placid reality. To insist on
> the value of Jewishness in the present is to

---

719 Bari Weiss, "Stop Being Shocked," *Tablet*, October 15, 2020, https://www.tabletmag.com/ sections/news/articles/stop-being-shocked.

> commit to its remaking. Such a commitment requires us to confront the fact that, admirable though she was, it is materially impossible for us to carry forward the legacy of Ruth Bader Ginsburg.

What do the editors of *Jewish Currents* offer liberal Jews to begin their new path? Nothing less than the dismantling of the old version of liberal American Jewish identity, smashing it, in their words, as Moses smashed the Tablets of the Covenant. "When we perform *teshuva* [repentance], we similarly begin from the premise that the pursuit of justice in a terribly unjust world requires a process of smashing and remaking. A Jewishness that has locked itself in a fantasized vision of the recent American past is deferring its panic about the inability to imagine where we're headed. We won't know the shape of what we must build until we've taken a nice, long look into the abyss."

At exactly the time of a deep moral crisis among liberal American Jews, who search for a new Jewish, moral, universal foothold in the face of assimilation, the disintegration of communities, and the increasing alienation from Israel, the Israeli Century will require, more than anything else, Jewish creativity that is both rooted and cosmopolitan, which will find a new balance among the threats, both from within and without, facing Jews in Israel and across the Diaspora.

This struggle will be decided in a wide variety of contexts, forums, and communities around the world, but the most important battlefield will be the norms, laws, and values that define the Jewish state itself.

Acknowledgments

The Israeli Century was first published in Hebrew in 2019. It was an Israeli bestseller and was translated into English with great skill by Eylon Levy (with Ronnie Hope) and I am grateful for their work. Many amendments were made and new materials were added to the English version. I was helped in this process by David Hazony's vision and intellectual insights. My deepest gratitude belongs to Daniel Goldman, whose passion for the Jewish people, friendship, and generosity facilitated the publication of this version.

I am deeply grateful to Erez Casif and Michal Shwartz for their extraordinary collaboration while I was working on the Hebrew version. Many other scholars were generous with their time, ideas, and suggestions and I could not have completed this work without them. Sarah Fainberg, Toby Green, and Meirav Jones were wonderful partners and coauthors along the way. Alex Yakobson was critical in the shaping of my ideas and correcting my mistakes. I also benefited from the insights and feedback of my esteemed colleagues, Bezalel Bar-Kochva, Azar Gat, David Vital, Shlomo Avinery, Alon Gal, Yagil levy, Guy Ben Porat, Evitar Matania, Michal Kochin, Uriel Abulof, Yoav Fromer, Aharon Kleiman, Amos Zehavi, Peter Berkowitz, Julie Cooper, and Hanni Lerner.

Peninah Moshe was a great assistant, and Limor Rachmanov supported this project in so many ways.

Many research assistants deserve my thanks: Aliza Furman, Joseph Benedict, Tomer Fadlon, Eyal Feldman, and Evgeny Klauber. The book benefited from the hospitality and intellectual environment of my academic homes at Tel-Aviv University and Georgetown University.

Finally, I'm indebted to my editor Adam Bellow and to Heather King at Wicked Son.

Index